# IRREGULAR MIGRANTS AND THE RIGHT TO HEALTH

In our globalised world, where inequality is deepening and migration movements are increasing, states continue to maintain strong regulatory control over immigration, health and social policies. Arguments based on state sovereignty can be employed to differentiate irregular migrants from other groups and reduce their right to physical and mental health to the provision of emergency medical care, even where resources are available. Drawing on the enabling and constraining factors of human rights law and public health, this book explores the scope and limits of the right to health of migrants in irregular situations, in international and European human rights law. Addressing these people's health solely with an exceptional medical paradigm is inconsistent with the special attention granted to people in vulnerable situations and non-discrimination in human rights, the emerging rights-based approach to disability, the social priorities of public health and the interdependence of human rights.

DR STEFANO ANGELERI is a Marie Skłodowska-Curie scholar at Queen's University Belfast and Universidad del Rosario Bogotá. Formerly he researched and lectured at the Irish Centre for Human Rights, NUI Galway where he also acted as Irish project manager for the FRANET project funded by the EU Agency for Fundamental Rights.

T0384518

# Irregular Migrants and the Right to Health

## STEFANO ANGELERI

Queen's University Belfast

Shaftesbury Road, Cambridge CB2 8EA, United Kingdom

One Liberty Plaza, 20th Floor, New York, NY 10006, USA

477 Williamstown Road, Port Melbourne, VIC 3207, Australia

314–321, 3rd Floor, Plot 3, Splendor Forum, Jasola District Centre, New Delhi – 110025, India

103 Penang Road, #05–06/07, Visioncrest Commercial, Singapore 238467

Cambridge University Press is part of Cambridge University Press & Assessment, a department of the University of Cambridge.

We share the University's mission to contribute to society through the pursuit of education, learning and research at the highest international levels of excellence.

www.cambridge.org
Information on this title: www.cambridge.org/9781009054805

DOI: 10.1017/9781009051750

First paperback edition 2023

*A catalogue record for this publication is available from the British Library*

ISBN    978-1-316-51191-6    Hardback
ISBN    978-1-009-05480-5    Paperback

# Contents

# Acknowledgements

This book could not have come to fruition without the support and contribution of several people I have met during the last six years. A very special thank you goes to my PhD supervisor, Dr Ciara Smyth, and my postdoc mentor, Professor Siobhán Mullally, who have encouragingly pushed me to improve my academic skills throughout these years. I am very grateful to current and past postgraduate students and staff at the Irish Centre for Human Rights and School of Law of National University of Ireland, Galway, and in particular to Professor Eilionóir Flynn, Dr Noemi Magugliani and Keelin Barry for their technical and professional advice. Special mentions of acknowledgement go to Dr Rebecca Downes for her tireless proofreading activities and to Professor Audrey Chapman for her insightful feedback as external examiner of the PhD dissertation on which this book is based.

An endless thank you goes to my parents, Patrizia and Loris, and my broader family, who love me so much and have unconditionally supported my choices, even when they entailed living 2,000 km from home. Many thanks to my close friends in Galway, Milano, Cologne, Karlsruhe, Galicia, Lleida, Toronto, Dublin and Verona. I always feel at home with you around, and you have helped me to maintain good emotional health during all these years. Thanks also to my partner, Edgar. You have been so patient and loving during this book preparation, before and during pandemic times.

# Table of Cases

## European Committee of Social Rights

## INTERNATIONAL

### UN Human Rights Treaty Bodies

## Other International Cases

# Abbreviations

| | |
|---|---|
| AAAQ | availability, accessibility, acceptability and good quality |
| CAT | Convention against Torture |
| CEDAW | Convention on the Elimination of All Forms of Discrimination against Women |
| CERD | Convention on the Elimination of Racial Discrimination |
| CESCR | Committee on Economic Social and Cultural Rights |
| COs | concluding observations |
| CRC | Convention of the Rights of the Child |
| CRPD | Convention on the Rights of Persons with Disabilities |
| CSDH | Commission on the Social Determinants of Health |
| ECHR | European Convention on Human Rights |
| ECSR | European Committee of Social Rights |
| ECtHR | European Court of Human Rights |
| ESC | European Social Charter |
| HRC | Human Rights Council |
| HRCtee | Human Rights Committee |
| ICCPR | International Covenant on Civil and Political Rights |
| ICERD | International Convention on the Elimination of All Forms of Racial Discrimination |
| ICESCR | International Covenant on Economic Social and Cultural Rights |
| ICMW | International Convention on the Protection of the Rights of All Migrant Workers and Members of Their Families |
| OHCHR | Office of the United Nations High Commissioner for Human Rights |
| PHC | primary health care |
| SDH | social determinants of health |
| UDH | underlying determinants of health |

| | |
|---|---|
| UDHR | Universal Declaration of Human Rights |
| UHC | universal health coverage |
| UN | United Nations |
| UNCHR | UN Commission on Human Rights |
| UNGA | United Nations General Assembly |
| WHA | World Health Assembly |
| WHO | World Health Organization |

# Introduction

As far back as 1966, Martin Luther King Jr, the charismatic leader of the American civil rights movement, affirmed that 'of all the forms of inequality, injustice in health is the most shocking and inhuman'.[1] Although his statement referred to the imbalance that the American private insurance system generated at the domestic level, it can easily be applied to the situation that community outsiders, such as irregular migrants or people who are not affiliated with a health system, encounter today in many parts of the world.[2]

Health-, social- and immigration-related policies and rights are areas over which states exercise particularly strict sovereign control, and this has meant that irregular migrants and the right to health, whether considered individually or jointly, have struggled to receive consistent recognition in the international human rights project over the last seventy years. Indeed, an orthodox approach to the interpretation of international and European human rights obligations has long displaced both the declared all-embracing personal scope of application of these legal frameworks where the rights of migrants are

---

[1]  Reference to M. L. King's remarks, on 25 March 1996, at the press conference following the annual meeting of Medical Committee for Human Rights, in 'Physicians for a National Health Program' note <http://pnhp.org/news/dr-martin-luther-king-on-health-care-injustice/> accessed 1 March 2021.

[2]  Regarding the situation in Europe see, for instance, Sarah Spencer and Vanessa Hughes 'Outside and In: Legal Entitlements to Health Care and Education for Migrants with Irregular Status in Europe' (2015) *Oxford Compas Report* <www.compas.ox.ac.uk/2015/outside-and-in/>; Isabel Noret 'Access to Health Care in 16 European Countries', Legal Report of the European Network to Reduce Vulnerabilities in Health & Médecins du Monde (2017) <https://mdmeuroblog.files .wordpress.com/2014/01/2017_final-legal-report-on-access-to-healthcare-in-16-european-countries .pdf> accessed 1 March 2021.

concerned[3] and the indivisibility or equal importance of all human rights, thereby reducing state accountability for failures to adequately implement social rights.[4] Thus, the adoption of selective approaches to human rights, where 'not all [avoidable] suffering and ill-health' are understood and addressed by social and legal communities,[5] is somewhat embraced and tolerated at different levels of governance. As such, the status and quality of the right to health of irregular or undocumented migrants remain contested within and across different legal frameworks. This anomaly is not only concerning from the point of view of human rights holders and advocates but also because it challenges the internal consistency and moral legitimacy of a legal framework based on dignity and equality that lawmakers and interpreters cannot overlook.

Migration and health are particularly urgent and interconnected areas of human rights enquiry in the twenty-first century for many reasons, which include those mentioned in the following non-exhaustive list. First, international migration rates have significantly increased over the last twenty years.[6] Second, economic inequalities within and across most countries have generally widened.[7] Third, the economic and health crises of the last two decades have exacerbated inequalities and social vulnerabilities affecting the worst off.[8] Fourth, human rights work has shifted from the drafting of binding standards to the context-sensitive implementation and clarification of the former.[9] Finally, important global actors, such as the European Union (EU), still insist on cracking down on irregular migration without opening

---

[3]   Marie-Bénédicte Dembour and Tobias Kelly (eds) *Are Human Rights for Migrants? Critical Reflections on the Status of Irregular Migrants in Europe and the United States* (Routledge 2011) 1–22.

[4]   Mashood Baderin and Robert McCorquodale (eds) *Economic, Social, and Cultural Rights in Action* (OUP 2007) 10–11.

[5]   Alicia Ely Yamin, *Power, Suffering and the Struggle for Dignity: Human Rights Frameworks for Health and Why They Matter* (Penn Press 2016) 4–5.

[6]   International Organization for Migration (IOM), 'World Migration Report 2020' (IOM 2020) 10, reports that international migrants were estimated to be 150 million in the year 2000 and 272 million in 2019.

[7]   UN Department of Economic and Social Affairs, 'World Social Report 2020 – Inequality in a Rapidly Changing World' (UN Publishing 2020) 19.

[8]   Aoife Nolan (ed) *Economic and Social Rights after the Global Financial Crisis* (CUP 2014) 2; European Committee of Social Rights (ECSR), 'Statement on Covid-19 and Social Rights' (24 March 2021) 4, 7, 14.

[9]   Helen Keller and Geir Ulfstein (eds) *UN Human Rights Treaty Bodies – Law and Legitimacy* (CUP 2012) 1.

up avenues for regular migration, while the continent is still beset by various armed conflicts and widespread socioeconomic deprivation.[10]

Despite this challenging context, over the last three decades, gradual but significant developments in European and international human rights have reduced the conceptualisation and implementation gaps between classical liberal rights and socioeconomic rights (including the right to health), particularly where particularly vulnerable or disadvantaged people or communities are concerned.[11] Furthermore, the number of migration cases adjudicated on by European courts and tribunals and the migrant-focused standard setting, monitoring and quasi-judicial activities at international level have spiked in recent years.[12]

This book invites readers to reflect on a series of questions: Why is it so difficult to equalise the rights of irregular migrants with those of citizens and regular migrants in a genuine *human* rights law? How have human rights bodies who are entrusted with the interpretation of legal obligations navigated the divide between human and migrant rights? How is the right to health conceptualised across different legal systems? How does this relate to public health and the concept of vulnerability? Why should its implementation prioritise vulnerable people? Why should such a categorisation of disadvantage include irregular migrants? To what levels of health care should irregular migrants and subgroups of the same have access according to the currently fragmented status of human rights law? How can the right to the social determinants of health facilitate the realisation of human and social rights, which are relevant to health promotion, for irregular migrants? And what are the conceptual and operational barriers to the implementation of this right? How can vulnerability- and disability-related arguments within human rights practice be strategised to support a right to mental health and social support for people with mental health issues or disabilities?

These questions can be summarised in the following central research question: Are international and European human rights frameworks sufficiently equipped to interpret and develop the right to health of irregular migrants towards meaningful levels of holistic health care provision and health promotion? The analysis and systematisation of applicable human

---

[10] The EU approach towards irregular migration is focused on prevention and border control and well as return legislation, see European Commission, 'A European Agenda on Migration' (Communication) (13 May 2015) COM(2015) 240 final, 7–10; European Commission, 'New Pact on Migration and Asylum' (23 September 2020) COM(2020) 609 final, Section 2.5.

[11] See Sections 2.4 and 2.5.

[12] Regarding European Courts, see Moritz Baumgärtel, *Demanding Rights: Europe's Supranational Courts and the Dilemma of Migrant Vulnerability* (CUP 2019) 3–4.

rights law and jurisprudence (of a binding, authoritative, persuasive or recommendatory nature) I have conducted for this book has left me moderately confident in offering a positive answer. However, to avoid being naïve, it is worth clarifying the boundaries of the current analysis and positioning this research in relation to the existing literature by starting with some working definitions.

## I.1 PRELIMINARY DEFINITIONS: IRREGULAR MIGRANTS AND THE RIGHT TO HEALTH

For the sake of academic integrity, it is important to be clear on the meaning of certain key terms employed in this book. In terms of personal scope, this study focuses on 'undocumented' or 'irregular' migrants; its material scope encompasses the 'right to physical and mental health' and its interconnections with other human rights in international and European human rights law.

This study refers interchangeably to 'irregular' and 'undocumented' migrants or people to refer to those foreign nationals who do not comply with immigration law requirements for entry or stay in a country and are, therefore, susceptible to deportation.[13] This wording is in line with the recommendations of various international bodies and the practice of specialised non-governmental organisations (NGOs), although there is no consensus on the correct term to use.[14]

In 1975, the United Nations General Assembly (UNGA) passed a resolution requiring the 'United Nations organs and specialised agencies concerned to use in all official documents the term "non-documented or irregular migrant workers" to define those workers that illegally and/or surreptitiously enter another country to obtain work'.[15] The UN Committee on Migrant Workers (CMW Committee) recently declared that 'the use of the term "illegal" to describe migrant workers in an irregular situation is inappropriate and should be avoided as it tends to stigmatise them by associating them with

---

[13] Elspeth Guild, 'Who Is an Irregular Migrant?' in Barbara Bogusz et al. (eds) *Irregular Migration and Human Rights: Theoretical, European and International Perspectives (Immigration and Asylum Law and Policy in Europe)* (Martinus Nijhoff Publishers 2004) 3.

[14] Magdalena Perkowska, 'Illegal, Legal, Irregular or Regular – Who Is the Incoming Foreigner?' (2016) *Studies in Logic, Grammar and Rhetoric* 45(58) 187. The Platform for International Cooperation on Undocumented Migrants (PICUM) <https://picum.org/> and Migrant Rights Centre Ireland (MCRI) <www.mrci.ie/> (accessed 1 March 2019) mainly employ 'undocumented migrants'.

[15] UNGA Res 3449 'Measures to Ensure the Human Rights and Dignity of All Migrant Workers' (9 December 1975).

criminality'.[16] The UN Committee on Economic, Social and Cultural Rights (CESCR) – the monitoring body of the UN International Covenant on Economic, Social and Cultural Rights (ICESCR) – has recently demonstrated a preference for the term 'undocumented migrants', whereas the International Organization for Migration prefers to employ the term 'irregular' migrants.[17] In the European context, the Parliamentary Assembly of the Council of Europe (PACE) has expressed a preference for 'irregular migrant' over 'illegal migrant' or 'migrant without papers', and other monitoring bodies employ similar terminology.[18] In addition, the European Court of Human Rights (ECtHR) seems to have finally accepted the terminology of 'irregularity' over 'illegality'.[19]

Furthermore, the word 'migrants' in conjunction with 'irregular' is employed not only to embrace people who are in the process of moving through an international border but also those people who have long settled in a country where they do not hold authorisation to stay or reside. Irregular migration is a 'multifaceted and dynamic' phenomenon, as individual circumstances, such as labour opportunities, age, protracted time spent living in a country and migratory background, may change a person's actual migratory status across the lifespan. Although doubts remain concerning the real number of irregular migrants in countries, regions and globally,[20] estimated figures are significant, and how states respond to this phenomenon gives rise to conceptual, legal and policy challenges at different levels of governance.[21]

---

[16] Committee on the Protection of the Rights of All Migrant Workers and Members of Their Families (CMW Committee), 'General Comment No. 2: The Rights of Migrant Workers in an Irregular Situation and Members of Their Families' (23 August 2013) CMW/C/GC/2, para 4. Similarly, UNHRC, Statement of the Special Rapporteur on the Human Rights of Migrants, 'Mainstreaming a Human Rights-Based Approach to Migration within the High-Level Dialogue' UNGA Plenary Session – Criminalization of Migrants (2 October 2013).

[17] IOM Key Migration Terms <www.iom.int/key-migration-terms> accessed 1 March 2021.

[18] Parliamentary Assembly of the Council of Europe (PACE) Res 1509 'Human Rights of Irregular Migrants' (2006). See also the European Commission against Racism and Intolerance of the Council of Europe (ECRI), 'General Policy Recommendation No.16: Safeguarding Irregularly Present Migrants from Discrimination' (16 March 2016).

[19] Cfr *Ponomaryov and Others v Bulgaria* App no 5335/05 (ECHR 2011) para 54 and *Chowdury and Others v Greece* App no 21884/15 (ECHR 2017) 95, 97.

[20] Irregularity of status means that it is impossible to have a census of irregular migrants, who by definition do not wish to be tracked by state authorities. Several studies estimate their number between 5 and 20 per cent of all migrant population, with significant differences across continents. See IOM's Global Migration Data Analysis Centre, 'Irregular Migration' in *Migration Data Portal* (last updated 9 June 2020) <https://migrationdataportal.org/themes/irregular-migration> accessed 10 May 2021.

[21] Sarah Spencer and Anna Triandafyllidou (eds) *Migrants with Irregular Status in Europe – Evolving Conceptual and Policy Challenges* (Springer 2020) 1–2.

In relation to health, the Constitution of the World Health Organization (WHO) defines the concept as a 'state of complete physical, mental and social well-being and not merely the absence of disease or infirmity'.[22] International human rights law has reduced the corresponding legal standard to the 'right to the highest attainable standard of physical and mental health' because it was seen as impossible to impose on states a duty to guarantee a 'state of complete [...] health' for everyone.[23] Health is a public good and a human right,[24] and the enjoyment of good health, although not directly acknowledged or theorised in international conventions, is crucial for us to flourish as human beings.[25] Therefore, fair and equal access to services should be available to meet basic health needs and ensure equality of opportunity to function in society.[26]

This 'highest attainable standard of health', for individuals and communities, must be realised through intersectoral measures concerning both health care and other social determinants of health.[27] In 1978, discussions between health experts and world leaders led to the adoption of the Declaration of Alma-Ata on 'primary health care'.[28] The approach of this milestone public health document, which was endorsed by the WHO and followed and consistently confirmed at other international fora,[29] has influenced the way in which the CESCR, *inter alia*, has framed the normative content of the right to health and its correlative general and core international obligations.[30] Therefore, states are urged, under international human rights

---

[22] Constitution of the World Health Organization (Adopted 22 July 1946, entry into force 7 April 1948) Off. Rec. WHO 2, 100, Preamble.

[23] International Covenant on Economic, Social and Cultural Rights (adopted 16 December 1966, entry into force 3 January 1976) (ICESCR) UNGA Res 2200A (XXI) Article 12. For further details, see Section 4, Ch 2.

[24] Francesco Francioni, 'Sovranità Statale e Tutela della Salute come Bene Pubblico Globale' in Laura Pineschi (ed) *La Tutela della Salute nel Diritto Internazionale ed Europeo tra Interessi Globali e Interessi Particolari* (Editoriale Scientifica 2017) 51–66.

[25] Amartya Sen, 'Elements of a Theory of Human Rights' (2004) *Philosophy and Public Affairs* 32 (4) 315, 332; Martha Nussbaum, *Creating Capabilities: The Human Development Approach* (Belknap Press 2011) 20–26.

[26] Norman Daniels, *Just Health: Meeting Health Needs Fairly* (CUP 2007) 20–21.

[27] Committee on Economic Social and Cultural Rights (CESCR) 'General Comment No. 14: The Right to the Highest Attainable Standard of Health (article 12 of the International Covenant on Economic, Social and Cultural Rights)' (11 August 2000) E/C.12/2000/4, paras 4, 11.

[28] Declaration of Alma-Ata – Health for All, International Conference on Primary Health Care (6–12 September 1978). For further details, see Chapter 2.

[29] Ottawa Charter for Health Promotion (21 November 1986); Programme of Action adopted at the International Conference on Population and Development, Cairo (5–13 September 1994).

[30] CESCR, GC14 (n 27) para 43.

law and global health law, to take measures to 'address [...] the main health problems in the community, providing promotive, preventive, curative and rehabilitative services' through the implementation of public health, medical and socioeconomic measures.[31] In doing so, under both public health and human rights law, state authorities should target health equity and embrace approaches of substantive equality to implement the right to health. This means targeting the elimination of 'systematic disparities in health (or in the major social determinants of health) between groups with different levels of underlying social advantage/disadvantage' to allow every population group 'equal opportunities to be healthy'.[32]

By writing on the right to health of irregular migrants, I not only encourage the reader to critically question how health care–related human rights obligations are (somewhat inconsistently) interpreted and implemented but also – given the expansive scope of this right, which embraces the social determinants of health – attempt to shed light on overly restrictive treaty interpretations in the context of migrant rights and several intersectional forms of systemic oppression and rights violations that must be addressed to meet the minimum requirements of inclusiveness and coherence of the human rights project.

## I.2 THE CONTOURS OF THIS HUMAN RIGHTS ANALYSIS: INTERNATIONAL LAW AND PUBLIC HEALTH

A number of dynamic and challenging issues exist at the intersection of migration, health and human rights, including how the experience of migration and holding a certain migration status can affect, either positively or negatively, the health and well-being of individuals and populations; how migration law and health policies can restrict access to necessary care and the enjoyment of human rights; and how the violations of a broad array of human rights norms can have detrimental consequences on individual health, as in the context of irregular employment and exploitative working conditions.[33]

This analysis is premised on the consideration that to approach these regulatory challenges, human rights law should give adequate weight to

---

[31] Declaration of Alma-Ata (n 28) para VII, 2–4, emphasis added.

[32] Paula Braveman and Sophia Gruskin, 'Defining Equity in Health' (2003) *Journal of Epidemiology and Community Health* 57 254, 257.

[33] These relations are partly modelled on the reflections of Jo Vearey, Charles Hui and Kolitha Wickramage, 'Migration and Health: Current Issues, Governance and Knowledge Gaps' in IOM (n 6) 209 and Johnathan Mann et al., 'Health and Human Rights' (1994) *Journal of Health and Human Rights* 1.

public health and social disability paradigms, as these can complement each other in working towards a human-centred, difference-sensitive and holistic regulation of health and well-being for irregular migrants, who constitute a multifaceted and marginalised group. Above domestic legal sources, human rights law is composed of a number of international and regional legal systems, but human rights is an intrinsically interdisciplinary subject.[34] Indeed, since the 1990s, health and human rights studies have significantly grown, and the new field of global health law, which incorporates human rights–based approaches, has emerged.[35] Furthermore, the social model of disabilities is embedded, with some adjustments, in the UN Convention on the Rights of Persons with Disabilities.[36] For both public health and disability scholars, the significance of human rights law derives, *inter alia*, from the fact that this is arguably the only source of law that legitimises international scrutiny of the standards of treatment of disadvantaged populations, such as irregular migrants with health issues or disabilities, and ensures a multilevel accountability for abusive law, policies and practices that fall within state jurisdictions and sovereign control.[37]

This work synergises a doctrinal analysis of the scope and content of the right to health for irregular migrants in international and European human rights law, including the root causes of inequality of standards and health determinants, with certain items of public health and disability literature to complement the definition and operationalisation of health standards. This entails regarding (human rights) 'law as a means to an end', which, in this case, is the realisation of the 'highest attainable standards of physical and mental health' for everyone.[38] This approach means analysing sources of human rights law and legal arguments[39] while also mitigating the criticism that a purely doctrinal approach to law would operate within a 'socio, political,

---

[34] Michael Freeman, *Human Rights: An Interdisciplinary Approach* (2nd edn, Polity Press 2011).

[35] Lawrence O. Gostin and Benjamin Mason Meier (eds) *Foundations of Global Health and Human Rights* (OUP 2020).

[36] Convention on the Rights of Persons with Disabilities (adopted 13 December 2006, entry into force 3 May 2008) (CRPD) UNGA Res 61/106, Preamble.

[37] Lance Gable and Laurence Gostin, 'Human Rights of Persons with Mental Disabilities: The European Convention of Human Rights' in Lawrence Gostin et al. (eds) *Principles of Mental Health Law and Policy* (OUP 2010) 104, referencing to Louis Henkin, *The Age of Rights* (Columbia University Press 1990) 20–21.

[38] Brian Tamanaha, *Law as a Means to an End* (CUP 2006); Dabney Evans and Megan Price 'Measure for Measure: Utilizing Legal Norms and Health Data in Measuring the Right to Health' in Fons Coomans, Fred Grünfeld and Menno T. Kamminga (eds) *Methods of Human Rights Research* (Intersentia 2009) 111.

[39] Richard A. Posner, 'Legal Scholarship Today' (2002) *Harvard Law Review* 115 1314, 1316.

and economic vacuum'.[40] For instance, irregular migration is scrutinised as a subject of legal interpretation and a human experience characterised by actual health, social and institutional vulnerabilities, and health is analysed as a 'status' and an 'entitlement', in the light of hard and soft law and public health material, keeping in mind the rules of international (human rights) law and 'striking a balance between foolish utopianism and grim realism'.[41]

For the purposes of this research, 'international human rights law' refers to the UN machinery of human rights, particularly the nine UN human rights treaties and the special procedures of the Human Rights Council.[42] 'European human rights law' refers to the instruments adopted in the context of the Council of Europe but excludes the legal standards and case law that have developed in EU law.[43] The exclusion of EU law is based on the fact that although irregular migration is a shared competence of the EU and its member states, health remains an exclusive competence of member states, albeit one that is supported and complemented by various provisions of the Treaty on the Functioning of the EU. The right to health is stated in the Charter of Fundamental Rights of the EU but applies only within the scope of EU law. The net effect is that the Court of Justice of the EU has pronounced on the right to health of an irregular migrant only once and only in the context

---

[40] David Ibbetson, 'Historical Research in Law' in Mark Tushnet and Peter Cane (eds) *Oxford Handbook of Legal Studies* (OUP 2003) 863, 864.

[41] David J. Bederman, 'Appraising a Century of Scholarship in the American Journal of International Law' (2006) *American Journal of International Law* 100 20, 22.

[42] International Convention on the Elimination of All Forms of Racial Discrimination (adopted 21 December 1965, entry into force 4 January 1969) (ICERD) UNGA Res 2106 (XX); International Covenant on Civil and Political Rights (adopted 16 December 1966, entry into force 23 March 1976) (ICCPR) UNGA Res 2200A (XXI); ICESCR (n 23); Convention on the Elimination of All Forms of Discrimination against Women (adopted 18 December 1979, entry into force 3 September 1981) (CEDAW) UNGA Res 34/180; Convention against Torture and Other Cruel, Inhuman or Degrading Treatment or Punishment (adopted 10 December 1984, entry into force 26 June 1987) (CAT) UNGA Res 49/46; Convention on the Rights of the Child (adopted 20 November 1989, entry into force 2 September 1990) (CRC) UNGA Res 44/25; International Convention on the Protection of the Rights of All Migrant Workers and Members of Their Families (adopted 18 December 1990, entry into force 1 July 2003) (ICMW) UNGA Res 45/158; International Convention for the Protection of All Persons from Enforced Disappearance (adopted 20 December 2006, entry into force 23 December 2010) (ICPED) UNGA Res 61/177; CRPD (n 36). For further details, including on the UN human rights bodies and their procedures, see <www.ohchr.org/EN/pages/home.aspx> accessed 1 March 2019.

[43] This research is primarily focused on the law and jurisprudence that is developed in the context of the Convention for the Protection of Human Rights and Fundamental Freedoms (adopted 4 November 1950, entry into force 3 September 1953) ETS 5 (ECHR); European Social Charter (adopted 18 October 1961, entry into force 26 February 1965), ETS 35; Revised European Social Charter (adopted 3 May 1996, entry into force 1 July 1999) ETS 163 (ESC).

of deportation-related inhuman or degrading treatment.[44] Accordingly, there is currently very little to be gleaned from EU law concerning the right to health of irregular migrants. Regarding the regional legal frameworks examined in this research, the choice to exclude from the analysis the instruments of the Organisation of American States and the African Union was made in the interest of avoiding excessively general statements and conclusions on migration and health situations in Africa and the Americas. However, it is worth noting that migration and socioeconomic rights in the American regional systems, which are briefly referred to in Chapter 1 and in the Conclusion, may become suitable subjects for further future research because of the rapid *pro homine* developments of these systems in the last few years.

As this examination is both expository and evaluative, the norms of human rights treaties are assessed in the light of relevant legal principles of interpretation, case law, jurisprudence, extra-legal sources and interdisciplinary scholarly analyses.[45] Although no hierarchical relation exists between international and regional legal frameworks, all chapters juxtapose and compare the standards developed within the European context – for instance by the binding judgments of the ECtHR – with those elaborated by prevalently non-binding procedures with regard to UN human rights treaties. Although the practices of UN human rights bodies differ in nature and legal value (e.g. case-specific views, state-specific findings on reporting procedures, general comments, reports of special rapporteurs), my position is that these instances of 'soft law' are not without legal importance. Indeed, human rights bodies are explicitly mandated to review state practices and perform interpretative activities, *inter alia*, by either a treaty or a resolution adopted by a state body. Furthermore, they have accumulated an impressive volume of human rights jurisprudence, which has contributed to elaborating broadly shaped human rights standards at the UN human rights level. These, when aligned with the criteria for interpretation of international (human rights) law, can be particularly authoritative.[46] Knowledge of this jurisprudence may prove particularly useful in the

---

[44] European Parliament and Council Directive 2008/115/EC of 16 December 2008 laying down common standards and procedures in Member States for returning illegally staying third-country nationals [2008] OJ L348/98; Case C-562/13 *Centre public d'action sociale d'Ottignies-Louvain-la-Neuve v Moussa Abdida* [2014] paras 62–64.

[45] Robert Cryer et al., *Research Methodologies in EU and International Law* (Hart Publishing 2011) 9.

[46] Helen Keller and Leena Grover 'General Comments of the Human Rights Committee and their Legitimacy' in Keller and Ulfstein (n 9) 193; Urfan Khaliq and Robin Churchill, 'The Protection of Economic and Social Rights: A Particular Challenge?' in Keller and Ulfstein (n 9) 205–208.

European legal context, where human rights discussions are overly dominated by the European Convention on Human Rights (ECHR) framework.

While I link my analysis to the general criteria for the interpretation of international law,[47] the operationalisation of which is 'not an exact science',[48] the contribution of human rights bodies to the elaboration and use of certain equalitarian arguments to human rights (vulnerability and non-discrimination, core obligations, positive obligations and the human rights approach to disability) constitutes the conceptual spine of this monograph. These arguments are qualified with reference, as previously mentioned, to certain extra-legal and meta-legal standards, namely, the concepts of 'primary health care' and the 'social determinants of health', as interpreted by the WHO,[49] which is the guardian of global health law and policy.

Finally, I must restate that although international human rights courts and bodies have contributed to the development of progressively more generous standards concerning irregular migrants and while many institutional follow-up measures have been implemented, the enforcement of these laws and rights-based policies are heavily reliant on the political willingness of state powers to adjust their domestic legal systems to align with internationally recognised norms. This leads me to clarify that this book is primarily – although not exclusively – concerned with the interpretation of human rights law to reduce the gap between the health-related entitlements of irregular migrants and those of the registered population while also respecting the prerogatives of the international and European legal frames. Although references are made to national practices and cases, I do not particularly focus on the implementation or assess the effectiveness of international frameworks in any specific domestic setting.

## I.3 THE PLAN OF THIS BOOK

In addition to this introduction, this study is composed of five substantive chapters and a concluding chapter. The first two chapters address the root causes of the inability of international law to generate sufficiently clear and consistent standards on the health rights of irregular migrants while highlighting certain progressive trends. Chapters 3–5, respectively, describe and

---

[47] These are codified in the Vienna Convention on the Law of Treaties (adopted 23 May 1969, entry into force 27 January 1980) 1155 UNTS 331 (VCLT), Article 31 and 32.
[48] ILC, 'Yearbook of the International Law Commission', II (1966) 218, para 4.
[49] Reference is made both to WHO-commissioned studies and World Health Assembly resolutions.

critically analyse three contested areas of international and European human rights as they apply to irregular migrants, namely how thick the protection of their right to health is with regard to access to health care beyond emergency treatment, the social or underlying determinants of health and the unexplored area of migrant mental health and disabilities.

More specifically, Chapter 1, entitled 'Sovereignty and the Human Rights of Irregular Migrants', situates the human rights of irregular migrants within the legal frames of reference chosen for this study. This chapter contrasts the principle of sovereignty in international law with the universal personal scope of application of human rights. The tension between the two foundational principles is a major root cause of the oscillation of international and European case law on the rights of irregular migrants between sovereigntist and human-centred tendencies. The trend is also visible in relation to migrants' entitlement and enjoyment of social rights.

Chapter 2, entitled 'The Normative Contours of a Vulnerability- and Equity-Oriented Right to Health', provides an overview of the public health–inspired conceptualisation of the right to health and its correlative obligations in international and European human rights law. It demonstrates a certain engagement of international bodies with the protection of health while also arguing that a structural and conceptual bias against socioeconomic rights has posed an obstacle for the universal protection and accountability of the right to health of vulnerable people, a category to which irregular migrants de jure or de facto belong. For instance, the analysis reveals a disjunct between regulatory obligations and high-threshold rights within the ECHR framework on the one hand and the targeting of comprehensive care while respecting non-discrimination in the ICESCR's typologies system on the other. The chapter concludes with a close examination of the conceptual and normative value of vulnerability in human rights theory and practice, which should also apply in relation to the implementation of an equity-based right to health.

Chapter 3, entitled 'The Right to Health Care of Irregular Migrants: Between Primary Care and Emergency Treatment', builds on the structural and conceptual challenges outlined in the preceding chapters to describe, compare and analyse the international and European jurisprudence on the right to health care or medical care of undocumented people. The assessment uncovers several inconsistencies. While international human rights law elaborates, *inter alia*, on the concepts of 'primary health care' and non-discrimination of vulnerable people, including irregular migrants, in its scope of application, European human rights law entitles irregular migrants to a level of health protection that equates to 'urgent' or 'life-saving' treatments. Although international human rights bodies employ vulnerability and core and positive obligations to urge states to implement measures in this area of law and policy, the chapter recommends a more substantive-oriented approach to health care obligations by international bodies aligned to the accessible level of health care specified in the WHO recommendations on 'primary health care' and greater rigour and consistency in health-related terminology and legal arguments to increase persuasiveness. In both this and Chapter 4, special remarks are dedicated to irregular migrant children and to women's access to reproductive services and care.

Chapter 4 is entitled 'The Determinants of the Health of Irregular Migrants: Between Interrelatedness and Power'. This chapter explores whether international and European human rights laws provide for the determinants of health of irregular migrants. The determinants of health, together with health care, are part of the scope of the right to health and constitute a particularly important area within the field of public health. Indeed, the enjoyment of human and social rights that support the determinants of health is in keeping with the concepts of empowerment, indivisibility, interrelatedness and vulnerability, which ground human rights law. However, an examination of the applicable human rights jurisprudence reveals that where irregular migrants are concerned, these narratives often – but not always – dissipate in the face of the imperative, as states see it, to control immigration, resulting in the social rights – other than the right to health care – of irregular migrants being guaranteed at only a basic or survival level.

Chapter 5 is entitled 'Mental Health, Irregular Migration and Human Rights: Synergising Vulnerability- and Disability- Sensitive Approaches'. This chapter evaluates what the international and European human rights frameworks can offer, in terms of standard setting and avenues for international legal development and protection, to those irregular migrants who experience either mental health difficulties or have a psychosocial disability. The analysis in this chapter extends the normative frames of reference to encompass 'disability', which is reconceptualised in the Convention on the Rights of Persons with Disabilities (CRPD) as a transformative status and a human rights argument. This chapter triangulates human rights, public health and disability-sensitive arguments to assess the relations between mental health and human rights in the context of irregular migration in human rights law and jurisprudence. While the ECtHR's deportation cases concerning people with mental health issues tend to reflect an overall emergency-oriented and predominantly biomedical approach to mental health, several UN human rights treaty bodies set out a more holistic conceptualisation of mental health and psychosocial disability. The latter approach promotes non-discriminatory psychosocial interventions to guarantee access to community-based mental health care services and the underlying determinants of mental health for everyone regardless of migration status.

The Conclusion synthesises the fragmented standards of the chosen legal frameworks on the subject, restates each chapter's findings, makes recommendations for the progressive development of the law and highlights areas worthy of further research.

# 1

## Sovereignty and the Human Rights of Irregular Migrants

This chapter presents a first set of arguments that explain why irregular migrants are often prevented from enjoying health-related rights on an equal basis with others with reference to international law-making and adjudication. Neither the form of international law nor the developing content and redress mechanisms of international human rights law facilitate the enjoyment of human rights by irregular migrants. This results in an expansion of domestic law and state discretion where the rights of irregular migrants are concerned. This analysis begins by providing an overview of two interacting normative pillars that are crucial in this regard, namely state sovereignty and human rights in international law. They are often presented as contrasting concepts, and the clash is particularly acute in relation to irregular migrants. Thus, over the last 130 years, a significant amount of domestic and international case law has referred to immigration control – understood as the executive power to exclude undesired aliens who are not refugees through the establishment of domestic laws regulating their legal entry, stay and return in a territory – as a corollary of state sovereignty.[1] By contrast, international human rights standards are aimed at limiting the arbitrary treatment of persons in the light of a common belonging to the human family.[2] The tensions between state self-determination and universal principles and between human rights and a subset of rights for irregular migrants lie at the heart of the philosophy and organisation of liberal democracy, which 'draws boundaries and creates

---

[1] James A. R. Nafziger, 'The General Admission of Aliens under International Law' (1983) *The American Journal of International Law* 77(4) 804, 822.
[2] Universal Declaration of Human Rights (adopted 10 December 1948) UNGA Res 217 A(III) (UDHR) Preamble: 'Whereas recognition of the inherent dignity and of the equal and inalienable rights of all members of the human family is the foundation of freedom justice and peace in the world.'

closures'.[3] Thus, the unequal treatment of irregular migrants in both law and practice puts to the test the coherence of international and European human rights law and personhood as a source of human rights.[4] This chapter conducts such a test by providing examples of the acute violations of human rights that irregular migrants have experienced in the context of border control. The intention is to give a flavour of the fragility – reflected in European and international case law – of the human rights of these migrants when they are subject to administrative detention, when they are deported and when they attempt to enjoy their right to family life. Furthermore, the unequal and somewhat inconsistent entitlement recognition in the European Social Charter (ESC) and the UN International Convention on Migrant Workers (ICMW) – partially remedied by the interpretative activities of their monitoring bodies – is revealed to demonstrate the dramatic extent to which sovereign state interests have shaped international human rights law-making with regard to these migrants. A brief reference to the jurisprudence of the inter-American system of human rights demonstrates that the 'sovereignty–human rights' relationship can also be shaped by a *pro homine* approach and that there is nothing natural in considering sovereignty as the starting point from which to grapple with immigrant-related cases.[5] However, the relatively recent intergovernmental negotiations on the Global Compact for Migration confirm the reliance on the 'guiding principles' of both national sovereignty and human rights in dealing with the challenges of international migration.

## 1.1 SOVEREIGNTY AND HUMAN RIGHTS OBLIGATIONS

### 1.1.1 *State Sovereignty in International Law*

Public international law,[6] here commonly referred to as international law, is the body of laws that, since the sixteenth century, has traditionally regulated

---

[3]   Dembour and Kelly (n 3, Introduction) 8; Seyla Benhabib, *The Rights of Others: Aliens, Residents and Citizens* (CUP 2004) 2.

[4]   Sylvie Da Lomba, 'Immigration Status and Basic Social Human Rights – A Comparative Study of Irregular Migrants' Right to Health Care in France, the UK and Canada' (2010) *The Netherlands Quarterly of Human Rights* 28(1) 6, 7.

[5]   Marie-Bénédicte Dembour, *When Humans Become Migrants: Study of the European Court of Human Rights with an Inter-American Counterpoint* (OUP 2015) 6–7.

[6]   Public international law differs from private international law, which is that body of domestic law that comes into play when a controversy contains a foreign element. In that case, the conflict of laws is resolved by this body of domestic law that identifies the law and jurisdiction applicable to the case. See Paul Torremans et al. (eds), *Cheshire, North and Fawcett: Private International Law* (OUP 2017).

the relationships between independent and sovereign nation-states.[7] Its first interpreters founded international law and its principles on the universal law of nature, to be discovered using reason and to be binding on all states.[8] By contrast, from the nineteenth century on, the dominant positivist doctrine has grounded international law in the 'theory of consent', according to which states could only be bound by those rules to which they had first agreed to be bound.[9] Until the twentieth century, the rules of this legal framework were concerned with interstate relations, and this is still largely the case today. However, regarding the role of people in international law, legal theories have reached different conclusions. For instance, in the nineteenth century, G. W. F. Hegel thought that individuals were subordinate to the state because the latter enshrined the wills of all citizens and, thus, evolved into a higher will.[10] From an international perspective, this state-centred approach meant that the state was sovereign and supreme, and people were merely objects of international law. Hersch Lauterpacht, an influential twentieth-century internationalist who witnessed the birth of the new post–World War II international community, considered the achievement of peoples' well-being as the primary function of all laws and advocated that international law based on human rights was the best way of achieving this purpose.[11] Contemporary international law recognises individuals as subjects of international law: states are primary subjects of international law, whereas individuals are – for the purposes of this discussion – rights holders in international and European human rights law.[12]

As for the principle of sovereignty, it is commonly understood as 'supremacy in respect of power, domination, or rank; supreme dominion, authority, or rule'.[13] Although sovereignty has existed since ancient times in different fashions within and between polities, the conceptual elaboration of modern sovereignty,[14] as an institutional attribute, is owed to the French philosopher

---

[7]  Antonio Cassese, *International Law* (2nd edn, OUP 2003) 3; Patrick Daillier and Alain Pellet, *Droit International Public* (7th edn, LGDJ 2002) 35.

[8]  Francisco de Vitoria and Hugo Grotius belonged to the school of natural law, see Malcolm N. Shaw, *International Law* (7th edn, OUP 2014) 16–18; Daillier and Pellet (n 7) 4–57.

[9]  Daillier and Pellet (n 7) 59, 98–100.

[10]  Shaw (n 8) 21.

[11]  Hersch Lauterpacht, *International Law and Human Rights* (Stevens & Sons 1950).

[12]  Cassese (n 7) 142–150; Shaw (n 8) 188–189.

[13]  *Oxford English Dictionary*, 'Sovereignty' <www.oed.com/view/Entry/185343?redirectedFrom= sovereignty#eid> accessed 1 April 2021.

[14]  For an overview on the nature, subject and source of sovereignty, see Samantha Besson, 'Sovereignty' (2011), in *Max Planck Encyclopaedia of Public International Law* <http://opil .ouplaw.com/home/MPIL> accessed 1 April 2021.

and jurist Jean Bodin, who defined it as the absolute and perpetual power of the *République*.[15] His views, together with those of Hugo Grotius,[16] contributed significantly to the appearance of state sovereignty as a key principle of the international legal order since the adoption of the seventeenth-century Treaties of Westphalia.[17] The essence of this double-sided concept is clearly captured in the influential *Palmas Island Case* award of the Permanent Court of Arbitration:

> Sovereignty in the relations between states signifies independence. Independence in regard to a portion of the globe is the right to exercise therein, to the exclusion of any other state, the functions of a state. The development of the national organization of states during the last few centuries and, as a corollary, the development of international law, have established this principle of the exclusive competence of the state in regard to its own territory in such a way as to make it the point of departure in settling most questions that concern international relations.[18]

Sovereignty means both independence from the interference of other states and supreme authority within a territory and over the population located therein.[19] In international law, the former (which is related to power and authority *between* states) is referred to as external sovereignty, and the latter (which concerns the power and authority *of* or *within* the state) is the internal component of sovereignty. This body of law concerns both aspects of the content of sovereignty, and since 1945, it has increasingly imposed obligations concerning how states behave in their jurisdictions and how they exercise their public power in relation to people and markets.[20]

As explained above, sovereignty is a structural principle of the international legal order, which locates the state at the centre of the stage of international relations, indeed as the primary subject.[21] Nevertheless, given that international law in the era of the UN has rapidly switched from being the law

---

[15] Jean Bodin, *Les Six Livres de la République* (first published 1579, Alden Press 1955) ch 7.

[16] Hugo Grotius, *De Jure Belli ac Pacis* (Buon 1625) book I.3.8.1.

[17] The peace process of Westphalia is associated with the birth of modern international law, as created by sovereign and equal states. For an overview, see Rainer Grote, 'The Westphalian System' (2006), in *Max Planck Encyclopaedia of Public International Law* <https://opil.ouplaw.com/home/MPIL> accessed 1 April 2021.

[18] *Island of Palmas Case (the Netherlands v USA)* (Merits) [1928] 2 UN Reports of International Arbitral Awards 829, para 8.

[19] *Customs Régime between Germany and Austria* (Advisory Opinion) [1931] PCIJ Series A/B No 41 [Individual Opinion of M. Anzilotti] 57, emphasis added.

[20] Emmanuelle Jouannet, *The Liberal-Welfarist Law of Nations: A History of International Law* (CUP 2012) 4, 64.

[21] Cassese (n 7) 71.

of coexistence to being the law of cooperation and has many inroads into matters traditionally considered to be of a domestic nature, some scholars have begun to question the view that state sovereignty is or should be the central feature of international society.[22] These debates focus on whether and, if so, to what extent the participation of new subjects in law-making marks a paradigm shift in the structural order of international law[23] and on whether it is desirable that sovereignty remains a guiding principle to address the contemporary legal and political problems of the international community.[24] While such debates constitute insightful critical approaches to the orthodoxy of international law, the dominant doctrine still considers (state) sovereignty to be a fundamental principle governing international relations and an organising principle of international law.[25] Nevertheless, there is substantial agreement on the point that the *exclusive* sovereignty of the *Palmas Islands* case is not a synonym for *unlimited* sovereignty.[26] The limit, as far as international law is concerned, is represented by state duties to comply with customary international law and treaty law,[27] including in the field of human rights.

### 1.1.2 *Human Rights Law*

International human rights law, as a comprehensive legal framework, was born in the aftermath of World War II. The horrors of the Holocaust and the war had shocked the world, and the international community mobilised around the idea that the treatment of people within states' borders could not be left to the exclusive discretion of states and domestic laws.[28] The dominant modern conception of human rights has its roots in several seventeenth- and eighteenth-century theories of natural law and rights, according to which (very

[22] See reference made by José E. Alvarez, 'State Sovereignty in Not Withering Away: A Few Lessons from the Future' in Antonio Cassese (ed) *Realizing Utopia* (OUP 2012) 26, 29.

[23] McCorquodale claims a 'participatory approach to sovereignty' and describes it as a relational concept shared by all subjects that engage in the international community. See chapters 'International Community and State Sovereignty: An Uneasy Symbiotic Relationship' and 'An Inclusive International Legal System' in Robert McCorquodale, *International Law beyond the State: Essays on Sovereignty, Non-state Actors and Human Rights* (CMP 2011) 401, 427.

[24] Don Herzog, *Sovereignty: RIP* (Yale University Press 2020) ix.

[25] See, Cassese (n 7) 46.

[26] Besson (n 14) para 75; and Christopher Greenwood, 'Sovereignty: A View from the International Bench' in Richard Rawlings, Peter Leyland and Alison Young (eds) *Sovereignty and the Law* (OUP 2013) 251, 254.

[27] VCLT (n 47, Introduction) Article 27: 'a party may not invoke the provisions of its internal law as justification for its failure to perform a treaty'.

[28] Johannes Morsink, *The Universal Declaration of Human Rights: Origins, Drafting, and Intent* (University of Pennsylvania Press 1999) 36–51.

briefly) there existed a reason-based moral framework with which positive man-made laws had to comply, and men were endowed with some innate tendencies and freedoms – natural rights – that were cognisable though the use of reason.[29] In the mid-twentieth century, these theories – often infused with moral, liberal and Western visions – led to a cosmopolitan conceptual-isation of human rights according to which 'all human beings are born free and equal in dignity and rights'[30] and every state must exercise its powers in a way that is compatible with these universal freedoms and entitlements. The Charter of the United Nations, the document that set out a new international order based on the prohibition of the use of force and maintenance of peaceful international relations, declared the promotion of human rights to be one of the purposes of the organisation and a value to be reaffirmed.[31] This statement represented the first encroachment of the naturalist logic into the revisited post-war international law. Human rights gained their first recogni-tion in an international legal document, and this 'value-based approach' to international law[32] has since been secured with the adoption of the morally authoritative Universal Declaration of Human Rights (UDHR) – containing civil, political, economic, social and cultural rights[33] – through binding human rights treaties[34] and with the recognition of some rights as customary norms, *jus cogens* and legal positions that can give rise to obligations *erga omnes* in international law.[35]

In the second half of the twentieth century, international law became progressively more engaged with the protection of human rights, and this has had an impact on the legitimate exercise of jurisdictional functions by

---

[29] For example, see John Finnis, *Natural Law and Natural Rights* (OUP 1980).

[30] UDHR (n 2) Article 1.

[31] Charter of the United Nations (UN Charter) (Adopted 26 June 1945, entry into force 24 October 1945) 892 UNTS 119, Preamble, Articles 1(3) and 55(c).

[32] Ilias Bantekas and Lutz Oette, *International Human Rights Law and Practice* (3rd edn, CUP 2020) 52.

[33] UDHR (n 2) Preamble: 'the General Assembly proclaims this Universal Declaration of Human Right as a *common standard of achievement* for all people and all nations', emphasis added.

[34] Including those mentioned at nn. 42 and 43, Introduction.

[35] Human rights as *customary international law* means that some of these norms are embraced via general state practice and are considered binding, regardless of their recognition in treaties; see American Law Institute, 'Restatement (3rd) of the Foreign Relations Law of the US' (1986) Section 701; *jus cogens* is a synonym of 'peremptory norms' [VCLT (n 47, Introduction) Article 53], which means that certain human rights norms, such as the prohibition of genocide and freedom from torture, are considered non-derogable under any circumstance, see *Questions Relating to the Obligation to Prosecute or Extradite (Belgium v Senegal)* (ICJ 2012) para 99; Obligations *erga omnes* highlight the fundamental nature of a human rights norm in relation to which all states have an interest and standing, see *Barcelona Traction case (Belgium v Spain)* (ICJ 1970) para 33.

states. However, it is worth noting that the UN Charter had not empowered the UN with any direct competence for the protection of human rights. Rather, states delegated to the organisation the *promotion* of the law and of cooperation in the area. In the first decades of the UN's existence, these loose textual state obligations allowed for an interpretation of Article 2(7) of the UN Charter to protect state sovereignty in the area of human rights as a matter 'essentially within the domestic jurisdiction of any State'. However, in the 1970s, the UNGA openly acknowledged that the protection of human rights was a predominantly international issue because human rights had an entrenched relation with the purposes of the organisation, including the maintenance of global peace and security.[36]

The negotiation of binding treaties in international and regional fora had, since the late 1940s, given legal recognition to the idea of the international protection of human rights. These human rights regimes have further developed through the creation of monitoring bodies, some of which allow individuals or groups of individuals to bring claims against states for human rights violations. This revolutionary development attributed elements of international legal personality to individuals by empowering them to claim their rights and hold states, as international duty bearers, to account.[37] Nevertheless, while international and regional human rights law, as a set of substantive rules, might be considered to be internationally led, the enforcement of such rules and the establishment of associated redress systems primarily take place at the domestic level. As such, the legal system is built around the principle of subsidiarity (states are, in the first instance, responsible for addressing human rights violations),[38] and this has significant implications for the actual enjoyment of migrant rights.

### 1.1.3 *The Mutual Impact of Sovereignty and Human Rights*

State sovereignty and human rights are often presented as opposing principles: the former is state-centred, and the latter is person-focused. They are synonyms of power and the limitation of power, respectively. To assess their relationship, it seems appropriate to distinguish between sovereignty as content and sovereignty as structure and, in relation to the former, between

---

[36] The UNGA Res 3219 (XXIX)/1974 on Chile was 'the real watershed in UN practice in this area'. See Israel de Jesús Butler, *Unravelling Sovereignty: Human Rights Actors and the Structure of International Law* (Intersentia 2007) 34–44.

[37] Irene Khan, *The Unheard Truth: Poverty and Human Rights* (W.W. Norton & Company 2009).

[38] See Section 1.3, *infra*.

authority and independence. Ultimately, I show that sovereignty is embedded in international human rights law and is, therefore, confirmed as a structural principle of international law to which human rights belong.

Based on Articles 2(1) and 2(4) of the UN Charter, sovereignty, as independence from external intervention, has been besieged by the doctrines of humanitarian intervention and responsibility to protect, two contested concepts that qualify sovereignty as responsibility, albeit to different extents. These doctrines hold that every state is internationally responsible for the treatment of people within its jurisdiction while also justifying the collective use of force in response to severe human rights violations within a state. However, such clashes of norms and goals in international law fall beyond the scope of this study.[39]

Sovereignty, as state authority to enact laws, adjudicate, draw up policies and enforce laws within a domestic jurisdiction, is a central feature of international law. The evolution of human rights as a branch of international law over the last seventy years has been aimed at preventing the arbitrary treatment of people through the establishment of a minimum content for state obligations in this regard. Accordingly, although logic may lead one to conclude that there is an inherent clash between this aspect of sovereignty and human rights, the *legal* understanding of these concepts points to a softer confrontation, at least with respect to the current state of the art. Indeed, on the one hand, regarding the broader picture of international law, it must be acknowledged that the international legal concept of sovereignty is not intended as unrestricted power and that international law works by imposing legal obligations regarding state behaviours by 'validating some claims of sovereign powers and refusing to validate others'.[40] On the other hand, most human rights, as legal rights, have not been conceptualised as absolute vis-à-vis other public interests. Human rights treaties allow reservations – although special rules apply[41] – and many rights contain limitation clauses that allow for the rights to be balanced against other private and public interests.[42] Furthermore, the formal

---

[39] For an overview of this debate, see Ramesh Thakur, 'The Use of International Force to Prevent or Halt Atrocities: From Humanitarian Intervention to the Responsibility to Protect' in Dinah Shelton (ed) *The Oxford Handbook of International Human Rights Law* (OUP 2013) 815 and Amitai Etzioni, 'Sovereignty as Responsibility' (2006) *Orbis* 50(1) 71–85.

[40] Patrick Macklem, *The Sovereignty of Human Rights* (OUP 2015) 29.

[41] See Ineke Boerefijn, 'Impact on the Law on Treaty Reservations' in Menno T. Kamminga and Martin Scheinin (eds) *The Impact of Human Rights Law on General International Law* (OUP 2009) 63; International Law Commission, 'Guide to Practice on Reservations to Treaties' (2011) *Yearbook of the International Law Commission* II(II) Ss. 4.5.1, 4.5.3.

[42] This broad wording means both 'derogations' in time of emergency, for example, Article 15 ECHR (n 43, Introduction), Article 4 ICCPR (n 42, Introduction), or common 'limitations'

incorporation of international human rights law into the domestic legal order, at least in dualist states, appears to be key for its applicability.[43] In addition, international treaties on human rights require the state to establish domestic means of redress for cases of violation[44] and to subject individual complaints made before international bodies to admissibility criteria, such as the exhaustion of domestic remedies, which are normally strictly scrutinised.[45] All of these structural, procedural and substantive features constitute an encroachment of state sovereignty into the legal sphere of human rights, which is based on the principle of subsidiarity. Subsidiarity – a central feature of human rights law – means that, in systems of multilevel governance, the most local level of governance is considered best equipped to exercise sovereign regulatory functions.[46] Notwithstanding some erosion of the domestic domain as a result of international and regional human rights law in relation to the internal aspect of sovereignty, human rights seem to 'qualify, rather than displace, the sovereignty of states' in international law.[47]

Finally, in relation to the impact of human rights on sovereignty as a 'structural' principle of international law, the conclusions cannot divert much from the above. Nevertheless, there are scholars who argue that the proliferation of international subjects or legal persons in the context of law-making and monitoring jeopardises the positioning of state sovereignty as a key organising principle of the international legal order.[48] The impact of civil society organisations, the delegation of power to international organisations, and the increasing role of individuals and corporations in the field of human

---

or 'restrictions' of rights, for example, Articles 9, 12, 13, 18, 19, 21, 22 ICCPR, Articles 5, 8–11 ECHR.

43  The 'incorporation' or 'transposition' of international law into domestic legal order is necessary for the domestic applicability of treaties only when states are 'dualist'. Dualism, as opposed to monism, is a legal tradition according to which international law and domestic law are two separate spheres of law. Therefore, for the applicability of international treaties at the domestic level, national acts incorporating international norms need to be enacted. See, Davíd Thór Björgvinsson, *The Intersection of International Law and Domestic Law: A Theoretical and Practical Analysis* (Edward Elgar Publishing 2015).

44  For example, ICCPR (n 42, Introduction) Article 2.3(a) and ECHR (n 43, Introduction) Article 13.

45  For example, ECHR (ibid), Article 35 and Optional Protocol to the International Covenant on Economic, Social and Cultural Rights (adopted 10 December 2008, entered into force 5 May 2013) ('OP-ICESCR') A/RES/63/117, Articles 2–5.

46  For details Gerald L. Neuman, 'Subsidiarity' in Shelton (n 39) 360, and Isabel Feichtner 'Subsidiarity' (2007), in *Max Planck Encyclopaedia of Public International Law* <https://opil.ouplaw.com/home/MPIL> accessed 1 April 2021.

47  James Crawford, 'Sovereignty as a Legal Value' in James Crawford and Martti Koskenniemi (eds) *The Cambridge Companion to International Law* (CUP 2012) 122.

48  For instance, see De Jesús Butler (n 36), and McCorquodale (n 23).

rights law is undeniable. Nevertheless, due to the fact that the structure of international law is still state-oriented, states appear to retain key de jure and de facto powers in this field. For example, the implementation of human rights treaties and the 'enforcement' of the decisions of their monitoring bodies are mainly contingent on the willingness of states to comply. In relation to the latter, the findings of most international human rights bodies have only moral or recommendatory authority, and even when they are legally binding, as is the case of a handful of courts, the execution of their judgments is left to state compliance in good faith and mediated through political bodies.[49] The concept of sovereignty is, therefore, built into human rights instruments. Since subsidiarity may be regarded as a structural principle of human rights law,[50] state sovereignty remains a valid lynchpin of international law. Overall, the relationship between human rights and general international law is characterised by a 'tension between substance and form'.[51] While human rights are designed as universally valid propositions, human rights law presupposes the nation-state as the venue for human rights implementation.[52] Human rights, by becoming international legal rights, have had to surrender to the structural logic of public international law.

## 1.2 MIGRANTS: BETWEEN SOVEREIGNTY AND HUMAN RIGHTS

Building on the above debates, the core aim of this section is to assess whether and, if so, to what extent human rights have 'qualified' sovereignty in relation to the treatment of migrants or whether the opposite is the case.

### 1.2.1 *Migrants and Sovereignty*

The Westphalian system of states, although it is qualified and limited in the exercise of both internal and external sovereign powers, is still the reference

---

[49]   For example, on the role of the intergovernmental body of the Council of Europe, the Committee of Ministers, on the execution of binding judgments and non-binding decisions on human rights. See ECHR (n 43, Introduction) Article 46, and the Additional Protocol to the European Social Charter Providing for a System of Collective Complaints (adopted 9 November 1996, entry into force 1 July 1998) ETS. No. 158.

[50]   Paolo G. Carozza 'Subsidiarity as a Structural Principle of International Human Rights Law' (2003) 97 *American Journal of International Law* 38.

[51]   Frédéric Mégret, 'Nature of Obligations' in Daniel Moeckli, Sangeeta Shah and Sandesh Sivakumaran (eds) *International Human Rights Law* (OUP 2018) 86, 88.

[52]   Benjamin Gregg, *The Human Rights State: Justice within and beyond Sovereign Nations* (Penn Press 2016) 44, as referred to in Lindsey N. Kingston, *Fully Human: Personhood, Citizenship, and Rights* (OUP 2019) 32.

model of the international community.[53] Intimately linked to this is state-led immigration management,[54] which has been regarded as a defining aspect of state sovereignty since the end of the nineteenth century.[55] Indeed, 'sovereignty's inherent powers within the nation-state system' are considered to include the state's power to control and manage the entry, residence and expulsion of aliens.[56] This is the result of a series of historical contingencies that occurred at the end of the nineteenth century, including political and economic tensions between states, which resulted in the spread of protectionism and nationalism[57] and the 'appearance of non-European foreigners on the migratory landscape' after four centuries of European explorations, colonisation, international business journeys and emigration.[58] For example, when these new migrants, mostly Asians, were drawn by the colonial interest in recruiting labour on a temporary basis, governing elites in both Australia and the USA proved reluctant to grant them entry.[59] One of the outcomes was the development of a common law jurisprudence that interpreted international legal theories as condoning the absolute state power to regulate immigration.[60] Therein, the texts of the authoritative international jurist Emer De Vattel were misinterpreted and bent to the political-judicial intent to regulate race and labour.[61] Indeed, in his *The Law of Nations*, Vattel set forth that:

> The lord of the territory may, whenever he thinks proper, forbid its being entered [. . .] he has, no doubt, a power to annex what conditions he pleases

---

[53] Alvarez (n 22) 26.

[54] In general, the last forty years of the European history have seen a gradual narrowing of the legal possibilities for aliens to immigrate and settle in European countries. See Boeles et al., European Migration Law (2nd edn, Intersentia 2014) 25. For example, in the post-World War II era and during the 1970s, French policy on immigration was not aimed at combating irregular immigration but rather was informally but deliberately focused on tolerating it. See Godfried Engbersen and Dennis Broeders, 'The State versus the Alien: Immigration Control and Strategies of Irregular Immigrants' (2009) *West European Politics* 32 867, 874.

[55] Catherine Dauvergne, 'Sovereignty, Migration and the Rule of Law in Global Times' (2004) *The Modern Law Review* 67(4) 588, 590; Eve Lester, *Making Migration Law: The Foreigner, Sovereignty and the Case of Australia* (CUP 2018) 81–111.

[56] Nafziger (n 1) 822.

[57] Ibid 816.

[58] Lester (n 55) 82, 84.

[59] Ibid.

[60] *Nishimura Ekiu v United States* [1892] 142 US 651 (US Supreme Court); *Fong Yue Ting v United States* [1893] 149 US 698 (US Supreme Court); *Musgrove v Chun Teong Toy* [1891] AC 272 (Privy Council of the United Kingdom). For details and other jurisprudential references see Lester (n 55) 94–107.

[61] Lester (n 55) 99–100; Nafziger (n 1) 813–814.

to the permission to enter. This, as we have already said, it is a consequence of the right to domain.[62]

However, he identified several qualifiers to this power in his writings, including the stipulation that 'every nation has the right to refuse to admit a foreigner into the country, when he cannot enter without putting the nation in evident danger, or doing it a manifest injury'.[63] Vattel added that the sovereign's 'duty towards all mankind obliges him on other occasions to allow free passage through, and residence in, his state'.[64] These rights of passage and residence could not be refused without 'particular and important reasons' and were extended to the case of 'a foreigner who comes into the country with the hope of recovering his health, or for the sake of acquiring instruction in the schools and academies'.[65] As for the right of establishment of foreigners, sovereign discretion would take precedence and establishment could be refused if it represented 'too great an inconvenience or danger'.[66] Vattel even stated that in Europe, unlike in Japan and China, the general rule was 'open frontiers', except in relation to 'enemies of the state'. State power to exclude was not absolute in Vattel's writings but was framed and limited by the above situations.[67] However, since the late nineteenth century, Vattel has often been associated with a maxim of international law according to which states have absolute power to regulate the entry of non-nationals who are not asylum seekers or refugees.

This exclusionary approach has survived until the present time, and the case law of the ECtHR, since the landmark case of *Abdulaziz, Cabales and Balkandali v. the United Kingdom*,[68] has made wide use of the 'long-established maxim of international law' according to which immigration control and the right to exclude are prerogatives of sovereign states. The constant repetition of this maxim encapsulates the idea of 'fixed and exclusive territoriality that is associated with the rise of the modern nation-state' and with sovereignty.[69] This suggests a natural state of the world divided into territories,

---

[62] Emer de Vattel, *The Law of Nations* (first published 1787, Liberty Fund 2009) Book II, ch VIII, para 100.

[63] Ibid, Book I, para 230.

[64] Ibid, Book II, ch VIII, para 100.

[65] Ibid, Book II, ch X, para 135.

[66] Ibid, Book II, ch X, para 136, emphasis added.

[67] Ibid, Book II, ch IX, paras 119–125; Nafziger (n 1) 810–815.

[68] *Abdulaziz, Cabales and Balkandali v the United Kigndom* App nos 9214/81, 9474/81 (ECHR 1985) para 67; New York Declaration for Refugees and Migrants (16 September 2016) UNGA Res 71.1, A/RES/71/1, para 24.

[69] Dora Kostakopoulou, 'Irregular Migration and Migration Theory: Making State Authorisation Less Relevant' in Bogusz et al. (n 13, Introduction) 45.

whereby people are associated inextricably with their state of origin or nationality. However, this idea of foreigners as outsiders with no right to enter countries that are not their own was the result of historical contingencies and was deeply linked to political-economic interests, the rise of non-European immigration and nativism.[70]

The doctrine of the 'integrity of national borders' and the exercise of sovereign power to determine who is entitled to enter and stay in a given state territory gave rise to different categories of people: nationals and non-nationals, with the latter being subdivided into authorised immigrants and irregular or undocumented migrants. The very presence of irregular migrants within a state jurisdiction is perceived as a de facto erosion of the state's territorial sovereignty and a violation of the state's power to determine the composition of its *demos* or national community.[71] The sovereign state's right 'to exclude' through refusal of admission or deportation is characterised by extensive executive discretion, but it is not unrestricted: slim but significant limitations are stipulated in refugee law and in certain provisions of human rights law. For this reason, Section 1.2.2 examines whether migrants in general and irregular migrants in particular enjoy the protection of human rights law and the extent to which this tool manages to counterbalance the sovereignty-related right to exclude.

### 1.2.2 *Migrant Rights or Human Rights?*

#### 1.2.2.1 International Law and the Standards of Civilisation

The treatment of foreigners was a topic of international law long before human rights (law) was officially recognised within that legal framework. This trend originated at the beginning of the sixteenth century with a series of intellectual and legal arguments that were designed to protect Western nationals while they were conducting business and expanding their interests in the non-European world during the colonial era. Fathers of international law, such as Francisco de Vitoria and Hugo Grotius, dealt with 'civilised' Christian European foreigners by resorting to theories of natural law to

---

[70] Lester (n 55) 77–86; Nafziger (n 1) 816.
[71] Linda S. Bosniak, 'Human Rights, State Sovereignty and the Protection of Undocumented Migrants under the International Migrant Workers Convention' in Bogusz et al. (n 13, Introduction) 311, 329; Dembour and Kelly (n 3, Introduction) 6–10.

articulate the 'rights of aliens to trade and preach' in the New World.[72] Francisco de Vitoria, in justifying the Spanish expansion in the Indies, defended the 'humane and dutiful' obligation to welcome strangers:[73] the stranger's (that is, the European coloniser's) right to receive hospitality, to trade, to travel and to reside within a territory were central to his thinking.[74]

A century after Vitoria's speculations, Hugo Grotius also defended the mobility of European traders in Europe and outside the continent as the natural order of things by asserting the rights to trade and hospitality.[75] Although the starting point was the right to free movement, the rights of foreigners could be restricted when their intentions were not 'benign'.[76] It is interesting to note that Grotius went as far as recognising the (limitable) right of foreigners to enjoy 'basic necessities'.[77] Although he is commonly regarded as one of the theorists who excluded foreigners' rights from international law, his arguments are similar to those put forward by Vattel.[78]

By the end of the nineteenth century, international law had also developed the doctrine of state responsibility for injuries to aliens. This meant that the treatment of a non-national below certain minimum 'standards of civilisation' (which were not clearly defined)[79] constituted a wrongful act towards the state of nationality of that person, which gave rise to interstate responsibility. The state of nationality, at its own discretion,[80] could exercise diplomatic protection in favour of its national. These relations constituted an exercise of state

---

[72] Anthony Anghie and Wayne McCormack, 'The Rights of Aliens: Legal Regimes and Historical Perspectives' in Thomas N. Maloney and Kim Korinek (eds) *Migration in the 21st Century: Rights, Outcomes and Policy* (Routledge 2010) 23, 30.

[73] Francisco de Vitoria, 'On the American Indians' in Anthony Pagden and Jeremy Lawrance (eds) *Vitoria: Political Writings* (CUP 1991) 250, 278–282.

[74] Ibid; Lester (n 55) 54–60.

[75] Hugo Grotius, *De Jure Praedae Commentarius* (first published 1604, Clarendon Press 1950) 218–220.

[76] Hugo Grotius, *De Jure Belli ac Pacis Libri Tres* (first published 1646, Clarendon Press 1925) Book II, ch II 192, 198, 201–202.

[77] Ibid, 192–195, 201.

[78] See *supra* at Section 1.2.1.

[79] Debates about 'civilisation' are controversial, interdisciplinary and beyond the scope of this study. As per Westlake, the 'test of civilisation' could consist in the capacity of the government to guarantee both the life and security of aliens and the security and well-being of locals. According to many colonial doctrines, when a 'country' was not considered civilised, it lacked sovereignty and therefore was suitable for conquest as *terra nullius*. See Anthony Anghie, 'The Evolution of International Law: Colonial and Postcolonial Realities' (2007) *Third World Quarterly* 27(5) 739, 745.

[80] *Barcelona Traction case* (n 35) para 79, ICJ stated that 'the State must be viewed as the sole judge to decide whether its protection will be granted, to what extent it is granted, and when it will cease'.

sovereignty and were the result of a traditional paradigm of international law whereby individuals were mere objects of interstate relationships and not active subjects.[81] Therefore, during the pre–human rights era, an individual classed as an alien often enjoyed greater protection under international law than as a national in his home country, since the latter was the exclusive domain of national law. For these reasons, the law of diplomatic protection has been defined as the forerunner of human rights in international law.[82] This conclusion may be an oversimplification, however, as the standard of civilisation doctrine and the related practice of 'capitulation agreements'[83] were legal constructs of the abusive colonial period aimed at protecting citizens of European countries as they went about their expansionist business in the 'uncivilised' colonies. When human mobility started to flow significantly in the opposite direction, with migrants tending to belong to lower social classes, contemporary international law shifted to play a marginal normative role with regard to migration.[84]

### 1.2.2.2 Human Rights for Migrants

In the contemporary legal world, the standard of civilisation law has been replaced by international human rights law.[85] However, during the first three decades after the adoption of the UDHR, international human rights were purely formal in relation to migrants and were mainly designed to empower citizens vis-à-vis abuses committed by their state of nationality. This international project 'made assumptions about [national] identity and membership' of rights holders, which 'placed limitations on its inclusiveness'.[86] Furthermore, the rights of aliens were associated with colonialism as a result of which core pieces of human rights law allowed developing states to restrict

---

[81]  On diplomatic protection and minimum standards of treatment for aliens, see Vincent Chetail, 'The Human Rights of Migrants in General International Law: From Minimum Standards to Fundamental Rights' (2014) *Georgetown Immigration Law Journal* 28 225, 231 and Annemarieke Vermeer-Kunzli, 'Diplomatic Protection as a Source of Human Rights' in Shelton (n 39) 250, 251.

[82]  Ibid (Vermeer-Kunzli) 262.

[83]  Capitulations were bilateral agreements whose purpose was essentially to insulate European expatriates or colonisers from the domestic jurisdiction of the forum state. For further details, see Christine Bell, 'Capitulations' (2009) in *Max Planck Encyclopaedia of Public International Law* <https://opil.ouplaw.com/home/MPIL> accessed 1 April 2021; Cassese (n 7) 26–28.

[84]  E. Achiume Tendayi, 'Reimagining International Law for Global Migration: Migration as Decolonization?' (2017) *American Journal of International Law* 111 142–146.

[85]  See the ICJ acknowledgement in *Ahmadou Sadio Diallo* (*Guinea v Dem. Rep. Congo*), (Preliminary Objections) [2007] 599 para 39.

[86]  Kingston (n 52) 30.

the economic rights of non-nationals in their jurisdictions.[87] The change began in the 1970s, when the mass expulsion of Asians from Uganda operated as a catalyst for greater involvement of the UN in the protection of the rights of non-nationals.[88] Since then, debates within the UNGA and its ancillary bodies brought about, *inter alia*, the adoption of the declaration on the human rights of non-citizens,[89] the Convention on the Rights of Migrant Workers,[90] the Durban Declaration[91] and, more recently, the New York Declaration for Refugees and Migrants and the Global Compacts.[92]

Apart from these migrant-specific initiatives, the general human rights treaties were worded to embrace every human being as a human rights holder by virtue of their common humanity or personhood,[93] irrespective of their migration status. As such, human rights conventions apply *ratione personae* to 'everyone' or 'all individuals'[94] in a state territory or jurisdiction,[95] and this includes non-citizens and, among them, irregular migrants. While this is the general rule, some treaty provisions and their interpretations allow for differential treatment on the grounds of nationality and immigration status. The Human Rights Committee (HRCtee), which is the monitoring body of the

---

[87] Article 2(3) ICESCR (n 23, Introduction) allows developing countries to restrict the enjoyment of economic rights for non-nationals. Regarding colonialism-related reasons for this rule, see Chetail (n 81) 235, 248–249; for the restricted applicability of this article, see Manisuli Ssenyonjo, *Economic, Social and Cultural Rights in International Law* (Hart Publishing 2016) 147–150.

[88] Stefanie Grant, 'The Recognition of Migrants' Rights within the UN Human Rights System: The First 60 Years' in Dembour and Kelly (n 3, Introduction) 33.

[89] Declaration on the Human Rights of Individuals who are not nationals of the country in which they live (13 December 1985) UNGA Res 40/144.

[90] ICMW (n 42, Introduction).

[91] This declaration reiterated that state sovereignty should be consistent with the human rights of all migrants, regardless of their legal status. See World Conference against Racism, Racial Discrimination, Xenophobia and Related Intolerance, Durban Declaration and Programme of Action) (8 September 2001) A/CONF.189/12, paras 26 and 39.

[92] New York Declaration (n 68); Global Compact for Safe, Orderly and Regular Migration (19 December 2018) UNGA Res 73/195; Global Compact on Refugees (17 December 2018) UNGA Res 73/151.

[93] UDHR (n 2) Article 2 stipulates that 'everyone is entitled to all the rights and freedoms set forth in this Declaration, without distinction of any kind'. See also ICCPR (n 42, Introduction) Article 2(1); CRC (n 42, Introduction) Article 2(1); CMW (n 42, Introduction) Article 7; American Convention on Human Rights (adopted 22 November 1969, entry into force 18 July 1978) (ACHR) Article 1(1); African Charter on Human and Peoples' Rights (adopted 27 June 1981, entry into force 21 October 1986) (ACHPR) OAU Doc. CAB/LEG/67/3 rev. 5, Article 2.

[94] ECHR (n 43, Introduction), Article 1; ICCPR (n 42, Introduction).

[95] For example, the ECtHR acknowledges the existence of the application of the ECHR *ratione loci* when a violation of human rights takes place in a state party's territory and exceptionally when, extraterritorially, the state exercises control and authority over an individual. See *Hirsi Jamaa and Others v Italy* App no 27765/09 (ECHR 2012) paras 70–82.

International Covenant on Civil and Political Rights (ICCPR), made clear, in its General Comment No. 15, that non-citizens must enjoy, without discrimination, all human rights set forth in the Covenant, with the exclusion of the right to vote.[96] In addition to the above, the right to freedom of movement and freedom to choose a residence within the territory (Article 12 ICCPR) and the guarantees of due process in relation to expulsion from the territory (Article 13 ICCPR) were intended to apply only to 'lawfully residing aliens'.[97]

In all other areas, the interpretation of the principle of non-discrimination is central for framing the actual enjoyment of human rights law by non-nationals. The contemporary concepts of equality and non-discrimination are deeply influenced by the Aristotelian maxim that 'things that are alike should be treated alike'.[98] Applying this to people, modern scholars have criticised this concept as being entirely 'circular', because it does not clarify what is meant by 'like people', which generates confusion regarding what defines comparable situations.[99] Accordingly, differential treatment has been justified because the comparators – irregular/regular migrants or migrants/citizens – are not always deemed sufficiently similar to warrant similar treatment in various legal frameworks. While the prohibited grounds for discrimination in international human rights law do not explicitly include nationality or the legal status of people, the normative interpretation by most international bodies has partly covered this gap.[100] Therefore, prima facie, all migrants enjoy a broad catalogue of human rights on a non-discriminatory basis. In legal practice, 'distinction, exclusion, restriction or preference based on [legal status and nationality] which has the purpose or effect of [...] impairing the recognition, enjoyment or exercise, on an equal footing, of human rights and fundamental freedoms [that admit limitations]'[101] may be legally

---

[96] Human Rights Committee (HRCtee) 'General Comment No. 15: The Position of Aliens under the Covenant' (11 April 1986) para 2.

[97] Ibid, paras 8, 9, 10. Similarly, the ECtHR, in *Maaouia v France* App no 39652/98 (ECHR 2000), held that the right to fair trial in Article 6 ECHR does not apply to immigration proceedings.

[98] David Ross, *The Nicomachean Ethics/Aristotle* in John Loyd Ackrill and James Opie Urmson (eds) (OUP 1980) 112–117.

[99] Peter Westen, 'The Empty Idea of Equality' (1980) *Harvard Law Review* 95(3) 537; Christopher J. Peters, 'Equality Revisited' (1997) *Harvard Law Review* 110 1211.

[100] HRCtee, GC15 (n 96); CESCR, 'General Comment No. 20: Non-discrimination on Economic, Social and Cultural Rights' (2 July 2009) E/C.12/GC/20, para 30. Nationality and legal status, as prohibited grounds of discrimination, are covered by the phrase 'other status' in Articles 2(1) ICCPR and 2(2) ICESCR. See *Ibrahima Gueye et al. v France* Com no 196/1985 (HRCtee 1989); *Gaygusuz v Austria* App no 17371/90 (ECHR 1996).

[101] HRCtee, 'General Comment No. 18: Non-discrimination' (1989) para 6; CESCR, GC20 (ibid) para 7.

acceptable only when restrictive state measures have a domestic legal basis, pursue a legitimate aim (such as immigration control or protecting the economic well-being of the country) and remain reasonable and proportionate.[102] In the concrete assessment of this issue, the proportionality test between means and aim usually plays a crucial role.[103] The prohibition of discrimination is also of pivotal relevance for socioeconomic rights, since, in relation to societal inequalities and concrete situations of vulnerability, it was interpreted in international law as requiring states to take appropriate measures to address structural and substantive forms of discrimination.[104] The CESCR clearly states that socioeconomic rights, although to be realised progressively, apply to 'everyone including non-nationals, such as refugees, asylum seekers, stateless persons, migrant workers and victims of international trafficking, regardless of legal status and documentation',[105] and that very limited circumstances allow restrictions of the personal scope of these rights.[106] Against this background, at a domestic level, socioeconomic rights are often restricted for irregular migrants, which underscores the state belief that the limitation of these subsistence rights reduces the 'pull factor' of immigration and deters people from infringing immigration law.[107] As explained in the following chapters, socioeconomic rights have always been regarded as resource demanding, so states have tended to limit their enjoyment by community outsiders such as certain categories of undesired immigrants. Even if international human rights law regards universality and personhood as principles governing its scope of application, in practice, other statuses, such as

---

[102] *Gaygusuz* (n 100) para 42; *Case 'Relating to Certain Aspects of the Laws on the Use of Languages in Education in Belgium' v Belgium* App nos 1474/62, 1677/62, 1691/62, 1769/63, 1994/63, 2126/64 (ECHR 1968) para 10. See also HRCtee, GC18 (ibid) para 13; CESCR, GC20 (n 100) para 13; Manfred Nowak, *UN Covenant on Civil and Political Rights – Commentary* (2nd edn, NP Engel Publishing 2005) 31–51; Ciara Smyth, 'Why Is It So Difficult to Promote Human Rights-Based Approach to Immigration?' in Donncha O'Connell (ed) *The Irish Human Rights Law Review 2010* (Clarus Press 2010) 83, 89.

[103] See examples provided in Section 1.3, *infra*.

[104] The former means equality of everyone before the law, without consideration of individual or group-related disadvantaged situations. The latter means that the state – to avoid de facto discrimination – should abandon the neutrality of a non-discrimination approach to law and actively adopt all necessary measures to equalise people's starting points and opportunities to attain real equality. For further details, see Section 2.7.

[105] CESCR, GC20 (n 100) para 30; CERD Committee, 'General Recommendation No. 30 on Discrimination against Non-citizens' (2005).

[106] ICESCR (n 23, Introduction) Article 4. See also Section 3.3.1. See also Office of the High Commissioner for Human Rights, *The Economic, Social and Cultural Rights of Migrants in an Irregular Situation* (UN Publications 2014) 31–32.

[107] Bosniak (n 71) 324.

nationality, citizenship or residence, continue to play key roles in empowering human beings vis-à-vis the state where they live.[108]

Furthermore, even where irregular migrants are entitled to their human rights, the actual enjoyment of those rights can prove problematic because of their irregular migratory status. For them – perceived as people that have infringed a state's territorial sovereignty – universal human rights may be just illusionary rhetoric, since rights exercise at local and national level and access to domestic and international redress mechanisms normally 'presuppose that migrants entertain contacts with the hosting state organs', which may report them to immigration authorities.[109] Irregular migratory status acts as a structural barrier to the enjoyment of rights, which makes this group particularly vulnerable because of 'their inability to call upon the basic protective functions of the state in which they reside for fear of deportation'.[110] Therefore, as exemplified in the sections that follow, irregular or undocumented migrants are *sui generis* subjects of human rights law: while some international treaties plainly limit their human rights, the interpretation of universal treaty obligations, which also permits rights limitation, is unsettled with respect to irregular migration.

To conclude, human rights law is framed in a way that oscillates between statements of universalism on the one hand and 'the attraction of particularism or closure', whereby 'only those who are recognised as belonging to the polity' have full access to jurisdictional human rights guarantees.[111] As far as the rights of vulnerable migrants such as undocumented people are concerned, exclusionary justifications based on the concepts of dependency, national identity and costs,[112] which are supported by a liberal and negative idea of human rights, seem to have negatively affected the character of migrant rights. People who do not hold legally recognised membership to a Westphalian polity may see the enjoyment of their human rights reduced to the maintenance of 'bare life',[113] thus bringing into question the consistency of a model of international

---

[108] Constantin Sokoloff and Richard Lewis, 'Denial of Citizenship: A Challenge to Human Security' (2005) 28 *European Policy Centre – Issue Paper* 3–4, <www.epc.eu/en/Publications/Denial-of-Citizenship–A-Chal~22ed68> accessed 2 April 2021.

[109] Gregor Noll, 'Why Human Rights Fail to Protect Undocumented Migrants' (2010) *European Journal of Migration and Law* 12 241, 243.

[110] Jaya Ramji-Nogales, '"The Right to Have Rights": Undocumented Migrants and State Protection' (2015) *Kansas Law Review* 63 1045.

[111] Dembour (n 5) 251; See also Dembour and Kelly (n 3, Introduction) 6–11.

[112] Baumgärtel (n 12, Introduction) 138–139.

[113] Giorgio Agamben, *Homo Sacer: Sovereign Power and Bare Life* (Stanford University Press 1998).

constitutionalism based on universal rights which are grounded on equal worth and dignity of every human being.

## 1.3 TRENDS IN THE EUROPEAN AND INTERNATIONAL JURISPRUDENCE ON THE HUMAN RIGHTS OF MIGRANTS WITH IRREGULAR OR PRECARIOUS STATUS

Having clarified the undertones of the human rights–sovereignty tension in the context of (irregular) migration, I now demonstrate how the clash plays out in pieces of international and European human rights law. This section aims to give a flavour of both exclusionary and protective jurisprudential tendencies in the contemporary human rights practice of the ECtHR and the UN treaty bodies. This helps to set the stage for later chapters, which extensively detail state obligations regarding the complex relations between health and irregular migration in human rights law, as complemented by public health arguments.

### 1.3.1 Instances of Immigration Cases before the Strasbourg Court

The ECHR is a multilateral human rights treaty between forty-seven countries across Europe and Western Asia, signed in the context of the Council of Europe in 1950. It is probably the most visible and celebrated of all human rights instruments, partly because its monitoring body, the ECtHR, is empowered to receive individual applications claiming violations of the ECHR and to deliver international judgments that are binding for the member states of the Council of Europe.[114] Like many other general human rights instruments of the same period, the original purpose of the ECHR was to protect citizens against arbitrary state treatment. This is clear from the drafting history: the Convention's personal scope was universally extended as a result of the Italian delegation's dissatisfaction with a proposal to link the rights in the Convention to people's residence in a member state, because that protection gap would have threatened the position of Italian nationals living in other European countries, at a time when Italy was a migrant-sending rather than a migrant-receiving country.[115]

Although the ECHR has been a treaty of universal personal application since its adoption, the case law of the Strasbourg Court concerning migrant rights has mainly developed over the last forty years and more intensively in

---

[114] ECHR (n 43, Introduction) Articles 32, 46.
[115] As explained by Dembour (n 5) 35–45.

the last two decades.[116] However, some provisions of the ECHR and some authoritative precedents of the ECtHR provide for a blunt asymmetric implementation of rights where migrants are concerned. For example, Articles 5(1) (f) and 16 ECHR (dealing with the right to liberty and restrictions on the political activities of aliens, respectively) explicitly authorise limitations of the rights of migrants.[117] Furthermore, Article 6(1) ECHR is consistently interpreted as excluding conventional fair trial guarantees from asylum, deportation and related procedures. In the landmark case of *Maaouia v. France*, Article 6(1) was not considered applicable to cases concerning migrant removal from state territories or exclusion orders because these circumstances would 'not involve a determination of [a person's] civil rights and obligations or of any criminal charge against [them]' and 'major repercussions on the applicant's private and family life or on [their] prospects of employment cannot suffice to bring those proceedings within the scope of civil rights'.[118] Not all the ECtHR judges considered these justifications to be convincing; some believed that because the 'rescission of an exclusion order' was an available legal remedy, 'the applicant's claim concerned the determination of a "civil" right'.[119] While it is beyond the scope of this chapter to provide a detailed analysis of the Court's jurisprudence in the field of immigration,[120] I examine here a sample of the applicable case law to present how, either directly or indirectly, state sovereignty impacts on the immigration case law of the ECtHR and to foreground some instances of *pro homine* findings.

Prior to examining the Court's findings on the merits of cases, it is worth mentioning the exceptional interim measures jurisdiction of the ECtHR (*per* rule 39 of the Rules of the Courts) in cases of deportation. This jurisdiction arises when an applicant would face a real risk of serious and irreversible harm involving violations of Articles 2 (life), 3 (torture or inhuman or degrading treatment or punishment) or 8 (right to private and family life) ECHR if the deportation was not suspended while the Court was considering the merits of

---

[116] The case of *Abdulaziz* (n 68) in 1985 was the first case decided on the merits which concerned the rights of immigrants.
[117] Furthermore, in *Saadi v the United Kingdom* App no 13229/03 (ECHR 2008), analysed in the main body, the Court made clear that immigration detention is justified even when it is not the measure of last resort.
[118] *Maaouia* (n 97), paras 36, 38.
[119] Ibid, Dissenting opinion of Junge Loucaides, joined by Judge Traja.
[120] European Court of Human Rights (Jurisconsult), 'Guide on the Case-Law of the European Convention on Human Right – Immigration – Updated on 31 August 2020', <https://echr.coe .int/Documents/Guide_Immigration_ENG.pdf> accessed 2 April 2021.

the case.[121] This practice, which concerns only a small number of migrant-related cases, demonstrates a certain prima facie commitment by the Court to the human rights of migrants with precarious status. Indeed, virtually all well-known health-related cases – which are analysed in detail in Chapter 3 – have been accompanied by the application of interim measures to protect migrants from irreparable harm to their freedom from inhuman or degrading treatment.[122] The recently initiated case of the search-and-rescue vessel *Sea-Watch 3* is instructive in this regard. In January 2019, this boat was prevented from harbouring in Sirausa (Italy) because forty-seven non-authorised migrants were on board, and the Italian government did not want them to go ashore, pursuant to a newly launched and particularly restrictive immigration policy. In light of the 'poor health' of the migrants on board, some of whom were children, the Court requested Italy 'to take all necessary measures, as soon as possible, to provide all the applicants with adequate medical care, food, water and basic supplies as necessary' to avoid any irreparable harm to their human rights.[123] Although this was an undeniably protective-oriented measure, it is interesting to note that the Court did not order Italy to allow the migrants to disembark to obtain assistance, thus demonstrating a lack of willingness to directly challenge sovereign immigration policies.

### 1.3.1.1 The Prohibition of Refoulement and Collective Expulsions

The principle of non-refoulement is ostensibly the strongest weapon against the sovereign right to control immigration and to deport non-nationals in all human rights frameworks. This principle, which is now an essential component of human rights law, originated in international refugee law.[124] It prevents states from transferring people, either nationals or non-nationals, to a country where they face a real risk of irreparable harm or a serious violation of human rights.[125]

---

[121] European Court of Human Rights – Press Unit, 'Interim Measures – Factsheet' (January 2019) <www.echr.coe.int/Documents/FS_Interim_measures_ENG.pdf> accessed 2 April 2021.

[122] See *D. v UK* App no 30240/96 (ECHR 1997); *N. v UK* App no 26565/05 (ECHR 2008), and *Paposhvili v Belgium* App no 41738/10 (ECHR 2016).

[123] Registrar of the European Court of Human Rights, 'ECHR Grants an Interim Measure in Case Concerning the SeaWatch 3 Vessel' *Newsletter* (February 2019) <www.coe.int/en/web/special-representative-secretary-general-migration-refugees/newsletter-february-2019 > accessed 2 April 2019.

[124] Convention Relating to the Status of Refugees (adopted 28 July 1951, entry into force 22 April 1954) 189 UNTS 137 (Refugee Convention) Article 33.

[125] Maarten Den Heijer 'Whose Rights and Which Rights? The Continuing Story of Non-refoulement under the European Convention on Human Rights' (2008) *European Journal of*

The ECtHR began to apply and develop this preventive and complementary protection in its case law on the prohibition of torture and inhuman or degrading treatment (Article 3 ECHR).[126] In *Soering* v. *the UK*, the Court held, for the first time, that an extradition that resulted in exposure to a real risk of treatment prohibited by Article 3, 'while not explicitly referred to in [its] brief and general wording', would 'plainly be contrary to the spirit and intendment of the Article'.[127] The right to life, fundamental aspects of the right to liberty and the right to fair trial were successively considered relevant human rights in this regard.[128] More recently, in *Hirsi* v. *Italy*, a case relating to the 'push-back' of migrants to Libya by the Italian Revenue Police and Coastguard, the ECtHR recalled the absolute character of non-refoulement and its applicability even in the maritime context when extraterritorial interceptions of migrants take place and when the return operations are grounded in a bilateral agreement between two countries as a part of a state migration policy to combat irregular migration.[129] The Court gave weighty evidentiary value to the reports of civil society organisations and international agencies working in the field to rule out the acceptability of immigration policies which are systematically designed to return migrants to a country where there are substantive grounds to believe that returnees are subjected to severe inhuman or degrading treatment and are likely to be refouled back further to their origin country, where they are also likely to be subject to abusive treatment.[130]

A few months previously, the Court had adopted the celebrated *M.S.S.* v. *Belgium and Greece* judgment, a seminal decision that has impacted states' interpretation and implementation of EU law in the area of immigration and asylum. Belgium had sent an asylum seeker back to Greece under the EU Dublin Regulation, which generally allocates responsibility for processing asylum claims to the first EU member state into which the asylum seeker enters.[131] Greece was held liable for violating the ECHR because reception

---

*Migration and Law* 10(3) 277; Guy Goodwin-Gill and Jane McAdam, *The Refugee in International Law* (OUP 2007) chapters 5 and 6.

[126] *Soering v UK* App no 14038/88 (ECHR 1989) paras 85–91; *Chahal v UK* App no 22414/93 (ECHR 1996) paras 74, 83–107; *D. v UK* (n 121) para 49.

[127] *Soering* (ibid) para 88.

[128] For example, *Bader and Kanbor v Sweden* App no 13284/04 (ECHR 2005); *Othman (Abu Qatada) v the UK* App no 8139/09 (ECHR 2012).

[129] *Hirsi* (n 94) paras 70–82. For a detailed analysis, see Maarten Den Heijer, 'Reflections on *Refoulement* and Collective Expulsion in the *Hirsi* Case' (2013) *International Journal of Refugee Law* 25(2) 265.

[130] *Hirsi* (n 95) paras 123–136.

[131] European Parliament and of the Council Regulation (EU) No. 604/2013 of the of 26 June 2013 establishing the criteria and mechanisms for determining the member state responsible for

conditions and procedures for processing asylum claims were largely dysfunctional and asylum seekers were either detained or left to fend for themselves on the street in dire socioeconomic conditions. Furthermore, the applicant had no access to a serious examination of his asylum claim and risked being denied international protection and potentially expelled to Afghanistan.[132] Against a background of violations of Articles 3, 5 and 13 (the right to an effective remedy) ECHR by Greece, Belgium was also held accountable because its decision to return the applicant to Greece had exposed him to inhuman or degrading treatment in Greece, about which Belgium should have known. Under such circumstances, instead of transferring the asylum seeker to the EU country of first entry, Belgium could have drawn on the 'sovereignty clause' in the Dublin Regulation to take responsibility for the case.[133] This judgment is an important example of how the Court, in cases of exceptionally severe circumstances, can reach findings favouring migrants in precarious situations. Linked to this jurisprudential trend, in *Tarakhel* v. *Switzerland*, a case involving a family of asylum seekers who were due to be transferred from Switzerland to Italy under the EU Dublin Regulation, the Court held that – in the light of the vulnerability of asylum seekers (particularly children) and the deficient reception conditions for families in Italy – Article 3 ECHR required the returning country to obtain sufficient assurances that the actual accommodation facilities for the returnee family in Italy were human rights compliant.[134]

It is also worth noting that neither of these cases, which were assessed for compliance with a provision that cannot be limited or derogated under any circumstances (Article 3), mentions the well-established maxim of the sovereign right to control immigration. Push-backs at sea or removals from a state territory of non-nationals may also raise concerns regarding violation of Article 4 of Protocol 4 to the ECHR, which prohibits collective expulsions. This procedural guarantee has been subject to oscillating interpretation. In the above-mentioned *Hirsi* case, the state obligation to conduct a reasonable and objective examination meant an assessment of 'the particular case of each individual alien of the group', whereby everyone was 'given the opportunity to put arguments against his expulsion to the competent authorities', resulting in

---

examining an application for international protection lodged in one of the member states by a third-country national or a stateless person, OJ L 180.

[132] *M.S.S. v Belgium and Greece* App no 30696/09 (ECHR 2011) paras 207–234, 254, 300.

[133] Dublin Reg (n 130); Violeta Moreno-Lax, 'Dismantling the Dublin System: M.S.S. v Belgium and Greece' (2012) *European Journal of Migration and Law* 14 1, 29.

[134] *Tarakhel v Switzerland* App no 29217/12 (GC ECHR 2014), para 120.

a suspensive effect on deportation enforcement.[135] In the more recent and controversial *Khlaifia* v. *Italy* judgment,[136] which concerned the lawfulness of the removal of three migrants from the First Aid and Reception Centre of Lampedusa to Tunisia via Palermo, the Grand Chamber of the ECtHR reversed the arguments of the Chamber (and of *Hirsi*) on the requirements of collective expulsion in the following terms:

[The collective expulsion of aliens] does not guarantee the right to an individual interview in all circumstances; the requirements of this provision may be satisfied where each alien has a genuine and effective possibility of submitting arguments against his or her expulsion.[137]

This opinion was considered a retrograde step in human rights protection by the dissenting judge Serghides, who, *inter alia*, held that the findings of the majority of the Grand Chamber might lead to:

Giving the authorities the choice of deciding to abstain from upholding the rule of law, i.e., from the fulfilment of their said procedural obligation, at the expense of satisfying the principles of effectiveness and legal certainty; [. . .] making the Convention safeguards dependent merely on the discretion of the police or the immigration authorities, [. . .] thereby not only making the supervisory role of the Court difficult, but even undermining it and rendering it unnecessary.[138]

This restrictive trend continued with *N.D. and N.T.* v. *Spain* that concerned the infamous 'systematic practice of collective summary expulsions at the border fence' of the Spanish enclave of Melilla.[139] The Court held that the expulsion of migrants was not technically 'collective' because, while Spain had provided evidence of 'genuine and effective means' to claim asylum or obtain a visa, the lack of individualised assessment was attributable to the situation 'in which the conduct of persons who cross a land border in an unauthorised manner, deliberately take advantage of their large numbers and use force, is such as to create a clearly disruptive situation which is difficult to control and endangers public safety'.[140] The weight of this precedent – which seems to condone indiscriminate push-backs and solidify previous *obiter dicta* on the relevance of the conduct of migrants at border crossing – on the case

---

[135] *Hirsi* (n 95) paras 184–185, 205–206.
[136] *Khlaifia and Others v Italy* App no 16483/12 (ECHR 2015) and (GC ECHR 2016).
[137] Ibid (*Khlaifia* 2016) para 248, emphasis added.
[138] Ibid, Partly Dissenting Opinion of Judge Serghides, para 12(a).
[139] *N.D. and N.T. v Spain* App nos 8675/15 and 8697/15 (GC ECHR 2020) para 81.
[140] Ibid, paras 198–201, 231.

law of the Court is yet to be appreciated. Early comments suggest that its scope of application should be narrowly circumscribed, as 'an overly broad interpretation of the judgment would damage the "broad consensus within the international community" concerning compliance with [...] the obligation of non-refoulement'.[141] Finally, on the migrant-protective side, the circumstances of the case of *M.K.* v. *Poland* convinced the ECtHR judges that even when individual interviews designed to put forward protection grounds are conducted, they may be a mere formality to hide a systematic policy of removal. In these circumstances, expulsion from the territory may well be considered 'collective' and in violation of Article 4 Protocol 4.[142]

### 1.3.1.2 The Right to Personal Liberty and to Fair and Decent Conditions of Detention and Living

In the above-mentioned *Khlaifia* case, the Court declared other breaches of the ECHR, including the right to liberty and security of person set out in Article 5(1), because the detention of the applicants in a migrant reception centre had no legal basis.[143] Generally, when a limitation of liberty is justified by a legal basis and a legitimate aim, the legality of detention is further scrutinised under the umbrella of the proportionality test, which means adopting the least restrictive alternative and ensuring that the detriment to the person is not excessive in relation to the benefits for the state. However, in immigration detention cases – which are explicitly foreseen in Article 5(1)(f) – the case law of the ECtHR has been overall consistent with *Saadi* v. *the UK* precedent and does not require a 'full' test of necessity and proportionality,[144] as far as 'adults with no particular vulnerabilities' are concerned.[145] Accordingly, unlike all other types of detention listed in Articles 5(1)(a)–5(1)(e) and regardless of a substantially similar wording, the detention of unauthorised migrants, which is deemed a 'necessary adjunct' of the power to control entry and stay of aliens on a state's territory, is permissible without

---

[141] *Asady and Others v Slovakia* App no 24917/15 (ECHR 2020), Dissenting Opinion of Judges Lemmens, Keller and Schembri Orland, para 25.

[142] *M.K. and Others v Poland* App nos 40503/17, 42902/17, 43643/17 (ECHR 2020) paras 204–211.

[143] *Khlaifia* (n 136) paras 66–72.

[144] ECHR (n 15, Introduction) Article 5(1): 'No one shall be deprived of his liberty save in the following cases and in accordance with a procedure prescribed by law [...] f) the lawful arrest or detention of a person to prevent his effecting an unauthorised entry into the country or of a person against whom action is being taken with a view to deportation or extradition'; *Saadi* (n 117) paras 72, 73.

[145] ECHR, Case law guide on immigration (n 119) para 18.

checking the 'necessity' of the measure, provided that it is 'closely connected' to the purpose of preventing unauthorised entry or processing viable deportation procedures and, thus, not arbitrary.[146] This is a clear example of how the principle of Westphalian sovereignty and its immigration-related corollary frame the interpretation of human rights provisions in a way that undermines their universal personal scope and dilute human rights.[147] However, in cases concerning children, the Strasbourg Court has adopted a full test of proportionality to scrutinise the legality of immigration-related detention. For instance, in *Rahimi* v. *Greece*, the Court held that the placement of a minor in a detention centre with dire conditions had been arbitrary – and thus illegal – because the 'best interest of the child' and the extreme vulnerability of unaccompanied minors would have required a less restrictive measure.[148]

In *Rahimi*, the Court also held a violation of Article 3 ECHR on the accounts provided by a series of NGOs and the European Committee for the Prevention of Torture, which described the material conditions of the Pagani camp as 'abominable'.[149] Indeed, a post-entry or pre-deportation detention in unsuitable locations may lead to violations of Article 3 ECHR, a human rights provision that admits no derogation under any circumstance. In this respect, the ECHR case law shows that violations of the freedom from inhuman or degrading treatment require a minimum level of severity to be met and are more likely to be ascertained as a result of the cumulative effect of certain risk factors in the concrete circumstances.[150] Poor conditions of detention might amount to violations of minimum subsistence rights and serious violations of human dignity,[151] which may increase the vulnerability of individuals and groups that the Court already recognises as socially and legally vulnerable, such as asylum seekers, children and elderly people.[152]

Finally, outside cases of migration detention, the Court found, in *Kahn* v. *France*, that the neglect of an unaccompanied migrant child, who was not

---

[146] *Saadi* (n 117) paras 72–74.
[147] For further details Galina Cornelisse, 'A New Articulation of Human Rights, or Why the European Court of Human Rights Should Think beyond Westphalian Sovereignty' in Dembour and Kelly (n 3, Introduction) 99.
[148] *Rahimi v Greece* App no 8687/2008 (ECHR 2011) paras 108–111.
[149] Ibid, paras 85, 95–96.
[150] These include the excessive length of detention, lack of privacy, overcrowding, lack of basic hygiene requirements, restricted access to the open air and the external world, lack of ventilation, scarce means of subsistence, lack of access to social and legal assistance, and inadequate medicine or medical care. For example, *S.D. v Greece* App no 53541/07 (ECHR 2007) paras 52–53; M.S.S. (n 132) paras 223–234; *Khlaifia* (2016) (n 136) paras 163–174.
[151] M.S.S. (n 132) para 233.
[152] *Khlaifia* (2016) (n 136) para 194.

provided state protection and social care and who was left in a shanty town near Calais in France, constituted inhuman or degrading treatment contrary to Article 3 ECHR.[153] This judgment relied heavily on the findings of Rahimi to establish that France had failed to consider the extreme situation of vulnerability of the child, which would give rise to positive obligations, displace any considerations pertaining to irregularity of status and lower the threshold of severity that triggers Article 3 ECHR.[154]

### 1.3.1.3 The Protection of Family Life

Another highly controversial area where European human rights law has encroached upon the sovereign state power to regulate the entry and stay of non-nationals, although only partially, is the protection of family life in Article 8 ECHR. This is a limitable or qualified right insofar as it is susceptible to any interference that is lawful and necessary in a democratic society in the interest of national security, public safety or the economic well-being of the country; for the prevention of disorder or crime; for the protection of health or morals; or for the protection of the rights and freedom of others.[155]

The case law of the Court has elaborated extensively on what 'family life' means, which includes married couples who are presumed to be a family[156] and those situations that demonstrate de facto family ties, such as people living together who are in a long-term relationship with each other or who have children.[157] The 'mutual enjoyment by parent and child of each other's company constitutes a fundamental element of family life'.[158] By contrast, the relatively recent case of *Narjis v. Italy* illustrated that, in the context of deportation, an unmarried and childless adult who had 'not demonstrated additional elements of dependence other than normal emotional ties towards his mother, sisters and brother', all of whom were adults, did not fall within the ambit of migrant family life.[159]

---

[153] *Khan v France* App no 12267/16 (ECHR 2019) paras 74, 81, 92.
[154] On 'child's extreme vulnerability [as a] decisive factor [that] takes precedence over considerations relating to the status of illegal immigrant' see also *Mubilanzila Mayeka and Kaniki Mitunga v Belgium* App no 13178/03 (ECHR 2007) para 55 and *Popov v France* App nos 39472/07 and 39474/07 (ECHR 2012) para 91.
[155] ECHR (n 43, Introduction) Article 8(2).
[156] *Marckx v Belgium* App no 6833/74 (ECHR 1979).
[157] *Johnston and Others v Ireland* App 9697/82 (ECHR 1986) para 56; *X, Y and Z v the UK* App no 21830/93 (ECHR 1997) para 36.
[158] *B. v the UK* App 9840/82 (ECHR 1987). For further details, see Council of Europe, *Guide on Article 8 of the European Convention on Human Rights* (COE–ECHR 2018) 46.
[159] *Narjis v Italy* App 57433/15 (ECHR 2019) para 37.

The immigration case law of the ECtHR actually began with the aforementioned family life case of *Abdulaziz, Cabales and Balkandali*, which concerned three women of foreign origin resident in the UK whose applications to be reunited with their husbands were rejected by the UK authorities. This case has become 'infamous' for setting the precedent – and premise of most of the immigration cases pending in Strasbourg – whereby, as a 'matter of well-established international law', immigration control is a sovereign state power that may counterbalance the enjoyment of human rights by migrants. Accordingly, while the Court recognised that Article 8 ECHR may give rise to 'positive obligations inherent in an effective "respect" for family life' and is *in abstracto* applicable to migrants, '[t]he duty imposed by Article 8 cannot be considered as extending to a *general* obligation on the [...] state to respect the choice by married couples of the country of their matrimonial residence and to accept the non-national spouse for settlement in that country'.[160] The ECtHR ultimately rejected the applicants' claims on the grounds that they had not, *inter alia*, shown that 'there were obstacles to establishing family life in their own or their husbands' home countries'.[161]

Therefore, although there is no general state duty to guarantee the right to enter or stay in a country to enjoy family life, under certain circumstances, 'the removal of a person from a country where close members of his family are living may amount to an infringement' of Article 8 ECHR.[162] In cases of alleged violation of Article 8 ECHR, the Court seeks to ascertain whether a 'fair balance' has been struck between the competing interests of protection of family life in paragraph 1 and any relevant state interest in paragraph 2, while affording states 'a certain margin of appreciation' in that regard. This means that the ECtHR must undertake, on a case-by-case basis, a 'legitimacy' and 'proportionality test' concerning the acceptability and necessity of the deportation or refusal of entry of a family member in relation to the applicant's right to family life. For example, the Court has found that immigration measures 'may be justified by the preservation of the country's economic well-being, by the need of regulating the labour market and by considerations of public order weighing in favour of exclusion'.[163] However, the case law of the ECtHR has indicated several factors that must be considered by the state in such cases. These include the best interest of family children, the existence of

---

[160] *Abdulaziz* (n 68) 68, emphasis added.
[161] Ibid.
[162] *Al-Nashif v Bulgaria* App 50963/99 (ECHR 2002) para 114.
[163] *Berrehab v the Netherlands* App 10730/84 (ECHR 1988) para 26; *Rodrigues da Silva and Hoogkamer v the Netherlands* App 50435/99 (ECHR 2006) para 38.

insurmountable obstacles to the relocation outside of the country, the potential rupture of the family, immigration control and public order considerations, and 'whether family life was created at a time when the persons
involved were aware that the immigration status of one of them was such that
the persistence of that family life within the host State would from the outset
be precarious.'[164]

Although 'very weighty reasons' are necessary to justify the deportation of a
settled migrant who, for example, has regularly spent most of her childhood or
youth in the deporting state or who is disabled or where serious impediments
prevent the establishment of family life in the country of deportation,[165] the
assessment of proportionality in the area of immigration adds a wide degree of
unpredictability to the findings of the Court. This unpredictability of outcomes in cases of migrant family life is evident in the comparison between
findings of the Chamber and those of the Grand Chamber in the case of *Biao
v. Denmark*. The responding state refused to grant a residence permit for
family reunion to one of the applicants because her husband – a naturalised
Danish citizen and co-applicant in the proceedings – had not demonstrated
sufficient 'attachment' to Denmark insofar as he did not meet the twenty-
eight-year citizenship requirement to bring his spouse into the country without undertaking an 'attachment' test. The Court's Chamber judgment
assessed the permissible interference with Article 8 ECHR by recalling the
maxim of state sovereignty in immigration management and without attaching
importance to the several years of Mr Biao's regular residence in Denmark.
Furthermore, considering the alleged ties of the applicants to countries other
than Denmark and the couple's awareness of the precarious status of one of
them when the relationship started, the Court concluded that there were no
insurmountable obstacles that prevented the family from moving to another
country and thus considered the balance struck by the state as fair and
compliant with Article 8 ECHR.[166] The Court also rejected the argument
that the twenty-eight-year citizenship prerequisite for family reunification
constituted indirect discrimination on the grounds of ethnic origin. The
Grand Chamber of the Court reversed the above findings and considered
that Article 14 on non-discrimination and Article 8 ECHR were jointly
violated. It held that Denmark had failed to show that there were:

---

[164] *Jeunesse v the Netherlands* App no 12738/10 (ECHR 2014) paras 107–109.
[165] *Maslov v Austria* App no 1638/03 (ECHR 2008) para 75; *Nasri v France* App 19465/92
    (ECHR 95).
[166] *Biao v Denmark* App 38590/10 (ECHR 2014) paras 52–60.

Compelling or very weighty reasons unrelated to ethnic origin to justify the indirect discriminatory effect of the 28-year rule. That rule favours Danish nationals of Danish ethnic origin, and places at a disadvantage, or has a disproportionately prejudicial effect on persons who acquired Danish nationality later in life and who were of ethnic origins other than Danish.[167]

### 1.3.2 A Glimpse at the UN Treaty Bodies' Jurisprudence Concerning Migrant Human Rights

The nine UN human rights treaties are monitored by ten independent treaty bodies, which were 'established specifically to supervise the application of [each] treaty' and provide interpretation of treaty obligations to which states should 'ascribe great weight'.[168] While the International Court of Justice is referring to the HRCtee in the above quotes, the general comments, recommendations and case-based views of all treaty bodies have an authoritative legal significance in international human rights law, although they are not a source of binding rules.[169] However, the normative legitimacy of their mandated activities arguably depends on a number of factors, including the determinacy of their reasonings, the coherence of the activities with the treaty system and the adherence of their findings to the sources and rules of interpretation of international (human rights) law.[170] Several of these bodies have made clear their commitment to the rights of migrants with precarious or irregular status, with arguments that are worth comparing with those of the Strasburg Court. Some examples of this general commitment are provided in this section, whereas a systematic analysis of the health-related jurisprudence of these treaty bodies is provided in Chapters 2–5.

#### 1.3.2.1 Authoritative Interpretative Statements on the Rights of Migrants

One of the first migrant-related interpretative statements was the 1986 General Comment No. 15 of the HRCtee, according to which aliens and citizens should, in principle, enjoy equal human rights and that prima facie embeds a less deferential approach to the idea of state sovereignty than that of the ECtHR:

---

[167] *Biao v Denmark* App 38590/10 (ECHR 2016) para 138.

[168] *Ahmadou Sadio Diallo (Republic of Guinea v Democratic Republic of the Congo)*, Merits 2010 ICJ Reports 639 (Judgment of 30 November 2010) para 66, emphasis added.

[169] See Section I.2.

[170] Brigit Schlutter, 'Aspects of Human Rights Interpretation by the UN Treaty Bodies' in Keller and Ulfstein (n 9, Introduction) 269, referring to Thomas Franck, *The Power of Legitimacy among Nations* (OUP 1990) 17.

The Covenant does not recognize the right of aliens to enter or reside in the territory of a State party. It is *in principle* a matter for the State to decide who it will admit to its territory. However, in certain circumstances an alien may enjoy the protection of the Covenant *even in relation to entry or residence*, for example, when considerations of non-discrimination, prohibition of inhuman treatment and respect for family life arise.[171]

Furthermore, General Recommendation No. 30 of the Committee on the Elimination of Racial Discrimination (CERD Committee), for reasons of system consistency with other UN human rights instruments and in consideration of the concerns raised in the state reporting mechanisms, reinterpreted the personal scope of application of the Convention on the Elimination of Racial Discrimination (CERD) as extending to racial discrimination against non-citizens, regardless of their immigration status.[172] This conclusion reversed the previous approach, according to which the Convention did not apply to state differentiations between citizens and aliens, which were in principle permissible under the Convention.[173]

More recently, in 2017, the CESCR issued a statement on the rights of migrants and refugees, which specified that all people in a situation of human mobility, particularly undocumented migrants, should be considered especially vulnerable people with regard to the enjoyment of socioeconomic rights.[174] This statement relies heavily on the concept of 'core obligations' to recommend that states guarantee to everyone the enjoyment of minimum essential levels of rights, an approach that is drawn upon in subsequent chapters and contributes to justifying a convincing road ahead for extending the depth and quality of migrant social rights as human rights.

Finally, in the same year, the Committee on the Rights of the Child (CRC Committee) and the CMW Committee issued two groundbreaking joint general comments on general principles and state obligations in relation to migrant children.[175] These collaborative statements of interpretation reiterated

---

[171] HRCtee, GC15 (n 96) paras 1, 2, 4, 5, emphasis added.

[172] CERD Committee, GR30 (n 105) paras 2, 4, 7.

[173] CERD (n 42, Introduction) Article 1.2 and CERD Committee, General Recommendation No. 11: 'Non-citizens' (1993) para 1.

[174] CESCR, 'Statement: The Duties of States towards Refugees and Migrants under the International Covenant on Economic, Social and Cultural Rights' (13 March 2017) E/C.12/2017/1.

[175] Committee on the Protection of the Rights of All Migrant Workers and Members of Their Families and Committee on the Rights of the Child, 'Joint General Comment No. 3/22 on the general principles regarding the human rights of children in the context of international migration' (16 November 2017) CMW/C/GC/3-CRC/C/GC/22; 'Joint General Comment No. 4/23 on the state obligations regarding the human rights of children in the context of

that international children's rights apply to all children, regardless of their or their parents' nationality or migration status. It is worth highlighting that these committees, among their various advances, plainly prohibited the detention of migrant children by establishing that the *ultima ratio* principle – which is currently employed by the ECtHR – should not apply to migrant children.[176]

### 1.3.2.2 Jurisprudential Trends from Treaty Bodies' Communication Procedures

Research on the databases of the UN Office of the High Commissioner of Human Rights demonstrates that, in their communication procedures concerning failed asylum seekers and non-authorised migrants, the UN treaty bodies have been particularly concerned by alleged violations of the right to freedom from torture or inhuman or degrading treatment and of the prohibition of refoulement.[177] As explained above, the latter requires states to refrain from deporting an individual when there are substantial grounds for believing that the person concerned would be at 'foreseeable, personal, present and real' risk of torture in that country'[178] or at real and personal risk of irreparable harm.[179]

While for both the ECtHR and the HRCtee, the identification of a real and personal risk of degrading or undignified treatment in the country of removal should, in principle, inhibit the enforcement of a return, the Committee of the Convention against Torture (CAT Committee) interprets the principle of non-refoulement as protecting the complainant against a risk of being subjected to 'torture' in the event of removal. Torture is defined in the Convention as the intentional infliction of severe pain or suffering, whether physical or mental, by the state. This fact raises considerably the threshold of potential human rights abuse that may prevent a removal within that legal framework. In such an assessment, 'the existence of a consistent pattern of gross, flagrant or mass violations of human rights' in the country of deportation

---

international migration in countries of origin, transit, destination and return' (16 November 2017) CMW/C/GC/4-CRC/C/GC/23.

[176] Ibid (JGC 4/23) para 5. For further details, see Ciara M. Smyth, 'Towards a Complete Prohibition on the Immigration Detention of Children' (2019) *Human Rights Law Review* 19 (1) 1.

[177] Research performed on <http://juris.ohchr.org/> accessed 2 April 2021.

[178] CAT Committee, 'General Comment No. 4 (2017): The Implementation of Article 3 of the Convention in the Context of Article 22' (4 September 2018) CAT/C/GC/4, para 11.

[179] HRCtee, 'General Comment No. 31: The Nature of the General Legal Obligation Imposed on States Parties to the Covenant (26 May 2004) CCPR/C/21/Rev.1/Add. 13.

is considered together with the complainant's personal risk of being tortured[180] and in the light of their vulnerabilities and medical records.[181]

The HRCtee, in the context of deportation, has demonstrated particular sensitivity with regard to family- and child-related situations. In *O.A. v. Denmark*, which concerned the removal of an unaccompanied minor from Denmark to Greece under the EU Dublin System, this Committee held that the child would be exposed to a high risk of irreparable harm because of the still ongoing substandard state of the Greek reception system.[182] In particular, the Committee held that the state party failed to undertake an individualised assessment of the risk of subjection to inhuman and degrading treatment that a vulnerable person, in this case a child, would face if deported.[183] In *Y.A.A. & F.H.M. v. Denmark*, the Committee reached similar conclusions in relation to the deportation of a family with four children to Italy, where they had previously encountered extreme hardship in securing basic social assistance, including shelter, work and health care. In this case, the state had failed to give enough weight to the situation of vulnerability of the complainants and their family and 'to seek proper assurances from the Italian authorities that the authors and their four children would be assured of living conditions that are compatible with Article 7 (prohibition of torture and inhuman or degrading treatment) ICCPR'.[184] In another case against Denmark, *Warda*, although similar circumstances of material deprivation in the 'first country of asylum' led the HRCtee to hold a violation of Article 7 ICCPR, the concurring opinion of two judges clarified the exceptional and particular factors that grounded that decision.[185] Similarly, in *I.A.M.*, the principles of precaution and the best interest of the child were employed by the CRC Committee to oppose the Danish decision to repatriate a Somali mother and her daughter to (an area of) their country of origin where female genital mutilation was widely practised.[186]

The protection of the family was also one of the main arguments in the *Mansour* case, which concerned the refusal to grant a visa to an Iranian father

---

[180] For example, see *M.A.M.A. et al. v Sweden* Com 391/2009 (CAT Committee 2012); *Rouba Alhaj Ali v Morocco* Com no 682/2015 (CAT Committee 2016).

[181] *J.B. v Switzerland* Com no 721/2015 (CAT Committee 2017); *A.N. v Switzerland* Com no 742/2016 (CAT Committee 2018). Further details on these and other mental health-related cases are provided in Chapter 5.

[182] *O.A. v Denmark* Com no 2770/2016 (HRCtee 2017) para 8.9.

[183] Ibid, para 8.11.

[184] *Y.A.A. and F.H.M. v Denmark* Com no 2681/2015 (HRCtee 2017) para 7.9.

[185] *Warda v Denmark* Com no 2360/2014 (HRCtee 2015) Appendix II.

[186] *I.A.M. v Denmark* Com no 3/2016 (CRC Committee 2018); Similarly, *Kaba v Canada and Guinea* Com no 1465/2006 (HRCtee 2010).

who had lived regularly for more than sixteen years in Australia because of insufficiently clarified 'compelling reasons of national security'. The HRCtee held that the state's procedure lacked due process of law and violated Articles 17 (private and family life) and 23 (protection of the family and rights associated with marriage) ICCPR because it did not provide 'adequate and objective justification for the interference with [the applicant's] long-settled family life'.[187] In another case of expulsion from Australia, the same Committee clarified that the state interest in expelling a long-term settled person to his country of nationality, where he had no family bonds, might be considered – as it was in the case in question – a disproportionate interference with the right to family life as per Article 17 ICCPR.[188]

In relation to detention, unlike the ECtHR, the HRCtee considers that the prolonged detention of 'unauthorised arrivals', while not prohibited in principle, 'could be considered arbitrary if it is *not necessary* given all the circumstances of the case'.[189]

The tension between sovereign immigration enforcement and human rights clearly underlies the recent *Toussaint* case, in which the HRCtee grappled, for the first time, with an alleged violation of the ICCPR on the grounds of a lack of access to urgent health care of an irregular migrant. The applicant was denied health care because the state authorities claimed that the 'operative cause' of the risk to her life and health was her own decision to irregularly remain in the country. The domestic court had stated that: 'The exclusion of immigrants without legal status from access to health care is justifiable as a reasonable limit under section 1 of the Canadian Charter because appropriate weight should be given to the interests of the state in defending its immigration laws.'[190] However, the Committee held the opinion that a differentiation based on the applicant's 'immigration status' that 'could result in the author's loss of life or in irreversible negative consequences for the author's health' was not based on reasonable and objective criteria and was therefore a discriminatory interference with the right to life (in dignity) of Article 6 ICCPR: 'Aliens have an "inherent right to life". States therefore cannot make a distinction, for the purposes of respecting and protecting the right to life, between regular and irregular migrants.'[191]

---

[187] *Mansour Leghaei et al. v Australia* Com no 1937/2010 (HRCtee 2015) para 10.5.
[188] *Stefan Lars Nystrom v Australia* Com no 1557/2007 (HRCtee 2011).
[189] *Madafferi v Australia* Com no 1011/2001 (HRCtee 2004) para 9, emphasis added. See Section 5.4.1 for further details on this case.
[190] *Toussaint v Canada* Com no 2348/2014 (HRCtee 2018) para 2.12.
[191] Ibid, paras 11.7, 11.8.

The advocacy of UN treaty bodies for migrant rights has exceeded the articulation of substantive arguments, and the 2021 decisions in *A.S. et al.* v. *Italy* and its twin case against *Malta* are important examples of how expansive rules on jurisdiction may contribute to developing a favourable case law for non-nationals with precarious legal status and at risk of dying.[192] These cases concerned the joint failure of Malta and Italy, in 2013, to rescue more than 200 migrants whose vessel sank six hours after the initial call to the Italian authorities. The case against Italy is particularly significant, as it shows how state obligations vis-à-vis the right to life of migrants at sea may be expanded as a result of a 'functional' approach to state jurisdiction. The HRCtee endorsed this approach in its General Comment No. 36 by favouring the idea that extraterritorial state responsibility for the protection of human rights not only exists where states have effective control *over the victims* but also where they (may) have *control over the enjoyment of the victim's human rights*, which may be foreseeably hindered by certain state actions or inactions, including in situations of distress and rescue at sea.[193] In this case, the HRCtee considered that although the vessel was located outside Italy's territorial sea and its search-and-rescue area, 'in the particular circumstances of the case, a special relationship of dependency had been established between the individuals on the vessel in distress and Italy'.[194] These circumstances included the fact that the people on the sinking boat had several contacts with the Italian search-and-rescue coordination centre and that an Italian navy ship was relatively close (an hour's sailing) to the place where the incident occurred but was required to move away from the sinking boat, as well as the 'relevant legal obligations incurred by Italy under the international law of the sea'.[195] In consideration of this, the rights of people onboard the vessel in distress 'were directly affected by the [delayed] decisions taken by the Italian authorities in a manner that was reasonably foreseeable in light of the relevant legal obligations of Italy, and that they were thus subject to Italy's jurisdiction for the purposes of the Covenant'.[196]

On the merits, the Committee found that Italy failed to act with due diligence to protect the right to life of the applicants.[197] The tension between sovereign migration policies and expansive human rights obligations lies at the

---

[192] A.S., D.I., O.I. and G.D. v Italy Com no 3042/2017 (HRCtee 2021).

[193] HRCtee, 'General Comment No. 36: Article 6 of the International Covenant on Civil and Political Rights on the right to life' (30 October 2018) para 63.

[194] A.S. et al. (n 192) para 7.8.

[195] Ibid.

[196] Ibid.

[197] Ibid, para 8.5.

heart of this case, as cooperating in the search and rescue of migrants at sea may have implications in terms of admissions and reception of those migrants, recognition of their rights (including their right to asylum) and redistribution of public resources. With this decision – which was criticised by scholars and dissenting judges because of the alleged inconsistent legal grounding of some of its arguments[198] – the HRCtee in its majority chose to embrace a marked *pro homine* approach on the spectrum of possible decisions by increasing state duties of due diligence at sea borders vis-à-vis migrant rights.

### 1.3.3 *The Different Approaches of European and International Case Law*

Instances of deportation from a country and irregular stay are particularly delicate circumstances in which human rights abuses are likely to take place and executive powers of immigration control are strong vis-à-vis a situation of concrete and legal vulnerability. Against this backdrop, the ECtHR has established certain procedural and substantial minimum standards, which, to different extents, limit the sovereign power to exclude. However, state sovereignty considerations, reminders of our Westphalian system of international law, are subsumed in the ECHR and in the Court's case law. On the one hand, the Court has relied on Article 3 ECHR concerning the prohibition of degrading treatment to rule out situations of appalling migration detention, extreme poverty outside of the detention context and cases of refoulement but only where a high threshold of severity of abuse is met. On the other hand, the Court has been hesitant to challenge restrictive state practices that impinge on migrants' right to family life. Furthermore, settled case law excludes the requirement to assess the migration-related detention of adults by reference to its 'necessity', as is the case for other types of detention. Finally, procedural guarantees against collective expulsions have evolved as particularly qualified standards, and fair trial guarantees do not generally apply to immigration proceedings. The migration-focused jurisprudence of the most widely known human rights Court is extremely complex and case-specific, making it difficult to establish long-lasting trends and general standards. This enables states to limit the impact of the Court's findings, which is why its case law has been described as 'dilemmatic'.[199] As for the UN treaty bodies, they

---

[198] Ibid, Annexes I and II; Marko Milanovic, Drowning Migrants, the Human Rights Committee, and Extraterritorial Human Rights Obligations (*EJIL:Talk! Blog of the European Journal of International Law*, 16 March 2021) <www.ejiltalk.org/drowning-migrants-the-human-rights-committee-and-extraterritorial-human-rights-obligations/> accessed 8 April 2021.

[199] Baumgärtel (n 12, Introduction) 101–120.

place less emphasis on the state power to regulate immigration than the ECtHR does in its case law. Indeed, none of the individual communications mentioned in Section 1.3.2, which are not formally binding for responding states, contains any *obiter dicta* regarding the 'long-established maxim' of state sovereignty in the area of immigration, and failed communications tend to be based on the applicants' lack of evidence or the failure to meet a prima facie standard of proof in relation to a human rights violation.[200] The HRCtee, in the case of *Toussaint*, even relies on the jurisprudence of the Inter-American Court of Human Rights, which, as explained in Section 1.5.1, is particularly progressive and *pro homine*–oriented in relation to migrants' rights.[201]

## 1.4 EXPLICIT LIMITATIONS ON THE RIGHTS OF IRREGULAR MIGRANTS IN HUMAN RIGHTS TREATY PROVISIONS

Not only has the uneasy balancing of sovereign interests and powers in the field of immigration with human rights law led to qualified judicial or quasi-judicial decisions on migrant rights, but it is directly enshrined in the texts of some human rights treaties, such as the ICMW and the ESC.

### 1.4.1 *The Convention on Migrant Workers*

Unlike the ICCPR, the ICESCR and the ECHR, the ICMW explicitly regulates differential treatment for regular as opposed to irregular migrants as human rights holders. On the one hand, this instrument represents an overall improvement in the protection of the rights of migrant workers and makes them visible within international human rights law,[202] emphasising 'the situation of vulnerability in which migrant workers and members of their families frequently find themselves'.[203] On the other hand, it 'constitutional-ises' a double divide (citizens v. non-citizens and regular v. irregular migrants) in international human rights law. Hence, the ICMW has been described as a 'hybrid instrument',[204] aimed at achieving greater protection of migrants'

---

[200] For example, *M.P. v Denmark* Com no 2643/2015 (HRCtee 2017); *E.A. v Sweden* Com no 690/2015 (CAT Committee 2017).

[201] *Toussaint* (n 190) para 11.7. See *infra* at Section 1.5.

[202] Isabelle Slinckx, 'Migrants' Rights in UN Human Rights Conventions' in Paul De Guchteneire, Antonie Pécoud and Ryszard Cholewinski (eds) *Migration and Human Rights – The United Nations Convention on Migrant Workers' Rights* (CUP 2009) 122, 146.

[203] ICMW (n 42, Introduction) Preamble.

[204] Bosniak (n 71) 316. See in particular Articles 34 and 79 of the ICMW, which recall the exclusive state right to regulate immigration.

rights while also reaffirming state territorial sovereignty as a well-founded principle of international and immigration law. For example, the unequal treatment of irregular migrants and documented migrant workers emerges in relation to social and health care entitlements. Whereas the Convention is generally silent regarding irregular migrants' social rights, Article 28 ICMW stipulates the following:

> Workers and members of their families shall have the right to receive any medical care that is *urgently required for the preservation of their life or the avoidance of irreparable harm to their health* on the basis of equality of treatment with nationals of the State concerned. Such *emergency* medical care shall not be refused [to anyone] by reason of any irregularity with regard to stay or employment.[205]

By contrast, Article 43 ICMW establishes that documented or regular migrant workers 'shall enjoy *equality of treatment* with nationals of the State of employment in relation to [...] access to housing, including social housing schemes [and] access to social and health services'.[206]

Although the ICMW is not widely ratified outside Latin America and western Africa[207] and its treaty body has encouraged a contextual interpretation of its text (in the light, e.g. of the ICESCR-related obligations) that aligns with the recommendation of the ILC's Fragmentation Report' to extend access to essential social services using the more favourable treaty norms among those applicable,[208] the differential treatment it textually condones has been openly written into a binding and a specialised human rights document.

### 1.4.2 *The European Social Charter*

The second example of a treaty text that clearly restricts the human rights of irregular migrants in the context of social and medical assistance and beyond

---

[205] ICMW (n 42, Introduction) Article 28, emphasis added.

[206] Ibid, Article 43, emphasis added.

[207] As of April 2021, only fifty-six states are parties to this Convention, neither of them from the EU, Euan MacDonald and Ryszard Cholewinski, *The Migrant Workers Convention in Europe: Obstacles to the Ratification of the International Convention on the Protection of the Rights of All Migrant Workers and Members of Their Families: EU/EEA Perspectives* (UNESCO Publishing 2007) 51.

[208] CMW Committee, 'General Comment No. 1 on Migrant Domestic Workers' (23 February 2011) CMW/C/GC/1, para 44; CMW Committee, GC2 (n 16, Introduction) paras 7, 8, 10, 72; Study Group of the International Law Commission, 'Fragmentation of International Law: Difficulties Arising from the Diversification and Expansion of International Law', UNGA Report, finalised by Martti Koskenniemi (13 April 2006) A/CN.4/L.682, para 108.

is the ESC.[209] This is the sister treaty, in the area of socioeconomic rights, of the ECHR. In contrast to the European Convention, which applies to 'everyone' within state jurisdictions,[210] the Appendix of the Charter places irregular migrants outside the personal scope of the treaty: 'the persons covered [...] include foreigners only in so far as they are nationals of other contracting parties lawfully resident or working regularly within the territory of the contracting party concerned'.[211] This ideological fault line (in the context of a human rights treaty) stems from the fact that the drafters of the Charter, in the mid-1950s, were principally concerned with eliminating barriers to the equal enjoyment of labour and social rights for the nationals of European countries.[212] However, this limited personal scope has been kept in the protocols to the ESC and the Revised Charter, which resulted from the reform of the ESC system in the late 1980s and early 1990s.[213] This confirmed the assumption that socioeconomic rights are prevalently considered a matter solely for nationals and 'legal communities' as identifiable taxpayers.[214] Justifications based on 'identity' and 'costs'[215] that are embedded in this status quo prima facie undermine the conceptualisation of equal migrant social rights in this legal framework.

Having said this, a contextual and purposive interpretation of the ESC and its Appendix, in conjunction with a series of substantive rights within the Charter, has led the European Committee of Social Rights (ECSR) – the quasi-judicial body that oversees the implementation of the ESC – to gradually grant basic social rights to irregular migrants. The turning point occurred in 2004 with the *FIDH* v. *France* case,[216] which concerned access to medical

---

[209] European Social Charter and European Social Charter (Revised) (n 43, Introduction).

[210] ECHR (n 43, Introduction) Article 1.

[211] ESC (n 43, Introduction) Appendix, para 1.

[212] PACE, 'Common Policy of Member States in Social Affairs – Debate on the Report of the Committee on Social Questions' (23 September 1953) 20–21: PACE, 'Debate on the Report of the Committee on Social Questions Expressing an Opinion on ... the Social Programme of the Council of Europe' (28 May 1954) 31, in *Collected Edition of the 'Travaux préparatoires'* Volume 1 (1953–1954) <www.coe.int/en/web/european-social-charter/preparatory-work> accessed 15 March 2021.

[213] Charte-Rel Committee, 'Final Activity Report (adopted by the Committee on the European Social Charter', Charte-Rel (94) 23, 19 October 1994, Appendix IV, 58: 'The majority of delegates had difficulty with the proposed change to the scope, *ratione personae*, of the Charter as a whole.'

[214] Francesca Biondi Dal Monte, 'Lo Stato Sociale di Fronte alle Migrazioni: Diritti Sociali, Appartenenza e Dignità della Persona' (2012) *Rivista del Gruppo di Pisa* 3(12).

[215] Baumgratel (n 12, Introduction) 138–139.

[216] *International Federation of Human Rights League (FIDH) v France* Com no 14/2003 (ECSR 2004).

care by irregular migrant children. On that occasion, the ECSR, arguing for the complementary nature of the ESC and the ECHR, the interdependence and indivisibility of all human rights, and the protection of human dignity, concluded that a 'legislation or practice which denies entitlements to medical assistance to foreign nationals, within the territory of a State Party, even if they are there illegally, is contrary to the Charter'.[217] In subsequent cases concerning housing and social and medical assistance, the ECSR extended its legal reasoning beyond the ordinary meaning of the words of the Appendix, stating that the Charter must be interpreted 'in the light of other applicable rules of international law'[218] that are truly universal, such as the Convention of the Rights of the Child (CRC) and the ICESCR.

This teleological and evolutionary interpretative extension of the personal scope of the Charter is considered the exception rather than the rule and is linked to certain circumstances. For example, most of the cases of the 'irregular migrant saga' have concerned 'unlawful children' who were deemed particularly vulnerable because of their limited autonomy.[219] Nevertheless, the ECSR reached the conclusion that at least the right to 'emergency assistance' (either social or medical) of Article 13(4) ESC – which is linked to the 'preservation of most fundamental rights of these persons, as well as their human dignity'[220] – should apply to all irregular migrants, including adults.[221] This creative interpretation constitutes a progressive step towards the universal personal application of the ESC, even though social rights for irregular migrants in the European human rights system are clearly not ultimately framed in equal terms for everyone, regardless of migration status.[222]

The variety of legal sources and bodies that interpret human rights provisions generates some confusion regarding the character, shape and content of the human rights of irregular or undocumented migrants. The legal uncertainty concerns, first and foremost, whether irregular migrants hold human rights or simply some rights, and, as in the case of social rights, what the 'levels'

---

[217] Ibid, paras 26–32.
[218] *Defence for Children International (DCI) v the Netherlands* Com no 47/2008 (ECSR 2009) para 35; *Defence for Children International (DCI) v Belgium* Com no 69/2011 (ECSR 2012) paras 29, 33; *Conference of European Churches (CEC) v the Netherlands* Com no 30/2013 (ECSR 2014) para 68.
[219] *DCI v Belgium* (ibid) para 35; *CEC* (ibid) para 71.
[220] *CEC* (ibid) para 74. See also *DCI v Belgium* (ibid) para 36.
[221] *CEC* (ibid) paras 73, 75; *European Federation of National Organisations Working with the Homeless (FEANTSA) v the Netherlands* Com no 86/2012 (ECSR 2014) paras 171, 173, 182–183, 186.
[222] Stefano Angeleri, 'Article 13: The Right to Social and Medical Assistance' in RACSE/ANESC (eds) *A Commentary on the European Social Charter*, Vol 3 (2023, Brill-Nijhoff 2023).

and 'qualities' of these guarantees are. Although not without contradictions, international and European human rights law has served to open international legal avenues to protect the human rights of irregular migrants in terms of providing fora for discussion, standard setting and interpretation. The partial achievements reported in this chapter bear witness to the fact that debates on the depth of irregular migrants' rights are yet to be resolved.


## 1.5  BROADENING CONTEXTUAL REFLECTIONS ON MIGRANT RIGHTS

### 1.5.1  *The Pro-migrant Approach of the Inter-American System of Human Rights*

The previous sections in this chapter demonstrate certain oscillations within international and European law between the need for immigration law enforcement and the necessity of human rights implementation. At this juncture, it is useful to briefly reference the jurisprudence of the inter-American bodies to show that limiting migrant rights is not inevitable in human rights law. While European human rights law has recognised violations of the human rights of irregular migrants in exceptional and severely abusive cases,[223] the inter-American human rights system has been particularly responsive to the call of equality vis-à-vis sovereign powers with respect to immigration management. This approach is especially evident in the Inter-American Court's advisory opinion on the rights of undocumented migrants.[224] This was the result of a request filed by Mexico regarding the treatment and rights of Mexican undocumented migrant workers in the USA. In particular, the question posed to the Inter-American Court was whether excluding undocumented migrants from labour rights was human rights compliant. It is interesting to note that the Court essentially acknowledged the vulnerability of undocumented migrants, referring to an 'individual situation of absence or difference of *power* with regard to non-migrants', and recognised them as people who are particularly exposed to various forms of discrimination.[225] In the advisory opinion, the principles of non-discrimination and equality are deemed so essential to the entire human rights legal framework to be considered part of *jus cogens* and, thus, as norms

---

[223] See *supra* at Sections 1.3.1 and 1.3.2; and *infra* at Chapters 3 and 4.
[224] *Juridical Condition and Rights of the Undocumented Migrants*, Advisory Opinion OC-18, IACtHR Series A no 18 (17 September 2003).
[225] Ibid, para 112, emphasis added.

that should prevail over any other in international law norms. According to this decision, human rights, including labour rights, which are essential to 'develop fully as a human being', must be enjoyed by everyone without discrimination, including discrimination on the grounds of legal status.[226] The maxims of this opinion are consistently restated in several judgments of the Inter-American Court,[227] and even recalled in a concurring opinion to an ECtHR ruling.[228]

Ten years after the above opinion was issued, the Court reiterated these highly protective conclusions in another advisory opinion on the rights of migrant children, which unequivocally stated that the 'State must ... respect the said rights, because they are based, precisely, on the attributes of the human personality [...] regardless of [...] whether the person is there temporarily, in transit, legally, or in an irregular migratory situation.'[229] This brief account of the approach of the inter-American system shows that the restrictive approach to the rights of undocumented people justified by the principle of state sovereignty is not the only option but instead is a deliberate choice of certain legal systems, including certain branches of international human rights law.

### 1.5.2 *The Global Compact for Migration*

This analysis would be incomplete without briefly mentioning that, since 2016, the adoption of the New York Declaration and the outcomes of the two Global Compacts, under the auspices of the UN, have shaped a non-binding cooperative framework to address large movements of migrants and refugees.[230] Although these instruments are not legally binding, they can play an important role in consolidating human rights–based norms and

---

[226] Ibid, paras 158, 169, 170. For further analysis, see Dembour (n 5) 296–304; Beth Lyon, 'Inter-American Court of Human Rights Defines Unauthorized Migrant Workers' Rights for the Hemisphere: A Comment on Advisory Opinion 18' (2003) *NYU Review of Law & Social Change* 28 547.

[227] *Vélez Loor v Panama* (IACtHR 2010) Series C No. 218, paras 98–100; *Pacheco Tineo Family v Bolivia* (IACtHR 2013) Series C No. 272 para 128; *Expelled Dominicans and Haitians v Dominican Republic* (IACtHR 2014) Series C No. 282, para 197.

[228] *De Souza Ribeiro v France* App no. 22689/07 (ECHR 2012) Concurring Opinion of Judge Pinto de Albuquerque.

[229] *Rights and Guarantees of Children in the Context of Migration and/or in Need of International Protection*, Advisory Opinion OC-21, IACtHR (19 August 2014) para 62.

[230] New York Declaration (n 68); Global Compact for Safe, Orderly and Regular Migration and Global Compact on Refugees (n 92).

collaborative approaches, including with regard to irregular migrants.[231] Indeed, they restate existing international obligations and set out relatively detailed priorities, good practice, action plans and follow-up mechanisms to deal with the challenges of international migration.

The Compact for Migration, like the documents analysed in this chapter, constantly wavers between the principle of state sovereignty, with all its negative implications for irregular migrants, and a genuine commitment to the holistic protection of the rights of all migrants. This tension was palpable in the negotiations that led to the text adopted at the Conference of Marrakech and endorsed by the UNGA in December 2018.

The zero draft of the Compact did not contain any explicit distinction between the treatment of regular and irregular migrants.[232] However, the paragraph on 'national sovereignty' as a *guiding principle* in the final draft, which was insisted upon by the EU bloc during the negotiations, reads as follows:

> The Global Compact reaffirms the sovereign right of States to determine their national migration policy and their prerogative to govern migration within their jurisdiction, in conformity with international law. Within their sovereign jurisdiction, States may distinguish between regular and irregular migration status, including as they determine their legislative and policy measures for the implementation of the Global Compact.[233]

It is also significant that, in relation to the actual enjoyment of rights by irregular migrants, the zero draft contained several references to the establishment of 'firewalls', which refers to the structuring of public service provision or labour inspection so as not to expose irregular migrants to immigration enforcement authorities, whereas the final draft makes this separation less clear.[234] The final text requires states to 'ensure that cooperation between service providers and immigration authorities does not exacerbate the vulnerabilities of irregular migrants by compromising' their human rights.[235]

---

[231] Alexander Betts, 'Towards a "Soft Law" Framework for the Protection of Vulnerable Irregular Migrants' (2010) *International Journal of Refugee Law* 22(2) 209–236.

[232] Zero Draft of the Global Compact for Safe, Orderly and Regular Migration (5 February 2018) para 13, <https://refugeesmigrants.un.org/sites/default/files/180205_gcm_zero_draft_final.pdf> accessed 1 March 2021.

[233] GCM (n 92) para 15; Elspeth Guild and Katharine T. Weatherhead, 'Tensions as the EU Negotiates the Global Compact for Safe, Orderly and Regular Migration' (*EU Migration Law Blog*, 6 July 2018) <http://eumigrationlawblog.eu/tensions-as-the-eu-negotiates-the-global-compact-for-safe-orderly-and-regular-migration/> accessed 1 March 2021.

[234] Zero Draft (n 232) paras 20.j; 21.g; 29.c.

[235] GCM (n 92) para 31.b.

However, it does not incontrovertibly dictate that public service providers should refrain from reporting situations of irregularity to the immigration authorities.

Finally, as far as immigration detention is concerned, Objective 13 of the Global Compact reads as promising on paper, since it requires states to ensure that detention is a measure of last resort and that it 'follow[s] due process, is non-arbitrary, based on law, necessity, proportionality and individual assessments'.[236] This emphasis on the procedural guarantees and on the necessity of detention is at odds with the limited applicability of the proportionality test of the ECtHR judgment in the case of *Saadi*.[237]

## 1.6 CONCLUSIONS

This chapter attempted to clarify, in relation to the topic at hand, the concepts of sovereignty and human rights and how their interrelations shape human rights treaty provisions, their interpretation and, ultimately, the enjoyment of human rights by irregular migrants. In doing so, it shows that the Westphalian system of international society, based on the inviolability of state borders and territories, has been a central argument in the establishment of immigration control as an exclusively domestic and sovereign power. However, the doctrine of absolute sovereignty in relation to immigration is not a 'natural' feature of the Westphalian system but instead is the result of a practice that has grown since the late nineteenth century and that is still upheld today. Even certain norms of international and European human rights law, which are naturally aimed at limiting the exercise of exclusive state authority in a territory and over a population, have recognised state control over migration flows as a legitimate state power and a well-established principle of international (human rights) law. The case law of the human rights bodies has navigated between a universally oriented human rights approach and a respect for sovereign domestic policies while also demonstrating an awareness that the vulnerability of irregular migrants to human rights abuses is high in the context of immigration control. These clashes have contributed to the development of asymmetric conceptualisations that human rights law will need to resolve to avoid excessive expansion of domestic law and state discretion where the rights of irregular migrants are concerned. The brief look at the inter-American jurisprudence reveals a different way of grappling with the rights of migrants in international law, whereby sovereign powers to regulate immigration are not

---

[236] Ibid.
[237] *Saadi* (n 117).

the starting point for human rights monitoring and adjudication. The case of the right to health provides a significant example of the structural difficulty of applying human rights regimes universally, regardless of immigration status. The legal and structural difficulties that irregular migrants encounter with regard to their right to health are not only a consequence of the harsh impact of sovereign powers in the areas of immigration. The non-neutrality of international and European human rights law in relation to socioeconomic rights and the sovereign dimensions of health governance – which are fleshed out in Chapter 2 – are important factors that constrain the full realisation of the right to health of irregular migrants.

# The Normative Contours of a Vulnerability- and Equity-Oriented Right to Health

This chapter outlines the development of the right to health in international and European human rights law while being cognisant that health is an area where states have maintained high levels of discretion or state sovereignty. The 'sovereignty–human rights' clash in the context of immigration, developed in Chapter 1, and the struggle for international recognition and consistent operationalisation of the human right to health in international legal frameworks – which has resulted in an excessive broadening of the margin of discretion in national rights implementation – are the two major barriers to the enjoyment of the international right to health for all, regardless of legal status. This chapter summarises the history of the 'right to health' in different treaty systems. The analysis is supplemented with reference to the meta-legal contributions of global public health, which have the potential to enhance protective human rights standards. Section 2.1 discusses the emergence of health as a subject of international interest since the nineteenth century, with an emphasis on the emergence of public health priorities. The literature in this field helps to flesh out and clarify the normative content of the human right to health. Section 2.2 gives a brief account of health as a social right in the mid-twentieth century, when socioeconomic rights were officially included in the human rights project. Section 2.3 locates the right to health within philosophical debates on human rights and social justice to identify the valued interests behind its normative scope. Sections 2.4 and 2.5 provide an extensive overview of the elaboration, monitoring and implementation of the right to health in the context of the ICESCR and demonstrates how this right is vulnerability-oriented and anchored in the aims and targets of public and global health studies. This section also assesses the contribution of other UN bodies to the development of health-related entitlements. Section 2.6 extends the scope of the analysis to the justiciability of certain health issues before the ECtHR and the ECSR. Finally, Section 2.7 focuses on non-discrimination and vulnerability, which are essential features of the human rights approach to health and which push international human rights obligations and, at times, European human rights law towards the realisation of meaningful standards of substantial equality and health equity, a process that must necessarily encompass the disadvantaged and marginalised social position of irregular migrants.

## 2.1 THE ORIGINS OF HEALTH AS A SOCIAL INTEREST IN THE LAST TWO CENTURIES

The roots of the right to health are deeply connected to the history of 'public health',[1] which is why this analysis relies on some contemporary standards of global public health as sources of applicable rules. According to an authoritative early definition, public health is:

> The science and the art of preventing disease, prolonging life, and promoting physical health and efficiency through organized community efforts for the sanitation of the environment, the control of community infections, the education of the individual in principles of personal hygiene, the organization of medical and nursing services for the early diagnosis and preventive treatment of disease, and the development of the social machinery which will ensure to every individual in the community a standard of living adequate for the maintenance of health.[2]

While medicine traditionally revolves around the provision of health care and treatment to individuals, public health addresses threats to the health of populations and communities by focusing on disease prevention and health promotion campaigns and programmes.[3]

Transmissible diseases, inadequate drinking water and sanitation, and a lack of access to medical care have been, to varying degrees, public social concerns throughout human history from Ancient Egypt through the Middle Ages to

---

[1]  For example, Brigit Toebes, *The Right to Health as a Human Right in International Law* (Hart Publishing 1999) 7; John Tobin, *The Right to Health in International Law* (OUP 2012) 9.

[2]  Charles-Edward Amory Winslow, *The Evolution and Significance of the Modern Public Health Campaign* (Yale University Press 1923), reprinted in (1984) *Journal of Public Health Policy* 1, 3, emphasis added.

[3]  Johnathan Mann, 'Medicine and Public Health, Ethics and Human Rights' (1997) *Hasting Centre Report* 27 6, 7; Audrey R. Chapman, 'Core Obligations Related to the Right to Health' in Audrey R. Chapman and Sage Russell (eds) *Core Obligations: Building a Framework for Economic, Social and Cultural Rights* (Intersentia 2002) 185, 187.

the present day.[4] However, prior to the eighteenth century, responsibility for cases of disease or illness fell mainly to private entities, such as churches or charities. Furthermore, natural and liberal rights theories, as well as notable declarations of rights, focused exclusively on civil rights. These did not apply to health nor did they create any inherent entitlement to protection vis-à-vis state authorities.[5] However, in response to the unhealthy working and living conditions of the working class in the nineteenth century, public health and social medicine movements began to advocate for a greater 'role of the state in securing the health of individuals', although without using the terminology of natural, fundamental or inalienable rights.[6] During the Industrial Revolution(s) in Europe, dire living and working conditions were seen as risk factors for epidemic diseases and social instability and as threats to the strategic capacity of modern nation-states. It was generally agreed that a healthy working class would benefit society and the economy,[7] which constituted an essentially utilitarian approach, distant from the mid-twentieth-century culture of dignity-based human rights.

Growing health-related concerns for people and national communities, together with the willingness to coordinate efforts for the prevention of transmissible disease at an international level, led to a series of international sanitary conferences, the first of which was held in Paris in 1851. At the 11th Sanitary Conference, it was agreed that an international health office would be established, and this process led to the creation of the Office international d'hygiène publique, which would subsequently be replaced by the Health Organisation of the League of Nations, the predecessor of today's WHO. In the nineteenth century, another branch of international law that was rich in health-related components emerged. This was the *corpus legis* known today as international humanitarian law, which deals, *inter alia*, with medical treatment for persons 'hors de combat' – sick and wounded soldiers at sea or on land, prisoners of war and civilians during armed conflicts.[8]

---

4   Jonathan Mann, *Health and Human Rights: A Reader* (Routledge 1999) 11. For further details on the historical perspective of public health, see George Rosen, *A History of Public Health* (first published 1958, John Hopkins University Press 1993).

5   Ed Bates, 'History' in Moeckli et al. (n 51, Ch 1) 3–9. Neither the 1776 United States Declaration of Independence nor the 1789 French Declaration on the Rights of Men explicitly mention health as a fundamental right.

6   Gerald M. Oppenheimer, Ronald Bayer and James Colgrove, 'Health and Human Rights: Old Wine in New Bottles?' (2002) *Journal of Law, Medicine & Ethics* 30(4) 522.

7   Rosen (n 4) 170.

8   Since the 1864, some states adopted the Geneva Convention for the Amelioration of the Condition of the Wounded in Armies in the Field. For further details, see Katherine H. A.

In the early twentieth century, health was also a strategic tool in international relations. As part of the Paris Peace Conference, held in 1919 after the end of World War I, the League of Nations was established with the aim of achieving global peace and security while preserving national sovereignty.[9] Article 25 of the Covenant of the League of Nations recognised the strategic role of health in achieving and maintaining global peace.[10] Against the same historical backdrop, the growing ideal of social justice and concerns regarding the conditions of workers throughout the world led to the foundation of the International Labour Organization. Since its establishment, this organisation has actively addressed work-related risks to health and has played a prominent role in international standard setting in the field of occupational health and safety.[11]

An analysis of the historical factors that resulted in international recognition of the modern right to health as a social right, with several interdependent connections with other rights, would be incomplete without considering the supportive voices and experiences that came from the Americas, which significantly influenced the drafting of the UDHR. The Latin American approach to human rights was greatly influenced by socialist ideologies and Catholic values and focused on the material needs of the poor and a common belonging to the human family.[12] These underlying values contributed to shaping how socioeconomic rights were formulated in the UDHR, which, as discussed in Section 2.2, includes health in its holistic sense as a core component of the right to an adequate standard of living as set out in its Article 25.[13]

---

Footer and Leonard S. Rubenstein, 'A Human Rights Approach to Health Care in Conflict' (2013) *International Review of the Red Cross* 95(889) 167.

[9] Tobin (n 1) 23.

[10] Covenant of the League of Nations (28 April 1919, entry into force 10 January 2020) Article 25: 'The Members [...] agree to encourage [...] national Red Cross Organisations having as purposes the improvement of health, the prevention of disease, and the mitigation of suffering throughout the World.'

[11] The Preamble of the Constitution of the International Labour Organization (adopted 1 April 1919 entry into force 28 June 1919) mentions 'the protection of the workers against sickness, disease and injury arising out of his employment' as one of the goals of the organisation. For details, see Benjamin O. Alli, *Fundamental Principles of Occupational Health and Safety* (2nd edn, ILO Publishing 2008) 17.

[12] For further details, see Mary Ann Glendon, 'The Forgotten Crucible: The Latin American Influence on the Universal Human Rights Idea' (2003) *Harvard Human Rights Journal* 16 27, 32, 36–37; Paolo G. Carozza, 'From Conquest to Constitutions: Retrieving a Latin American Tradition of the Idea of Human Rights' (2003) *Human Rights Quarterly* 25(2) 281.

[13] For further analysis, see Section 2.2, *infra*.

The history of public health and social medicine over the previous two centuries, the shift in their governing ideologies from instrumentalism to humanitarianism, the Industrial Revolution, emerging social movements and the contribution of Latin American Catholic values and views on social justice to the UDHR may all be read as important catalysts for the emergence of the right to health as a social human right in the aftermath of World War II. Finally, it is worth remembering that the United States government had supported the idea of socioeconomic rights as an issue of primary concern before the rise of the Cold War. Former US President F. D. Roosevelt, influenced by the legacy of the Great Depression and the emergence of the modern welfare state,[14] famously included 'freedom from want' and a call to widen the opportunities for medical care in his 1941 'Four Freedoms' speech.[15]

## 2.2 EARLY PROCLAMATIONS OF THE RIGHT TO HEALTH, SOVEREIGNTY AND THE UNIVERSALISATION OF SOCIAL RIGHTS AS HUMAN RIGHTS

In 1945, the Charter of the UN was adopted with the primary aim of establishing a new international order based on international peace and security. Both 'health' and 'human rights' featured in Article 55 of the Charter, which stipulated that their promotion was instrumental to the 'creation of conditions of stability and well-being [...] among Nations'.[16]

Furthermore, the drafting of the 1946 WHO Constitution, also considered the Magna Carta of health,[17] reflected the idea that health is an essential factor in the attainment of security, peace and well-being for individuals and nations. In the constitutive document of the WHO, health is regarded as a 'state of complete physical, mental and social well-being and not merely as the absence of disease or infirmity'. It is seen as a 'value', and, for the first time,

---

[14] The welfare state is a system whereby the 'state undertakes to protect the health and well-being of its citizens, especially those in financial or social need, by means of grants, pensions, and other benefits', <https://en.oxforddictionaries.com/definition/welfare_state> accessed 1 March 2021. This rests on the idea that the social provision of goods must 'be treated as rights possessed by all people as citizens', see David Kelly, *A Life of One's Own: Individual Rights and the Welfare State* (Cato Institute 1998) 1. See also, Luca Baccelli, 'Welfare, Diritti Sociali, Conflitti: Ci Salveranno i Barbari?' (2014) *Ragion Pratica* 87 according to whom 'socio-economic rights represent the legal dimension of the welfare state'.

[15] Franklin Delano Roosevelt, 'The State of the Union Address to Congress' (6 January 1941).

[16] UN Charter (n 31, Ch 1) Article 55: 'With a view to the creation of conditions of stability and well-being [...] among Nations [...] the UN shall promote the solution of international [...] health [...] related problems [...] and universal respect for [...] human rights.'

[17] Thomas Parran, 'Charter for World Health' (1946) *Public Health Reports* 61 1265.

as a 'fundamental human right' of every human being.[18] This text gathered key elements of debates around health, which it framed as a multilayered interdisciplinary concept with medical, ethical, strategic, political and legal connotations. The WHO's approach and the composition of its staff combine the 'negative aspects of public health', including vaccination and other specific means of combating infection, with its 'positive aspects', that is, the 'improvement of public health by better food, physical education, medical care, [and] health insurance'.[19] Accordingly, incorporating a socio-medical approach, the WHO Constitution established that 'governments have a responsibility for the health of their peoples which can be fulfilled only by the provision of adequate health and social measures'.[20]

Nevertheless, it is worth noting that the rise of health protection as a priority issue at the domestic and international levels, over the last seventy years, has not led to any substantive relinquishment of state sovereignty or to a large expansion of the regulatory force of international law in this field. Health governance was, and still largely is, a sovereign competence. As Article 3 of the 2005 International Health Regulations (IHR) clarifies, '[s]tates have, in accordance with the Charter of the United Nations and the principles of international law, the sovereign right to legislate and to implement legislation in pursuance of their health policies'.[21] This is reflected in the fact that the WHO, despite its potentially expansive constitutional mandate, has only adopted one treaty (the Framework Convention on Tobacco Control) and two regulations (the Nomenclature Regulations and the IHR) since its establishment. Furthermore, the right to the highest attainable standard of health in the Preamble to the WHO Constitution has long remained a dormant clause, and the organisation has mainly limited its operations to technical cooperation and acted with a recommendatory approach.

Furthermore, state sovereignty may be referred to as a critical *political determinant* of health because only where there is a functioning and democratic government can health promotion and care be guaranteed with respect to freedom and entitlements. The precarious living conditions and standards

---

[18] WHO Constitution (n 22, Introduction) Preamble, emphasis added.
[19] Andrija Stampar, 'Suggestions Relating to the Constitution of an International Health Organization' (1949) *WHO Official Records* 1 (Annex 9), as referred to in Lawrence O. Gostin and Benjamin Mason Meier, 'The Origins of Human Rights in Global Health' in Benjamin Mason Meier and Lawrence O. Gostin (eds) *Human Rights in Global Health: Rights-Based Governance for a Globalizing World* (OUP 2018) 28.
[20] WHO Constitution (n 22, Introduction) Preamble, emphasis added.
[21] World Health Organization, *International Health Regulations* (2005) (2nd edn, WHO 2008) Article 3(4).

of health protection in states at war and in those experiencing institutional crises, such as Libya and Venezuela, demonstrate the importance of functioning state apparatuses for guaranteeing the respect, protection and fulfilment of the right to health in the context of a state-based international society.[22] Whereas state sovereignty is a precondition of effective health protection, a significant number of international instruments have been agreed upon to qualify standard setting and health policies in the fields of infectious disease control (under the binding though 'not so hard' IHR regime)[23] and human rights law (to which the right to health and other interconnected rights belong).[24]

As well as its inclusion in the WHO Constitution, the right to health is recognised as an international human right in Article 25 of the UDHR, according to which 'everyone has the right to a standard of living adequate for the health and well-being of himself and of his family, including, food, clothing, housing, medical care, and necessary social services, and the right to security'.[25] Although this wording does not grant to the right to health any conceptual autonomy, its significance lies in the fact that the Declaration appeared to adopt a holistic approach to health – one that is still valid today – by considering both health care and other social factors of health as constitutive elements of the right to an adequate standard of living. The drafting history of the UDHR provides evidence that an autonomous right to health care – or to medical care – had been under debate in the UN Commission on Human Rights (UNCHR). The Commission, however, preferred to eventually link this right to what contemporary human rights and public health would define as the 'underlying determinants of health' to highlight the composite nature of 'adequate living standards'.[26] Even though this choice may have reduced the visibility of the right to health in this resolution, this effect is mitigated by the fact the Declaration was conceived to contain a set of principles to be spelled out in greater detail in subsequent legal instruments of

---

[22] Francioni (n 24, Introduction) 57.

[23] Pedro Villareal, 'The (Not So) Hard Side of the IHR: Breaches of Legal Obligations' (*Global Health Law Groningen Blog*, 26 February 2020) <www.rug.nl/rechten/onderzoek/expertisecentra/ghlg/blog/the-not-so-hard-side-of-the-ihr-breaches-of-legal-obligations-26–02–2020> last accessed 20 October 2020.

[24] Francioni (n 24, Introduction) 51–66.

[25] UDHR (n 2, Ch 1) Article 25.

[26] Commission on Human Rights (UNCHR) – Drafting Committee, Draft Outline of International Bill of Rights (4 June 1947) E/CN.4/AC.1/3. See also Meier and Gostin (n 19) 29–31. For further details on the 'travaux préparatoires', see Section 4.3.1.

a binding nature, which would also set out corresponding state obligations.[27] Another merit of the drafting choices of the UDHR is the absence of any explicit hierarchy or priority of rights, along with the delineation, in the same document, of civil, political, economic, social and cultural rights that *everyone has*. Furthermore, in referring to the goal of achieving 'better standards of life in larger freedom', the Preamble to the Declaration evokes the universal necessity of meeting the material needs of people while defending their autonomy and dignity. This corresponds to guarantees of equality and freedom for everyone, two major underlying principles of human rights law, in a system where all rights were originally conceived to have the same worth and to mutually reinforce each other.[28]

Although the Declaration was not designed to be legally binding on states, it represented authoritative international recognition of the importance of welfare and health for the 'dignity and free development of human personality'.[29] Until that moment, welfare measures and social rights had belonged exclusively to the domestic domain, and their implementation constituted a way of guaranteeing political stability for market-based Western economies vis-à-vis emerging radical labour movements and socialist states. Domestic welfare benefits played a stabilising role in the shift from absolute monarchy to mass democracy,[30] and the institutionalisation of these provisions and rights of a redistributive nature within domestic legal frameworks gave birth to the modern welfare state.[31] T. H. Marshall, one of the most authoritative sociologists of the mid-twentieth century, linked the recognition of social rights to the evolution of national citizenship in the twentieth century. Citizenship was intended as 'a status bestowed on those who are full members of a community'.[32] However, social citizenship can be seen as a crucial aspect of sovereignty whereby states allocate social benefits to stable members of a national community. This is what makes modern citizenship a 'basic form of spatial

---

[27] Asbjørn Eide and Wenche Barth Eide, 'Article 25' in Gudmundur Alfredsson and Asbjørn Eide (eds) *The Universal Declaration of Human Rights: A Common Standard of Achievement* (Martinus Nijhoff Publishers 1999) 523.

[28] World Conference on Human Rights, Vienna Declaration and Programme of Action Vienna (12 July 1993) A/CONF.157/23, para 5: 'All human rights are universal, indivisible and interdependent and interrelated. The international community must treat human rights globally in a fair and equal manner, on the same footing, and with the same emphasis.' For further details see Section 4.1.3.

[29] UDHR (n 2, Ch 1) Article 22.

[30] Bard-Anders Andreassen, 'Article 22' in Alfredsson and Eide (n 27) 453.

[31] Ulrich Preuss, 'The Concept of Rights and the Welfare State' in Gunter Teubner (ed) *Dilemmas of Law in the Welfare State* (Walter de Gruyter 1986) 151.

[32] Thomas Humphrey Marshall, *Citizenship and Social Class* (CUP 1950) 28.

closure'.[33] Both the European social model and constitutionalism were influenced by this definition; nonetheless, it must be noted that in twentieth-century Europe, social rights in 'social states'[34] were not meant 'to generate subjective individual rights enforceable against the state by Courts',[35] particularly in the case of community outsiders.

Unlike the case of the UDHR, where social rights were not grounded in any explicit political ideology,[36] the Western liberal position embraced by Marshall regarded social rights as necessary to balance the inequality created by the capitalist system and essential for the enjoyment of a 'modicum of economic welfare and security' of community members.[37] In contrast, the broad principles of the UDHR were meant to apply universally:[38] everyone – not only certain citizens – had prima facie the right to a minimum of social goods and services to meet their basic material needs.

Unfortunately, with the rise of the Cold War, the ideological clash between the free market–oriented world and the socialist bloc undermined, for decades, the equal value and the effective enforcement of socioeconomic rights vis-à-vis civil and political rights. The disagreement within the UN member states on the nature and form of implementation of these ostensibly different categories of human rights led the UNGA to pass the 'Separation Resolution', which mandated the UNCHR to discuss and draft two different

---

[33] Maurizio Ferrara, 'Towards an "Open" Social Citizenship? The New Boundaries of Welfare in the European Union' in Gráinne de Búrca (ed) *EU Law and the Welfare State: In Search of Solidarity* (OUP 2005) 11.

[34] Colm O'Cinneide, 'Austerity and the Faded Dream of "Social Europe"' in Nolan (n 8, Introduction) 169, 172. Social states are a subcategory of welfare states where the state assumes constitutional obligations to intervene in the economic and social spheres, in some instances by constitutionalising social rights. This model originated from the German 'Sozialstaat', see George S. Katrougalos, 'The (Dim) Perspectives of the European Social Citizenship' (2012) *Jean Monnet Working Paper NYU School of Law* 5(7) 9.

[35] Colm O'Cinneide, 'The Present Limits and Future Potential of European Social Constitutionalism' in Katharine G. Young (ed) *The Future of Economic and Social Rights* (CUP 2019) 326–327.

[36] Ulrike Davy, 'Social Citizenship Going International: Changes in the Reading of UN-Sponsored Economic and Social Rights' (2013) *International Journal of Social Welfare* 22 (SUPPL.1) S15, S22–23 argues that UN-sponsored economic and social rights drew on three main ideologies: developmentalism, socialism and liberalism.

[37] Marshall (n 32) 11.

[38] The adjective 'universal' has at least a double meaning in this context: it refers both to the targeted geographical application of the Declaration as a moral rights framework and to the personal application of the same, which encompasses every people who are present in a state jurisdiction, regardless of their nationality *inter alia*.

general treaties on human rights: the ICCPR and the ICESCR.[39] Similarly, in the European and American regional human rights systems, separate treaties were being designed to protect civil rights and socioeconomic rights.[40] The principle of the indivisibility of human rights, which means that all human rights have the same worth, was set off course for decades, and the situation has still not been completely reversed today.

## 2.3 PHILOSOPHICAL JUSTIFICATIONS FOR THE RIGHT TO HEALTH

Before discussing the elaboration and development of the right to health in international human rights instruments, it is worth briefly considering how philosophical debates on human rights law and social justice regard health as a key element of a rights-based moral framework, especially when the terminologies of 'human needs' or 'capabilities' are employed.

This section does not provide a full and detailed account of all applicable theories but rather grapples with a few of them to reflect on what the international right to health can actually protect and why mere 'human survival' – which often grounds the operationalisation of rights for irregular migrants – is not a sufficient foundation or target of this right.

The orthodox philosophical approach to human rights is that all human beings possess such rights by virtue of their humanity; these rights are regarded as inherent in humans' dignity. This suggests that human rights exist independently of, and prior to, any legal recognition. This view is rooted in the school of natural rights, which has developed since the seventeenth century and which generally recognises the existence of pre-institutional moral rights that can be identified using reason.[41] Early philosophers of this school, such as Thomas Hobbes and John Locke,[42] identified a few civil liberties as natural rights. The value that underpinned most of the theories of the Enlightenment was human freedom, especially freedom from state interference in people's lives, liberty and property.

While a naturalistic view eventually made its way into Article 1 UDHR, which states that 'all human beings are born free and equal in dignity and

---

[39] UNGA Res 543(VI) 'Preparation of Two Draft International Covenants on Human Rights' (5 February 1952). ICCPR, ICESCR (n 13, Introduction).

[40] ECHR, ESC (n 43, Introduction), ACHR (n 93, Ch 1), Additional Protocol to the American Convention on Human Rights in the Area of Economic, Social and Cultural Rights (adopted 17 November 1988, entry into force 16 November 1999) A-52.

[41] Bates (n 5) 3–8.

[42] Thomas Hobbes, *Leviathan* (first published 1651, OUP 2008); John Locke, *Second Treatise of Government* (first published 1690, Hackett Publishing 1980).

rights', the inclusion of socioeconomic rights within human rights moral frameworks required a partial reshaping of the fundamental values underlying the philosophy and practice of human rights: freedom and the role of the state in human rights theories had to be reconfigured.[43] Freedom, rather than being understood as the absence of state interference, can be conceptualised as the removal of constraints on human agency. For example, the contemporary scholar Amartya Sen identifies poor economic opportunities, systematic social deprivation and tyranny as such constraints.[44] Individuals cannot achieve their potential and develop true agency and freedom without an adequate social context and social inputs.[45] Moreover, respecting human dignity – the value meant to underlie human rights law[46] – as a socio-relational concept means recognising the equal worth of everyone and redressing the disadvantages of the worst off by creating opportunities for the development of capabilities for the benefit of individuals and society as a whole.[47] Martha Nussbaum makes this clear: 'A dignified free being shapes his or her life in cooperation and reciprocity with others [...]. A life that is really human is one that is shaped throughout by these human powers of practical reason and sociability.'[48]

During the second half of the twentieth century, both legal positivism – which is concerned with the analytical study of law – and those political philosophies that focus on the role that human rights play in society resulted in a paradigmatic shift in the justification of human rights.[49] Over the last few decades, there has been less speculation about their metaphysical justification and more on what having rights means, what valued features of human lives are protected by human rights and how a comprehensive theory of rights, capable of justifying the practice of human rights, should be designed.[50] Thus, the main contemporary approaches to the justification of human rights tend to

---

[43] Sandra Fredman and Meghan Campbell, 'Introduction' in Fredman and Campbell (eds) *Social and Economic Rights and Constitutional Law* (Edward Elgar 2016) xii–xviii.

[44] Amartya Sen, *Development as Freedom* (OUP 1999) 3.

[45] Jürgen Habermas, *Between Facts and Norms* (MIT Press 1997); Joseph Raz, *The Morality of Freedom* (Clarendon Press 1986) 124.

[46] ICCPR, ICECSR (n 42, Introduction) Preamble(s): 'these rights derive from the inherent dignity of the human person'.

[47] Sandra Liebenberg, 'The Value of Human Dignity in Interpreting Socio-economic Rights' (2005) *South African Journal on Human Rights* 21(1) 1.

[48] Martha Nussbaum, *Women and Human Development – The Capabilities Approach* (CUP 2000) 72.

[49] John Rawls, 'The Law of People' in Stephen Shute and Susan Hurley (eds) *On Human Rights – The Oxford Amnesty Lectures 1993* (Basic Books 1983) 41, 68.

[50] Siegfried Van Duffel, 'Moral Philosophy' in Shelton (n 39, Ch 1) 32.

frame rights in instrumentalist or practice-based terms rather than considering their inherent nature. Instrumental justifications frame human rights as essential means to realise the 'valued features of human lives'.[51] These features or values to which human rights contribute vary across theories and include agency,[52] a good life,[53] basic needs[54] and capabilities.[55]

Theories that focus on agency hold that human rights protect the capacity to pursue autonomous choices without interference and, thus, tend to frame human rights protection in generally negative terms. For instance, James Griffin rejected the idea of the 'right to the highest attainable standard of health' because this attainment would not be a necessary condition to protect the foundational value of human rights, which for him is human agency or autonomy. According to Griffin, 'we have a right to life because it is a necessary condition of agency; and a right to health "care" for our functioning effectively as agents'.[56] As he regards human rights as minimalist and urgent moral claims, while this conceptualisation may fit with indirect health protection through the protection of civil and political rights or a claim to urgent care, it does not fully justify the existence of broader socioeconomic obligations. Other authoritative Western philosophers have dismissed the concept of the 'highest attainable standard of health' as utopian and unachievable at a global level: since universal health cannot be provided, the assertion of a human right to health is mistaken, and correlative state obligations cannot be held by any agent of international law.[57] Other scholars have also demonstrated unease in dealing with the concept of health, as it seems to imply the 'right to be healthy'; accordingly, they recognise only 'health care' as a legitimate right worthy of ethical and legal justification.[58]

---

[51] Rowan Cruft, S. Matthew Liao and Massimo Renzo, 'The Philosophical Foundations of Human Rights: An Overview' in Cruft, Liao and Renzo (eds) *Philosophical Foundations of Human Rights* (OUP 2015) 11.

[52] James Griffin, *On Human Rights* (OUP 2008) 180.

[53] S. Matthew Liao, 'Human Rights as Fundamental Conditions for a Good Life' in Cruft, Liao, Renzo (n 51).

[54] David Miller, 'Grounding Human Rights' (2012) *Critical Review of International Social and Political Philosophy* 15(4) 407.

[55] Nussbaum (n 25, Introduction) 20–26.

[56] James Griffin, 'Discrepancies between the Best Philosophical Account of Human Rights and the International Law of Human Rights' (2001) *Proceedings of the Aristotelian Society* 7.

[57] Onora O'Neill, 'The Dark Side of Human Rights' (2005) *International Affairs* 81 427.

[58] Kristen Hessler and Allen Buchanan, 'Specifying the Content of the Human Right to Health Care' in Rosamond Rhodes, Margaret P. Battin and Anita Silvers (eds) *Medicine and Social Justice: Essays on the Distribution of Health Care* (OUP 2002) 84; Norman Daniels, *Just Health Care* (CUP 1985) 6.

By contrast, justice theories centred on a good life and basic needs appear to be more consistent with the grounding, development and aim of socioeconomic rights. Indeed, such theories assert that human rights are conditions for pursuing either a good or a minimally decent life through the meeting of certain human needs. Norman Daniels, a scholar of 'human needs', draws on Rawls' theory of justice as fairness to argue that the right to health – including prevention via public health interventions, restoration through health care and its promotion via the social determinants of health – provides a fair range of equal opportunities for people to pursue their life plan, function and have their basic material and health needs met.[59] However, Daniels does not resolve the priority-setting issue or specify detailed state obligations regarding health, as, according to his theory, these are for deliberative processes to shape.[60]

Other scholars, most notably Sen and Nussbaum, adopt a capability approach to social justice and rights, according to which human rights should protect certain human capabilities that are necessary to choose, to act and, ultimately, to achieve certain functionings or a flourishing life.[61] Capability theories understand well-being in terms of capabilities and functionings. Whereas the former are 'doings and beings that people can achieve if they so wish', the latter are realised or achieved capabilities.[62] For capability scholars, focusing on a distribution of means and resources is not sufficient to achieve equality and social and individual well-being because individuals 'vary in their abilities to convert resources into functionings'[63] and what ultimately matters is 'what people are able [and willing] to do and to be'.[64] Thus, the capability approach is respectful of human diversity and agency[65] without neglecting the key role played by 'conversion factors' (of a personal,

---

[59] Daniels (n 26, Introduction) 14–15, 96–97.

[60] Ibid 24–26, Ch 4; See also Alicia E. Yamin and Ole F. Norheim, 'Taking Equality Seriously: Applying Human Rights Framework to Priority-setting in Health' (2014) *Human Rights Quarterly* 36(2) 296.

[61] Nussbaum (n 25, Introduction) 20–26; Sen (n 25, Introduction) 320.

[62] For an overview, see Ingrid Robeyns and Morten Byscov, 'The Capability Approach' in Edward N. Zalta et al. (edn) *The Stanford Encyclopedia of Philosophy* (first published 14 April 2011; substantive revision 10 December 2020) <https://plato.stanford.edu/entries/capability-approach/#:~:text=The%20capability%20approach%20purports%20that,are%20effectively%20able%20to%20lead.&text=Sen%20calls%20this%20notion%20capabilities,their%20potential%20doings%20and%20beings> accessed 10 March 2020.

[63] Caroline Harnacke, 'Disability and Capability: Exploring the Usefulness of Martha Nussbaum's Capabilities Approach for the UN Disability Rights Convention' (2013) *Journal of Law, Medicine and Ethics* 4 768, 770, referring to Nussbaum (n 47) 164–165.

[64] Nussbaum (n 48) 5.

[65] Robeyns and Byscov (n 62) para 2.5.

social and environmental nature) that social institutions must consider when adopting measures to enable a real freedom, opportunity or 'capability to be healthy'.[66]

Nussbaum recognises that 'capabilities are understood as ways of realizing a life with human dignity in the different areas of life with which human beings typically engage'[67] and that her theory is 'a species of a human rights approach'.[68] Unlike Sen, she draws – but does not describe in detail – a list of 'central human capabilities', all of which are critical for individual and collective health.[69] She specifies that all human rights 'understood as entitlements to capabilities, have material and social preconditions, and all require government action'.[70]

Jennifer Ruger also criticised Rawlsian approaches to welfare for adopting a 'resource-oriented' paradigm that focuses on 'inputs for health, means and goods' rather than on 'outputs, results and capabilities'. Ruger holds that human rights – including the right to health – play a critical role in identifying the nature and scope of obligations for realising the necessary human capabilities and functions to achieve the Aristotelian concept of a flourishing life.[71] Ruger's theory combines Sen's theoretical approach with the 'incompletely theorised agreements' of Cass Sunstein. She defines international human rights treaties as instances of incompletely theorised socio-legal-institutional 'practice', which express overlapping consensus and moral commitment to the fact that health is an interest and a right worthy of recognition.

Although treaties have failed to reach agreement on the conceptual foundation of the right to health or on the specific outcomes of the controversies that may arise, 'human needs' and 'capabilities' theories seem to capture the interests that the international right to health targets. They do so in a way that generally corresponds to the level of entitlement pursued by socioeconomic treaties, a level that should be progressively increased and pitched significantly higher than mere bare survival. However, all of these theories have both

---

[66] Sridhar Venkatapuram, *Health Justice: An Argument from the Capabilities Approach* (Polity Press 2011) 19.

[67] Martha Nussbaum, *Frontiers of Justice* (Harvard University Press 2006) 161.

[68] Martha Nussbaum, 'Human Rights and Human Capabilities' (2007) *Harvard Human Rights Journal* 20 20–24.

[69] These are 'Life, Bodily Health, Bodily Integrity, the Development and Expression of Senses, Imagination and Thought, Emotional Health, Practical Reason, Affiliation (both personal and political), Relationships with Other Species and the World of Nature, Play, and Control over One's Environment (both material and social)'. See Nussbaum (n 48) 33–43.

[70] Nussbaum (n 68) 20.

[71] Jennifer Ruger, 'Towards a Theory of a Right to Health: Capability and Incompletely Theorised Agreements' (2006) *Yale Journal of Law & the Humanities* 18 273.

potential and limitations in terms of providing a conceptual foundation for the human right to health. For instance, Daniels' theory does not set out universally valid norms but instead guides actions that remain society-specific in terms of funding priorities, and capability approaches 'fail to identify the content of specific rights and obligations'.[72]

While the analytical exercise of this book is not exclusively grounded on any one of these theories, needs-based arguments and capability theories have an undeniable impact on my arguments because they are able to accommodate the desirability of combining human rights and social justice arguments to enhance health standards progressively while also establishing a 'healthy survival threshold' for state provisions and reducing inequalities in state jurisdictions.[73] In particular, capability approaches, which require active state measures and target real freedom of opportunities, are particularly suited to accommodating instances of substantive equality and autonomy and are consistent with a human rights approach to disability.[74] Throughout the remainder of this chapter and book, public health concepts and general principles for the operationalisation of the right to health, such as primary health care and the social determinants of health, are frequently used to explain the scope of this international health claim. I argue that these elements of the right to health, which are equity-based ethical strategies to reduce avoidable and unfair inequalities in health, can reinforce the normative concepts of substantive equality and vulnerability to call for the realisation of international positive obligations of a certain quality regarding the health of irregular migrants. Without denying their distinctive features and histories, social justice, public health and human rights law are here employed as complementary strategies for advancing standards to enable everyone to pursue health justice.[75]

## 2.4 THE RIGHT TO THE HIGHEST ATTAINABLE STANDARD OF HEALTH IN THE CONTEXT OF THE ICESCR

As this book strives to identify the normative contributions that international and European human rights law can offer to enhance the protection of the

---

[72] Audrey Chapman, 'The Foundations of a Human Right to Health: Human Rights and Bioethics in a Dialogue' (2015) *Health and Human Rights Journal* 17(1) 6, 13.

[73] On the concepts of minimum core obligations and social minimum threshold, see *infra* at Section 2.4.2.4.

[74] This is the main conceptual and normative framework employed in Chapter 5.

[75] Lawrence O. Gostin, Matiangai V. S. Sirleaf and Eric A. Friedman, 'Global Health Law: Legal Foundations for Social Justice in Public Health' in Gostin and Meier (n 35, Introduction) 49.

right to health of irregular migrants, this section starts by exploring how the ICESCR – which provides 'the fullest and most definitive conception of the right to health' in general international human rights law[76] – unpacks the scope of this right and the corresponding state obligations.

As stated in Section 2.2, ideological disagreement on the nature of socio-economic human rights led states to engage in parallel negotiations on two separate treaties at the UN level, as well as in the European region. The ICCPR was designed to generate immediate binding state obligations 'to respect and to ensure' people's civil and political rights.[77] In contrast, Article 2(1) of the ICESCR urges ratifying states to:

> Take steps, individually and through international assistance and cooperation, [...] to the maximum of its available resources, with a view to achieving progressively the full realisation of the rights recognised in the present Covenant by all appropriate means, including particularly the adoption of legislative measures.[78]

This provision is crucial for a full understanding of state obligations under the ICESCR and has a dynamic relationship with all the other provisions of the Covenant, including Article 12 on the right to health. Most importantly, Article 2 imposes the general obligation to 'progressively' realise each of the substantive rights set out in the treaty to its full extent over a period (of unspecified duration) by adopting appropriate steps or measures.[79] The rationale for this type of state duty was the belief that the implementation of socioeconomic rights required positive state measures involving the allocation of economic resources, and that countries with different degrees of development could not meet the same goals at the same time.[80] Social rights, at the time the ICESCR was being negotiated (and still today in many countries), were considered to be akin to programmatic directives or policies rather than

---

[76] Audrey R. Chapman, 'Conceptualizing the Right to Health: A Violation Approach' (1998) *Tennessee Law Review* 65 389, 398.

[77] ICCPR (n 42, Introduction) Article 2(1).

[78] ICESCR (n 23, Introduction) Article 2(1).

[79] UNCHR, '*Note verbale dated 5 December 1986 from the Permanent Mission of the Netherlands to the United Nations Office at Geneva addressed to the Centre for Human Rights ("Limburg Principles")*' (8 January 1987) E/CN.4/1987/17, para 21, interpreted this temporal requirement as the state duty to 'move as expeditiously as possible towards the realisation' of the Covenant's rights; CESCR, 'General Comment No. 3: The nature of States parties' obligations (Article 2, para 1, of the Covenant) (14 December 1990) E/1991/23.

[80] For further details, see ibid (CESCR, GC3) para 9.

legal entitlements for immediate implementation and enforcement.[81] Closely connected to the rule of progressive realisation, the obligation to devote the maximum available resources to securing socioeconomic rights, while representing a limit for the immediate realisation of rights, also creates a duty with regard to budget allocation and public expenditures that cannot be unduly deferred.[82]

The above remarks demonstrate that the margin of discretion granted to states for meeting international obligations in the socioeconomic field is undeniably broad. States maintain competence over the form of incorporation and on the nature of the concrete measures adopted, although they must causally pursue the progressive realisation of the elements of the rights of the Covenant to the maximum of available resources[83] with 'deliberate, concrete and targeted' steps or actions.[84] However, Articles 2 and 3 ICESCR explicitly establish at least two different types of immediate obligations of states: to take (immediate) steps towards the full realisation of rights and regulate the enjoyment of existing socioeconomic rights or provisions in a non-discriminatory manner on a series of specified but non-exhaustive grounds.[85] Finally, it is worth noting that permissible interferences with these rights, which should be interpreted restrictively,[86] are only possible when they are in the form of law that is 'compatible with the nature' of these rights and for the purpose of promoting 'general social welfare'.[87]

### 2.4.1 A Textual Analysis of Article 12 ICESCR in the Light of Its Travaux Préparatoires

In the 1950s, during the early stages of the drafting of a UN binding instrument on human rights, the WHO secretariat assumed leadership in debates on health issues in the UNCHR. A draft proposal from the WHO included a

---

[81] Daniel J. Whelan and Jack Donnelly, 'The West, Economic and Social Rights, and the Global Human Rights Regime: Setting the Record Straight' (2007) *Human Rights Quarterly* 29(4) 908. For further details, see Sections 2.4.2 and 2.7, *infra*.

[82] CESCR, GC14 (n 27, Introduction) para 31; Limburg Principles (n 80) para 21.

[83] CESCR, 'General Comment No. 9 (the Domestic Application of the Covenant)' (3 December 1998) E/C.12/1998/24.

[84] CESCR, 'General Comment No. 13 (the Right to Education – Article 13 of the Covenant)' (8 December 1999) E/C.12/1999/10, para 43.

[85] For further details, see Sections 2.4.2 and 2.7, *infra*.

[86] Nihal Jayawickrama, *The Judicial Application of Human Rights Law* (CUP 2002) 184–185.

[87] Article 4 ICESCR (n 23, Introduction), as elaborated by the CESCR, in *Rosario Gómez-Limón Pardo v Spain* Com No 52/2018 (CESCR 2020) para 9.4; See also, Ssenyonjo (n 87, Ch 1) 150–154.

definition of health and emphasised social measures for realising conditions that constitute positive underlying determinants of health.[88] However, with the beginning of the Cold War, the WHO stopped actively engaging with the drafting of international human rights instruments and began to position itself as a 'technical' organisation, abandoning, for decades, an explicit human rights approach.[89]

The compromises reached within the Commission, under the influence of US and Russian proposals, led to an early draft article on the right to health, which included more detailed general state obligations of conduct and a more extensive list of the social or underlying determinants of health than those featuring the final text of the ICESCR while limiting medical services to *state nationals* or *citizens*.[90] Further debates and proposals in the Commission involving US representatives, who eventually dismissed socioeconomic rights as aspirational, resulted in the exclusion from the final 1957 draft article on the right to health of any reference to a definition of health, the concept of social well-being or an extensive list of extra-medical determinants of health.[91]

Article 12 ICESCR, in its adopted formulation, establishes both obligations of result and obligations of conduct in its first and second paragraphs, respectively.[92] The first paragraph of Article 12 stipulates that 'the States Parties to the present Covenant recognise the right of everyone to the enjoyment of the highest attainable standard of physical and mental health'. The universal

---

[88] UNCHR, 'Suggestions Submitted by the Director of the World Health Organisation' (18 April 1951) E/CN.4/544 2.

[89] Benjamin Mason Meier and Florian Kastler, 'Development of Human Rights through WHO' in Meier and Gostin (n 19) 111, 112–126.

[90] UNCHR, 'Summary Record of the 223rd Meeting' (13 June 1951) E/CN.4/SR.223. Draft text (emphasis added): 'The States parties to this Covenant recognize the right of everyone to the enjoyment of the highest standard of health obtainable. With a view to implementing and safeguarding this right, each State party hereto *undertakes to provide legislative* measures to promote and protect health and in particular: 1. to reduce infant mortality and to provide for healthy development of the child; 2. to *improve nutrition, housing, sanitation, recreation, economic and working conditions* and other aspects of environmental hygiene; 3. to control epidemic, endemic and other diseases; 4. to provide conditions which would assure the right of *all its nationals* to a medical service and medical attention in the event of sickness' (emphasis added).

[91] UNGA, 'Draft International Covenants on Human Rights' (28 January 1957) A/C.3/SR.743. The draft article on the right to health therein is the same as that of the 1966 ICESCR. For an overview of the *travaux préparatoires*, see Toebes (n 1) 40–51.

[92] In international law, obligations of conduct are state duties that require a certain course of action by the state, while obligations of result require the ratifying state to 'achieve, or prevent, a particular result by means of its own choice'. See International Law Commission, *Yearbook of the International Law Commission* (1999 vol. II part 2) A/CN.4/SER.A/1999/Add.1 (Part 2) 57–62.

application of the right to health is conveyed by the word 'everyone': the right to health as a human right is therein grounded in the 'dignity' of every 'human person' as a rights holder, regardless of their geographical location.[93] This unqualified formulation suggests that the personal scope of application is not limited to state nationals, as it was in previous drafts.[94] Furthermore, the choice of the verb 'recognise' appears to grant less immediate operative force to the provision than having a right to something. Unlike the unaccepted draft proposal drawn up by the director of the WHO, which had included the formulation 'every human being *shall* have the right to' something,[95] the adopted terminology undeniably grants state parties a certain degree of discretion[96] in selecting the type of measures and the time span for their progressive domestic implementation of 'the highest attainable standard of physical and mental health' for everyone. Therefore, the full realisation of this right requires the creation of conditions, within and outside medical systems, that are conducive to this optimum at both the individual and collective levels. States are not bound to guarantee a 'state of complete physical, mental and social well-being' for every individual.[97] In other words, the right to health is not to be understood as the right to be 'healthy'[98] but rather as the right to be afforded the conditions or capabilities to achieve the highest attainable level of physical and mental health, which may be different for everyone. Finally, references are made to both physical and mental health, which is a crucial acknowledgement of the twofold dimension of health.[99]

Additionally, the second paragraph of Article 12 prescribes that states take necessary steps to fully realise this human right, which 'include' those necessary for:

> (a) The provision for the reduction of the stillbirth rate and of infant mortality and for the healthy development of the child; (b) The improvement of all aspects of environmental and industrial hygiene; (c) The prevention, treatment and control of epidemic, endemic, occupational and other diseases; (d) The creation of conditions which would assure *to all* medical service and medical attention in the event of sickness.[100]

---

[93] ICESCR (n 23, Introduction) Preamble.
[94] UNCHR (n 89).
[95] UNCHR (n 91) 1.
[96] Ssenyonjo (n 87, Ch 1) 514–515.
[97] WHO Constitution (n 22, Introduction).
[98] CESCR, GC14 (n 27, Introduction) para 7.
[99] See Chapter 5 for a specific analysis on the right to mental health (of irregular migrants).
[100] ICESCR (n 23, Introduction) Article 12, emphasis added.

This is a non-exhaustive list of broadly shaped obligations of conduct for states, which are deemed necessary to fully realise the right to health. Regarding subparagraph (a), the drafting history of the article demonstrates state agreement on the prioritisation of maternal and children's health, with particular emphasis on the latter because of the special health vulnerabilities of children during their first years of life.[101] Since poor health during childhood can result in poor health as an adult, health measures targeted at children can be read as an important socio-developmental factor of health.[102] Subparagraph (b) above emphasises that the realisation of the right to health is deeply linked to certain environmental standards. This wording focuses on industrial health and compels states to take measures to avoid the risk of harm in the workplace, as well as on the 'reduction of the population's exposure to harmful substances' and access to water and basic sanitation which are particularly critical to prevent harm and ill health.[103] Subparagraph (c), regarding measures to avoid the spread of diseases, with a focus on prevention, treatment and control, requires individualised and collective measures to be taken by medical and public health decision-makers. This obligation bears witness to an embryonic acknowledgement that human rights and public health are mutually reinforcing strategies for the protection and promotion of the health and well-being of people.[104] Finally, subparagraph (d) refers to the establishment of an equitable health care system with medical services and staff that are accessible to *all*, regardless of personal or group status that might be considered justification for exclusion.

Even while adopting a formalistic approach to human rights obligations, Article 12(2) explicitly lists key elements that characterise the contemporary approach to the right to health: the targeting of vulnerable groups (such as children and pregnant women), a focus on the underlying environmental and occupational preconditions of health, the need to combine collective measures with individual treatment and a health care system with universal personal scope that targets the health needs of the entire population.

### 2.4.2 *The Normative Content of the International Right to Health and the Correlative State Obligations*

This section describes the genesis and development of a series of analytical frameworks that the human rights community has employed over the last

---

[101] Toebes (n 1) 48.

[102] M

[103] CESCR, GC14 (n 27, Introduction) paras 4, 11, 15.

[104] Ibid, para 16; Mann et al. (n 33, Introduction) 6, 7; Sophia Gruskin et al. (eds) *Perspective on Health and Human Rights* (Routledge 2005) 35, 40.

thirty years to clarify and operationalise international obligations regarding the right to health in law and policy. This analytical exercise, which is based on a teleological interpretation of the right to health, demonstrates that all such classifications, and the jurisprudence of the CESCR in general, prioritise the adoption of state measures that target health and social needs of vulnerable populations.

### 2.4.2.1 The Complex Scope of the Right to Health

The right to health is not the right to be healthy but the right 'to enjoy a variety of facilities, goods, services and conditions necessary for the realization of the highest attainable standard of health'.[105] Its scope, therefore, extends 'to timely and appropriate health care' and 'to the underlying determinants of health'.[106] The CESCR elaborates these formulations in General Comment No. 14, which is arguably the most referenced and authoritative interpretative document on the normative content of the right to health and related state obligations at UN level, although it has been criticised for exceeding the formal and textual scope set out in Article 12 ICESCR.[107]

The right to health entails entitlements and freedoms concerning its broad scope of material application. Regarding entitlements, the right to health care includes adopting positive 'preventive, promotional, curative and palliative health' measures.[108] Furthermore, states should take measures addressing the underlying determinants of health which refer to 'a wide range of socio-economic factors that promote conditions in which people can lead a healthy life', such as 'food and nutrition, housing, access to safe and potable water and adequate sanitation, safe and healthy working conditions, and a healthy environment'.[109] Public health maxims are incorporated in this approach,[110] and not only do living and working conditions affect, either positively or negatively, the enjoyment of the highest attainable standard of physical and mental health, but they are also protected interests of the scope of other

---

[105] CESCR, GC14 (n 27, Introduction) para 9.
[106] Ibid, para 11.
[107] Tobin (n 1) 108.
[108] CESCR, GC14 (n 27, Introduction) paras 16–17; Maite San Giorgi, *The Human Right to Equal Access to Health Care* (Intersentia 2012) 20–25.
[109] CESCR (ibid) para 4.
[110] WHO – Commission on Social Determinants of Health (CSDH), *Closing the Gap in a Generation: Health Equity through Action on the Social Determinants of Health: Final Report of the Commission on Social Determinants of Health* (World Health Organization 2008) 1. See further details on the 'determinants of health' in Chapter 4.

human rights, such as the right to an adequate standard of living in Article 11 of the Covenant.

Regarding freedoms, the normative scope of the right to health covers the 'right to control one's health and body, including sexual and reproductive freedom, and the right to be free from [...] non-consensual medical treatment and experimentation', which are also specifications of the right to personal integrity and freedom from ill treatment.[111] These overlaps between rights demonstrate the principle of the interdependence and interrelatedness of human rights, according to which the enjoyment of a particular right is dependent upon the enjoyment and realisation of other rights.[112] As such, this interrelatedness facilitates the indirect protection of health in those legal systems where the social entitlement to health does not constitute a legally enforceable right, including before the HRCtee and the ECtHR.[113]

### 2.4.2.2 The 'Tripartite Typology'

The major conceptual framework for human rights obligations is arguably the 'tripartite typology', which clarifies the nature of legal state duties at an international level, moving away from the categorisations of first- v. second-generation rights or negative v. positive rights. This framework, originally presented by Shue,[114] developed by Eide[115] and finally endorsed by the CESCR,[116] classifies state obligations for the realisation of human rights law in domestic jurisdictions according to three groups: the obligation to respect, the obligation to protect and the obligation to fulfil.

The obligation to respect the right to health requires states to refrain from any act that negatively interferes, directly or indirectly, with this right. For example, states should refrain from denying or limiting equal access to health care services on a discriminatory basis, marketing unsafe drugs, withholding or misrepresenting health information or unlawfully polluting air, water or soil.[117]

---

[111] CESCR, GC14 (n 27, Introduction) para 8.

[112] Vienna Declaration and Programme of Action on Human Rights (n 28).

[113] See the case law of the HRCtee and the ECtHR, respectively at Sections 2.5.1, and 2.6.1, *infra*.

[114] Shue asserts that for every basic right (of either a civil, political, economic, social or cultural nature) there are three types of correlative obligations: 'to avoid depriving'; 'to protect from deprivation'; and 'to aid the deprived'. Henry Shue, *Basic Rights: Subsistence, Affluence, and U.S. Foreign Policy* (first published 1980, Princeton University Press 1996).

[115] Asbjørn Eide, 'Report of the Special Rapporteur on the Right to Adequate Food as a Human Right – The New International Economic Order and the Promotion of Human Rights' (7 July 1987) E/CN.4/Sub.2/1987/23.

[116] CESCR, GC14 (n 27, Introduction) paras 33–37.

[117] Ibid, para 34. For further examples, see Ssenyonjo (n 87, Ch 1) 532–535.

The obligation to protect the right to health obliges states to take measures to prevent third parties from engaging in activities that might affect the right to health of individuals and communities. For instance, states should ensure that health professionals provide care to persons with their free and informed consent and that the privatisation of the health sector does not constitute a threat to the availability, accessibility, acceptability and quality of health services and conditions, in particular for vulnerable people.[118] Finally, the obligation to fulfil binds states to adopt appropriate legislative, administrative, budgetary, judicial and promotional measures to ensure for each person within their jurisdiction 'opportunities to obtain satisfaction of those needs, recognised in the human rights instruments, which cannot be secured by personal efforts'.[119] States must, *inter alia*, adopt active budget-sensitive measures to:

> Ensure provision of health care, including immunisation programmes against the major infectious diseases, and ensure equal access for all to the underlying determinants of health, such as nutritiously safe food and potable drinking water, basic sanitation, and adequate housing and living conditions.[120]

Upon ratification of the ICESCR, states commit to respect, protect and fulfil the right to the highest attainable standard of health 'through numerous, complementary approaches, such as the formulation of health policies, the implementation of health programmes developed by the WHO, [...] the adoption of specific legal instruments'[121] and any other appropriate measure of an 'administrative, judicial, economic, social and educational' nature.[122]

### 2.4.2.3 The AAAQ-AP Framework

Since 1991, the CESCR has complemented the normative analysis of the substantive rights of the ICESCR with an identification of 'certain aspects' that must be considered to fully understand and specify the scope of rights and their correlative state obligations.[123] In relation to the right to health, these

---

[118] CESCR, CG14 (n 32, Introduction) para 35; Ssenyonjo (ibid) 535–537.
[119] Eide (n 116) 37.
[120] The obligation to fulfil can be break down into the obligations to 'facilitate', 'promote' and 'provide', see CESCR, GC14 (n 27, Introduction) paras 36–37.
[121] CESCR GC14 (n 27, Introduction) para 1.
[122] Limburg Principles (n 80) para 17.
[123] CESCR, 'General Comment No. 4 (the Right to Adequate Housing – Article 11 (1) of the Covenant) (13 December 1991) E/1992/23, para 8.

aspects or 'elements'[124] or 'guiding principles'[125] have led to the development of the AAAQ framework (meaning 'availability, accessibility, acceptability and good quality'), which is particularly useful for human rights–based policy-making. This interpretative approach urges states to guarantee available, accessible, acceptable and good quality health services, goods and facilities, as well as extra-medical factors and conditions that positively affect health outcomes.

The element of availability requires the distribution of functioning facilities, goods, services and programmes related to health care and the underlying determinants of health in sufficient quantity within a state. Accessibility, which has four overlapping subdimensions that are critical for this analysis, means that health-related services, goods, facilities and conditions must be physically accessible, affordable and enjoyable by all without discrimination. The element of accessibility also implies securing the right of all people to seek, receive and impart health-related information in an accessible format by guaranteeing data confidentiality. Providing access to acceptable facilities, goods and services requires states to ensure that these are gender-sensitive, culturally appropriate and respectful of medical ethics. Finally, ensuring quality in this context signifies that health services must be scientifically and medically appropriate, providing, for example, trained health professionals, scientifically approved hospital equipment, unexpired drugs, adequate sanitation and safe drinking water.[126]

In addition to the four core elements of the AAAQ framework, accountability and participation are two more essential dimensions of the human rights approach to health that are increasingly referred to (thus AAAQ-AP). Accountability includes the establishment of processes through which domestic authorities show, explain and justify how they have discharged their health-related duties, such as state reporting procedures and the creation of redress mechanisms for rights violation.[127] Participation, which includes a bottom-up approach to norms, means that the general public and vulnerable groups, also via the involvement of civil society organisations, should be consulted as part of the process of implementing the right to health. This includes the

[124] CESCR, GC14 (n 27, Introduction) para 12.
[125] Brigit Toebes et al., *Health and Human Rights in Europe* (Intersentia 2012) 94–96.
[126] CESCR, GC14 (n 27, Introduction). For an overview of the case law on the 'AAAQ framework', see Ssenyonjo (n 87, Ch 1) 525–523.
[127] Helen Potts, 'Accountability and the Right to the Highest Attainable Standard of Health' (2008) University of Essex Human Rights Centre 13 <http://repository.essex.ac.uk/9717/1/accountability-right-highest-attainable-standard-health.pdf> accessed 1 March 2021.

establishment of public policies and decision-making that guarantees fair and transparent processes.[128]

The success of this analytical framework in contemporary human rights practice is apparent in the text that the drafters of the CRPD adopted in 2006. Indeed, its Article 25 CRPD focuses on non-discrimination on the basis of disability with respect to the enjoyment of the right to health. States are required to 'provide those health services needed by persons with disabilities specifically because of their disabilities',[129] covering the 'availability' dimension. Furthermore, health care must be 'affordable', 'geographically accessible' and of good 'quality'.[130]

### 2.4.2.4 The Core Framework

A distinctive feature of international socioeconomic rights and obligations, including the right to health and related obligations, is that they are to be realised and implemented in 'stages, as resources permit'.[131] Even though the ICESCR also creates obligations to implement immediately or expeditiously (e.g. to take steps to realise social rights and of non-discrimination) and, in principle, prevents retrogressive measures, the general rule of progressive realisation grants states a broad margin of discretion, which, if abused, can constitute a real loophole for states wishing to shirk their obligations.

Hence, since the 1980s, for the purposes of clarifying international socioeconomic commitments, preventing socioeconomic rights from losing their raison d'être,[132] assisting with their monitoring and strengthening their justiciability,[133] scholars have been developing the concept of the core content of social rights. This development included Shue's 'basic rights to subsistence',[134] Andreassen's 'practical minimal floor of well-being'[135] and Örücü's 'core and essential rights'.[136]

---

[128] Helen Potts, 'Participation and the Right to the Highest Attainable Standard of Health' (2008) University of Essex Human Rights Centre 16 <http://repository.essex.ac.uk/9714/> accessed 1 March 2021.

[129] CRPD (n 36, Introduction) Article 25(b).

[130] Ibid, Article 25(a)(c)(d).

[131] Chapman and Russell (n 3) 4.

[132] CESCR, GC3 (n 80) para 10.

[133] Fons Coomans, 'In Search of the Core Content of the Right to Education' in Chapman and Russell (n 3) 217.

[134] Shue (n 115) 18.

[135] Bård-Anders Andreassen et al., 'Assessing Human Rights Performance in Developing Countries: The Case for a Minimal Threshold Approach to the Economic and Social Rights' in Bård-Anders Andreassen and Asbjørn Eide (eds) *Human Rights in Developing Countries* (Academic Press 1987) 333, 334.

[136] Esin Örücü, 'The Core of Rights and Freedoms: The Limits of Limits' in Tom Campbell et al. (eds) *Human Rights from Rhetoric to Reality* (Blackwell 1986) 47.

There are several theories that link 'rights' with the word 'core'.[137] Some refer to 'core rights', such as Shue's theory of 'basic rights' as 'preconditions for other rights', which implies a hierarchy of rights. Others refer to an 'inviolable core content of selected human rights' that cannot be limited vis-à-vis competing principles, rights or legitimate state interests. An example of the latter is Alexy's theory of rights, which differentiates between 'principles' (or human rights) that allow a process of weighing and balancing on the one hand and 'rules' (or core elements of human rights) that do not allow for such processes on the other.[138] Still more theories were developed to define the minimum content of socioeconomic rights, accord relative priority to certain entitlements, set high standards of justification for states to discharge their obligations and prevent their progressive implementation from delaying or impeding the realisation of social rights.[139]

This last group of core theories received embryonic recognition in the 1987 Limburg Principles on the implementation of the ICESCR. Therein, international obligations were interpreted, *inter alia*, as entailing the protection of 'minimum subsistence rights' and the 'provision of essential services'.[140] This approach has received both praise and criticism. On the one hand, it was welcomed as an attempt to concretise entitlements and obligations concerning economic and social rights, thereby establishing a 'survival kit' or a 'floor' below which socioeconomic conditions and services should not be permitted to fall without bringing about immediate breaches of human rights. On the other hand, it was criticised for lacking explicit grounding in any human rights treaty text,[141] for leaving room for the creation of maximum 'ceilings' of implementation rather than minimum floors[142] and for a generally unclear conceptualisation. For example, a 'survival-based' core would tend to protect bare life, whereas a 'value-based' core would emphasise human dignity and capabilities and set higher standards for 'what it means to be human'.[143]

The CESCR's General Comments Nos. 3 and 14 apply the core framework to the right to health. However, these two general comments exemplify two slightly different approaches. On the one hand, General Comment No. 3, on

---

[137] Martin Scheinin, 'Core Rights and Obligations' in Shelton (n 39, Ch 1) 527.
[138] Robert Alexy, A *Theory of Constitutional Rights* (first published 1994, OUP 2002).
[139] Katharine G. Young, 'The Minimum Core of Economic and Social Rights: A Concept in Search of Content' (2008) *The Yale Journal of International Law* 33 113, 116; Jeff King, *Judging Social Rights* (CUP 2012) 29–39.
[140] Limburg Principles (n 80) paras 25, 35, 47, 55.
[141] Tobin (n 1).
[142] Chapman and Russell (n 3) 9.
[143] Young (n 140) 126–138.

the nature of state obligations in the ICESCR, refers to a 'minimum core obligation to ensure the satisfaction of, at the very least, minimum essential levels of each right', including 'essential primary healthcare'. In this guiding documents on duty implementation, core obligations were susceptible to limitation, provided that the state had discharged its high burden of proof on the mobilisation and use of all available resources.[144] On the other hand, General Comment No. 14 lists a series of non-limitable and immediate core obligations. Although there are scholarly debates concerning the nature of the core obligations or their desirability and usefulness,[145] the approach of the two general comments suggests a general shift from 'core content' to 'core obligations' and to an 'immediate effect' of these obligations before the state 'moves into the territory of progressive realisation'.[146] Although the difference might be considered merely a nuance, the 'obligation-based approach' focuses more on timing, priorities and the structural aspects of health regulation and governance.[147] General Comment No. 14 spells out the core obligations by first referring to General Comment No. 3, which prescribes that states must 'ensure the satisfaction of, at the very least, minimum essential levels of each of the rights enunciated in the Covenant', including 'essential primary health care',[148] and then identifies the following set of core obligations:

> a) To ensure the right of access to health facilities, goods and services on a non-discriminatory basis, especially for vulnerable or marginalised groups; b) To ensure access to the minimum essential food which is nutritionally adequate and safe, to ensure freedom from hunger to everyone; c) To ensure access to basic shelter, housing and sanitation, and an adequate supply of safe and potable water; d) To provide essential drugs, as from time to time defined under the WHO Action Programme on Essential Drugs; e) To ensure equitable distribution of all health facilities, goods and services; f) To adopt and implement a national public health strategy and plan of action, on the basis of epidemiological evidence, addressing the health concerns of the whole population; [...] periodically reviewed, on the basis of a participatory

---

[144] CESCR, GC3 (n 80) para 10.
[145] For details, see Lisa Forman et al., 'Conceptualizing Minimum Core Obligations under the Right to Health: How Should We Define and Implement the "Morality of the Depths"' (2016) *The International Journal of Human Rights* 20(4) 531, 536.
[146] Chapman and Russell (n 3) 14.
[147] Forman et al. (n 146) 537; Chapman and Russell (n 3) 9.
[148] CESCR, GC14 (n 27, Introduction) para 43. This paragraph of the General Comment also refers to the Declaration of Alma Ata as a main tool of interpretation ('compelling guidance') of the core obligations. For further analysis, see Section 2.4.2.3, *infra*.

and transparent process; they shall include methods, such as right to health indicators and benchmarks, [...] with particular attention to all vulnerable or marginalised groups.'[49]

These six core obligations incorporate elements of the other two previously mentioned textual obligations of immediate realisation as per Article 2 ICESCR, namely, the principle of non-discrimination with regard to the enjoyment of rights (a) and the obligation to take immediate steps towards the realisation of rights (f). Overall, core obligations (in particular those spelled out in letters a, e and f) are more procedural than substantive; participation, monitoring and non-discrimination are central provisions, and the other obligations listed do not specify which goods, services, facilities or conditions should be immediately accessible, apart from essential drugs. That being said, the focus of these provisions – bearing in mind the CESCR's 'obligations of comparable priority'[50] – appears to be on vulnerable individuals and marginalised groups and on a holistic approach to health that would complement 'equitable' medical care with social measures. Although the core framework does not prescribe detailed health and social services as international obligations, in consideration of the fact that technology, care standards and needs evolve over time, the indisputable prioritisation of vulnerable people does give an indication of the health and social services that states must prioritise and fund, which are community settings, primary and preventive health care that can benefit a large portion of the population and prevent health conditions from becoming chronic and severe rather than 'expensive curative health services'.[51]

Although the theoretical grounding and the bundle of resources that the CESCR identify as the content of core obligations regarding the right to health is not fully clear, it can be inferred from the above that states should at least ensure that people are able to enjoy what Jeff King defines as a 'healthy subsistence threshold', as the references to essential primary health care and to a number of determinants of health related to material conditions suggests.

---

[49] Ibid, para 43 (a)–(f).

[50] CESCR, GC14 (n 27, Introduction) 44: 'The Committee also confirms that the following are obligations of comparable priority: (a) To ensure reproductive, maternal (pre-natal as well as post-natal) and child health care; (b) To provide immunization against the major infectious diseases occurring in the community; (c) To take measures to prevent, treat and control epidemic and endemic diseases; (d) To provide education and access to information concerning the main health problems in the community, including methods of preventing and controlling them; (e) To provide appropriate training for health personnel, including education on health and human rights.'

[51] CESCR, GC14 (n 27, Introduction) para 19; Chapman (n 3) 212, 214.

This exceeds a 'bare survival' threshold, and it means that states must immediately or promptly regulate the provisions to ensure that 'basic physical needs
for shelter, nutrition, childhood development, health and physiological integrity' are met.[152]

Unlike in international human rights law, minimum services are more
clearly identified in the 'essential health packages' that many countries, within
the ambit of policy-making, have decided to adopt.[153] These are 'health service
interventions that are considered important and that society decides should be
provided to everyone'.[154] Although their goals present some synergies with the
core obligations of the right to health, their concrete shaping is overall influenced by a neoliberal philosophy that encourages the framing of public health
intervention in *minimalist* terms so as to guarantee a consistent share to the
private health care sector.[155] It is worth mentioning the risk that essential
health packages may be confused with the minimum acceptable levels of
the universal right to health. In contrast to core obligations and the AAAQ
framework, essential health packages do not per se focus on equitable measures to protect vulnerable groups and individuals, either in terms of availability
or affordability of health services and care.[156]

### 2.4.2.5 International Meta-legal Health Standards: Primary Health Care and Universal Health Coverage

The CESCR's General Comment No. 14, on the interpretation of health-
focused state obligations in the context of the ICESCR – which embraces a
distinct public health approach to human rights resulting from the consultations that led to its adoption – explicitly states that 'the Alma-Ata Declaration
provides *compelling guidance* on the core obligations arising from article 12'.[157]

The Declaration of Alma-Ata was the outcome of the International
Conference on Primary Health Care, held in Almaty, Kazakhstan, under
the auspices of the WHO and UNESCO in 1978 and endorsed via resolution

---

[152] King (n 140) 29–37.
[153] Audrey R. Chapman, Lisa Forman and Everaldo Lamprea, 'Evaluating Essential Health
    Packages from a Human Rights Perspective' (2017) *Journal of Human Rights* 16(2) 141, 142.
[154] Eleuther Tarimo and World Health Organization, Division of Analysis, Research and
    Assessment, 'Essential Health Service Packages: Uses, Abuse and Future Directions' (1997)
    ARA *Paper number* 15 WHO/ARA/CC.7.
[155] Chapman, Forman and Lamprea (n 154) 143, 151; World Bank, *World Development Report
    1993 – Investing in Health* (OUP 1993) 8.
[156] Ibid (Chapman et al.) 153–154.
[157] CESCR, GC14 (n 27, Introduction) para 43, emphasis added.

by the UNGA in 1979.[158] This was one of the most important international events of the last five decades in the area of health and development and was attended by representatives from 134 states. Its purpose was to identify a model to tackle inequalities in health policy, practice and outcomes through intersectoral measures. The Declaration, which recognises health as a fundamental human right, clarifies that the highest attainable standard of health and the goal of 'health for all' may be achieved through health and social measures in accordance with a 'primary health care' (PHC) *strategy*.[159] Indeed, it clarifies that PHC:

> [A]ddresses the main health problems in the community, providing promotive, preventive, curative and rehabilitative services [and] includes at least [...health] education [...] promotion of food supply and proper nutrition; an adequate supply of safe water and basic sanitation; maternal and child health care, [...] immunization against the major infectious diseases; prevention and control of locally endemic diseases; appropriate treatment of common diseases and injuries; and provision of essential drugs.[160]

Primary (health) care, as a *level* of care, is defined as '[e]ssential healthcare [...] based on [...] scientifically sound [...] methods [...] made universally accessible [...] at a cost [...] [that is] affordable. [...] It is the first level of contact of individuals [...] with the national health system'.[161] In brief, the Declaration constituted a call to adjust health systems and public policy-making to reflect a 'spirit of social justice' and to reconceptualise health as a tool of social development.[162] Prevention, health education, the participation of communities and people, an interdisciplinary multisectoral approach, health vulnerability and equity are the core pillars of the Declaration.[163] This social approach to health was incorporated into the WHO's Health for All strategy during the 1970s,[164] which 'echo[ed] the needs approach of human

---

[158] Declaration of Alma-Ata (n 28, Introduction); UNGA Res 34/58, 'Health as an Integral Part of Development' (29 November 1979).

[159] Ibid, paras I, V, emphasis added.

[160] Ibid, para VII. See also, WHA Res 62.12 'Primary Health Care, Including Health System Strengthening' (22 May 2009) Doc A/62/8, para 1(3).

[161] Ibid, para VI.

[162] Ibid, para V; Marcos Cueto, 'The Origins of Primary Health Care and Selective Primary Health Care' (2004) *American Journal of Public Health* 94(11) 1864–1874, 1867.

[163] For further details, see Helen Potts, 'Public Health, Primary Health Care, and the Right to Health' in Gunilla Backman (ed) *The Right to Health: Theory and Practice* (Studentlitteratur 2012) 93, 98–104.

[164] Ceuto (n 163) 1864–1866.

rights advocates'.[165] After twenty years of neglect, the WHO was reformulating a human rights approach to health.[166]

PHC in the Declaration is a broader concept than just primary care in health systems: the former includes the latter, according to the Alma-Ata paradigm. On the one hand, primary care 'is what happens when someone who is ill (or thinks he or she is ill or wants to avoid getting ill) consults a health professional in a community setting for advice, tests, treatment or referral to specialist care'. It normally includes health check-ups and the 'treatment of relatively common minor illnesses provided on an outpatient or community care' basis.[167] On the other hand, the PHC approach in the Declaration of Alma-Ata targets global and jurisdictional health inequalities and encourages states to adopt intersectoral preventive, promotional and curative measures targeting health, social and environmental conditions, which includes the prioritisation of 'primary care' in health systems.[168] Both primary care and PHC 'evolved in response to health disparities among socioeconomic [...] groups' and 'the poorer health of disadvantaged is the basic problem addressed by both approaches'.[169] However, they differ in the strategies to achieve health equity and good health outcomes at the individual and population levels.

During the 1980s, several states, under pressure from medical elites and neoliberal agendas, pulled out of their community-based and equity-oriented commitments under the Declaration. However, the PHC approach has remained highly authoritative for human rights practice and development studies and health governance communities, particularly in advocating for enhanced health standards for women and children. An example, also referenced by the CESCR's General Comment No. 14, is the Programme of Action of the 1994 International Conference on Population and

---

[165] Benjamin Mason Meier et al., 'ALMA-ATA at 40: A Milestone in the Evolution of the Right to Health and an Enduring Legacy for Human Rights in Global Health' (*Health and Human Rights Journal Blog*, 5 September 2018) <www.hhrjournal.org/category/blog/> accessed 1 December 2018.

[166] Meier and Gostin (n 19) 35, 115–119.

[167] Fundamental Rights Agency of the European Union (FRA), 'Healthcare Entitlements of Migrants in an Irregular Situation in the EU–28' (30 May 2016) <https://fra.europa.eu/en/publication/2016/healthcare-entitlements-migrants-irregular-situation-eu-28> accessed 1 March 2021; CESCR, GC14 (n 32, Introduction) note 9.

[168] Helen Keleher, 'Why Primary Health Care Offers a More Comprehensive Approach for Tackling Health Inequalities than Primary Care' (2001) *Australian Journal of Primary Health* 7 (2) 57.

[169] Donelle Barnes et al., 'Primary Health Care and Primary Care: A Confusion of Philosophies' (1995) *Nursing Outlook* 43(1) 7–16, 9.

Development, a milestone document in the area of development and population policy, which placed new emphasis on the needs, aspirations and rights of women and children.[170] This document restated and developed a PHC approach to health care and recognised the right to sexual and reproductive health as an integral part of PHC and as a human right.[171] In international human rights law, Article 24 of the 1989 CRC, unlike Article 12 ICESCR, made explicit reference to the concept of PHC. Article 24 is a detailed provision that focuses on preventive, curative and rehabilitative measures and, *inter alia*, requires states 'to ensure the provision of *necessary* medical assistance and health care to *all* children with emphasis on the development of primary health care'.[172] This approach constituted an operationalisation of two principles of the rights of the child: the best interest of the child and the physical, mental, moral, spiritual and social dimensions of children's development.

Forty years after the Declaration of Alma-Ata, the Astana Declaration on Primary Health Care, adopted in October 2018, reaffirmed the commitment of the signatory member states and the WHO to the values and principles of Alma-Ata by confirming PHC as the most 'inclusive, effective and efficient approach to enhance people's physical and mental health', which is recognised as a 'fundamental right of every human being [to be enjoyed] *without distinction of any kind*'.[173] The Declaration of Astana recommends that states enhance the 'capacity and infrastructure for primary care – the first contact with health services – prioritising essential public health functions',[174] create health-conducing environments and empower individual and communities through intersectoral measures and strengthened partnerships and collaborations between all stakeholders.

The Astana Declaration – as well as the WHO by virtue of its resolution-based incorporation of the same[175] – recognises PHC as a cornerstone or 'necessary foundation' of the global community efforts to achieve 'universal

---

[170] Programme of Action, Conference on Population and Development (n 29, Introduction) Principles.

[171] Ibid, Chs 7.2, 7.6, 8.5–8.10.

[172] CRC (n 42, Introduction) Article 24.2(b). CRC Committee, 'General Comment No. 15 on the Right of the Child to the Enjoyment of the Highest Attainable Standard of Health (Article 24)' (17 April 2013) CRC/C/GC/15, para 73.

[173] Global Conference on Primary Health Care, Declaration of Astana (25–26 October 2018) WHO/HIS/SDS/2018.61, para I, emphasis added.

[174] Ibid, para V.

[175] Ibid, Preamble; WHA, 'Universal Health Coverage: Primary Health Care towards Universal Health Coverage – Report by the Director-General' (1 April 2019) A72.12; WHA Res 72.2, 'Primary Health Care' (24 May 2019).

health coverage' (UHC), a key goal of the UN Agenda for Sustainable Development.[176] UHC consists of 'access to quality essential health care services and access to safe, effective, quality and affordable essential medicines and vaccines for all'.[177] This means access 'without discrimination, to nationally determined sets of the needed promotive, preventive, curative and rehabilitative basic health services [...] with a special emphasis on the poor, vulnerable and marginalised segments of the population'.[178] This equity-based target also entails that such care should be affordable.[179]

It is worth noting that UHC, as a dimension of the 2030 Agenda, is a political commitment that requires a 'long-term process of progressive realization',[180] whereas the obligations regarding the right to health are legally binding on states and include obligations of both a progressive and an immediate nature. The achievement of UHC is explicitly linked to the realisation of Article 25 UDHR,[181] and the Agenda for Sustainable Development is grounded in the UDHR.[182] UHC has been defined as a 'practical expression of the right to health';[183] however, for UHC to be genuinely compliant with human rights and the right to health, its realisation needs to prioritise 'the worst off, expanding coverage to everyone and reducing out-of-pocket payments, all while ensuring that disadvantaged groups are not left behind'.[184]

A combination of textual and purposive interpretations of the right to health obligations in the context of the ICESCR – which target the highest attainable

---

[176] UNGA Res 70/1 'Transforming Our World: The 2030 Agenda for Sustainable Development' (25 September 2015) Goal 3.8.

[177] Ibid.

[178] UNGA Res 67/81 'Global Health and Foreign Policy' (12 December 2012); WHA Res 69.1. 'Strengthening Essential Public Health Functions in Support of the Achievement of Universal Health Coverage' (27 May 2016); Lisa Forman et al., 'What Do Core Obligations under the Right to Health Bring to Universal Health Coverage?' (2016) *Health and Human Rights Journal* 18(2) 23.

[179] Meier et al. (n 166).

[180] Audrey R. Chapman, *Global Health, Human Rights, and the Challenge of Neoliberal Policies* (CUP 2016) 284.

[181] WHA Res. 64.9 Agenda Item 31.4. 'Sustainable Health Financing Structures and Universal Coverage' (24 May 2011).

[182] UNGA (n 177) para 10.

[183] WHO, 'Positioning Health in the Post-2015 Development Agenda', WHO Discussion Paper (October 2012).

[184] WHO, 'Making Fair Choices on the Path to Universal Health Coverage: Final Report of the WHO Consultative Group on Equity and Universal Health Coverage' (2014) as referred to by Dainius Pūras, 'Report of the Special Rapporteur on the Right of Everyone to the Enjoyment of the Highest Attainable Standard of Physical and Mental Health (focus: Agenda 2030)' (5 August 2016) A/71/304, para 81.

standard of physical and mental health for individuals and communities, with an emphasis on the worst off and the determinants of health – seem overall to be aligned with embracing a cost-effective PHC approach to health and health care,[185] which is also a precondition for achieving development and policy goals like the UHC.

However, it is undeniable that, as health regulation remains a politically charged, technical, evolving and sovereignty-sensitive area of law and policy, human rights obligations and best practices regarding the right to health have been mostly set out, at an international level, in 'soft law' instruments that incorporate public health and development principles and declarations.[186] These instruments include general comments, recommendations and non-binding decisions on communications of treaty bodies, all of which form 'part of a process of slowly accumulating a corpus of related norms and embedding health-related rights in international law'[187] and which, at least when they are consistent with the text, purpose and spirit of the respective treaty, should be given weighty interpretative consideration.[188]

## 2.5 INTERNATIONAL MONITORING AND ACCOUNTABILITY FOR PROTECTING THE RIGHT TO HEALTH

The implementation of the right to health requires governments to operation-alise international standards through laws, policies and practices. Indeed, its full implementation requires collaboration between different actors in several sectors, including lawyers, health workers, policy-makers, advocates and economists. This multisectoral implementation requires 'an expansive under-standing of public health as well as an interdisciplinary approach to human rights'.[189] The ways in which human rights are implemented should match

---

[185] Gillian MacNaughton and Diane F. Frey, 'ALMA-ATA at 40: From Siloes to Synergy – Linking Primary Health Care to Human Rights' (*Health and Human Rights Journal Blog,* 7 October 2018) <www.hhrjournal.org/2018/10/alma-ata-at-40-from-siloes-to-synergy-linking-primary-health-care-to-human-rights/> accessed 1 October 2020.

[186] For instance, see CESCR, GC14 (n 27, Introduction); CRC Committee, GC15 (n 173).

[187] Alicia Ely Yamin and Andrés Constantin, 'The Evolution of Applying Human Rights Frameworks to Health' in Meier and Gostin (n 19) 48.

[188] In *Ahmadou Sadio Diallo (Republic of Guinea v Democratic Republic of the Congo)* (n 168, Ch 1) para 66; Keller and Grover (n 46, Introduction) and Khaliq and Churchill (n 46, Introduction).

[189] Gillian MacNaughton and Mariah McGill, 'The Office of the UN High Commissioner for Human Rights: Mapping the Evolution of the Right to Health' in Meier and Gostin (n 19) 480. See also, Paul Hunt, 'Report of the Special Rapporteur on the Right to [. . .] Health (focus: The health and human rights movement)' (17 January 2007) A/HRC/4/28; Freeman (n 35, Introduction) 13.

the ways in which authorities are held domestically and internationally accountable for failures to turn human rights standards into a reality. Enduring conceptual and policy differences between socioeconomic rights and civil and political rights – in particular, the fact that the former, unlike the latter, would be resource-dependant issues for governments to manage and, as such, are not fully enforceable or justiciable in courts[190] – have resulted in a narrow operationalisation of the right to health as an international norm and weak accountability for this process. This situation has widened the gap between reality and the rhetoric of 'indivisibility' in European and international human rights law, which has had critical consequences for human rights holders in vulnerable situations and has reduced the normative influence of treaty bodies that monitor and jurisprudentially develop social rights.

### 2.5.1 *State Reporting before the CESCR*

At the international level, the original absence of a treaty body entrusted with the supervision of the ICESCR demonstrated a weak approach to the implementation of social rights. Until the 1980s, the UN Economic and Social Council, a governmental UN entity, was entrusted with monitoring activities concerning the ICESCR's implementation.[191] When the CESCR was eventually established,[192] it was only competent to assess state reports and had no competence to receive individual or collective complaints. Only recently, with the adoption of the Optional Protocol (OP-ICESCR) in 2008 and its entry into force in 2013, was the CESCR made consistent with other UN treaty bodies.[193]

Periodic reporting before the CESCR is a procedural obligation of state parties to the ICESCR and allows the Committee to regularly monitor, through constructive dialogue with the representative of the state under review, the measures that have been adopted domestically to realise the rights recognised in the Covenant.[194] Relevant information for the review, apart

---

[190] For further details, see Paul O'Connell, *Vindicating Socio-Economic Rights* (Routledge 2012) 8. See also Table X in Gostin and Meier (n 35, Introduction) 52.

[191] ICESCR (n 23, Introduction) Articles 16–22 describe the functions of the ECOSOC in relation to socio-economic rights. On the general mandate of the ECOSOC, see Chapter X of the UN Charter (n 31, Ch 1).

[192] The Committee on Economic, Social and Cultural Rights (CESCR) was established under the ECOSOC (United Nations Economic and Social Council) Res 1985/17 (28 May 1985).

[193] OP-ICESCR (n 45, Ch 1).

[194] CESCR, 'General Comment No. 1, Reporting by States parties' (27 July 1981) E/1989/22. The 1991 Guidelines (E/C.12/1991/1) have been replaced by the CESCR, 'Guidelines on Treaty-

from the state report, can also be obtained from NGOs,[195] other international organisations and UN agencies. The procedure is, however, dependent on the quality of state cooperation – with respect to timely submissions and the accuracy of the information provided – and is hampered by the frequent inability of the Committee itself to respond in a timely manner.[196] The 'verdicts' of this review are the concluding observations (COs), which are not binding on states but instead rely on the card of persuasion to call for change.[197]

I now turn to provide an overview of the health-related trends in the CESCR's COs of the last ten years (2010–2020) to highlight the thematic priorities of this procedure. Unsurprisingly, stark majority of the COs criticise failures to formally incorporate the rights set out in the ICESCR into domestic legal orders,[198] thereby preventing these rights from being claimable standards before state organs.[199] On a systemic level, this is a major problem, as international human rights monitoring and adjudication are intended to be subsidiary and residual vis-à-vis domestic protection and redress.[200] Specifically regarding the right to health, inadequate budgetary allocation for health is a recurring concern in the COs.[201] The requirement to provide the maximum available resources has always been somewhat vague for monitoring purposes, in terms of both the type and measurement of resources to be

---

Specific Documents to be Submitted by State Parties under Articles 16 and 17 of the ICESCR' (23 March 2009) E/C.12/2008.2.

[195] CESCR, 'NGO Participation in Activities of the Committee on Economic, Social and Cultural Rights' (7 July 2000) E/C.12/2000/6.

[196] For details, see Marco Odello and Francesco Seatzu, *The UN Committee on Economic, Social and Cultural Rights: The Law, Process and Practice* (Routledge 2013) 155–185.

[197] Bantekas and Oette (n 32, Ch 1) 203–204.

[198] All CESCR's COs from 2015 onwards show 'concerns' about the lack of incorporation of either the treaty itself or its substantial provisions. See 'Concluding Observations' on the website of the CESCR: <www.ohchr.org/EN/HRBodies/CESCR/Pages/CESCRIndex.aspx> accessed 1 October 2020.

[199] As explained in Chapter 1, for those countries that model the relationship between international and domestic law according to a dualist tradition, international law must be transposed into the domestic legal order if it is to play a role among the sources of law, in and policy-making and judicial review.

[200] On the concept of 'subsidiarity', see Neuman (n 46, Ch 1).

[201] For example, CESCR, COs on the reports submitted by: Ireland (8 July 2015) E/C.12/IRL/CO/3, para 28; Greece (27 October 2015) E/C.12/GRC/CO/2, para 35; Italy (28 October 2015) E/C.12/ITA/CO/5, para 49; Uganda (7 July 2015) E/C.12/UGA/CO/1, para 32; Canada (22 March 2016) E/C.12/CAN/CO/6, para 9; Kenya (5 April 2016) E/C.12/KEN/CO/2–5, para 51; Lebanon (23 October 2016) E/C.12/LBN/CO/2, para 10; Philippines (25 October 2016) E/C.12/PHL/CO/5–6, para 15; Cyprus (28 October 2016) E/C.12/CYP/CO/6, para 39; Pakistan (20 July 2017) E/C.12/PAK/CO/1, para 75; Sri Lanka (4 August 2017) E/C.12/LKA/CO/5, para 57.

included in this assessment, although the CESCR has developed a doctrine with a number of circumstantial factors to bring states to account for allocations and actions.[202] Over the last decade, several European countries have been expressly advised to pay attention to the Committee's position letter on socioeconomic rights in economic and financial crises.[203] During the crisis that hit many world economies during the late 2000s and early 2010s, retrogressive measures in the form of budget cuts and austerity measures disproportionately affected the allocation of (maximum) available resources to public services and the equitable enjoyment of the right to health and other social rights.[204] For the CESCR, alternatives must be carefully considered,[205] and anti-crisis measures entailing legislative setbacks must be temporary, non-discriminatory and respectful of the core content of rights, particularly with respect to vulnerable people and groups.[206]

Another crucial concern has been the accessibility of primary or basic health services, facilities, goods, information and conditions, mostly in terms of geographical distribution[207] and for certain vulnerable groups, including migrants, ethnic minorities and people with disabilities.[208] Since the 1990s, sexual and reproductive health has received increasing attention. This terminology applies to those situations related to well-being and autonomy in relation

---

[202] Rodrigo Uprimny, Sergio Chaparro and Andres Castro, 'Bridging the Gap: The Evolving Doctrine on ESCR and Maximum Available Resources' in Young (n 37) 624–653; CESCR, 'An Evaluation of the Obligation to Take Steps to the "Maximum Available Resources" under an Optional Protocol to the Covenant – Statement' (21 September 2007) E/C.12/2007/1.

[203] Chairperson CESCR, 'Letter to States Parties on Economic, Social and Cultural Rights in the Context of the Economic and Financial Crisis' (16 May 2012); See CESCR, COs concerning reporting cycles of: Italy (n 201) para 9; Ireland (n 201) para 11; Greece (n 201) para 8; the UK (13 July 2016) E/C.12/GBR/CO/6, para 19; Cyprus (n 201) para 12.h.

[204] Magdalena Sepúlveda Carmona, 'Alternatives to Austerity: A Human Rights Framework for Economic Recovery' in Nolan (n 8) 23, 30–40.

[205] For example, CESCR, GC3 (n 80) para 9; CESCR GC14 (n 27, Introduction) para 32.

[206] CESCR, Letter (n 203).

[207] For example, CESCR, COs on the Reports of: FYROM (North Macedonia) (14 July 2016) E/C.12/MKD/CO/2–4, para 47; Lebanon (n 201) para 57; France (12 July 2016) E/C.12/FRA/CO/4, para 46; Honduras (10 July 2016) E/C.12/HND/CO/2, para 51; Kenya (n 201) para 51; Italy (n 201) para 46; Morocco (21 October 2015) E/C.12/MAR/CO/4, para 45; Sudan (26 October 2015) E/C.12/SDN/CO/2, para 21; Paraguay (19 March 2015) E/C.12/PRY/CO/4, para 28.

[208] Most of the CESCR's COs refer either directly or indirectly to 'vulnerability and non-discrimination'. For example, this is the case of the reporting procedures of: Australia (11 July 2017) E/C.12/AUS/CO/5, para 43; the Netherlands (6 July 2017) E/C.12/NLD/CO/6, paras 39, 46, 48; Tunisia (14 November 2016) E/C.12/TUN/CO/3, para 32; Cyprus (n 201) para 39; Philippines (n 201) para 15; Poland (25 October 2016) E/C.12/POL/CO/6, para 41; FYROM (n 208) para 47; the UK (n 203) para 55; Sweden (13 June 2016) E/C.12/SWE/CO/6, para 32; France (n 208) para 19; Honduras (ibid) paras 24–26; Kenya (n 201) para 22; Uganda (n 201) para 32; Ireland (n 201) para 14; Chile (6 July 2015) E/C.12/CHL/CO/4, para 28.

to sexuality and reproductive behaviour,[209] including contraception, education on sexual health, discrimination against women and LGBTQI+ (lesbian, gay, bisexual, transgender, queer and intersex) people, and accessibility of maternal health care and of services for preventing or terminating a pregnancy.[210] The Committee has also demonstrated an increased sensitivity to the need to adopt appropriate measures to safeguard mental health among the general population and specific vulnerable groups.[211] The above findings confirm the Committee's strong commitment to reviewing the situation of vulnerable groups and individuals for whom social rights, including the right to health, are extremely delicate tools with which to strive for a dignified standard of living.

To monitor whether domestic legislation and policies comply with international obligations of both an immediate and progressive nature, human rights bodies, including the CESCR, have begun to refer to human rights indicators. These are specific pieces of information on the state or condition of an object, event, activity or outcome that can be related to human rights norms and standards and that address and reflect human rights principles and concerns.[212] In the context of socioeconomic rights, indicators are deemed particularly important tools because they provide a methodology for evaluating the progressive realisation of these rights, and they hold the state accountable for the discharge of its responsibilities.[213] With regard to the right to

---

[209] The CESCR recently issued a General Comment in this area. CESCR, 'General Comment No. 22 on the Right to Sexual and Reproductive Health – Article 12 of the ICESCR (2 May 2016) E/C.12/GC/22.

[210] For example, CESCR, COs concerning reporting cycles of: Uruguay (20 July 2017) E/C.12/ URY/CO/5, para 52; Pakistan (n 201) para 78; Philippines (n 201) para 51; Poland (n 208) para 46; Costa Rica (20 October 2016) E/C.12/CRI/CO/5, para 53; Dominican Republic (20 October 2016) E/C.12/DOM/CO/4, para 60; FYROM (n 207) para 49; Burkina Faso (12 July 2016) E/ C.12/BFA/CO/1, para 47; Honduras (n 207) para 53; Kenya (n 201) para 53; Canada (n 201) para 51; Italy (n 201) para 49; Morocco (n 207) para 45; Thailand (12 July 2015) E/C.12/THA/CO/1–2, para 30; Uganda (n 201) para 35; Ireland (n 201) para 30; Venezuela (6 June 2015) E/C.12/VEN/ CO/3, para 28; Chile (n 208) para 29; Paraguay (n 207) para 29.

[211] For example, CESCR, COs concerning reporting cycles of: Sri Lanka (n 201) paras 59–60; Uruguay (n 210) para 53; Australia (n 208) para 45; Cyprus (n 201) para 39; Poland (n 208) para 51; UK (n 203) para 57; Sweden (n 208) para 43; Greece (n 201) paras 35–36; Uganda (n 201) para 34; Ireland (n 201) para 29.

[212] These can be both 'quantitative' and 'qualitative', the former being an equivalent of statistics (using numbers, percentages or indices), while the latter covers any information articulated as a narrative or in a 'categorical' form. Indicators can also be categorised as 'structural', 'process' or 'outcome' when they relate commitments, efforts or results, respectively. For examples of 'right to health' indicators, see OHCHR 'Human Rights Indicators, a Guide to Measurement and Implementation' (2012) HR/PUB/12/5 16, 90.

[213] Paul Hunt and Gillian MacNaughton, 'A Human Rights-Based Approach to Health Indicators' in Baderin and McCorquodale (n 4, Introduction) 303.

health, the CESCR has encouraged states to create and use indicators and set benchmarks to monitor the appropriateness of the health-related measures they adopt in relation to the various elements of the AAAQ-AP framework[214] and to disaggregate these indicators on various personal grounds to shed light on potential discrimination.[215]

### 2.5.2 *The Justiciability of Socioeconomic Rights and the Optional Protocol to the ICESCR*

The term 'justiciability' refers to the 'ability to claim a remedy before an independent and impartial body [in particular, a court] when a violation of a right has occurred or is likely to occur'.[216] This issue has been the Achilles' heel of socioeconomic rights for decades at different levels of governance. A conspicuous number of arguments have been put forward to deny the legal or jurisdictional nature of social rights, including the right to health. Common objections have pointed to their vague formulation and program-matic nature and the alleged lack of expertise of courts and tribunals to decide on complex policy issues. The main objection, however, revolves around 'fear' of an 'antidemocratic rise in judicial power', which, in connection with the principle of the separation of powers, would result in only elected and relevant government branches being entitled to make technical decisions involving the allocation of resources to economic and social issues.[217] Even though legal and quasi-legal adjudication of health rights have increased since the 1990s,[218] the full judicial recognition of these rights has not yet been realised. For example, in Ireland, social rights are referred to in the Constitution as non-justiciable 'directive principles of social policy', and health-related issues and

---

[214] CESCR, GC14 (n 27, Introduction) para 57; OHCHR (n 213) 32; Sophia Gruskin and Laura Ferguson, 'Using Indicators to Determine the Contribution of Human Rights to Public Health Efforts' (2009) *Bulletin of the World Health Organization* 87 714.

[215] OHCHR (n 212) 68.

[216] International Commission of Jurists, 'Report on Courts and the Legal Enforcement of Economic, Social and Cultural Rights: Comparative Experiences of Justiciability' (2009) 6 <www.icj.org/courts-and-the-legal-enforcement-of-economic-social-and-cultural-rights/> accessed 1 March 2021.

[217] King (n 140) 3–8; Katharine G. Young, 'Introduction' in Young (n 37) 8, regarding social rights in general. As far as healthcare is concerned, see San Giorgi (n 109) 80–81.

[218] Colleen M. Flood and Aeyal Gross, 'Litigating the Right to Health: What Can We Learn from a Comparative Law and Health Care Systems Approach' (2014) *Health and Human Rights Journal* 16(2) 62, 64; Alicia Ely Yamin and Fiona Lander, 'Implementing a Circle of Accountability: A Proposed Framework for Judiciaries and Other Actors in Enforcing Health-Related Rights' (2015) *Journal of Human Rights* 14(3) 312.

decisions lie with the government and the legislator.[219] Some legal traditions have responded to this criticism by arguing that the primary purpose of the separation of powers is to avoid a concentration of power that may lead to arbitrariness and that regulation of the exercise of power through mutual scrutiny by state apparatuses are democratically desirable.[220] Accordingly, checks and balances between state powers would allow the judicial review of policies and laws against a set of criteria, namely human rights law, as a means to protect individual rights – particularly those of the least privileged members of society – from arbitrary majoritarian decisions.[221]

Furthermore, the extent and the quality of domestic adjudication on the right to health depends on a series of factors, including the vertical sources that enshrine it (constitutional, legislative or jurisprudential), the 'form' in which the international treaties are 'incorporated' into domestic law[222] and the type of health care system established in a state (universalist, corporatist or private/public).[223] Health-related rights have been judicialised in many juris-dictions,[224] especially in middle-income countries such as South Africa and certain states in the Latin American region, which proves that there this right and other social rights are not inherently non-judicially enforceable.[225] The CESCR, in its General Comment No. 9, specified that it is a precise state duty to give effect to the rights contained in the ICESCR, including through appropriate means of redress or remedies – among them third-party independent adjudication – for individuals or groups.[226]

If we take this debate to an international level, we can reconstruct it in terms of the sovereignty–human rights clash: international adjudication of the right to health and of interconnected social rights would pierce state

---

[219] Constitution of Ireland (1 July 1937), Article 45.

[220] Eric Barendt, 'Separation of Powers and Constitutional Governments' (1996) *Public Law* 599, 606.

[221] International Commission of Jurists (n 216) 82; Jeanne M. Woods, 'Justiciable Social Rights as a Critique of the Liberal Paradigm' (2003) *Texas International Law Journal* 38 763, 773.

[222] CESCR, GC9 (n 84).

[223] Flood and Gross (n 218).

[224] According to Courtney Jung, Ran Hirschl and Evan Rosevear, 'Economic and Social Rights in National Constitutions' (2014) *American Journal of Comparative Law* 62 1043, approximately 70 per cent of countries worldwide have enacted constitutions that protect health rights in some form. Eleonor D. Kinney and Brian Alexander Clark, 'Provisions for Health and Health Care in the Constitutions of the Countries of the World' (2004) *Cornell International Law Journal* 37(2) 285 found that around 40 per cent of these constitutions make the right to health justiciable.

[225] Alicia Ely Yamin and Rebecca Cantor, *Litigating Health Rights: Can Courts Bring More Justice to Health?* (Harvard University Press 2011) 312.

[226] CESCR, GC9 (n 84) paras 1–2.

sovereignty in areas such as health and social policy, where states, in particular their non-judicial branches, have traditionally maintained a broad margin of regulatory discretion. The overall reluctance to qualify socioeconomic rights as fully justiciable rights in international law is reflected in the long and difficult process of negotiation of the OP-ICESCR, which introduced a complaint mechanism to support the monitoring of state accountability for implementing the ICESCR.[227] Twelve years after its adoption, only twenty-four states have ratified this instrument.[228]

With the adoption of this Protocol, individuals (and groups of individuals) can file communications with the CESCR alleging that a state has violated any of the substantive provisions of the ICESCR. This complaint procedure empowers individuals and groups to directly defend their socioeconomic rights by claiming their material needs or capabilities before an international body (albeit a subsidiary one) that has the power to issue non-binding views to which states must at least give 'due consideration'.[229] Considering the generally progressive nature of the ICESCR's obligations and the fact that state parties may adopt 'a range of possible policy measures' to implement the ICESCR, the CESCR's examination of communications is framed as an assessment of the reasonableness or appropriateness of the steps taken by states to realise the substantive treaty provisions.[230] This case-based evaluation, while structured to partly preserve state sovereign discretion in policy-making, assesses whether the respondent state has adopted all appropriate and reasonable measures,[231] with the least restrictive impact on the realisation of rights, either immediate or progressive.[232]

So far, the CESCR has decided seven cases on the merits, four of which were on the right to housing, two on social security and one on the right to health and gender equality. The latter, *S.G. and G.P. v. Italy*, concerned the examination of the forced transfer of an embryo generated via in vitro fertilisation into a woman's uterus for compliance with Articles 12 and 3 of the

---

[227] On the origins, evolution and legal status of the OP-ICESCR, see Odello and Seatzu (n 197) 47–78.

[228] Source: OHCHR website <http://indicators.ohchr.org/> accessed 14 March 2021.

[229] OP-ICESCR (n 45, Ch 1) Article 9(2).

[230] Ibid, Article 8(4); ICESCR (n 23, Introduction) Article 2: 'by all appropriate means'. For an analysis of the first cases decided by the CESCR see Sandra Liebenberg, 'Between Sovereignty and Accountability: The Emerging Jurisprudence of the United Nations Committee on Economic, Social and Cultural Rights under the Optional Protocol' (2020) *Human Rights Quarterly* 42(1) 48, 53.

[231] *Miguel Ángel López Rodríguez v Spain* Com no 1/2013 (CESCR 2013) para 11.3; *Ben Djazia et al. v Spain* Com no 15/2015 (CESCR 2017) paras 15.5, 16.6.

[232] *I.D.G. v Spain* Com no 2/2014 (CESCR 2015) paras 12.1, 14.

ICESCR. The Committee argued that the right to (sexual and reproductive) health 'includes the right to make free and informed decisions concerning any medical treatment' and that 'the restriction on the right to withdraw one's consent affects both sexes [but] places an extremely high burden on women['s bodies]' and illegitimately interferes with '*the very substance* of the right to health'.[233] The CESCR, in all seven decisions, demonstrated a reliance on the analytical frameworks set out in its general comments,[234] including the 'core framework'.[235] For example, in the case of *Trujillo* v. *Ecuador*, the CESCR held that the Ecuadorian social security regulation had failed to offer adequate and reasonable social security benefits. In particular, both contributory and non-contributory benefits were found to be discriminatory in their application to women engaged in unpaid domestic work, and the state was found not to have met its core obligations towards vulnerable people under Article 9 ICESCR.[236]

Apart from the high number of inadmissibility decisions, which highlight a rigorous take on its subsidiarity in deciding on human rights issues, these first opinions of the CESCR in its compliant procedure indicate that the review is conducted through a proportionality or reasonableness test of the state measures alleged to interfere with the rights of the ICESCR, whereas the intensity of the scrutiny largely depends on the circumstantial vulnerability of the author of the communication.[237]

### 2.5.3 A Sample of the Health-Related Views of the CEDAW Committee

Outside the framework of the OP-ICESCR, other human rights treaty bodies have made states accountable for the realisation of health-related obligations via their findings on both reporting and complaint procedures and through general comments or recommendations.[238] While it is beyond the scope of this analysis to provide a general overview of this jurisprudence,[239] this section provides a flavour of some relevant decisions of the Committee monitoring

---

[233] *S.G. and G.P. v Italy* Com no 22/2017 (CESCR 2019) paras 10, 11, emphasis added.
[234] CESCR (*I.D.G.*) (n 232) paras 11.3, 12.1, 16, 17(c).
[235] For example, CESCR (*López Rodríguez*) (n 231) para 10.3; CESCR (*S.G. and G.P.*) (n 233) paras 8 and 10; *Trujillo Calero v Ecuador* Com no 10/2015 (CESCR 2018) paras 14.2–3.
[236] Ibid (*Trujillo*) paras 14, 17, 19.
[237] Liebenberg (n 230) 83–84.
[238] Benjamin Mason Meier and Birginia Bras Gomez, 'Human Rights Treaty Bodies: Monitoring, Interpreting and Adjudicating Health Related Human Rights' in Meier and Gostin (n 19) 509.
[239] The emphasis of the HRCtee's views is on unhealthy detention conditions, for compliance with article 6 and 7 ICCPR. For example, *Turdukan Zhumbaeva v Kyrgyzstan* Com no 1756/2008 (HRCtee 2011); *McCallum v South Africa* Com no 1818/2008 (HRCtee 2010);

the Convention on the Elimination of All Forms of Discrimination against Women (CEDAW Committee), which are particularly responsive to discriminatory rights violations that have severe consequences for the health and well-being of women, in particular those in vulnerable or disempowered situations.

For instance, in the case of *Alyne da Silva Pimentel Teixeira*, concerning a Brazilian national of African descent who had died during childbirth, the CEDAW Committee restated the duty of states 'to ensure women's right to safe motherhood and emergency obstetric services, and to allocate to these services the maximum extent of available resources'.[240] The Committee found violations of Articles 2 (general non-discriminatory actions) and 12 (discrimination against women in the field of health) CEDAW because the death of the mother and the child resulted from a lack of adequate medical services to 'prevent detect and treat illnesses specific to women' and because such a situation constituted discrimination against women – and, in this case, discrimination on the ground of the woman's African descent and socioeconomic status[241] – in the health care system.[242] *L.C.* v. *Peru* was another dramatic case of discrimination against women, which concerned the lack of timely access to therapeutic abortion for a sexually abused and suicidal thirteen-year-old girl.[243] The Committee highlighted that it was cruel and stereotyping to blame and generate guilt in a girl 'for acts that were totally beyond her control, such as being sexually abused and consequently suffering a mental imbalance that worsened when she learned that she was pregnant'.[244] It also stated that the lack of legislative and administrative measures regulating access to therapeutic abortion in Peru 'condemn[ed] women to legal insecurity insofar as protection of their rights is completely at the mercy of gender prejudices and stereotypes'. In this case on structural inequalities, the 'sociocultural pattern based on a stereotypical function of a woman and her

---

*Tolipkhuzhaev v Uzbekistan* Com no 1280/2004 (HRCtee 2009); *Dorothy Kakem Titiahonjo v Cameroon* Com no 1186/2003 (HRCtee 2007); *F.K.A.G. et al.* v *Australia* Com no 2049/2011 (HRCtee 2013) para 9.8; *M.M.M.* v *Australia* Com no 2136/2012 (HRCtee 2013) para 10.7; *Joyce Nawila Chiti v Zambia* Com no 1303/2004 (HRCtee 2012) para 12.2–4. The CRPD Committee upheld significant decisions on rehabilitative care, finding that state practice that neglected this type of health care constituted discrimination on the grounds of disability in the enjoyment of the right to health, see, For example, *X. v Argentina* Com no 8/2012 (CRPD 2014) paras 8.1–8.10; *H.M.* v *Sweden* Com no 3/2011 (CRPD 2012) para 8.5.

[240] CEDAW Committee, 'General Recommendation No. 24: Article 12 of the Convention (Women and Health)' (1999) para 27.

[241] *Alyne da Silva Pimentel Teixeira v Brazil* Com no 17/2008 (CEDAW 2011) para 7.7.

[242] Ibid, paras 7.3, 7.4, 7.6.

[243] *L.C. v Peru* Com no 22/2009 (CEDAW 2011).

[244] Ibid, para 7.2.

reproductive capacity guided the medical decision', leading to detrimental and irreparable consequences for the victim's enjoyment of human rights on an equal footing with men.[245]

Gender stereotyping regarding the role and expected submissive attitude of women was found to be the root cause of the rights violations (Articles 2, 3, 5, 12 CEDAW) in *S.F.M.* v. *Spain*, the first case on obstetrical violence heard by the CEDAW Committee. This is a 'widespread and systematic' form of gender-based violence, which women may experience during facility-based childbirth, where, as exemplified by the experience of the author of the communication, their 'autonomy and their capacity to make informed decisions about their reproductive health' may be ignored by health care professionals, including through forced medication and medical interventionism.[246]

### 2.5.4 *The Contribution of the UN Charter–Based Mechanisms*

This overview of international mechanisms for ensuring state accountability for the protection of the right to health and health rights would not be complete without brief mention of the Special Procedures and the Human Rights Council (HRC). Several reports of the Special Procedures, in particular those of special rapporteurs, are referred to in Chapters 3–5 to demonstrate their support for standard setting in underdeveloped or insufficiently understood areas of human rights. These are ancillary independent bodies of the HRC that perform thematic or country-specific assessments, issue press statements and communications to intergovernmental actors and the public, and undertake annual reporting to the HRC and the UNGA.[247] Though their activities are non-binding on states and, as such, may be dismissed, there is evidence that they have been highly persuasive in several ways: their cooperation and dialogue with key stakeholders is widespread; Special Procedures have unique access to states, develop guiding principles and take joint actions; and their agenda-setting reports are employed by virtually all other UN human rights bodies, from the HRC to the treaty bodies.[248] Concerning the right to health, the UNCHR – today replaced by the HRC – appointed the first special

---

[245] Ibid, para 7.12.

[246] *S.F.M. v Spain* Com no 138/2018 (CEDAW 2020) para 7.

[247] See an Introduction to the Special Procedures at <www.ohchr.org/en/hrbodies/sp/pages/welcomepage.aspx> accessed 1 March 2021; For further analysis see Aoife Nolan, Rosa Freedman and Thérèse Murphy, *The United Nations Special Procedures System* (Nottingham Studies on Human Rights) (Brill 2017) 1–8.

[248] Thérèse Murphy and Amrei Müller, 'The United Nations Special Procedures: Peopling Human Rights, Peopling Global Health' in Meier and Gostin (n 19) 487–501.

rapporteur on the right to health in 2002 and the mandate has been periodically renewed by the HRC ever since.[249] The four mandate holders have worked closely with the CESCR and the WHO to develop a consistent analytical framework for the right to health to clarify its normative contours and make it an operational or practically implementable right.[250] It would be impossible to detail here the extremely wide-ranging activities and topics to which the rapporteurs have contributed through, *inter alia*, country visits, thematic annual reporting and public and scientific engagement. For example, they have conducted extensive studies on health-related issues that have yet to be crystallised in international law, such as the prohibition of criminalising sexual and reproductive health, the development of benchmarks and health indicators to monitor and guide the implementation of the right to health, health disparities and the determinants of health, the role of pharmaceutical companies and access to essential medicines, and, most recently, mental health and human mobility.[251] As reflected in the 'purpose of the mandate' on the website of the special rapporteur on the right to health,[252] the common features of these reports and missions are arguably the special attention granted to situations of discrimination and vulnerability and the significant emphasis on preventive, promotional and primary health measures.[253]

It is worth noting that the HRC, the intergovernmental body to which rapporteurs report their findings, runs, among other mechanisms, a special interstate peer review monitoring of the status of *all* 'indivisible, interrelated, interdependent, and mutually reinforcing' human rights in *all* UN member

---

[249] UNCHR Res no 2002/31 (April 2002); HRC Res no 6/29 (December 2007) and HRC Res no 42/16 (October 2019). The current mandate holder (4th SRH) was appointed in July 2020.

[250] Paul Hunt and Sheldon Leader, 'Developing and Applying the Right to the Highest Attainable Standard of Health: The Role of the UN Special Rapporteur' in John Harrington and Maria Stuttaford (eds) *Global Health and Human Rights: Philosophical and Legal Perspectives* (Routledge 2010) 28–61; Paul Hunt, 'Configuring the UN Human Rights System in the 'Era of Implementation': Mainland and Archipelago' (2017) *Human Rights Quarterly* 39 489.

[251] For an overview of the work of the mandate holders, see Dainius Pūras, 'Report of the Special Rapporteur on the Right to [. . .] Health' (2 April 2015) A/HRC/29/33, paras 13–31; Murphy and Muller (n 248) 494–496.

[252] Website of the OHCHR, Special Rapporteur on the Right of Everyone to [. . .] Health, <www.ohchr.org/en/issues/health/pages/srrighthealthindex.aspx> accessed 10 December 2020.

[253] For example, Dainius Pūras, 'Report of the Special Rapporteur on the Right to [. . .] Health (focus: the right to mental health of people on the move)' (28 July 2018) A/73/216; ibid '(focus: the right to health in early childhood)' (30 July 2015) A/70/213 2015; Anand Grover, 'Report of the Special Rapporteur on the Right to [. . .] Health (focus: migrant worker's right to health)' (15 May 2013) A/HRC/23/41 2013; ibid '(focus: right to health and criminalization of same-sex conduct and sexual orientation, sex work and HIV transmission)' (27 April 2010) A/HRC/14/20 2010.

states.[254] This Universal Periodic Review (UPR) is conducted through interactive non-confrontational and cooperative state dialogue on human rights information from a variety of sources, and its outcomes are peer recommendations. Constructed in this way, this mechanism may offer unique opportunities for realising the right to health by contributing a universal mechanism of accountability for the protection of socioeconomic rights. However, early studies of this unfolding mechanism, now in its third cycle, have reported that the UPR has granted socioeconomic rights less attention than civil and political rights.[255] Nevertheless, a study conducted by the University of Essex in partnership with the WHO, which specifically focused on the right to health and used an expansive definition of health-related issues, found that 22 per cent of the UPR's thousands of recommendations touched upon the right to health or its determinants. However, partly because of the limited involvement of relevant stakeholders, these often unspecific recommendations mainly concern top agenda issues, such as gender-based violence, children and maternal health.[256]

### 2.5.5 *Preliminary Conclusions*

In the UN human rights system, the right to health, health-related human rights and public health interests are located at the centre of a web of international accountability procedures which have, to different extents during the last seventy years, contributed to their conceptualisation and operationalisation as human rights law issues. Moreover, the wide global ratification of the international instruments containing right-to-health provisions – as recalled and elaborated by a wide array of supporting soft law instruments which highlight the existence of a consistent *opinio juris* – has led some commentators to hold that at least part of the scope of the right to health (i.e. the right to health care) has gained the status of a customary international norm.[257]

---

[254] UNGA Res 60/251 'Human Rights Council' (15 March 2006) A/RES/60/251.
[255] Center for Economic and Social Rights, 'The Universal Periodic Review: A Skewed Agenda? Trends Analysis of the UPR's Coverage of Economic, Social and Cultural Rights' (report, June 2016) <www.cesr.org/universal-periodic-review-skewed-agenda> accessed 1 March 2021. This report found that only 17 per cent of the recommendations generated by the UPR concerned socio-economic rights issues.
[256] Judith Bueno De Mesquita, 'The Universal Periodic Review: A Valuable New Procedure for the Right to Health?' (2019) *Health and Human Rights Journal* 21(2) 263.
[257] Eibe Riedel, 'The Human Right to Health: Conceptual Foundations' in Andrew Clapham et al. (eds) *Realizing the Right to Health* (Rüffer und Rub 2009) 21, 32.

Finally, to restate the international relevance of health protection, the priorities of health governance and the creation of conditions that are conducive to the realisation of the right to the highest attainable of health, it is worth mentioning a recent resolution that was adopted as a whole by the UNGA and that is, therefore, highly persuasive. This act called member states to realise the right to health and to address the underlying determinants of health by committing to, *inter alia*:

> [S]trengthen health systems, notably in terms of *primary health care*, in order to provide universal access to a wide range of health-care services that are safe, quality, *accessible*, available and *affordable*, timely, clinically and financially integrated, *people-centred, gender-sensitive and community-based*, which will help to empower those who are *vulnerable or in vulnerable situations* in addressing their physical and mental health needs, enhance health *equity and equality, end discrimination* and stigma, eliminate gaps in coverage and create a more inclusive society.[258]

## 2.6 EUROPEAN HUMAN RIGHTS LAW AND THE RIGHT TO HEALTH

Health, or the right to health, also falls within the protective scope of the two general human rights treaties of the Council of Europe family: the ECHR and ESC. Regional systems may be advantageous in principle with regard to the effective implementation of supranational norms because regions are relatively homogeneous, and regional adjudicators are 'likely to achieve greater enforceability of their decisions partly because of the political will [. . .] to do so by the regional system itself'.[259]

Although the justiciability of social interests or social rights in the European human rights system has increased over the last twenty years,[260] the supreme role that the civil rights–focused ECHR plays in the European human rights stage accounts for a reduced level of visible protection of (the right to) health in these legal framework compared to international human rights law. Although the ECHR is devoted to the protection of civil and political rights, the ECtHR – the most highly regarded human rights adjudicator in Europe – has developed sophisticated and domestically binding case law on the

---

[258] UNGA Res no 74/20, 'Global Health and Foreign Policy: An Inclusive Approach to Strengthening Health Systems' (28 January 2020) A/RES/74/20, 1, emphasis added.
[259] Jeremy Sarkin, 'The Role of Regional Systems in Enforcing State Human Rights Compliance' (2010) *Inter-American and European Human Rights Journal* 1(2) 199, 209–210.
[260] Carole Nivard, *La Justiciabilité des Droits Sociaux: Etude de Droit Conventionnel Européen* (Bruylant 2012) 701.

health-related components of various rights. By contrast, the 1961 ESC (and its revised 1996 version) is devoted to the protection of socioeconomic rights, including the (collectively) justiciable right to health. It should be noted, however, that the decisions of its monitoring body – the ECSR – are not technically binding. This again underscores the different approaches to civil and political rights on the one hand and socioeconomic rights on the other.

However, it is worth noting that the COVID-19 pandemic, which is ongoing at the time of writing, may constitute a real watershed moment in terms of enhancing the protection of social rights and the right to health in the context of the Council of Europe. A number of political and independent institutions are redoubling their interpretative and promotional efforts to make the right to health a social vulnerabilities–sensitive human right by drawing on public health arguments and documents.[261]

### 2.6.1 *The Strasbourg Court's Case Law: Health System Deficiencies and Regulatory Obligations*

The ECHR does not contain any clear-cut state obligation to realise the 'right to the highest attainable standard of health' for everyone in law or policies, whereas this is included in the ESC. Nevertheless, the ECtHR has recognised that 'health care is important in a democratic society'.[262] This Court has long acknowledged that many of its civil rights 'have implications of a socio-economic nature' and that 'there is no water-tight division' between 'different' categories of rights.[263] Therefore, health issues may be scrutinised through the lens of the provisions of the ECHR as health-related interests of civil rights, particularly under Articles 2 (the right to life), 3 (prohibition of torture and inhuman and degrading treatment), 5 (the right to liberty) and 8 (the right to respect for private and family life).

For instance, issues concerning violations of Article 8 ECHR have arisen in cases of restricted access to medical records, failure to obtain informed consent, breaches of the confidentiality of personal health-related

---

[261] Commissioner for Human Rights of the CoE, 'Protecting the Right to Health through Inclusive and Resilient Health Care for All', Issue paper (February 2021); PACE, Res 2329 'Lessons for the Future for an Effective and Rights-Based Response to the COVID-19 Pandemic' (June 2020); ECSR, 'Statement of Interpretation on the Right to Protection of Health in Times of Pandemic' (21 April 2020).

[262] *Villnow v Belgium* App no 16938/05 (ECHR Decision 2008); See also CoE/ECHR, 'Thematic Report – Health-Related Issues in the Case-Law of the European Court of Human Rights' (2015) <www.echr.coe.int/Documents/Research_report_health.pdf> accessed 1 March 2021.

[263] *Airey v Ireland* App no 6289/73 (ECHR 1979) para 26.

information[264] and exposure to environmental hazards.[265] Furthermore, forms of discrimination on the grounds of health (e.g. denial of a residence permit because a person had been found to be HIV positive) have also been deemed to violate Article 8 in conjunction with Article 14 ECHR (prohibition of discrimination).[266] However, it should be noted that where limitable rights, such as those contained in Article 8 ECHR, are concerned, socioeconomic deprivation must reach a certain level of severity to constitute an unjustified interference with this right of the Convention.[267] A fair balance needs to be struck between 'the general interest of the community [to limit economic expenditures] and the interests of the individual'.[268] Therefore, states enjoy:

> [A] wide margin [of appreciation] when it comes to general measures of economic or social strategy [...]. Because of their direct knowledge of their society and its needs, the national authorities are in principle better placed than the international judge to appreciate what is in the public interest on social or economic grounds, and the Court will generally respect the legislature's policy choice unless it is 'manifestly without reasonable foundation'.[269]

No assessment of competing interests or rights balancing is carried out where the Court assesses alleged violations of Articles 2 or 3 ECHR. Nevertheless, the threshold of severity to trigger the applicability of these articles is particularly high. For instance, Article 3 has been employed as a reference standard for adjudicating on the deportation of severely ill people,[270] the extradition of people with mental health conditions,[271] forcible medical interventions[272] and the living conditions of inmates, asylum seekers or migrants, either in detention or not.[273] Where people with mental health issues were denied their liberty, including in unsuitable and unhealthy penitentiary facilities, the Court found violations of both Articles 3 and 5.[274] In cases where deaths have

---

[264] *K.H. and Others v Slovakia* App no 32881/04 (ECHR 2009); *L.L. v France* App no 7508/02 (ECHR 2006).
[265] *Guerra and Others v Italy* App no 14967/89 (ECHR 1998); *Lopez Ostra v Spain* App no 16798/90 (ECHR 1994).
[266] *Kiyutin v Russia* App no 2700/10 (ECHR 2011).
[267] *Fadeyeva v Russia* App no 55723/00 (ECHR 2005) para 69.
[268] *Rees v UK* Application n. 9532/1981 (ECHR 1986) para 37.
[269] *Stec and Others v UK* App nos 65731/01 and 65900/01 (ECHR 2006) para 52.
[270] *N. v the United Kingdom* (n 122, Ch 1).
[271] *Aswat v the United Kingdom* App no 17299/12 (ECHR 2013), *Bensaid v UK* App no 44599/98 (ECHR 2001).
[272] *Jalloh v Germany* App no 54810/00 (ECHR 2006).
[273] *M.S.S.* (n 132, Ch 1); *Aden Ahmed v Malta* App no 55352/12 (ECHR 2013).
[274] *L.B. v Belgium* App no 22831/08 (ECHR 2012); *W.D. v Belgium* App no 73548/13 (ECHR 2016).

occurred because of flagrant or systemic malfunctioning of the health system, issues may arise under Article 2.[275]

To provide a thorough assessment of applicable case law is beyond the scope of this book, but it is worth noting that these cases target a broad array of situations constituting particularly unfavourable determinants of health, and where issues of 'access' and 'quality' of health care are concerned, the applicable case law of the Court has been particularly restrictive. The ECtHR carries out a concrete case-based assessment of health policies and health systems.[276] For instance, a violation of Article 2 ECHR 'may arise' when there is a systemic denial of health care to individuals,[277] including when the 'authorities of a contracting state put an individual's life at risk through the denial of health care that they have undertaken to make available to the population in general'.[278] The provision on the right to life in the ECHR may be substantively engaged in very exceptional circumstances when a patient's life is knowingly put in danger by the denial of access to life-saving treatment in a dysfunctional health care system.[279] In the case of *Câmpeanu*, the Court ruled on the case of a young Roma man who was HIV positive and mentally disabled and had been in state care all his life. He died in a psychiatric hospital because of the inappropriate medical care and treatment he had received. The Grand Chamber found that Romania had violated the applicant's right to life because, in a context of systemic deficiencies, the authorities had unreasonably put his life in danger, given his multilayered vulnerability and the proven inadequacy of the medical care he had received.[280] Similar importance was granted to a situation of severe socioeconomic deprivation, children's vulnerability and state awareness of the violation of rights in the case *Nencheva and others*, which resulted in a finding of violation of Article 2 ECHR. In this case, fifteen children and young people, who eventually died, had been entrusted to the care of the state, which failed to adequately protect them from serious and immediate threats to their lives, including cold and shortages of food, medicines and basic necessities.[281]

---

[275] *Centre of Legal Resources on behalf of Valentin Câmpeanu v Romania* App no 47848/08 (ECHR 2014); *Mehmet Şentürk and Bekir Şentürk v Turkey* App no 13423/09 (ECHR 2013) paras 84–97.

[276] *Hristozov et al. v Bulgaria* App nos 47039/11, 358/12 (ECHR 2012) para 105; *Cyprus v Turkey* App no 25781/94 (ECHR 2001) para 219.

[277] Ibid (*Cyprus v Turkey*).

[278] *Şentürk and Şentürk* (n 275) para 88.

[279] *Yirdem et al. v Turkey* App no 72781/12 (ECHR 2018); *Lopes de Sousa Fernandes v Portugal* App no 56080/13 (ECHR 2017).

[280] *Câmpeanu* (n 275).

[281] *Nencheva and Others v Bulgaria* App no 48609/06 (ECHR 2013).

Outside of cases of dire socioeconomic deprivation and structural or targeted dysfunctions of the emergency health care system, the Court consistently required states 'not only to refrain from the intentional taking of life, but also to take appropriate steps to safeguard the lives of those within its jurisdiction'.[282] As far as health care is concerned, states have a positive duty 'to put in place an effective regulative framework compelling hospitals whether private or public, to adopt appropriate measures for the protection of patients' lives'.[283] However, an 'error of judgment on the part of a health professional or negligent coordination among health professionals in the treatment of a particular patient' is not considered sufficient to give rise to a violation of Article 2 ECHR.[284] Additionally, the relatives of deceased patients should have effective access to independent judicial proceedings to determine who is responsible for the death of their next of kin.[285] This approach, even when complemented with protection from systemic deficiencies, exposes the ECtHR to the criticism of setting the threshold for a substantive violation of Article 2 in health care scenarios very high. Even some ECtHR judges have held that evidentiary rules regarding the full awareness of state authorities, the collective and severe nature of state deficiencies and their causal link with the individual harm disproportionally affect the indirect justiciability of the right to health in individual cases.

The 'partly concurring, partly dissenting opinion' of Judge Pinto de Albuquerque in the case of *Lopes de Sousa Fernandes* v. *Portugal* bears witness to the fact that the ECHR is an 'unfulfilled promise' in the field of health care. The standards of primary care and the provision of essential drugs are only relevant for the Court in relation to prisoners and servicemen.[286] The ECtHR's jurisprudential standards in the field of health care, which consider state actions or inactions legally relevant only in exceptionally severe cases, also fail to acknowledge the evolution, over several decades, of an expansive right to health and related obligations in several other international and regional frameworks.[287] The Court's narrow interpretation of life-related state obligations in the area of health care is the result of an interpretative choice which emphasises the textual material scope of the ECHR, limits the impact

---

[282] *Calvelli and Ciglio v Italy* App no 32967/96 (ECHR 2002) para 48.
[283] *Arskaya v Ukraine* App no 45076/05 (ECHR 2013) paras 84–97.
[284] *Lopes de Sousa Fernandes* (n 279) para 187.
[285] *Calvelli* (n 282) para 49. Similarly, *Oyal v Turkey* App no 4864/05(ECHR 2010) para 66.
[286] *Lopes de Sousa Fernandes* (n 279) Partly Concurring Partly Dissenting Opinion of Judge Pinto De Albuquerque, para III.A, paras 73–78, emphasis added.
[287] Ibid.

of contextual sources of human rights law[288] and, in practice, undermines the indivisibility of rights. Other interpretative approaches have been taken in other human rights frameworks, as demonstrated by the 'right to life in dignity' set out by the HRCtee,[289] and the new *pro persona* jurisprudence of the Inter-American Court of Human Rights on the full justiciability of socioeconomic rights under the ACHR, which refers to the international *corpus juris* of the UN human rights system.[290] Without going that far, Article 53 ECHR ('safeguard for existing human rights'), in which 'the more favourable protection clause' is embedded, could constitute an important, yet currently overlooked, interpretative principle vis-à-vis the fragmentation of human rights law.[291] This clause urges state parties to the ECHR to provide individuals with the highest level of protection established in different domestic and international law, even above and beyond the human rights contained in the ECHR. Lack of compliance with this rule would arguably constitute at least a 'procedural' breach of the ECHR.[292]

### 2.6.2 *The ESC: European 'Averages' and Socioeconomic Protection*

The ESC, the Council of Europe's general treaty on socioeconomic rights, contains a discrete number of health-related provisions setting out *legal* rights, including Articles 3 (the right to safe and healthy working conditions), 11 (the right to protection of health) and 13 (the right to social and medical assistance). In this legal system, the protection of health has a special legal value: 'human dignity is the fundamental value and indeed the core of positive human rights law [...] and health care is a prerequisite for the preservation of human dignity'.[293] Part I of the ESC, which establishes *policy objectives* for states, recognises that 'everyone has the right to benefit from any measures enabling him [or her] to enjoy the highest standard of health attainable'.[294]

---

[288] Through the VCLT (n 47, Introduction) Article 31(3)(c) – a treaty shall be interpreted by taking into consideration 'any relevant rules of international law applicable in the relations between the parties' – relevant instruments of international human rights law can be used to interpret the ECHR provisions. For example, *Demir v Baykara v Turkey* App no 34503/97 (ECHR 2008) 69–86.

[289] HRCtee, GC36 (n 193, Ch 1).

[290] See Section 1.5.2.

[291] Adamantia Rachovitsa, 'Treaty Clauses and Fragmentation of International Law: Applying the More Favourable Protection Clause in Human Rights Treaties' (2016) *Human Rights Law Review* 16 77.

[292] Ibid, 97.

[293] FIDH (n 216, Ch 1) para 31.

[294] ESC (n 43, Introduction) Part I para 11.

The extension of medical assistance to the nationals of other treaty member states, who are also legal residents, was one of the major goals of the Charter, as evidenced by its drafting history.[295]

While the ESC, in all its versions, is a particularly detailed treaty, it is also a *sui generis* international human rights instrument for at least three reasons. First, it is not entirely binding on state parties, but states can select a minimum number of articles (or paragraphs) and comply with the duties contained in those articles. Second, its personal scope normally only extends to the nationals of the member states. Finally, it provides 'collective accountability' mechanisms. However, unlike those of the ICESCR, the legal obligations under the substantive provisions of Part II of the Charter are shaped as duties of result with immediate or expeditious effects upon ratification, except where otherwise indicated.[296]

Article 11 is the key clause relating to the right to health in the ESC, although it is not ranked as a core provision.[297] It imposes negative and positive obligations,[298] of a preventive, promotional or curative nature, focusing in particular on state duties entailing the adoption of collective measures.[299] Although the text differs from that of Article 12 ICESCR, Article 11 ESC 'enshrines the right to the highest possible standard of health and the right of access to health care'.[300] Article 13 on social and medical assistance is one of the core provisions of the Charter and applies to people at risk of poverty by emphasising their individual right to have minimum social and health needs met.[301] While social assistance-related obligations require state

---

[295] For example, see Committee of Ministers of the Council of Europe (Social Committee) Third Session (8 November 1956) in Collected 'Travaux préparatoires' of the European Social Charter, 870–872, which refers to the European Convention on Social and Medical Assistance (11 December 1953) ETS No. 14.

[296] Stein Evju, 'Application by Domestic Courts of the European Social Charter' (2010) *Nordic Journal of Human Rights* 28(3–4) 401, 406.

[297] ECS (n 43, Introduction) Article 20(1) of the 1961 Charter and article A(1) of the 1996 Charter.

[298] ECSR, Conclusions 2005, Statement of Interpretation of Article 11.

[299] ESC (n 43, Introduction) Article 11: 'With a view to ensuring the effective exercise of the right to protection of health, the Contracting Parties undertake, either directly or in co-operation with public or private organisations, to take appropriate measures designed inter alia: 1 to remove as far as possible the causes of ill health; 2 to provide advisory and educational facilities for the promotion of health and the encouragement of individual responsibility in matters of health; 3 to prevent as far as possible epidemic, endemic and other diseases.'

[300] *Transgender Europe and ILGA Europe v Czech Republic* Com no 117/2014 (ECSR 2018) para 71. See also commentary on article 11 ESC in ECSR, *Digest of the Case Law of the European Committee of Social Rights* (December 2018) 128–136.

[301] ESC (n 43, Introduction) Article 13: 'With a view to ensuring the effective exercise of the right to social and medical assistance, the Contracting Parties undertake: 1. to ensure that any person who is without adequate resources and who is unable to secure such resources either by his own efforts or from other sources, in particular by benefits under a social security scheme, be

parties to make means-based social benefits in kind or in cash – which are important determinants of health – accessible to poor people, medical assistance relates more to the affordability of health care. It is intended to ensure 'free or subsidised health care or payments to enable persons [without adequate resources] to pay for the care required by their condition'.[302]

The ECSR has developed an analytical framework for the monitoring of state reports based on disaggregated thematic indicators and has interpreted the collected data by reaching conclusions on the 'conformity' of state measures with the Charter where there is a progressive enhancement of standards, also in consideration of the 'European averages'.[303] The ECSR has also heard and adjudicated (collective) complaints in a series of health-related cases that were brought before the Committee by a number of authorised international NGOs and trade unions.[304] On the accessibility of curative health care for irregular migrant children, the ECSR has adopted a particularly protective approach since 2004.[305] Within the context of the 'irregular migrant saga', analysed in other chapters of this book, the ECSR has extended the personal scope of the treaty to guarantee the right to health to undocumented people, pursuant to a contextual and teleological interpretation of the international treaty.

Regarding the availability and accessibility of health care services, in two cases against Italy, the ECSR has stated that 'once states introduce statutory provisions allowing abortion in some situations, they are obliged to organise their health service system' in a way that ensures both the effective exercise conscientious objections by health professionals and that patients are not prevented 'from obtaining access to services to which they are legally entitled under the applicable legislation'.[306]

The removal of 'causes of ill-health resulting from environmental threats such as pollution' was the subject matter of the case of *Marangopoulos*

---

granted adequate assistance, and, in case of sickness, the care necessitated by his condition [. . .] .' See Angeleri (n 222, Ch 1).

[302] ECSR, Conclusions XIII–4 (1996), Statement of Interpretation of Article 13.

[303] Claire Lougarre, 'What Does the Right to Health Mean? An Interpretation of Article 11 of the European Social Charter by the European Committee of Social Rights' (2015) *Netherlands Quarterly of Human Rights* 33(3) 326, 344–354. For example, ECSR, Conclusions 2005, *Lithuania*.

[304] ESC-Revised (n 43, Introduction) Article D; Markus Jaeger, 'The Additional Protocol to the ESC Providing for a System of Collective Complaints' (1997) *Leiden Journal of International Law* 10 (1) 69; Regis Brillat, 'The Supervisory Machinery of the European Social Charter: Recent Developments and Their Impact' in Gráinne de Búrca and Bruno de Witte (eds) *Social Rights in Europe* (OUP 2005) 31.

[305] *FIDH* (n 216, Ch 1).

[306] *IPPF EN v Italy* Com no 87/2010 (ECSR 2013) para 69; *CGIL v Italy* Com no 91/2013 (ECSR 2015) paras 166–167.

*Foundation* v. *Greece*.[307] This case concerned the disposal of highly polluting industrial waste into the Asopos river for over forty years. On the merits, the ECSR concluded that Greece had failed to fulfil its obligations under Articles 11(1) and 11 (3) of the Charter by failing to take appropriate measures to, as far as possible, remove causes of ill health, prevent diseases and provide advisory and educational facilities for the promotion of health, as required by Article 11(2).

In assessing whether the right to protection of health can be effectively exercised, the ECSR pays particular attention to the situation of disadvantaged and vulnerable groups, as required by the joint interpretation of the non-discrimination clause in the Charter and the latter's substantive rights. The ECSR '[a]ssesses the conditions under which the *whole* population has access to health care, taking into account also the Council of Europe Parliamentary Assembly Recommendation 1626 (2003) on "reform of health care systems in Europe: reconciling equity, quality and efficiency"'.[308] On the basis of these premises, the ECSR held that France had violated Article 11 ESC by not adopting sufficient targeted preventive and promotional health care measures, including screening, for Roma children and pregnant women. The social context in which Roma people live required 'the Government to take specific measures in order to address their particular problems' as 'treating the migrant Roma in the same manner as the rest of the population when they are in a different situation constitutes discrimination'.[309]

Even though the decisions of the ECSR, in these and other cases, have established particularly protective standards, their legal analysis and effects at the domestic level are at risk of being overshadowed by the binding judgments of the ECtHR. In spite of their substantial differences, both the decisions of the ECSR and the judgments of the ECtHR capture a distinctive feature of human rights: the protection of vulnerable people from discrimination. This feature can be useful in enhancing disease prevention, health promotion and treatment of irregular migrants' health in human rights law.

## 2.7 THE PRINCIPLE OF NON-DISCRIMINATION, VULNERABLE GROUPS AND THE RIGHT TO HEALTH

### 2.7.1 *Equality, Non-discrimination and Marginalisation*

Non-discrimination and equality are basic general principles of human rights; they appear in the Preambles and the substantive provisions of all human

---

[307] *Marangopoulos Foundation for Human Rights v Greece* Com no 30/2005 (ECSR 2006) paras 195, 202.
[308] *Médecins du Monde International v France* Com no 67/2011 (ECSR 2012) para 163, emphasis added.
[309] Ibid.

rights instruments.[310] Equality is a relatively modern construct in the area of law and is commonly associated with the Aristotelian maxim 'likes should be treated alike'.[311] This apparently intuitive sentence harbours several controversial debates. These include the comparability problem mentioned in Chapter 1, which is particularly acute in the context of irregular migration. Furthermore, the equality maxim does not specify the 'equal' level of dignified treatment that should be enjoyed or the kind of equality worth targeting and achieving, which is left to standard setters, policy-makers or the interpretative community, at different levels of regulation, to decide.[312] Furthermore, the prohibition of discrimination does not mean that every instance of differential treatment on suspect grounds is prohibited. An instance of differentiation is deemed not to constitute discrimination and is thus permissible if it has a legal basis, is aimed at protecting legitimate public interests and is proportional.[313] Such justification lies at the core of many condoned differentiations involving irregular migrants.

The prohibition of discrimination has been traditionally understood as the negative restatement of the principle of equality because when prohibited grounds and characteristics are removed from decision-making processes, everyone is prima facie treated equally.[314] According to the type of equality that one embraces, non-discrimination obligations will vary. Formal equality (equality before the law) – which corresponds to a liberal notion of human rights that is centred on an abstract person (everyone) – is, for instance, particularly controversial because offering the same treatment to people in different personal or socioeconomic situations may give rise to substantive discrimination or inequities, exacerbate patterns of disadvantage and ultimately hinder the effective enjoyment of human rights.

Martha Nussbaum has lucidly written that 'what people can achieve is influenced by economic opportunities, political liberties, social powers and enabling conditions of good health, basic education and the encouragement and cultivation of initiatives'.[315] The removal of barriers to full equality

---

[310] Jarlath Clifford, 'Equality' in Shelton (n 39, Ch 1) 420, 430 describes the impact and the role of equality in human rights law as a 'preambular objective' and as performing a 'descriptive' and a 'substantive' function.

[311] Ross/Aristotele (n 98, Ch 1).

[312] On these debates, see Sandra Fredman, *Discrimination Law* (2nd edn, OUP 2011) 8–14; Clifford (n 310) 424.

[313] For instance, CESCR, GC20 (n 100, Ch 1) para 13. See also Sections 1.2.2.2 and 3.3.1.

[314] Klaartje Wentholt, 'Formal and Substantive Equal Treatment: The Limitations and Potential of the Legal Concept of Equality' in Peter R. Rodrigues and Titia Loenen (eds) *Non-discrimination Law: Comparative Perspectives* (Kluwer/Brill 1999) 54.

[315] Nussbaum (n 48) 90–91.

requires an acknowledgement of human diversity, differences in starting positions and the targeting of social and personal disadvantage. Accordingly, drawing on values such as human dignity and distributive justice, proponents of the concept of 'substantive equality' have elaborated two main forms: 'equality of opportunities' and 'equality of results'.[316] This means that states, through law and policy, should abandon the neutrality of the formal equality paradigm and treat people differently according to their capacity to enjoy human rights. This approach generally corresponds to a route to achieve equity, which is an ethical principle of social justice and public health that includes disadvantage, or needs, as a key or preferential criteria for policy planning and service provisions.[317]

Therefore, acknowledging power asymmetries entails the adoption of the necessary measures, including those of a positive nature, to either equalise people's starting points or capabilities or to directly achieve equality of outcomes, even if this signifies, at least temporarily, more favourable treatment for certain disadvantaged individuals and groups.[318] A step forward would mean embracing a transformative approach to substantive equality that can redress disadvantage and stigma and support participation and social inclusion while also appreciating differences and pursuing structural change.[319]

Discrimination is normally linked to the marginalisation of specific individuals or groups and is at the root of fundamental structural inequalities in society. An essential feature of the human rights–based approach is the commitment to protecting the rights of vulnerable and disadvantaged individuals and groups.[320] After all, human rights law is founded on the fundamental principle of the inherent dignity and equal worth of every human being, and sets out minimum conditions for a dignified life for all: not only should the worst off not be left behind but they should be prioritised in the realisation of

---

[316] Fredman (n 312) 14–19; Daniel Moeckli, 'Equality and Non-Discrimination' in Moeckli et al. (n 51, Ch 1) 148, 149–151.

[317] Braveman and Gruskin (n 32, Introduction).

[318] Mark Bell, 'The Right to Equality and Non-Discrimination' in Tamara Hervey and Jeff Kenner (eds) *Economic and Social Rights Under the EU Charter of Fundamental Rights – A Legal Perspective* (Hart Publishing 2003) 95; Hilary Charlesworth, 'Concepts of Equality in International Law' in Grant Huscroft and Paul Rishworth (eds) *Litigating Rights: Perspectives from Domestic and International Law* (Hart Publishing 2002) 137.

[319] Sandra Fredman, 'Substantive Equality Revisited' (2016) *International Journal of Constitutional Law* 14 712.

[320] Audrey R. Chapman and Benjamin Carbonetti, 'Human Rights Protections for Vulnerable and Disadvantaged Groups: The Contributions of the UN Committee on Economic, Social and Cultural Rights' (2011) *Human Rights Quarterly* 33 682, 683; Paul Hunt, 'Report of the Special Rapporteur on the Right to [. . .] Health (focus: A human rights-based approach to health indicators)' (3 March 2006) E/CN.4/2006/48, 25.

rights.[321] Indeed, even if 'human rights are [theorised as] universal, the risk of having one's rights violated is not universal',[322] but it is deeply connected to people's social position and personal characteristics. Therefore, the vulnerability approach to human rights law may require the adoption of measures to combat both formal and substantial discrimination, although the concept may inherently hide inclusionary and exclusionary effects.

### 2.7.2 *What Is Vulnerability in Human Rights?*

The word 'vulnerability' comes from the Latin *vulnerare*, which means 'to hurt' or 'to wound'. Accordingly, to be vulnerable is to be 'exposed to the possibility of being attacked or harmed, either physically or emotionally' and to be 'in need of special care, support'.[323]

The concept of vulnerability, as employed in the social sciences and legal scholarship and indeed throughout these pages, is as popular and attractive as it may be complex and confusing.[324] This concept, although it has not been clearly conceptualised,[325] has, along with the concepts of 'marginalisation' and 'disadvantage', been widely used by international and regional human rights bodies[326] and is a mantra for the CESCR.

Human rights and vulnerability are conceptually linked. Indeed, the UDHR, drafted in the aftermath of World War II, stated that 'disregard and contempt for human rights have resulted in barbarous acts which have outraged the conscience of mankind'.[327] This appears to be an implicit acknowledgement that human vulnerability and dignity are threatened by the arbitrary exercise of state powers. Furthermore, vulnerability has entered the arena of human rights law because vulnerable individuals can find it more difficult to exercise their human rights and are more likely to become or remain victims of formal or substantive discrimination. Human rights apply, in principle, to everyone, and positive state duties to rebalance opportunities by

---

[321] Ibid (Chapman and Carbonetti) 726.

[322] Paul Farmer, *Pathologies of Power: Health, Human Rights, and the New War on the Poor* (University of California Press 2003) 231.

[323] Oxford Dictionaries, 'vulnerable', <https://en.oxforddictionaries.com/definition/vulnerable> accessed 1 March 2021.

[324] Kate Brown, Kathryn Ecclestone and Nick Emmel, 'The Many Faces of Vulnerability' (2017) *Social Policy and Society* 16(3) 497.

[325] Chapman and Carbonetti (n 320) 725.

[326] For example, see Ingrid Nifosi-Sutton, *The Protection of Vulnerable Groups under International Human Rights Law* (Routledge 2017).

[327] UDHR (n 2, Ch 1) Preamble.

removing obstacles to their exercise in order to tackle situations of individual vulnerability are a distinctive feature of contemporary human rights law.

Scholarship is divided on the conceptualisation of vulnerability. On the one hand, vulnerability is described as a universal constant, an inherent trait of the human condition,[328] which represents the raison d'être of human rights.[329] On the other hand, the dominant doctrine and practice make use of this concept in relation to specific groups and individuals who, due to their group membership or individual characteristics, find themselves in a marginalised or disadvantaged position in society.[330] Furthermore, this elevated risk of harm can be classified as *inherent* vulnerability, which arises from corporeality or dependence on others, or *situational* vulnerability, which is context-specific. The latter underlines the fact that individual or group situations of vulnerability may be caused or exacerbated by exogenous factors, such as the social, cultural and political contexts in which people live.[331] Considered in this way, vulnerability may be framed as a 'socially induced condition'.[332]

A useful and comprehensive 'taxonomy of vulnerability' developed by feminist philosophical scholars identifies three different complementary and non-exclusionary 'sources' of vulnerability (inherent, situational and pathogenic) and two 'states' of vulnerability (dispositional and occurrent). Pathogenic vulnerability, which adds to the two above-mentioned types of human vulnerability, is a subset of situational vulnerability in which the sources of harm lie in interpersonal relationships and institutional structures, as in the case of 'paternalistic social policy responses'.[333] The distinction between dispositional and occurrent vulnerability lies in the state of potential or actual risk of harm.[334] Classifying conceptualisations of vulnerability plays an important role in identifying protective measures in regulatory frameworks, such as human rights law, that aim to respond to the 'dynamic and dialectical

---

[328] Martha Albertson Fineman, 'The Vulnerable Subject: Anchoring Equality in the Human Condition' (2008) *Yale Journal of Law and Feminism* 20(1) 1; and Bryan Turner, *Vulnerability and Human Rights* (The Pennsylvania State University Press 2006) 2, 89.

[329] Ibid (Turner) 1.

[330] Francesca Ippolito and Sara Iglesias Sánchez (eds) *Protecting Vulnerable Groups – The European Human Rights Framework* (Bloomsbury-Hart 2015) 1–5.

[331] Catriona Mackenzie, Wendy Rogers and Susan Dodds, 'Introduction: What Is Vulnerability and Why Does It Matters for Moral Theory?' in Catriona Mackenzie, Wendy Rogers and Susan Dodds (eds) *Vulnerability: New Essays in Ethics and Feminist Philosophy* (OUP 2014) 1.

[332] Judith Butler, 'Rethinking Vulnerability and Resistance' in Judith Butler, Zeynep Gambetti and Leticia Sabsay (eds) *Vulnerability in Resistance* (Duke University Press 2016) 25.

[333] Mackenzie, Rogers and Dodds (n 331) 9.

[334] Ibid, 8.

relationships between institutional precariousness and ontological vulnerability'.[335]

In relation to the sources of potential harm, for authoritative human rights scholars, vulnerability means to be at risk[336] of suffering harm of a physical, moral, psychological, economic or institutional nature.[337] A brief digression to some aforementioned cases heard by the ECtHR may help to clarify the different sources of vulnerability. For instance, in *Rahimi* v. *Greece*, a case that concerned the placement of an irregular migrant child in an immigration detention camp, the Strasbourg Court, in finding a violation of Article 5 ECHR on the right to liberty, took into consideration the special physical and psychological risk of harm for an unaccompanied minor, who is inherently and situationally vulnerable. Indeed, the applicant's socioeconomic vulnerability, due to the 'abominable' material conditions of the refugee camp, contributed to the Court's finding of a violation of Article 3 ECHR.[338] *M.S.S.* v. *Belgium and Greece* is another notorious example of a case in which the risk of harm to the physical, mental and socioeconomic well-being of particularly vulnerable people was considered central in the arguments of the Court. In this case, which concerned the return of an Afghan asylum seeker to Greece from Belgium, both the economic and institutional aspects of this risk were highlighted.[339]

### 2.7.3 *Non-discrimination and Vulnerability for the CESCR, the ECtHR and the ECSR*

In essence, the aim of the ICESCR may be defined as 'to encompass and appeal to equality'.[340] Article 2(2) ICESCR stipulates that states '[u]ndertake to guarantee that the rights enunciated in the [. . .] Covenant will be exercised

---

[335] Turner (n 328) 32.

[336] For reflections on a vulnerability-related 'risk of suffering' v 'actual suffering', elsewhere defined dispositional or occurrent vulnerability, see Robert Chambers, 'Vulnerability, Coping and Policy' (2006) *Institute of Development Studies Bulletin* 37(4) 33.

[337] Lourdes Peroni and Alexandra Timmer, 'Vulnerable Groups: The Promise of an Emerging Concept in European Human Rights Convention Law' (2013) *International Journal of Constitutional Law* 11(4) 1056, 1058.

[338] *Rahimi* (n 148, Ch 1) paras 62, 85–86, 95–96, 108–110.

[339] *M.S.S.* (n 132, Ch 1) para 263; Stefano Angeleri, 'The Impact of the Economic Crisis on the Right to Health of Irregular Migrants, as Reflected in the Jurisprudence of the UN Committee on Economic, Social and Cultural Rights' (2017) *European Journal of Migration and Law* 19(2) 165, 170.

[340] Matthew Craven, *The International Covenant on Economic, Social, and Cultural Rights: A Perspective on Its Development* (Clarendon Press 1995) 153, 192.

without discrimination of any kind as to race, colour, sex, language, religion, political or other opinion, national or social origin, property, birth or other status'.[341] 'Other status' must be interpreted flexibly for the CESCR, and 'additional grounds are commonly recognised when they reflect the experience of social groups that are vulnerable and that continue to suffer marginalisation'.[342] In practice, several grounds of discrimination can overlap in individual experiences, and this may give rise to the phenomenon of compounded or intersectional discrimination, which further exacerbates the vulnerability of victims of discrimination.[343]

Against a backdrop of general obligations regarding progressive realisation, the use of the term 'guarantee' in the text of Article 2(2) ICESCR, as confirmed by the CESCR's jurisprudence, qualifies protection from discrimination in relation to enjoying a certain level of fulfilled rights as an obligation of immediate application.[344] Accordingly, to avoid both formal and substantial discrimination, which are relevant for the CESCR, formal barriers restricting socioeconomic rights must be lifted, and special measures must be adopted 'to bring disadvantaged or marginalised persons or groups of persons to the same substantive level as others'.[345]

Discrimination and vulnerability are deeply interlinked concepts: formal or substantive discrimination generates situations of personal vulnerability, and the identification of vulnerabilities often exposes inadequacies and bias in state or state-backed practice. Despite the fact that vulnerable individuals and groups are central in shaping the normative content of social rights and the priorities of state obligations, there is no agreement on the criteria for identifying vulnerable and disadvantaged populations, no accepted definition of vulnerability and no standard list of vulnerable groups.[346]

---

[341] Analogous provisions are contained at Article 2 UDHR (n 2, Ch 1); Article 2(1) ICCPR; Article 1 (1) ICERD; Article 1 CEDAW (n 42, Introduction); Article 14 ECHR (n 43, Introduction). An authoritative interpretation of Article 2(2) ICESCR is given by the CESCR, GC20 (n 100, Ch 1).

[342] CESCR, GC20 (ibid) para 27.

[343] For the concept of intersectional discrimination in human rights, see Bantekas and Oette (n 32, Ch 1) 531 referring to Kimberlé Crenshaw, 'Mapping the Margins: Intersectionality, Identity Politics, and Violence against Women of Color' (1991) *Stanford Law Review* 43 1241. See also, GC20 (n 100, Ch 1) para 27.

[344] Ssenyonjo (n 87, Ch 1) 134; CESCR, GC3 (n 80) para 1 and GC14 (n 27, Introduction) para 30.

[345] CESCR, 'General Comment No. 16, the equal right of men and women to the enjoyment of all economic, social and cultural rights' (Article 3 of the ICESCR)' (11 August 2005) E/C.12/2005/4/Corr.1, para 15.

[346] Chapman and Carbonetti (n 320) 683, 724.

Although the CESCR largely uses the terminology of vulnerability to identify priorities in human rights monitoring and in state implementation, as exemplified by the above-mentioned frameworks for state obligations, it fails to provide a definition or conceptualisation of vulnerability, which is sometimes linked to some fixed or variable status or to the personal impact of human rights violations.[347] It also fails to systematically identify who vulnerable human rights holders are, although it has drafted a list of 'non-exhaustive examples' of statuses relevant for protection against discrimination, thus indirectly identifying possible vulnerable individuals and groups.[348] A provisional list, as the practice of the CESCR indicates, should include at least women, children, refugees and migrants, internally displaced people, stateless people, ethnic minorities, people with disabilities, elderly persons, people with marginalising health statuses, such as HIV positive persons, and LGBTQI people. In addition, poverty and economic vulnerability are confirmed as relevant factors for assessing the effective enjoyment of human rights, and, as highlighted in a case recently decided on by the CESCR, any added conditions to the exercise of social rights should not perpetuate the 'systemic discrimination and stigmatization of those who live in poverty'.[349]

Since the year 2000, the ECtHR has also increasingly made use of this concept by referring to the 'special' vulnerability of certain groups of human rights victims: first, Roma people and, subsequently, people with disabilities, HIV positive people and asylum seekers.[350] The ECtHR's acknowledgement of this relational, particular and harm-based vulnerability has affected the decision-making of this body in cases where these people are the alleged victims of human rights violations. This trend has included the elaboration of positive obligations, such as the exceptional obligation 'to secure shelter to particularly vulnerable individuals' under Article 8 ECHR.[351] Other consequences of the case law on special vulnerabilities are the ECtHR lowering of the level of severity that must be attained to trigger the violation of an absolute right and the limiting of the state margin of appreciation in the context of the

---

[347] Ibid, 721.

[348] CESCR, GC20 (n 100, Ch 1) paras 15–35; ibid, 723–724.

[349] *Maribel Viviana López Albán v Spain* Com no 37/2018 (CESCR 2019) para 10.1.

[350] *Chapman v UK* App no 27238/95 (ECHR 2001) para 96: 'the vulnerable position of Gypsies as a minority means that some special consideration should be given to their needs and their different lifestyle both in the relevant regulatory planning framework and in reaching decisions in particular cases'. Similarly, for example, *D.H. and Others v the Czech Republic* App no 57325/00 (ECHR 2007) para 182; *Alajos Kiss v Hungary* App no 38832/06 (ECHR 2010) para 42; *M.S.S.* (n 132, Ch 1) para 251; *Kiyutin* (n 266) para 63.

[351] *Yordanova v Bulgaria* App no 25446/06 (ECHR 2012) para 130.

proportionality test of a limitable right.[352] In the European context, the concept of vulnerability has allowed the ECtHR to 'address several aspects of substantive equality' for certain 'identified' disadvantaged groups who, according to the Court, are likely to be exposed to harm and to experience, *inter alia*, material deprivation and social exclusion more than other people. Although this approach is a feature of several judgments of the Court, it may have exclusionary consequences and has not reached the status of consistent practice or a criterion of interpretation with foreseeable outcomes.[353]

In cases when state law and practice fail to fully realise the rights of the ESC, the ECSR has used the terminology of vulnerability in relation to Roma people, people with disabilities, pensioners, migrant children and, in general, people who fall below the threshold of poverty.[354] In the complaints procedure before the ECSR, the normative concept of vulnerability has been employed to emphasise inappropriate measures of a responding state in dealing with certain people's 'particular' situation of socioeconomic deprivation, which should receive special attention and be responded to with positive measures. Indeed, states are required to 'pay particular attention to the impact of their choices on the most vulnerable groups and on the other persons concerned'.[355] Interestingly, the Committee has complemented this 'vulnerable groups' approach with measures targeting 'human' or 'situational' vulnerability. For example, in relation to irregular migrant adults, it stated that 'the right to emergency shelter and to other emergency social assistance is not limited to those belonging to vulnerable groups, but extends to all individuals in a precarious situation pursuant to their human dignity'.[356]

### 2.7.4 *Non-discrimination and Health*

In the context of health, the concepts of discrimination and vulnerability generate a number of interlinked relations in human rights and public health. First, 'health status' is one of the prohibited grounds of discrimination in the

---

[352] Ibid 129–133; *M.S.S.* (n 132, Ch 1) paras 232, 233, 251, 259, 262; *Kiyutin* (n 266) para 63. For further analysis, see Peroni and Timmer (n 337) 1074–1082.

[353] Ibid, 1084.

[354] For example, *European Roma Rights Centre v Bulgaria* Com no 46/2007 (ECSR 2008) para 38; *European Roma and Travellers Forum (ERTF) v Czech Republic* Com no 104/2014 (ECSR 2016) para 119; *DCI v Belgium* (n 218, Ch 1) para 141; *International Association Autism-Europe v France*, Com no13/2002 (ECSR 2003) para 53; *Federation of Employed Pensioners of Greece (IKA-ETAM) v Greece* Com no 76/2012 /ECSR 2012) paras 73, 81.

[355] *DCI v Belgium* (n 218, Ch 1) para 72.

[356] *FEANTSA* (n 221, Ch 1) paras 184–185.

enjoyment of human rights, including the right to health.[357] Discrimination on the grounds of health was repeatedly held by the ECtHR when Russia, on a series of occasions, refused to issue residence permits on the grounds that the foreign national applicants in question were HIV positive.[358] Second, while the concept of 'health vulnerability' in health care concerns how people can anticipate, grapple with, resist and recover from the impacts of diseases or epidemics,[359] social status, isolation, discrimination and stigma have a negative impact on health vulnerability and threaten the enjoyment of the right to the highest attainable standard of health for specific vulnerable individuals or groups.[360] An ECSR case regarding limited and discriminatory access to health care by Romani people in Bulgaria exemplifies this relationship:

> In assessing whether the right to protection of health can be effectively exercised, the Committee pays particular attention to the situation of disadvantaged and vulnerable groups. Hence, it considers that any restrictions on this right must not be interpreted in such a way as to impede the effective exercise by these groups of the right to protection of health. This interpretation imposes itself because of the non-discrimination requirement [in the ESC] in conjunction with the substantive rights of the Charter.[361]

All the operational frameworks for human rights obligations mentioned earlier in this chapter appear to be vulnerability cognisant, which means that negative and positive anti-discriminatory measures regarding vulnerable people are central for discharging state obligations of all types. Indeed, a violations-based approach to identifying the content of rights and obligations[362] and the

---

[357] CESCR, GC20 (n 100, Ch 1) para 33: 'Discrimination on the ground of health status takes place [...] for example, when HIV status is used as the basis for differential treatment with regard to access to education, employment, health care, travel, social security, housing and asylum. States party should also adopt measures to address widespread stigmatisation of persons on the basis of their health status, such as mental illness, diseases such as leprosy and women who have suffered obstetric fistula, which often undermines the ability of individuals to enjoy fully their Covenant rights. Denial of access to health insurance on the basis of health status will amount to discrimination if no reasonable or objective criteria can justify such differentiation.'

[358] *Kiyutin* (n 266); *Novruc and others v Russia* App nos 31039/11, 48511/11, 76810/12, 14618/13 and 13817/14 (ECHR 2016).

[359] Cristina Grabovschi, Christine Loignon and Martin Fortin 'Mapping the Concept of Vulnerability Related to Health Care Disparities: A Scoping Review' (2013) *BMC Health Services Research* 13 94.

[360] Grover (n 253) para 64.

[361] ERTF (n 354) para 112, see also *Médecins du Monde* (n 308) para 144.

[362] Audrey R. Chapman, 'A Violations Approach for Monitoring the International Covenant on Economic, Social and Cultural Rights' (1996) *Human Rights Quarterly* 18 23.

frameworks of core obligations, the 'tripartite typology' and AAAQ-AP all highlight the degree of priority that should be given to the needs of particular groups or individuals when the state implements its obligations to respect, protect and fulfil the right to health.[363] Furthermore, as previously mentioned, the CESCR, in its General Comment No. 3 on state obligations, states that even in times of severe resource constraints, socially vulnerable people must be protected by the adoption of relatively low-cost targeted programmes.[364] Thus, it is not an overstatement to assert that vulnerability considerations lie at the core of progressive and immediate measures concerning the realisation of the right to health.

## 2.8 CONCLUSIONS

Like migration, the field of health is extremely sovereignty-sensitive; states are at the centre of health regulation and health care provision. Building on this premise, this chapter provided an overview of the complex development of the normative content of the right to health and the corresponding state obligations to which standards of public health have – although to different extents in international or European conceptualisations – contributed.

Sections 2.1 and 2.2 demonstrated how, in different fields of governance and regulation, the protection of human health has become an issue of international concern over, at least, the last century. Furthermore, public health principles have qualified the nature of the right to health and its formulations since its first international recognition, whereby states were required to implement and progressively enhance measures concerning elements of disease prevention, health promotion and curative care.

During the years of the Cold War, the right to health as an international social right largely remained a dormant or, at best, a weak treaty provision requiring states to take programmatic commitments. During this period, the WHO disengaged with the human rights community and it timidly restarted employing rights terminology in the 1970s with the 'health for all' campaign. This led to the adoption of the Declaration of Alma-Ata on PHC, which the WHO identified as the best strategy to achieve health justice and realise the right to health. Since the 1990s, a gradually increasing number of multidisciplinary initiatives and instruments elaborating on what protecting and promoting health in international law or having a right to health grounded in human rights law means have been launched and adopted, and the

---

[363] CESCR, GC14 (n 27, Introduction) paras 43, 50–52.
[364] CESCR, GC3 (n 80) para 12.

jurisprudence of courts and quasi-legal bodies on the right to health and health-related matters has since grown.

Vis-à-vis this increased interest, Section 2.3 overviewed some authoritative philosophies that can provide a moral foundation for the right to health: while the legal right to health can be described as an incompletely theorised norm in the international agreements of the twentieth century, growing jurisprudence and studies around health and human rights seem to articulate a number of equalitarian theories of (health) justice that have conceptually grounded this right in either expansive health needs or capabilities arguments. Although they fail to specify the *detailed* content of obligations regarding the right to health, these philosophical and justice frameworks generally agree on the necessary role of the state in realising health and social needs or capabilities, in a holistic way and outside of an emergency paradigm.

The stratification of international normative contributions in the technical field of health has raised concern in terms of the quality of international obligations. Textual treaty obligations allow for a wide margin of discretion in domestic implementation, although these have been specified through the interpretative activities, of either a binding or persuasive nature. Several international courts and quasi-legal tribunals have established criteria, often based on a teleological interpretation of international law and drawing on interdisciplinary sources, to discharge state obligations. In a non-hierarchical international legal system, these activities have led to certain inconsistencies within and between different legal frameworks, particularly given the different legitimacy statuses of human rights treaty bodies. For example, in Europe, the special reliance on the ECHR, together with the ECtHR as the legitimate source and guardian of European human rights, has contributed to the perception that safeguarding the right to health care means bringing states to account only where systemic and regulatory deficiencies occur. This is in stark contrast with state obligations under the ESC and the ICESCR, as interpreted by their monitoring bodies, which adopt a more demanding approach to health protection and promotion. This is the reason why the following chapters will particularly rely on and develop the arguments of international human rights law rather than stretching European human rights law. Having said this, it is worth recalling that greater emphasis on systemic interpretation and on the ECHR's 'most favourable treatment clause' could, in principle, redirect the Strasbourg's Court's case law, especially since the ECtHR has not proved to be neutral vis-à-vis vulnerability arguments.

Even though the veil of state sovereignty on health and social policies and rights is difficult to pierce with international human rights law, it can be inferred that all normative activities at the international and European levels are, although to different extents, supportive of tightening human rights scrutiny – and thus of increasing their normative persuasiveness – where the rights of vulnerable people are concerned. Furthermore, the development of equity-oriented law, policies and practice and the favouring of preventive measures, primary care and health-supportive living environments is not only contained in certain pieces of human rights law but is also supported by a broad array of international political commitments and technical resolutions, adopted by, *inter alia*, the UNGA and the World Health Assembly (WHA).

The priorities set out in these declarations, which are frequently recalled by the health and human rights communities, orient the discussions on health as a human right towards the concepts of PHC, the social determinants of health and UHC, all of which present certain synergies with the operationalisation of the principles of non-discrimination and vulnerability in human rights practice. These meta-legal concepts can contribute to the interpretation of the core obligations regarding the right to health and other health-related obligations of all international and European human rights frameworks in a human health–centred and non-emergency–oriented ways, making exclusions on the grounds of migratory status difficult to defend.

Indeed, even though the concept of core obligations may not be entirely agreed upon, the priority assigned to vulnerable groups and equitable access is either clearly developed or at least implied in several pieces of human rights law. For these reasons, vulnerability, non-discrimination and PHC are among the key transformative arguments for assessing the contribution of international and European human rights law to the right to physical and mental health of irregular migrants. They prevent the reduction of the complex and holistic conceptualisation of their right to health to life-saving treatment and support access to meaningful levels of health care and other social determinants of health, for everyone regardless of migrant status.

# 3

# The Right to Health Care of Irregular Migrants

## Between Primary Care and Emergency Treatment

Chapters 1 and 2 elaborated on the underlying difficulties involved in fully including the rights of irregular migrants within the human rights paradigm and in imbuing the right to health with clear normative content across different international legal frameworks. At the same time, they highlighted a number of expansive human rights arguments and the spirit of a non-discriminatory and vulnerability-oriented right to health. In this chapter, I critically assess whether international and European human rights law can help to realise elements of PHC – a priority in the field of public health – for irregular migrants. It is worth recalling that the components of the PHC approach, for the WHO, are as follows: '1. meeting people's health needs [...] throughout the life course, strategically prioritizing [...] primary care [...]; 2. [...] Addressing the broader determinants of health through multisectoral policy and action [...]; 3. Empowering individuals, families and communities to take charge of their own health.'[1]

This chapter mainly focuses on the first component and, in particular, on whether access to preventive and primary care is included in the scope of the right to health of irregular migrants. Although the scope of the right to health care has several components, issues concerning accessibility must be addressed as a precondition to discussions on the acceptability and quality of the services and are central for understanding the legal and circumstantial barriers that irregular migrants experience.

Section 3.1 briefly recalls the root causes of unequal treatment and presents an overview of how the concept of vulnerability applies to migrants and

---

[1] World Health Organization and the United Nations Children's Fund (UNICEF), 'A Vision for Primary Health Care in the 21st Century: Towards Universal Health Coverage and the Sustainable Development Goals' (2018) 2 <www.who.int/docs/default-source/primary-health/vision.pdf> accessed 25 September 2020.

irregular migrants. Section 3.2 sheds light on the generally restrictive European approach to the health of irregular migrants, which is mostly affected by the competence limitations of the ECtHR and the ECSR. Section 3.3 shows how the concepts of positive obligations, vulnerability, non-discrimination and core obligations in international human rights law can prevent the adoption of overly restrictive measures concerning access to health care by irregular migrants. This section describes, assesses and develops the arguments contained in key pieces of UN human rights law, in light of a number of meta-legal public health principles that have contributed to shaping the conceptualisation of the human right to health. Section 3.4 shows how a growing number of human rights bodies, particularly during the last decade, have levelled up state obligations regarding health care for irregular migrants and subgroups of the same.

## 3.1 IRREGULAR MIGRANTS: BETWEEN EXCLUSIONARY MEASURES AND VULNERABILITY

### 3.1.1 A Brief Recapitulation of the State Sovereignty Approach to Irregular Migration

During the twentieth century, the power to establish and enforce norms on the entry, residence and expulsion of aliens has become an entrenched element of state sovereignty and has gained recognition as an established maxim of international law.[2] However, this competence, which has been referred to as the 'last bastion of sovereignty',[3] is not absolute, and international asylum and human rights law can curtail the arbitrary treatment of people by national authorities. European and international human rights law sets forth, in principle, inalienable and universal rights that are inextricability linked to the concept of human dignity, regardless of a person's legal or administrative status.[4]

Nonetheless, when the rights of migrants are at stake, narratives of emergency, crisis, border control, security and limited resources are often employed to counterweigh the fact that migrants belong to the 'human family' and state communities and can lead to de jure (set out in law) and de facto

---

[2]  For example, New York Declaration for Refugees and Migrants (n 67, Ch 1); *Abdulaziz et al. v UK* (n 68, Ch 1) para 67; ICMW (n 42, Introduction) Article 79.
[3]  Dauvergne (n 55, Ch 1) 600–601.
[4]  Grant (n 88, Ch 1) 25–47.

(due to structural or situational circumstances) limitations of rights.[5] This phenomenon is even more acute in relation to irregular migrants, whose existence represents a breach of the sovereign power to enforce border control and to exclude aliens from state territories. Irregular migrants, who normally avoid contact with host states' authorities for fear of deportation, are often exposed to substandard living conditions, labour exploitation and social exclusion.[6] Against a background of particular exposure to material and multidimensional deprivation or poverty, not only is the enjoyment and defence of the rights of irregular migrants problematic – since it may require their engagement with state authorities – but the entitlements themselves are sometimes unevenly set out, including in human rights law.[7]

The clash between sovereignty and human rights in the field of immigration and the spread of bias against perceived resource-dependant and not easily justiciable or enjoyable socioeconomic rights has led to a situation in which states often neglect the health of irregular migrants, leave it up to NGO clinics to address or grapple with it only as a matter of emergency care. Indeed, to discourage undesired irregular migrants from entering and staying in their territories, states have resorted to restricting the fundamental rights of this group from 'the inside', for example, by raising legal or administrative barriers to accessing public service providers.[8] This strategy has often been justified for budget-related reasons, namely as a tool to contain public expenditure and to achieve sustainable public services.[9] Furthermore, the development of the right to health as a social right and its concrete operationalisation have undermined its universal reach, as the welfare state – the ideological and structural context within which social rights are normally implemented in the Global North – tend to create boundaries of 'belonging' separating those who

---

[5]   De Guchteneire, Pécoud and (n 202, Ch 1) 30–33; Marco Gestri, 'Conclusioni Generali' in Giuseppe Nesi (ed) *Migrazioni e Diritto Internazionale: Verso il Superamento dell'Emergenza?* (Editoriale Scientifica 2018) 643, 659–669.

[6]   For an overview of the precarious situations in which irregular migrants live, see Fundamental Rights Agency of the European Union, *Migrants in an Irregular Situation: Access to Healthcare in 10 European Union Member States – Comparative Report* (FRA Publishing 2011).

[7]   See Section 1.4.

[8]   Bosniak (n 71, Ch 1) 325; Alessia Di Pascale, 'Italy and Unauthorized Migration: Between State Sovereignty and Human Rights Obligations' in Ruth Rubio-Marín (ed) *Human Rights and Immigration* (OUP 2014) 278, 279.

[9]   Regarding the case of Spain, see Alex Boso and Mihaela Vancea, 'Should Irregular Migrants Have the Right to Healthcare? Lessons Learnt from the Spanish Case' (2016) *Critical Social Policy* 36(2) 225, 226, 235; in relation to the UK, see Platform for International Cooperation on Undocumented Migrants, 'PICUM Quarterly, January–March 2016' (2016) <https://picum.org/picum-quarterly-january-to-march-2016/> accessed 1 March 2021.

are members of the polity from those who are not, those 'strangers' who are deserving and those who are not.[10]

### 3.1.2 *Irregular Migrants and Their Vulnerability to Human Rights Abuse*

Where the phenomena of migration and human mobility are concerned, situations of special vulnerability and an increased risk of human rights abuse can originate from pre-migration factors, from events and living conditions that take place during transit or in the destination country or from an individual migrant's identity or personal situation.[11] Without detracting from the importance of pre-migration or journey-related risk factors, this analysis is particularly focused on the vulnerable positions of irregular migrant vis-à-vis the actions or inaction of public authorities, policy-makers and service providers in destination or transit countries.

Certain subgroups of migrants are generally considered more vulnerable than others in international law. For example, the 2014 Draft Articles on the Expulsion of Aliens by the International Law Commission identifies 'children, older persons, persons with disabilities, [and] pregnant women' as particularly vulnerable.[12] Furthermore, the 2016 New York Declaration for Refugees and Migrants explicitly presents the following non-exhaustive list of 'migrants in vulnerable situations':

> Women at risk, children, especially those who are unaccompanied or separated from their families, members of ethnic and religious minorities, victims of violence, older persons, persons with disabilities, persons who are discriminated against on any basis, indigenous peoples, victims of human trafficking, and victims of exploitation and abuse in the context of the smuggling of migrants.[13]

This exact list is recalled in the final text of the Global Compact for Migration.[14] Apart from a series of references to how gender can increase

---

[10] See Sections 2.2 and 3.1 on the welfare state and migrants' rights.
[11] OHCHR and GMG, 'Principles and Guidelines, supported by practical guidance, on the human rights protection of migrants in vulnerable situations' (OHCHR 2008) 6–7 <www.ohchr.org/EN/Issues/Migration/Pages/VulnerableSituations.aspx> accessed 1 March 2021. See also Francesca Ippolito, 'La Vulnerabilità come Criterio Emergente per una Maggiore Tutela del Migrante nel contesto Internazionale' in Nesi (n 5) 447–466.
[12] International Law Commission, *Draft Articles on the Expulsion of Aliens, Yearbook of the International Law Commission* 2(II) Article 15(1) <http://legal.un.org/ilc/texts/9_12.shtml> accessed 25 September 2020.
[13] New York Declaration (n 68, Ch 1) para 23.
[14] GCM (n 92, Ch 1), Preamble, recital 7. For further details on GCM, see Section 1.5.2.

migrants' vulnerability, the Compact's use of the term vulnerability mainly applies to migrant children.[15] This is not surprising; children have traditionally been associated with the concept of vulnerability because of the disproportionate impact of certain adverse and external factors on their ongoing development and, of particular interest here, their health.[16] In accordance with the focus on children and gender issues, addressing the vulnerability of migrants by providing access to health care is explicitly mentioned only in relation to women, girls and unaccompanied children.[17]

Thus, the Global Compact's idea of vulnerability is mainly linked to the personal situation of certain subgroups of migrants, such as children, women and people exploited in work environments, while irregular legal status, which is a state-made circumstance, is not explicitly indicated as a source of vulnerability per se. Nonetheless, the recommendations to facilitate case-by-case status regularisation and help those transitioning from one regular status to another implicitly indicate that irregularity of status is, as much as an issue for migration management, a major source of actual or circumstantial human vulnerability.[18]

The ECtHR also adopts, although not always consistently, a categorical approach to the qualification of 'vulnerable migrants', as indicated in the case of *Khlaifia and others* v. *Italy*:

> The applicants were weakened physically and psychologically because they had just made a dangerous crossing of the Mediterranean. Nevertheless, *the applicants, who were not asylum seekers, did not have the specific vulnerability inherent in that status*, and did not claim to have endured traumatic experiences in their country of origin [. . .] they belonged neither to the category of elderly persons nor to that of minors.[19]

The inclusion of irregular migrants in the overall category of vulnerable people is, however, openly accepted by, *inter alia*, the CESCR,[20] the Inter-

---

[15] Ibid, Objective 7.
[16] Brown, Ecclestone and Emmel (n 324, Ch 2) 499; Wadsworth and Butterworth (n 100, Ch 2) 31.
[17] CGM (n 92, Ch 1) Objective 7, para 23, letters (c) and (f).
[18] Ibid, Objective 7, para 23, letters (h) and (i); Idil Atak, 'GCM Commentary: Objective 7: Address and Reduce Vulnerabilities in Migration' (*Refugee Law Initiative Blog*, 30 October 2018) <https://rli.blogs.sas.ac.uk/> accessed 15 January 2021.
[19] *Khlaifia* (2016) (n 136, Ch 1) para 194, emphasis added.
[20] For example, CESCR, COs on the report of France (9 June 2008) E/C.12/FRA/CO/3, para 26; CESCR, List of issues in relation to the report of the Netherlands (22 December 2009) UN Docs E/C.12/NLD/4–5, para 27: 'the situation of the most disadvantaged and marginalized individuals and groups, such as immigrants without legal residence'.

American Court on Human Rights,[21] the UN special rapporteur on the right to health and the special rapporteur on the rights of migrants.[22] These human rights bodies accept migration status as either a suspect ground of differentiation or a prohibited ground of discrimination, thus implicitly acknowledging that irregular migrants are in a comparable situation to that of people with regular or citizenship status in relation to the enjoyment of their human rights.

Discussing the health-related rights of irregular migrants exposes the tensions that exist between human rights, citizenship and the construct of state sovereignty,[23] which are at the origin of all the various types of vulnerability experienced by these people. First, irregular migrants are especially vulnerable on an institutional level because they are unable to 'call upon the basic protective functions of the state in which they reside for fear of deportation'.[24] As a consequence of this disempowerment in relation to enjoying and claiming their human rights,[25] most irregular migrants live in the shadows, in precarious or poor living and working conditions, and are exposed to physical, moral, psychological and economic risks of harm. The experience of irregularity is not the only factor of disempowerment for undocumented people; 'racism, patriarchy, economic disadvantages and other discriminatory systems contribute to create layers of inequality that structures the[ir] relative positions'.[26] Against this background of social and institutional exclusion and disregard for the special needs of subgroups, they are often reliant on the protection of local NGOs.[27]

Recalling the approaches to vulnerability analysed at the end of Chapter 2, irregular migrants seem to qualify at least as de facto vulnerable right holders under both a group-based and an individual or circumstantial construct of

---

[21] IACtHR, Advisory Opinion OC-18 (n 224, Ch 1) para 112.

[22] The particular 'vulnerability' of undocumented migrants had been recognised since the document of appointment of the Special Rapporteur on the Rights of Migrants, pursuant to UNGA Res 1999/44 (27 April 1999) E-CN_4-RES-99–44; Anand Grover, 'Report on [...] migrant worker's right to health' (n 253, Ch 2).

[23] Turner (n 328, Ch 2) 2.

[24] Ramji-Nogales (n 110, Ch 1) 1045.

[25] Migrants' vulnerability has been described as essentially 'structural' and 'cultural', and therefore not natural but 'social' in nature by Jorge A. Bustamante, 'Immigrants' Vulnerability as Subjects of Human Rights' (2002) *International Migration Review* 36(2) 339.

[26] Achiume E. Tendayi, Report of the special rapporteur on contemporary forms of racism, racial discrimination, xenophobia and related intolerance (Focus: citizenship, nationality and immigration) (25 April 2018) A/HRC/38/52, 9.

[27] Maurizio Ambrosini and Joanne Van der Leun, 'Introduction to the Special Issue: Implementing Human Rights: Civil Society and Migration Policies' (2015) *Journal of Immigrant & Refugee Studies* 13(2) 103.

vulnerability. As a group, they encounter institutional aversion and structural and state-made vulnerabilities, which, in concrete terms, means they are targets of a state-supported narrative of exclusion, are liable to deportation measures and have less access to public services, including health care. This reduced accessibility is due both to laws and policies that restrict the possibility of providing health care to irregular migrants on an equal basis with citizens or regular migrants (with regard to the entitlement per se or the affordability of the service) and to factual barriers, such as language barriers and a lack of culturally appropriate care, a lack of information and a lack of responsiveness on the part of health care staff.[28] Beyond their group identity as intrinsically vulnerable human beings, undocumented individuals are generally socioeco-nomically vulnerable because of the lower quantity and quality of the resources and assets they normally command in concrete circumstances,[29] including health-related goods and services. These situations of disadvantage regarding the enjoyment of fundamental rights are described as precariousness by some scholars and by the ECSR. Unlike vulnerability, the term 'precar-iousness' places emphasis on the systemic and contextual state-produced precarious status and avoids victim-blaming.[30]

Whether irregular migrants are classed as a vulnerable group or human beings in vulnerable or precarious positions, the CESCR has long acknow-ledged that the legal and factual situations of this group contain elements of vulnerability that merit special attention in the assessment of state reports and qualify them as targets for protective initiatives.[31] It is worth noting that the

---

[28]  FRA Report (n 6) 71–83.
[29]  Fineman (n 328, Ch 2) 10 and Peadar Kirby, *Vulnerability and Violence* (Pluto Press 2005) 54–55.
[30]  Shauna Erin Labman, *At Law's Border: Unsettling Refugee Resettlement*, PhD thesis, University of British Columbia, 15 November 2012 <https://open.library.ubc.ca/cIRcle/collections/ubctheses/24/items/1.0071854>; Idil Atak, Delphine Nakache, Elspeth Guild and François Crépeau, 'Migrants in Vulnerable Situations and the Global Compact for Safe Orderly and Regular Migration' (16 February 2018) *Queen Mary School of Law Legal Studies Research Paper No. 273/2018* 4 <https://ssrn.com/abstract=3124392> accessed 1 March 2021; FEANTSA (n 221, Ch 1) paras 184–185.
[31]  For example, CESCR, COs on the reports submitted by: France (n 20) para 26: 'persons belonging to disadvantaged and marginalized groups, such as asylum-seekers and undocumented migrant workers'; Greece (n 201, Ch 2) para 36: 'The Committee recommends that the State party [...] take steps to ensure that all persons belonging to disadvantaged and marginalized groups, in particular asylum seekers and undocumented migrants [...] have access to basic health care'; Cyprus (n 201, Ch 2) para 270: 'Persons belonging to vulnerable groups, including illegal immigrants, prisoners, children of illegal immigrants, and asylum seekers, are entitled to the necessary medical care free of charge.' Periodic report of Ireland to the CESCR (8 November 2013) E/C.12/IRL/3, para 24: 'Vulnerable groups. One stakeholder expressed concern over the situation of undocumented persons in Ireland.'

CESCR, beyond making cursory mention in its reporting procedures, recently issued a statement that clearly qualified irregular migrants as 'specifically vulnerable' people, deserving of being targets of core obligations regarding the right to health and other social rights.[32] Before turning to this and other hard and soft law standards belonging to the UN rights law system, Section 3.2 provides an overview of applicable European human rights law, an examination which portrays a generally restrictive position on irregular migrant rights and sets the scene for the following sections to set out what a thicker and public health–inspired conception of the right to health care for irregular migrants might look like.[33]

## 3.2 EUROPEAN HUMAN RIGHTS APPROACHES TO HEALTH CARE FOR IRREGULAR MIGRANTS

The ECtHR and the ECSR, which oversee the ECHR and the ESC, respectively, have often grappled, although to different extents, with the socioeconomic conditions of irregular migrants. However, due to various competence restraints, both these human rights bodies have essentially reaffirmed an emergency approach, which seems difficult to reconcile with the realisation of the highest attainable standard of health for all and the PHC approach. Nonetheless, their jurisprudence has not been static, and it contains progressively enhanced standards.

### 3.2.1 *The ECtHR: Stretching a Constrained Material Competence*

Although the ECHR sets forth rights that are essentially civil and political, the ECtHR has long considered that 'many [ECHR rights] have implications of a social or economic nature',[34] and, thus, its material jurisdiction, in principle, covers health-related controversies concerning access and quality of care, under, for instance, the right to life, the prohibition from ill treatment and the right to respect for private life.[35] I have previously explained that Article

---

[32] CESCR, Statement on migrant rights (n 174, Ch 1) Section III.
[33] The critical remarks that follow acknowledge that all international treaties recognise that greater legal protection (including for the right to health of irregular migrants) may be granted by domestic statutes rather than at regional or international level. See for example, ECHR (n 43, Introduction), Article 53; ESC-Rev (n 43, Introduction) Article H. For an overview of the domestic legal guarantees in this area, see Spencer and Hughes (n 2, Introduction).
[34] *Airey* (n 263, Ch 2) para 26.
[35] For example, see Section 2.6.1.

2 ECHR (the right to life) has been interpreted as containing positive state obligations to regulate health protocols for health care providers and to prevent systemic state deficiencies in offering emergency health care, especially in consideration of the special vulnerabilities of victims who had lost their life.[36] The prohibition of torture and ill treatment, set forth in Article 3 ECHR, has also been relied upon in health-related cases, in particular for the provision of adequate health care for detained people. However, the established and widespread case law of the Court of Strasbourg indicates that ill treatment must be of a 'minimum level of severity' to trigger the applicability of this norm. Furthermore, 'the assessment of this minimum [level of severity] is, in the nature of things, relative, and it depends on all the circumstances of the case'.[37] These types of argument, which are indeed very critical for the development of a migrant health jurisprudence, indicate that interference with an individual's health must take a particularly abusive form to fit the material scope of these provisions and that no freestanding right to health (care) exists in the ECHR framework. Indeed, the Court considers that 'matters of health care policy [including preventive programmes] are in principle within the margin of appreciation of domestic authorities, who are best placed to access priorities, use of resources [and] social needs'.[38]

With regard to irregular migrants, a fluctuating body of case law has developed, involving cases where the principle of non-refoulement is employed to prevent the deportation, removal or extradition of people with severe health conditions.[39] In *D. v. the UK*, regarding the deportation of a person in the terminal stages of AIDS to St Kitts, the Court found that the existence of 'very exceptional circumstances', that is, a 'real risk of dying under distressing circumstances', could be invoked under Article 3 ECHR to prevent the removal.[40] By contrast, in *N v. the UK*, the applicant's health condition – she was suffering from AIDS but not in a terminal stage – was not considered critical enough to prevent her from travelling because she was not at imminent risk of dying.[41] The exceptional applicability or Article 3 ECHR is

---

[36] For example, *Câmpeanu; Şentürk and Şentürk* (n 275, Ch 2).

[37] *Kudła v Poland* App no 30210/96 (ECHR 2000) para 91, emphasis added.

[38] *Hristozov and Others v Bulgaria* App nos 47039/11 and 358/12 (ECHR 2013) paras 3, 119. *Shelley v UK* App no 23800/06 (Decision, ECHR 2008). When a case raises issues concerning the allocation of resources, the Court makes wide use of the concept of 'margin of appreciation', i.e., *Da Conceição Mateus and Santos Januário v Portugal* App nos 62235/12, 57725/12 (ECHR 2013, Decision) para 22.

[39] *D. v UK; N. v UK; Paposhvili* (n 122, Ch 1) paras 172–183.

[40] Ibid (*D.*) paras 43, 52–53.

[41] *N.* (n 122, Ch 1) paras 42–51.

reflected in an *obiter dictum* in the case of N. v. UK, also restated in other judgments, according to which this ECHR's article does not impose a state obligation to provide 'free and unlimited health care to all aliens without a right to stay within its jurisdiction. A[s a] finding to the contrary would place too great a burden on the contracting states' regulatory sovereignty and finances.[42]

The above approach was partly eased in the key case of *Paposhvili* v. *Belgium*, where the Grand Chamber of the ECtHR extended the scope of the exceptional circumstances in which severe health conditions can interrupt the deportation of irregularly staying people in the following terms:

> He or she, *although not at imminent risk of dying*, would face *a real risk*, on account of the absence of appropriate treatment in the receiving country or the lack of access to such treatment, *of being exposed to a serious, rapid and irreversible decline in his or her state of health resulting in intense suffering or to a significant reduction in life expectancy*.[43]

Whether evidence is adduced to demonstrate that 'there are substantial grounds for believing that [if deportation] were to be implemented, [applicants] would be exposed to a real risk of being subjected to treatment contrary to Article 3',[44] namely a 'serious, rapid and irreversible decline in his or her state of health', the Court would perform a more rigorous and *in concreto* assessment of the risk of ill treatment ex Article 3 ECHR in the country to which the non-national is about to be deported. This means that the returning states must verify whether available care is 'sufficient and appropriate in practice for the treatment of the applicant's [severe] illness' and assess 'the extent to which the individual in question will actually have access to this care', granting adequate weight to the 'cost of medication and treatment, the existence of a social and family network, and the distance to be travelled in order to have access to the required care'.[45] If doubts persist, sufficient and individual assurances should be obtained by the receiving state.[46] This criterion was criticised because it would downgrade the absolute protection from

---

[42] Ibid, para 44; *Yoh-Ekale Mwanje v Belgium* App no 10486/10 (ECHR 2011) para 82; *A.S. v Switzerland* App no 39350/13 (ECHR 2015) para 31, emphasis added.

[43] *Paposhvili* (n 122, Ch 1) para 183, emphasis added.

[44] *Savran v Denmark* App no 57467/15 (ECHR GC 2021) para 130.

[45] *Paposhvili* (n 122, Ch 1) paras 189–190; *Savran v Denmark* App no 57467/15 (ECHR 2019) paras 46–48, 51.

[46] Ibid, para 67.

refoulement and ill treatment, making it conditional on rather formal state declarations.[47]

As an aside, it can be noted that in these cases, the recognition of health care needs, in the context of deportation, directly clashes with the sovereign power to expel an irregular migrant because a certain severe state of health may prevent the person's deportation. Nonetheless, these situations differ conceptually and practically from those relating to the regulation of accessibility to health (and related social) services of undocumented populations in a state jurisdiction outside of deportation proceedings and without the granting of any regularisation of status (although temporarily for health reasons).

Considering that the Court has not specifically articulated the normative content of state obligations regarding health or medical care for the mainstream population, beyond regulatory duties and the avoidance of systemic deficiencies with severe individual consequences, it is not surprising that this 'deportation and health' saga is informed by a logic of emergency and exceptionality.[48] Furthermore, unlike asylum seekers in dire conditions, irregular migrants in need of social and medical protection have not, in a number of key cases, been considered especially vulnerable per se.[49] There are, however, cases where migrants – because of their irregular status, compounded by past and present emotional circumstances, gender and 'fragile' physical and mental health – are qualified as vulnerable, which is an important factor for meeting the threshold of severity for the applicability of Article 3 ECHR.[50]

In a nutshell, due to material limitations and interpretative restraints, including the limited value attributed to other sources of human rights treaty law, the ECtHR appears to be committed to the protection of undocumented people's health only in terms of survival and freedom from inhuman or degrading treatment rather than guaranteeing or targeting any broader standard of health.[51]

---

[47] Mark Klaassen, 'A New Chapter on the Deportation of Ill Persons and Article 3 ECHR: The European Court of Human Rights Judgment in Savran v. Denmark' (*Strasbourg Observers*, 19 October 2019) <https://strasbourgobservers.com/2019/10/17/a-new-chapter-on-the-deportation-of-ill-persons-and-article-3-echr-the-european-court-of-human-rights-judgment-in-savran-v-denmark/> accessed 18 December 2020.

[48] *Cyprus v Turkey* (n 276, Ch 2) para 219; Şentürk and Şentürk (n 275, Ch 2). Further examples in Section 2.5.

[49] M.S.S. (n 132, Ch 1) para 263: 'the Court considers that the Greek authorities have not had due regard to the applicant's vulnerability as an asylum-seeker'; cf. *Hunde v the Netherlands* App no 17931/16 (ECHR 2016, Decision) paras 45–60; *Khlaifia* 2016 (n 136, Ch 1) para 194.

[50] Aden Ahmed v Malta (n 273, Ch 2) para 97: 'The applicant was in a vulnerable position, not only because of the fact that she was an irregular migrant [. . .] but also because of her fragile health.'

[51] For further cases regarding mental health care and irregular migration in ECHR framework, see Section 5.3.

### 3.2.2 *The ECSR: Between Interpretative Courage and Limitations of Mandate*

Unlike the ECHR, the ESC, the Council of Europe's general human rights treaty in the field of socioeconomic rights, directly grapples with the right to health.[52] Most notably, Article 11 ESC sets forth obligations to provide curative, promotional and preventive health measures, and Article 13 ESC sets out the legal basis for the right to social and medical assistance for people 'without adequate resources'.

However, the Appendix to this treaty prima facie excludes from its personal scope people who do not work or who are not 'lawfully' resident. Nonetheless, as previously indicated,[53] this textual limitation has not prevented the ECSR, in key non-binding but authoritative decisions on collective complaints, from partially extending the personal scope of the treaty to irregular migrants. It has done so by employing a number of arguments, including the complementary nature of the ESC and the ECHR, human dignity, the indivisibility of human rights,[54] systematic interpretation of the rules of international law[55] and a teleological reasoning which would prevent excessively restrictive treaty interpretation that would deprive a human rights treaty of its spirit.[56] In brief, the Committee has made clear that at least emergency health care, which is connected to the realisation of *fundamental rights* such as those protecting life, personal integrity and health,[57] should be provided to all irregular migrants.[58]

Despite the use of creative 'ultra-textual' methods of interpretation, the ECSR pitches the legal standard of protection for irregular migrant adults at the level of emergency measures. A qualification of this rule, in relation to medical assistance, comes from an often-restated dictum, according to which, '[although] an individual's need must be sufficiently urgent and serious to entitle them to assistance under Article 13(4), this criterion must not be interpreted too narrowly'.[59] Since the ECSR's understanding of the right to

---

[52] ESC (n 43, Introduction).
[53] See Section 1.4.2.
[54] *FIDH v France* (n 216, Ch 1) paras 26–32.
[55] *DCI v the Netherlands* (n 218, Ch 1) para 35; *CEC v the Netherlands* (n 218, Ch 1) para 68.
[56] Ibid (*DCI*) para 36.
[57] Fundamental rights, for the ECSR, are 'the right to life, to the preservation of human dignity, to psychological and physical integrity and to health' *DCI v Belgium* (n 218, Ch 1) para 38; *FEANTSA* (n 221, Ch 1) para 58, emphasis added.
[58] *CEC* (n 218, Ch 1) paras 73, 75; *FEANTSA* (n 221, Ch 1) paras 171, 173, 182–183, 186.
[59] Ibid (*CEC*) para 105; (*FEANTSA*) para 171.

health is broad and interrelated with other social issues, a more detailed analysis of its contentious jurisprudence is carried out in Chapter 4, which addresses the determinants of health.[60] However, at this point, it must be remembered that the ECSR draws a distinction between groups traditionally regarded as vulnerable, such as children or ethnic minorities, and other people in a precarious situation, such as irregular migrants. Accordingly, at least emergency levels of social rights must be guaranteed to everyone to protect their human dignity from precarious circumstances,[61] and this includes the provision of 'emergency medical assistance to persons unlawfully present in [any state] territory'.[62] The special precariousness or circumstantial vulnerability of irregular migrants, who, in spite of their precarious socio-economic living conditions, are excluded from the personal scope of the treaty by its text, has led the ECSR to require states to adopt positive duties to protect and promote the health of this group, although these are framed at a broad level of generality and apply only in cases of a certain level of severity.

## 3.3 INTERNATIONAL HUMAN RIGHTS LAW AND LEVELS OF HEALTH CARE FOR MIGRANTS WITH IRREGULAR STATUS AS VULNERABLE PEOPLE

This section shows the extent to which UN human rights conventions and the jurisprudence of treaty bodies offer particularly protection-oriented arguments that support – by using the concepts of vulnerability, non-discrimination, positive and core obligations – the desirability of conceptualising and implementing a thicker right to health of irregular migrants that extends beyond the provision of emergency medical assistance. I begin by explaining the difference between emergency and urgent care in the right-to-life jurisprudence of the HRCtee, which is not merely a matter of nuance. I then explore the practice of the CESCR – which considers irregular migrants especially vulnerable per se – to reveal an implicit substantive approach that is grounded in

---

[60] See Section 4.2.2.

[61] *FEANTSA* (n 221, Ch 1) paras 184–185.

[62] This standard was repeated as a mantra, vis-à-vis situations of suspect conformity with the ESC, in most of the conclusions issued by ECSR in the last reporting cycle on Articles 11 and 13 ESC. See ECSR, Conclusions 2017, January 2018, Andorra, Armenia, Austria, Belgium, Bosnia and Herzegovina, Bulgaria, Estonia, Finland, France, Hungary, Ireland, Italy, Latvia, Lithuania, Malta, Moldova, Montenegro, Portugal, Romania, Serbia, Slovak Republic, FYROM (now North Macedonia), Turkey <https://rm.coe.int/compilation-of-conclusions-2017-by-country/1680786061>; ECSR, Conclusions XXI-2 (2017), January 2018, Denmark, Germany, Spain, UK, <https://rm.coe.int/compilation-of-conclusions-xxi-2-2017-by-country/1680786063> accessed 18 December 2020.

certain public health standards that the WHO and other UN bodies also recommend on a universal basis.[63] The WHO's vision is particularly relied upon because it is the 'health normative agency within the United Nations system'[64] and thus has a constitutional mandate to act as the 'directing and coordinating authority on international health work'.[65]

### 3.3.1 *The Human Rights Committee: Urgent Care and the Right to Life*

Before discussing state obligations regarding the right to health in detail, it is worth reflecting on how the broad protective scope of Article 6 ICCPR concerning the right to life relates to health care. Both General Comments No. 6 and No. 36 of the HRCtee, drafted thirty-six years apart, authoritatively establish that interpreting the right to life too narrowly is against the spirit of the ICCPR and that enjoying life 'in dignity' compels states to adopt positive obligations, including those regarding the protection of the health of individuals and populations.[66]

In *Toussaint* v. *Canada*, a pivotal case concerning the denial of urgent health care to an irregular migrant with serious health conditions, the HRCtee developed the maxims of the above-mentioned general comments, thereby helping to clarify the difference between emergency and urgent care in human rights law and their relevance under Article 6 ICCPR. The author of this communication was denied registration with the Canadian health system for migrants and access to necessary care because of her irregular status. Canadian authorities justified such an exclusion because 'appropriate weight should be given to the interests of the state in defending its immigration laws'.[67] On the substantive scope of the right to life in dignity, the HRCtee recalled that state parties 'have the [positive] obligation to provide access to existing health care services that are *reasonably available and accessible*, when lack of access to the health care would expose a person to a reasonably foreseeable risk that can result in loss of life', and that this assistance should exceed life-saving hospital treatment or emergency care.[68]

---

[63] For example, Declaration of Astana (n 174, Ch 2); Report by the Director-General of the WHO (n 176, Ch 2); WHA Res 72.2 (n 176, Ch 2); WHA Res 70.15 'Promoting the Health of Refugees and Migrants (31 May 2017); WHO, 'Promoting the Health of Refugees and Migrants – Draft Global Action Plan 2019–2023 – Report by the Director-General, A72/25, Rev.1 (25 April 2019).

[64] Ibid, (WHO, A72/25).

[65] Constitution of the WHO (n 22, Introduction) Article 2(a).

[66] HRCtee, 'General Comment No. 6: Article 6 ICCPR (Right to life) (sixteenth session 1982) para 5; HRCtee, GC36 (n 193, Ch 1) paras 3, 6–9, 24–26.

[67] *Toussaint* (n 190, Ch 1) para 2.12.

[68] Ibid, paras 11.3, 11.4, emphasis added.

Furthermore, the Committee held that everyone has an 'inherent right to life' and that states cannot, *in principle*, make distinctions between regular and irregular migrants. Finally, a differentiation based on the applicant's migratory status which '*could* result in the author's *loss of life* or in *irreversible negative consequences for the author's health*' would not be reasonable, objective or proportionate to the state interest of preventing irregular migration.[69] These findings grounded the decision of a violation of Article 6 (right to life) in conjunction with Article 26 (non-discrimination) of the ICCPR.

This case is significant for at least four reasons. First, it sheds light on a common state approach that restricts irregular migrants' health care to publicly funded medical care in life-saving situations (emergency care) while non-interfering with primary and preventive care provided by private actors such as NGOs. According to the HRCtee, the above practice is not sufficient to meet states' positive obligations regarding the right to life. I would add that these enhanced standards to comply with Article 6 ICCPR substantively align with the treaty-based duties under the ICMW to provide to migrants with 'medical care that is urgently required for the preservation of their life or the avoidance of irreparable harm to their health', regardless of irregularity of status.[70] Second, considering the facts of the case, the health care standards set out encompass the provision of appropriate care of chronic and continuous health needs to avoid irreparable harm rather than one-off medical treatment. Third, the HRCtee has launched a set of arguments which may be employed to push for minimum provisions that indirectly fall under the scope of other socio-economic rights, like urgent social care, the denial of which could jeopardise irreparably migrants' right to life in dignity.[71] Fourth, it rules out immigration control as a proportional justification to differentiate the level of social services that are urgently required for the realisation of the right to life. This means that denying any necessary health care able to prevent irreparable harm to life and health that exceeds emergency treatment as a way of implementing migration policies (to combat irregular migration) is not a reasonable and objective interference with the right to life. This particular argument may be exported to the context of the ICESCR, as discussed in Section 3.3.3, where similar practices are scrutinised for their reasonableness in interfering with the right to health.

---

[69] Ibid, paras 11.7, 11.8, emphasis added.
[70] ICMW (n 42, Introduction) Article 28.
[71] See further details at Section 4.3.2.3.

### 3.3.2 *The Committee on Economic Social and Cultural Rights: Irregular Migrants and the Typologies on Right to Health Obligations*

The CESCR classified human rights obligations and state actions of either an immediate or progressive nature that are helpful for clarifying states' duties concerning the right to health of irregular migrants.

Recalling the 'Respect, Protect, Fulfil' typology, states must meet their 'obligations to respect' the right to health by, *inter alia*, '[r]efraining from denying or limiting equal access for all persons, including prisoners or detainees, minorities, asylum-seekers and illegal immigrants, to preventive, curative and palliative health services [and] abstaining from enforcing discriminatory practices as a State policy.'[72] 'Obligations to protect' bind states to adopt measures, including legislation, to ensure equal access for irregular migrants to health care services provided by third parties. In this regard, privatisation of the health sector may constitute a threat to the availability, accessibility, acceptability and quality of health facilities, goods and services for irregular migrants, as their socioeconomic disadvantage and irregular legal status place them in an especially precarious or vulnerable position vis-à-vis third parties' market regulation of basic services.[73] Finally, 'obligations to fulfil' a genuinely universal right to health require states to grant recognition to the right to health of undocumented people in their legal system and to adopt a detailed national health policy that addresses their health needs. These obligations require that adequate health care information be provided in an understandable language and that the health care system be made genuinely accessible for undocumented people. The Committee, in this regard, has embraced the idea that the ICESCR is a source of 'positive duties to promote equality' in law and policy, which are particularly crucial for underrepresented, powerless and generally vulnerable groups, who may encounter difficulties in directly claiming their human rights in political and legal procedures.[74]

Considering all the various dimensions of health care separately, international human rights law, according to the AAAQ typology, requires states to make health care services, goods and facilities (as well as the underlying determinants of health) 'available', 'accessible' and 'acceptable' and ensure they are of 'good quality'. Scholars and practitioners in the field of human

---

[72] CESCR, GC14 (n 27, Introduction) para 34.
[73] Ibid, para 35.
[74] Fredman (n 312, Ch 2) 299–300.

rights have added 'accountability' and 'participation' to this list.[75] Arguably, the most critical dimensions for irregular migrants as a subgroup of people on the move are acceptability, accessibility, accountability and participation.

The health care system must be acceptable in terms of being culturally appropriate, that is, respectful of 'the culture of individuals, minorities, peoples and communities', including migrants.[76] One way of realising this health-related aim is to adopt a person-centred and differentiated approach to primary care.[77] Furthermore, discrimination in accessing health care, either in the form of ineligibility or excessive limitations on the use of health care services, is a major issue experienced by irregular migrants, as discussed in Section 3.3.3. Denial of accessible health care may also occur when requirements for excessive 'out-of-pocket payments' prevent poor undocumented people from accessing health services, thereby perpetuating discrimination based on their 'economic and social situation'.[78] Regardless of the public or private nature of the service provider, primary and emergency care must remain affordable for everyone. This is also one of the components of the progressive realisation of a UHC.[79] Furthermore, access is de facto restricted or prevented when health care staff have a duty to report irregular migrants to immigration authorities or when no mechanisms are in place to hold service providers to account for refusal of treatment. For instance, the law in Germany states that health care other than emergency treatment should not be free of charge. The cost of the service can be subsidised only if people enter into contact with a social security office, which has a duty to report the status of irregularity to the authorities.[80] In such a case, the entitlement is practically nullified by the combined effect of the non-affordability of the service (an element of 'accessibility' of the right to health) and the measures to combat irregular flows.[81] In Italy, a country where the law is among the least restrictive in the area of access to health care for everyone,[82] administrative barriers to

---

[75]  See *supra* at Section 2.4.2.2.
[76]  CESCR, GC14 (n 27, Introduction) para 12.c.
[77]  WHO and UNICEF (n 1) 14.
[78]  CESCR, GC20 (n 100, Ch 1) para 35.
[79]  UNGA Res 67/81; WHA Res 69.1 (n 179, Ch 2).
[80]  Spencer and Hughes (n 2, Introduction) 12, 16.
[81]  CESCR, CG14 (n 27, Introduction) para 12(b)(iii).
[82]  Legislative Decree no 286 of 25 July 1998, published in the Official Gazette no 191 of 18 August 1998 (Consolidated Immigration Act) Article 35(3): 'Aliens that are present on the national territory, who do not comply with the rules concerning entry and residence, are granted, in public and authorized structures, either *urgent* or *essential* outpatient and hospital treatment and continuative care for diseases and injuries, as well as programmes of preventive medicine for the protection of individual and collective health.'

recouping the cost of the health care service have often led hospitals to turn undocumented people away and informally recommend that they rely on NGO clinics.[83]

Thus, as migrants' legal status can considerably reduce access to health care, in law and in practice, international bodies are beginning to support the idea of 'firewalls', as discussed in Section 3.4.2. This leads to consideration of another critical dimension of the right to health: accountability. Administrative or judicial redress mechanisms must be structured to guarantee the anonymity of undocumented people when they access services to realise their social human rights.[84] Finally, participation is critical for similar reasons. Indeed, it remains difficult for undocumented people to have their voices heard due to their fear of deportation and to general institutional and state-made barriers to their enjoyment of their rights.

These problems were known to the drafters of the Global Compact for Migration, which, in relation to 'access to basic services' for migrants, stipulates that states should commit, *inter alia*, to '[i]ncorporate the health needs of migrants in national and local health care policies and plans, such as by strengthening capacities for service provision, facilitating affordable and non-discriminatory access, reducing communication barriers, and training health care providers on culturally-sensitive service delivery'.[85] However, the Global Compact interprets the principle of non-discrimination in a way that does not completely extend to differentiations based on legal status, stipulating that 'differential provision of services based on migration status might apply'.[86] This may comply with human rights law when differentiation is proportionate and does not result in an undue limitation of health care, which is an assessment that the final text of the Global Compact fails to include. The recommendations of the Global Compact, even though they do not refer explicitly to the establishment of firewalls, emphasise the need not only for formal legal entitlements but also for practical access to health care.[87]

---

[83] FRA (n 6) 41–43; NAGA ONLUS, 'Curare non è permesso: Indagine sull'accesso alle cure per i cittadini stranieri irregolari negli ospedali milanesi – Report' <www.naga.it> accessed 1 March 2020.

[84] See *infra* at Section 3.4.2 regarding 'firewalls'.

[85] GCM (n 92, Ch 1) para 31 (e).

[86] Ibid, 31 (a).

[87] Bethany Hastie, 'GCM Commentary: Objective 15: Provide Access to Basic Services for Migrants' (*Refugee Law Initiative Blog* 15 October 2018) <https://rli.blogs.sas.ac.uk/> accessed 1 March 2021.

### 3.3.3 *Non-discrimination in the Enjoyment of the Right to Health as a Core Obligation of Immediate Nature*

I now present a series of arguments on why the principle of non-discrimination in international human rights law, a rule that must be immediately realised in all human rights frameworks, and a reasonableness test for limitations of rights in the CESCR jurisprudence prevent states from whittling down the right to health of irregular migrants, as vulnerable people, to the provision of emergency or even urgent health care only. The starting point of this analysis is the reach of the CESCR's non-discrimination clause in relation to the unjustifiable differential treatment of similarly situated individuals on prohibited or suspect grounds, which have been interpreted to include nationality or other status: 'The Covenant rights apply to everyone including non-nationals, such as refugees, asylum-seekers, stateless persons, migrant workers and victims of international trafficking, regardless of legal status and documentation.'[88] Nonetheless, differential treatment of irregular migrants may be upheld if it is provided for by law, pursues a legitimate aim and remains proportionate to that aim. The questions of whether the aim of immigration control is a legitimate one and whether curtailing the right to health of irregular migrants is proportionate to that aim have been considered by the CESCR, whose responses are examined in the analysis that follows.

### 3.3.3.1 Emergency Treatment, Non-discrimination and Rights Limitations

Any measure, even if it is justified by reasons of budget or border control, that targets individuals exclusively on the basis of their administrative status and limits their right to health to the extent of providing only urgent or life-saving treatment would seem difficult to defend in the context of the ICESCR-related obligations, where, as we saw previous Chapter 2, the scope and spirit of the right to health is grounded in dignity, equality and equity.

A joint reading of the Preamble, Articles 2(1), 2(2) and 12 ICESCR, as textually and teleologically interpreted,[89] suggests that 'everyone' is prima facie entitled to the right to the highest attainable standard of health, which includes 'the creation of conditions which would assure *to all* medical service and medical attention' and measures targeting 'prevention, treatment and control of epidemic, endemic, occupational and other diseases'.[90] The object

---

[88] CESCR, GC20 (n 100, Ch 1) para 32.
[89] VCLT (n 47, Ch 1) Article 31.
[90] ICESCR (n 23, Introduction) Article 12(2)(c) and (d).

and purpose of the treaty (namely, the universal, progressive and best realisation of socioeconomic rights and the prompt elimination of discrimination in the enjoyment of these rights) would be hindered by too restrictive an interpretation of health-related duties, such as considering that the provision of emergency or urgent care is the adequate standard of care for irregular migrants, without any commitment to increase the scope of their rights. This treaty and the CESCR's jurisprudence subscribe to an idea of substantive equality with regard to access to health care, according to which equal opportunities to achieve the highest attainable standard of health or the enhancement of everyone's capability to be healthy cannot simply be met by the sole provision of emergency or urgent care in health systems.

Similar conclusions can be derived from Article 4 ICESCR. Indeed, legal rights limitations must be compatible with the 'nature' of rights: the spirit and scope of the right to health, as elaborated in the ICESCR, extend beyond life-saving treatment and are vulnerability- or equity-oriented. Furthermore, it is debatable, from both a public health and a budgetary perspective, whether the criterion of promoting the 'general welfare of a society as a whole' (another condition or legitimate aim for rights' limitations) is met by leaving irregular migrants, who are part of the state demos, without, *inter alia*, preventive and primary care that is made generally available in a particular country. Meeting only the emergency health needs of a part of the population without adopting a preventive approach – for instance, in relation to infectious diseases – may expose the population at large to higher public health–related risks.[91] Moreover, interdisciplinary studies with a focus on a budgetary (cost–benefit) analysis have demonstrated that the cost associated with urgent or emergency health interventions is higher than that of implementing preventive and essential primary care, whose function is to reduce requests for urgent and hospital care.[92]

---

[91] Vearey, Hui and Wickramage (n 33, Introduction) 209–228; CMW Committee, UN SR on the Human Rights of Migrants, OHCHR, SR on Refugees [...] and Migrant in Africa of the African Commission on Human and Peoples' Rights, the SR of the Secretary General on Migration and Refugees of the CoE and the Rapporteur on the Rights of Migrants of the IACmHR, 'Joint Guidance Note on Equitable Access to COVID-19 Vaccines for All Migrants' (8 March 2021) 2.

[92] European Union Agency for Fundamental Rights, *Cost of Exclusion from Healthcare: The Case of Migrants in an Irregular Situation* (EU Publishing 2015); Ursula Trummer et al., under the overall guidance of IOM Europe, 'Cost Analysis of Health Care Provision for Irregular Migrants and EU Citizens without Insurance. Final report' (December 2016); David Ingleby and Roumyana Petrova-Benedict 'Recommendations on Access to Health Services for Migrants in an Irregular Situation: An Expert Consensus' (2016) IOM Europe; WHO, *Technical Series on Primary Health Care – Building the Economic Case for Primary Health Care: A Scoping Review* (Doc no WHO/HIS/SDS/2018.48, 2018).

As the limitation to rights realisation at stake here targets a particular social group, it is worth examining the operationalisation of the non-discrimination principle in this legal framework. Where states put forward an economic argument to limit services to a part of the population, the rule of international human rights law is that, in general, the basis of a lack of available resources is not an objective and reasonable justification per se to operate differentiations targeting marginalised and disadvantaged groups.[93] Based on Article 2(2) ICESCR, read in conjunction with Article 2(1) ICESCR, the CESCR has established that when resources are available to realise elements of the right to health care, their use should not perpetrate unjustified detrimental differentiation (i.e. discrimination).[94]

Even considering the protection of public resources or the implementation of migration policies as elements of a legitimate state interest falling under 'the general welfare of the society as a whole',[95] the withdrawal of health care rights or their reduction to emergency care in the case of irregular migrants would constitute a detrimental differentiation and would be difficult to defend in a 'proportionality' test. This test would entail verifying whether the restrictive measure is suited to the legitimate purpose and ensuring that the relationship between the purpose of the measures or omissions and their effects on the rights of target people are reasonable. It would also include assessing whether the least restrictive measures have been considered and whether the measures adopted disproportionally impact on certain individuals or groups.[96] In relation to the latter, the existing case law of the CESCR, in communication procedures on other subject matters, demonstrates that the scrutiny of reasonableness and proportionality is assessed more strictly in relation to state measures affecting vulnerable people and groups.[97]

Despite the above remarks, policies on the removal of irregular migrants and the reduction of what states often define as 'pull factors'[98] have continued in many countries, where the health-related rights of migrants are severely

---

[93] CESCR, GC14 (n 27, Introduction) para 13.
[94] ICESCR (n 23, Introduction) Article 2(2): 'The States Parties to the present Covenant undertake to guarantee that the rights enunciated in the present Covenant will be exercised without discrimination of any kind'; CESCR, GC14 (n 27, Introduction) para 52 indicates as example of the violation of the obligation to fulfil the right to health 'insufficient expenditure or misallocation of public resources which results in the non-enjoyment of the right to health by individuals or groups, particularly the vulnerable or marginalized'.
[95] López Rodríguez v Spain (n 231, Ch 2) para 13.3.
[96] Yutaka Arai-Takahashi, 'Proportionality' in Shelton (n 39, Ch 1) 446.
[97] Liebenberg (n 230, Ch 2) 83–84; see also Sections 2.5.2 and 2.7.2– 2.7.4.
[98] Bernard Ryan and Virginia Mantouvalou, 'The Labour and Social Rights of Migrants in International Law' in Rubio-Marín (n 8) 177.

legally or factually curtailed.[99] This did not go unnoticed in the CESCR's COs, which, as previously explained, are the outcomes of the periodic state reporting mechanism.[100] In its assessment of state reports regarding non-discrimination and irregular migration, the Committee has adopted different approaches: (1) it has explicitly expressed concern about de facto and de jure discrimination affecting the right to health of irregular migrants;[101] (2) it has mentioned suspected differential treatment, often expressing concern about the accessibility of the health system, but without qualifying it as discrimination;[102] (3) notwithstanding the reference to non-justified or suspected differential treatment during the reporting cycle, it has not raised any specific issue in its final recommendations.[103] Regarding the first two points, since the purpose of the monitoring procedure is not to find violations but to make recommendations, the presence or the absence of the word 'discrimination' may not appear crucial. However, the absence of any mention of concern – the third point above – indicated missed opportunities for both developing a consistent international practice and pushing for the improvement of domestic standards.

Against this background, the adoption of the CESCR's 2017 statement on state duties towards refugees and migrants – which, in principle, considers as discrimination any differential treatment on the basis of irregular legal status and where irregular or undocumented migrants are qualified as especially vulnerable people that 'must enjoy the minimum content of the Covenant rights'[104] – may prove useful for the future development of a consistent and protective jurisprudence, including in the context of the CESCR's complaint

---

[99]  FRA Report (n 6) 71 and Spencer and Hughes (n 2, Introduction) 9–29.

[100]  See *supra* at Section 2.4.3.1.

[101]  For example, CESCR, List of issues in relation to the report of Cyprus (12 April 2013) E/C.12/CYP/Q/6, para 9; CESCR, COs on the report of Norway (13 December 2013) E/C.12/NOR/CO/5, paras 7 and 21.

[102]  See CESCR, COs on the report of Finland (17 December 2014) E/C.12/FIN/CO/6, para 27; CESCR, COs on the report of France (n 20) paras 21, 47.

[103]  See fourth periodic report submitted by Belgium to the CESCR (9 July 2010) E/C.12/BEL/4, para 243 'Although illegal immigrants can only claim emergency medical care [...]'. No further mention of undocumented migrants appears in subsequent documents or in the 2013 COs on Belgian report; CESCR, replies to the list of issues to the report of Sweden (6 April 2016) E/C.12/SWE/Q/6/Add.1, para 115: 'Asylum seekers and undocumented persons that are 18 years of age and above shall be offered health and dental care that cannot be deferred.' In the subsequent COs on the report of Sweden (n 208, Ch 2), while concern was raised in relation to the adequate access to healthcare for asylum seekers (paras 31–32), the Committee did not issue similar recommendations in relation to undocumented migrants despite the fact that they received the same restricted access according to the domestic legislation.

[104]  CESCR, Statement on migrant rights (n 174, Ch 1) 9–12.

procedure. Over the last two years, this approach has been explicitly mentioned in a significant number of COs touching upon discrimination against
migrant populations with regard to the enjoyment of and social rights.[105]

### 3.3.3.2 Core Obligations, Non-discrimination and the Levels of Accessible Care

The ICESCR normally imposes obligations on states to progressively realise
rights within the limits of available resources, thus granting states a certain
margin of appreciation. However, a textual interpretation of Article 2(2)
indicates that, regardless of the stage of realisation of a certain right, states
must make immediately accessible to all, without discrimination against
especially vulnerable people, those health-related services and goods that are
available to general users. In several countries of the Global North, the
Committee has raised particular concern about the lack of accessibility of
services for vulnerable groups, including irregular migrants, due to legal or
factual barriers rather than identifying problems about the very existence
(availability) of health care services for mainstream population.[106]

As previously indicated, the CESCR's General Comment No. 14 has
shaped the principle of non-discrimination as a fundamental element of state
core obligations concerning the right to health and health care, by listing,
*inter alia*, the core obligations to ensure access to existing health services and
essential drugs that are equitably distributed 'on a non-discriminatory basis,
especially for vulnerable or marginalized groups'. Core obligations also
include the adoption and implementation of 'a national public health strategy
and plan of action [. . .] addressing the health concerns of the whole population [. . .] with particular attention to all vulnerable or marginalized groups'.[107]

These baseline obligations reflect minimum initial steps that states
must take while working towards the goal of establishing a universally
inclusive health system,[108] based on substantive equality or equity and aimed

---

[105] For example, CESCR, COs on the report of South Africa (28 November 2018) E/C.12/ZAF/
CO/1, para 27; Slovakia (14 November 2019) E/C.12/SVK/CO/3, para 21; Belgium (26 March
2020) E/C.12/BEL/CO/5, para 23; Norway (2 April 2020) E/C.12/NOR/CO/6 para 39.

[106] For example, CESCR, COs on the report of Austria (13 December 2013) E/C.12/AUT/CO/4,
paras 21–22; list of issues in relation to the report of the UK (3 November 2015) E/C.12/GBR/Q/
6, para 26.

[107] CESCR, GC14 (n 27, Introduction) para 43, (a), (d), (e) and (f).

[108] CESCR, 'Guidelines on Reporting' (n 195, Ch 2) para 55: 'Indicate whether the State party has
adopted a national health policy and whether a national health system with universal access to
primary health care is in place.'

at meeting people's health needs or supporting their 'capability to be healthy'.[109]

Core obligations and rights – which are intensely debated concepts in the legal literature[110] – have been developed in order to prevent the progressive realisation of socioeconomic rights from undermining or delaying the implementation of minimum or essential levels of each right.[111] Although these have been criticised for creating 'ceilings' of protection with regard to social rights, this concern is arguably more relevant in relation to mainstream implementation rather than for those social groups who struggle to gain access to basic services. For the latter, core obligations, in conjunction with the non-discrimination rule, may be more beneficial than harmful.

With regard to the right to health, the Committee has established that, in accordance with the compelling findings of the Declaration of Alma-Ata on PHC,[112] states have a minimum duty to guarantee, at the very least, 'essential primary health care'.[113] Given that the non-discrimination clause in the ICESCR is not subject to the rule of progressive realisation and that core obligations apply particularly to vulnerable people or groups, states ought to guarantee irregular migrants access to services, conditions and goods that implement or at least do not contradict the operationalisation of the concept of PHC.

Recalling the findings of Chapter 2, it is important to clarify that the Alma-Ata standard of essential 'primary health care' does not only mean the provision of health care but also includes the social or underlying determinants of health within the scope of health-related measures.[114] Leaving the analysis of the determinants of health to Chapter 4, as far as health care is concerned, PHC means 'essential health care' that 'addresses the main health problems in the community, providing promotive, preventive, curative and rehabilitative services' and that 'includes at least [...] appropriate treatment of common diseases and injuries; [the] provision of essential drugs [and] immunization against major infectious diseases'.[115] Forty years after Alma-Ata, the WHO-backed Declaration of Astana on PHC clarified that '[m]eeting people's *health*

[109] Daniels (n 26, Introduction) 20–21; Venkatapuram (n 67, Ch 2).
[110] Legal scholars have not reached agreement on whether core obligations are to be intended as obligations of conduct or obligations of result, on whether they are non-derogable or retractable in nature, or on whether are universal or country-specific in application. See Section 2.4.2.4.
[111] CESCR, GC3 (n 80, Ch 2) para 10.
[112] Declaration of Alma-Ata (n 28, Introduction).
[113] CESCR, GC14 (n 27, Introduction) para 43.
[114] Declaration of Alma-Ata (n 28, Introduction); Potts (n 164, Ch 2) 93–111.
[115] Ibid (Alma-Ata) para VII; Toebes (n 1, Ch 2) 348.

*needs* through comprehensive and integrated health services (promotive, protective, preventive, curative, rehabilitative and palliative) throughout the life course [requires] *prioritizing primary care* and *essential public health functions*'.[116] An acknowledgement of this model can also be extracted from the list of CESCR's 'obligations of comparable priority' regarding the right to health.[117]

The frameworks of core obligations and those of comparable priority to core obligations are also substantially harmonised with the UN's recommendation for achieving UHC as an element of sustainable development, which is also focused on affordability and vulnerability and, as such, is able to shape particularly beneficial rules for irregular migrants in terms of policies and service provision. Indeed, on several occasions, the UNGA and the WHA have clarified that UHC includes 'access, without discrimination, to nationally determined sets of the needed promotive, preventive, curative and rehabilitative basic health services [. . .] with a special emphasis on the poor, vulnerable and marginalized segments of the population',[118] and that the PHC approach is instrumental for achieving UHC.[119]

A public health–oriented international human rights law requires states to regulate and extend to irregular migrants, at least, essential preventive and primary care services – which are critical to prevent and mitigate heath inequalities[120] – together with urgent and emergency treatment[121] and essential drugs[122] that are made available to the rest of population.[123]

Nevertheless, the COs of the CESCR have not always been unequivocal on this point. At times, reference has been made to the lack of 'adequate' health care for irregular migrants,[124] which seems to hint at a threshold of provision that is not so different from the health care that must be provided to citizens and regular migrants.[125] In other documents, it is noted that emergency health

---

[116] WHA 72.2 and WHO A72/12 (n 176, Ch 2), emphasis added.

[117] CESCR, GC14 (n 27, Introduction) para 44, at n 150, Ch 2.

[118] UNGA Res 67/81; WHA Res 69.1; Forman et al. (n 179, Ch 2) 23–34.

[119] WHO A72/12 (n 176, Ch 2).

[120] See Section 2.4.2.5.

[121] *Toussaint* (n 190, Ch 1).

[122] Provision of essential drugs are explicitly mentioned as mainstream and migrant related core obligations in CESCR, GC14 (n 27, Introduction) para 43 (d); CESCR, Statement on migrant rights (n 174, Ch 1) para 9.

[123] Similarly, see Pinto de Albuquerque (n 286, Ch 2).

[124] CESCR's COs on the reporting cycles of: France (n 20) para 47, Austria (n 105) para 21.

[125] Gillian MacNaughton, 'Beyond a Minimum Threshold: The Right to Social Equality' in Lanse Minkler (ed) *The State of Economic and Social Human Rights* (CUP 2013) 282–284.

care is not enough and that 'basic' services should be provided.[126] The word 'basic' is confusing: it can be understood as referring to rights that are preconditions of other rights,[127] the type of services that should be offered[128] or a minimal, although not specified, level of entitlement. Recent monitoring findings have even emphasised the need to provide irregular migrants with 'equal' access to care vis-à-vis the rest of the population to avoid discrimination or to make PHC accessible.[129] Considering the CESCR's quasi-judicial powers, which are based on persuasion rather than on formal legal power, greater rigour and consistency of arguments, resorting to legal and metal-legal sources and to explicit references to the techniques of interpretation of international law[130] could enhance the position of the Committee in providing useful ICESCR-based guidance on legal and policy change for those countries that guarantee either no health care services or only emergency treatment, thereby reducing, factually or administratively, access to health care for irregular migrants vis-à-vis other population groups.[131]

Before concluding the normative analysis of the right to health care of undocumented migrants in the ICESCR framework, it is worth making a brief digression to consider the human rights standards required by the ICMW. The text of this UN human rights treaty, which remains substantially unratified in Europe, reduces the enjoyment of the right to health by irregular migrants to 'medical care that is urgently required for the preservation of their life or the avoidance of irreparable harm to their health'. This adds a cause for confusion regarding the international obligations of states that have ratified both the ICESCR and ICMW.[132] While this text excludes non-urgent care for irregular migrants from the human rights standards under the ICMW, medical care that prevents 'irreparable harm to health' can constitute, as the HRCtee demonstrated, a potentially expansive standard that exceeds life-saving treatment.[133] Furthermore, the CMW Committee, in its General

---

[126] CESCR's COs on the reporting cycles of: Denmark (6 June 2013) E/C.12/DNK/CO/5, para 18; Greece (n 201, Ch 2) para 36.

[127] Shue (n 115, Ch 2).

[128] For example, the GCM (n 92, Ch 1) Objective 15 urges states to 'provide access to basic services for migrants'.

[129] For example, CESCR, COs on the report of Israel (12 November 2019) E/C.12/ISR/CO/4, para 57; Denmark (12 November 2019) E/C.12/DNK/CO/6, para 63; Finland (30 March 2021) E/C.12/FIN/CO/7, para 42; Norway (n 91) paras 38, 39.

[130] Angeleri (n 339, Ch 2) 190.

[131] FRA Report (n 6) 71–83.

[132] ICMW (n 42, Introduction) Article 28; see Section 1.4.1.

[133] This is one of the core arguments of *Toussaint* case (n 190, Ch 1). See Section 3.3.1.

Comment No. 2, resolved the clash between these treaty norms by favouring the more protective standards as follows:

> States parties are [...] obliged to ensure that all persons, irrespective of their migration status, have effective access to at least a minimum level of health care on a non-discriminatory basis. The Committee on Economic, Social and Cultural Rights considers this to encompass primary health care, as well as preventive, curative and palliative health services.[134]

In spite of its welcomed protective outcome, this approach has been criticised in the legal literature for failing to set out an explicit 'legal rationale' by recommending greater emphasis and reliance on the purposive criterion of interpretation of international law and on the Fragmentation Report of the International Law Commission,[135] again to enhance the credibility of the quasi-judicial findings of the UN treaty bodies.[136]

### 3.3.3.3 What Is 'Essential' Primary Health Care?

Core obligations regarding the right to health in the CESCR's General Comments 3 and 14 refer to the standard of 'essential primary health care'. While the meanings of 'primary care' and PHC were clarified and emphasised in Chapter 2 as key components of the scope of the right to health,[137] it is important to question what 'essential' stands for in the context of core obligations to limit the excessively discretional interpretation and implementation of human rights obligations. The adjective 'essential' is synonymous with 'extremely important' or 'fundamental'[138] or refers to something 'that is such by its essence'. Placed near 'health care' or 'care', it expresses an order of priorities in health care or medical care or a set of care and cure that are necessary to meet people's health needs or free individual health-related capabilities. If it accompanies 'primary health care', it indicates that at least key elements of the PHC model ought to be pursued by states and corresponding services should be made available and accessible to people.

---

[134] CMW, GC2 (n 16, Introduction) para 72.

[135] UNGA, Fragmentation of International Law (n 208, Ch 1).

[136] Claire Lougarre, 'The Protection of Non-nationals' Economic, Social and Cultural Rights in UN Human Rights Treaties' (2020) *International Human Rights Law Review* 9 252–290, referring in particular to the Fragmentation Report at 288: 'regard[ing] conflicts between human rights norms [...] the one that is more favourable to the protected interests is usually held overriding'.

[137] See Section 2.4.2.5.

[138] Oxford Dictionaries, 'essential' <https://en.oxforddictionaries.com/definition/essential> accessed 1 March 2021.

However, focusing on the 'level' of care rather than on the PHC 'strategy', it is worth noting that the specific human interest to which health care is essential is open to question in human rights law. Emergency or urgent care are, respectively, instrumental or essential for preserving a person's vital functioning or avoiding 'serious, rapid and irreversible decline in his or her state of health associated with intense suffering' (as related to the right to enjoying life in dignity and freedom from ill treatment).[139] Other levels of health care, including 'preventive', 'primary care', are instrumental or essential for securing good health outcomes or preserving capabilities to be healthy, normally outside life-saving situations and above a healthy subsistence threshold.[140]

A certain number of international documents, including the CESCR's General Comment No. 3 in relation to core obligations and the Declarations of Alma-Ata and Astana, employ 'essential' in relation to standards of treatment and health care.[141] These documents refer to 'essential' health care as something distinct from emergency care. For instance, the EU Return Directive, a piece of EU law which sets out rules governing the return of irregular migrants to their origin countries, mentions 'emergency health care and essential treatment of illness',[142] and the Declaration of Astana refers to states' commitment to:

> Enhance capacity and infrastructure for primary care – the first contact with health services – prioritizing essential public health functions [. . .] to meet all people's health needs across the life course through comprehensive preventive, promotive, curative, rehabilitative services and palliative care.[143]

The priority that global health initiatives – such as PHC and UHC – and human rights law accord to vulnerable people would be hindered if one vulnerable group, such as 'irregular migrants', received only emergency or urgent treatment and was thus ineligible for essential preventive and primary care services available in the country. Such a concern was raised by the CESCR in relation to the 2012 restrictive and retrogressive Spanish act that regulated access to health care for irregular migrants in terms of exceptional

---

[139] *Paposhvili* (n 122, Ch 1) para 183.
[140] King (n 140, Ch 2) 29.
[141] CESCR, GC3 (n 80, Ch 2); Declaration of Alma-Ata (n 28, Introduction); Declaration of Astana (n 174, Ch 2).
[142] European Parliament and Council Directive 2008/115/EC of 16 December 2008 laying down common standards and procedures in Member States for returning illegally staying third-country nationals [2008] OJ L348/98, Article 14.1(b).
[143] Declaration of Astana (n 174, Ch 2) para V.

and urgent treatment only. In that case, the CESCR pushed its jurisprudence to the point of urging Spain to take 'all necessary steps to ensure that irregular migrants have access to all necessary health-care services, without discrimination'.[144] This generous approach is confirmed in the COs on the 2018 report of Germany, in which the state is recommended to adopt 'all measures necessary to ensure that all persons in the State party [...] have equal access to preventive, curative and palliative health services, regardless of their legal status and documentation' and to review restrictive domestic law and policies.[145] Finally, the special rapporteur on the right to health stated that 'the principle of non-discriminatory access is eroded when irregular migrant workers are not allowed to access non-emergency health care services'.[146]

As such, placed near 'primary (health) care' (e.g. in General Comments 3 and 14), the world 'essential' is indicative of the fact that while states have a certain margin of discretion in shaping preventive and primary care policies and services (with regard to irregular migrants), these cannot exclude preventive check-ups, essential vaccinations and the treatment of common diseases in primary care settings. Furthermore, the establishment of UHC policies that explicitly commit to prioritising the poor and marginalised in the process of expanding coverage and in determining which services to provide in order to avoid entrenching inequalities in health[147] would inevitably encompass preventive and primary care.

While full clarity is still somewhat lacking on what 'essential' health care is in international law, it seems sufficiently clear that this does not correspond to 'emergency or urgent' medical treatment but extends to certain elements of the PHC approach, at least under international human rights law and the recommendations of global health governance.

### 3.4  LEVELLING-UP DEVELOPMENTS

This section sheds light on some important developments that confirm a progressive trend in human rights law concerning the conceptualisation and operationalisation of the right to health care of vulnerable people, including irregular migrants and subcategories of this group, beyond an emergency paradigm. These include, first, the statements of both the CESCR and the

---

[144] CESCR, COs on the report of Spain (25 April 2018) E/C.12/ESP/CO/6, paras 41–42.
[145] CESCR, COs on the report of Germany (27 November 2018) E/C.12/DEU/CO/6, para 59.
[146] Grover (n 253, Ch 2) para 40.
[147] Pūras (n 185, Ch 2) para 17. See also, UNGA Res 67/81; WHA Res 69.1, Forman et al. (n 179, Ch 2) 23–34.

ECSR on austerity measures and the statements of these and other treaty bodies on the response to the COVID-19 pandemic, which prioritise the protection of the worst off. Second, a growing number of international human rights bodies have started to support the idea that public service delivery should be strictly separated from public immigration authorities and, thus, be practically accessible. Third, especially protective human rights standards have been adopted in the areas of sexual and reproductive health and children's health to the extent that differentiations between irregular migrants and country nationals are, in these fields, largely outlawed in human rights law.

### 3.4.1 *Vulnerable Migrants and Their Protection in Economic and Health Crises*

The financial and economic crisis that began in 2007 and the intensification of austerity policies to mitigate the crisis over the following years proved particularly detrimental to the implementation of sustainable welfare models and the realisation of social rights in general.[148] Cuts to public spending have had a negative impact on socioeconomic rights because the latter are so sensitive to resource allocation. This has exposed the economic vulnerability of the worst off, including irregular migrants.[149]

For instance, in the 2010s, resource constraints were used to justify a substandard right to health care for migrants in an irregular situation. In Greece, severe public cuts generated a crisis in the health system,[150] justifying the retention of domestic legislation that bars irregular migrants from accessing health care, save for the most urgent and life-saving treatment. In the UK, where irregular migrants are entitled to free GP 'consultations' but only if they manage to be accepted onto a GP's list,[151] the health-related entitlements of irregular migrants have been restricted in recent years,[152] and public discussions on extending charges for primary care services have recently taken

---

[148] Nolan (n 8, Introduction) 2; Diego Giannone, 'Measuring and Monitoring Social Rights in a Neoliberal Age: Between the United Nations' Rhetoric and States' Practice' (2015) *Global Change, Peace & Security* 27(2) 173, 176–179.

[149] This section (particularly 3.4.1 and 3.4.1.1) is adapted from Angeleri (n 339, Ch 2) 182.

[150] CESCR, Replies to the List of issues to the second periodic report of Greece (6 August 2015) E/C.12/GRC/Q/2/Add.1, para 102.

[151] Milena Chimienti and John Solomos, 'How Do International Human Rights Influence National Healthcare Provisions for Irregular Migrants? A Case Study in France and the United Kingdom' (2015) *Journal of Human Rights* 1, 1–5.

[152] CESCR, COs on the periodic report of the UK (n 203, Ch 2) para 55.

place.[153] Spain is the most prominent example of a state where, during the last decade, unlawful, discriminatory and explicitly retrogressive measures have targeted irregular migrants. Criticism from advocacy and international bodies had been strong, and it is only recently, after most Spanish regions – taking advantage of their high degree of autonomy in the area of health – restored universal public health services for everyone, that the central government has lifted the limitations on access and care for irregular migrants.[154]

In consideration of the special vulnerability of disadvantaged and marginalised groups in crisis contexts and vis-à-vis financial adjustment measures, during the economic crisis of the last decade, both the CESCR and the ECSR have developed international legal arguments to resist retrogressive measures, including measures related to the accessibility and quality of health care. Other crisis-response statements have been adopted since the onset of the COVID-19 pandemic that have elaborated on the barriers to and actions for ensuring irregular migrants' access to essential services.

### 3.4.1.1 The CESCR's Approach vis-à-vis the Financial and Economic Crisis: Non-retrogression and Non-discrimination

The response of the CESCR to the economic crisis and austerity came a little late with the Committee Chairman's 2012 Open Letter to States Parties.[155] This statement, while loosening the prima facie ban on retrogressive measures,[156] insisted that the principle of non-discrimination in relation to vulnerable groups and the core content of rights should not be affected by temporary and proportionate austerity measures and legislative setbacks. As such, the

---

[153] Department of Health, 'Making a Fair Contribution: A Consultation on the Extension of Charging Overseas Visitors and Migrants Using the NHS in England' (2015) Visitor and Migrant NHS Cost Recovery Programme. For a 'clinical' perspective on this initiative, see Lucinda Hiam and Martin McKee, 'Making a Fair Contribution: Is Charging Migrants for Healthcare in Line with NHS Principles?' (2016) *Journal of the Royal Society of Medicine* 109 (6) 226.

[154] For further details, see Boso and Vancea (n 9) and PICUM (n 9); Real Decreto-ley 7/2018 'Acceso universal al Sistema Nacional de Salud' (27 July 2018) in Spanish <www.boe.es/diario_boe/txt.php?id=BOE-A-2018–10752> accessed 15 January 2021.

[155] CESCR, 'Letter to States Parties' (n 203, Ch 2).

[156] The 'Letter' (ibid) represented a paradigmatic shift from a 'business as usual model' within ICESCR that allowed flexibility through Article 2(1) and 4 but barred exceptional or emergency responses – reflected in the doctrine of non-retrogression – to an 'accommodation model' which allows derogation-style deviations from the Covenant. See the critical remarks of Ben T. C. Warwick, 'Socio-Economic Rights During Economic Crises: A Changed Approach to Non-retrogression' (2016) *International and Comparative Law Quarterly* 65(1) 249.

right to essential PHC of irregular migrants should be safeguarded against austerity measures and should not be subject to discriminatory retrogressive laws, policies or practices.

Against this human rights framework, the narrative of crisis has fuelled domestic setbacks in Spain, and in Greece it has justified the maintenance of a discriminatory status quo with the erroneous identification of emergency care as the minimum acceptable standard of care for people in irregular situations.[157] Economic justifications appeared to hide the ever-present tension between human rights regimes at the international level and those at the level of the nation-state and their different ideas about entitlement to rights.[158]

The reaction of the Committee to domestic reluctance to properly implement international standards of health care for irregular migrants in times of crisis has not always been unequivocal in terms of either legal argumentation or terminology. The Committee has more frequently mentioned its 2012 Open Letter (which set out the official approach to economic crisis-related retrogressive measures) in relation to those European countries that have used the 'narrative of crisis' in their reports[159] and has explicitly condemned the limitation of medical care to emergency care for people of irregular status in the cases of Greece, Spain and the UK.[160] Without reference to the crisis, concerns about retrogressive measures and the provision of only emergency health care were raised in the reporting documents of several northern European states.[161] The most recent COs regarding Norway explicitly raise human rights concerns about the fact that retrogressive measures affecting the availability and accessibly of PHC for irregular migrants have not been withdrawn in almost a decade.[162]

---

[157] In 2012, in consideration of the measures of austerity that hit the public services, the Minister of Health reminded public hospitals' personnel not to provide free medical care beyond 'emergency care'. Charges applies even to maternal care. See, PICUM, Picum Bullettin (29 May 2012) <https://picum.org/picum-bulletin-29-may-2012/> accessed 15 November 2020; Spencer and Hughes (n 2, Introduction) 17.

[158] Chimienti and Solomos (n 150) 1–5.

[159] For example, CESCR's COs on the periodic report of Spain (n 143); Iceland (11 December 2012) E/C.12/ISL/CO/4; Portugal (8 December 2014) E/C.12/PRT/CO/4; Czech Republic (23 June 2014) E/C.12/CZE/CO/2; Romania (9 December 2014) E/C.12/ROU/CO/3–5; Italy (n 201, Ch 2); Greece (n 201, Ch 2); Ireland (n 201, Ch 2); the UK (n 203, Ch 2).

[160] CESCR, COs on periodic report of Greece (ibid) para 35; Spain (ibid) paras 41–42; UK (ibid) paras 18, 55, 56.

[161] CESCR, COs on the report of Finland (n 100) para 27; Norway (n 101) para 21; similarly: 'The Committee is concerned that irregular migrants [. . .] do not have access to health-care services other than emergency health-care services'; Germany (n 144); Denmark (n 125) 12, 63.

[162] CESCR, COs on the report of Norway (n 101) paras 38–39.

### 3.4.1.2 The ECSR and Austerity in Europe

Before the CESCR issued its 'open letter', the ECSR had issued a clear-cut statement on the effective realisation of social rights in cases of budgetary austerity. This is included in the 2009 General Introduction to the Conclusions and spells out that 'governments are bound to take all necessary steps to ensure that the rights of the Charter are effectively guaranteed at a period of time when beneficiaries need the protection most'.[163]

Budget cuts to public spending may be a public interest worthy of consideration, but European social rights law, in relation to people's economic vulnerability in times of crisis, requires states to fully honour their international progressive duties under the ESC. In particular, the ESC requires states that wish to take urgent measures to combat the economic crisis to conduct 'the minimum level of research and analysis into the effects of such far-reaching measures that is necessary to assess in a meaningful manner their full impact on vulnerable groups in society'.[164]

As far as the undocumented are concerned, against the often-recalled background of retrogressive measures introduced in Spain in 2012 that withdrew irregular migrants' access to health care except in 'special situations', the ECSR expressed serious concerns about the legitimacy of such measures, stating, *inter alia*, that 'the economic crisis cannot serve as a pretext for a restriction or denial of access to health care that affects the very substance of that right'.[165] This conclusion seems to represent an advance vis-à-vis the position held in the collective complaints procedure that the health and social care of irregular migrants are of concern for the ECSR only when their health and social needs are sufficiently 'urgent and severe'.[166] The progressive full realisation of the social rights of people in vulnerable or precarious situations, including irregular migrants, remains a core issue for the ECSR to monitor, in times of economic crisis and austerity as at any other time.

### 3.4.1.3 The COVID-19 Pandemic and Vulnerability-Targeted Measures

The COVID-19 pandemic is having devastating consequences throughout the world in all spheres of life and has drawn the world's attention to the importance of having adequate public health policies, protocols for the

---

[163] ECSR, General Introduction to Conclusions XIX–2 2009, para 15.
[164] *IKA-ETAM v Greece* (n 354, Ch 2) para 79.
[165] ECSR, Conclusions XX–2 Spain, Article 11(1) ESC.
[166] See *supra* at Section 3.2.2.

surveillance and containment of highly infectious diseases and sufficiently funded and functioning health systems able to perform testing and tracing and provide treatment and care. Unfortunately, as the CESCR ascertained, 'health-care systems and social programmes' have been 'weakened by decades of underinvestment' – a process 'accelerated by the global financial crisis of 2007–2008' – and have thus proved overall 'ill equipped to respond effectively and expeditiously to the intensity of the current pandemic'.[167]

A significant number of human rights bodies, including the CESCR and ECSR, have embarked on the drafting of many interpretative statements, reports and operational guidelines on the respect for human rights during a pandemic, including on the socioeconomic rights of vulnerable groups.[168]

The pandemic itself and the corresponding containment measures have had an especially detrimental impact on the worst off, particularly migrants who work in the informal sector in unstable jobs and who live in substandard accommodation with reduced access to medical care, education and social welfare. All of these are risk factors for human rights violations of an inter-related nature because substandard living and working conditions expose people to higher risk of infection and to higher risk of not being able to cope with the socioeconomic consequences of stay-at-home orders and out-of-work periods: migrants 'who are in an irregular situation or undocumented are in a situation of even greater vulnerability' than regular migrants.[169] In the case of irregular migrants, precarious living conditions are exacerbated by their invisibility to state authorities and by the radical lack of social entitlements in several domestic legal frameworks. This situation represents a 'vivid illustrat [ion] of the importance of indivisibility and interdependence of human rights'.[170] As indicated in Section 3.4.2, the actual enjoyment of social rights via service provisions may necessitate, in pandemic times especially, the regulatory and administrative separation between immigration authorities and agencies entrusted with essential service provision.

---

[167] CESCR, 'Statement on the Coronavirus Disease (COVID-19) Pandemic and Economic, Social and Cultural Rights' (17 April 2020) E/C.12/2020/1, para 4.

[168] Many of these are collected at OHCHR, 'COVID-19 and Human Rights Treaty Bodies' <www .ohchr.org/EN/HRBodies/Pages/COVID-19-and-TreatyBodies.aspx>; OHCHR, 'Covid-19 and Special Procedures' www.ohchr.org/EN/HRBodies/SP/Pages/COVID-19-and-Special-Procedures.aspx; ECSR, 'Social Rights in Times of Pandemic' <www.coe.int/en/web/european-social-charter/social-rights-in-times-of-pandemic> accessed 15 December 2020.

[169] CMW Committee and Felipe González Morales as UN special rapporteur on the human rights of migrants, 'Joint Guidance Note on the Impacts of the COVID-19 Pandemic on the Human Rights of Migrants' (26 May 2020) para 1.

[170] CESCR, Statement on Covid-19 (n 166) para 3.

During the first year of the pandemic, the ECSR periodically issued statements to interpret the ESC-related obligations in times of pandemics while 'ensuring lasting progress with respect to social rights', starting with one six-page document on how to interpret Article 11 ESC. To comply with the Charter's health-related obligations, states must demonstrate their 'ability to cope with infectious diseases', which entails adopting targeted law, policy and practices of a preventive, curative and promotional nature.[171] Irregular migrants are highlighted as a group at 'particularly high risk' who 'must be adequately protected by the healthcare measures put in place'.[172] Indeed, this approach explicitly pursues '[h]ealth equity as defined by the World Health Organisation (WHO) [. . . and] specifically, the absence of avoidable, unfair, or remediable differences among groups of people, whether those groups are defined socially, economically, demographically or geographically or by other means of stratification'.[173] These rules are once again complemented by the aforementioned state obligations of non-retrogression and non-discrimination in enjoying the right to health and other socioeconomic rights, which remain fundamental normative cornerstones of human rights law, including during the COVID-19 pandemic and connected economic downturns.[174]

Finally, even before the start of the rollout of COVID-19 vaccinations, the CESCR made public a statement on 'universal and equitable access to vaccines for the coronavirus disease', based on 'medical needs and public health grounds', as a 'priority obligation concerning the right to health' and the right to enjoy the benefits of scientific progress under the ICESCR.[175] The CESCR considers the maintenance of discriminatory barriers to access to vaccines based on, *inter alia*, migration status, social status and poverty to be incompatible with the international human rights framework. The Committee emphasised that those people who are particularly exposed to the virus because of the interplay between several unfavourable determinants of health, such as those who live in 'informal settlements or other forms of dense or unstable housing, people living in poverty, indigenous peoples, racialized minorities, migrants, refugees, displaced persons, [and] incarcerated people', should be temporarily prioritised for affordable or free-of-charge coronavirus vaccines and necessary medical treatment.[176] This approach is

---

[171] ECSR, 'Statement of the right to [. . .] health' (n 264, Ch 2) paras 3–4.
[172] Ibid, 4.
[173] Ibid, 5.
[174] See Sections 3.4.1.1 and 3.4.1.2.
[175] CESCR, 'Statement on Universal and Equitable Access to Vaccines for the Coronavirus Disease (COVID-19)' (15 December 2020) paras 3, 5.
[176] Ibid, paras 4, 5, 12, emphasis added.

reinforced in the Joint Guidance note on the vaccination of migrant populations against COVID-19 as a human rights obligation, which was signed across several international legal frameworks.[177] In this document, international human rights bodies stated that 'distribution of the COVID-19 vaccines presents public health and human rights challenges' and that the principle of non-discrimination in human rights, in principle, rules out any differentiation based on nationality or legal status. Against this background and in consideration of the initial scarcity of vaccinations, priority in allocation 'must be given to *those* migrants who are *most exposed and vulnerable* to the SARS-COV-2 *due to social determinants of health*, such as migrants in irregular situations, low-income migrants, migrants living in camps or unsafe conditions, in immigration detention, [and] migrants in transit'.[178] In synergy with this approach, scholars have taken a human rights–based multidimensional vulnerability approach to establish a prioritisation model for the allocation of limited vaccines.[179] Accordingly, as the right to health prioritises vulnerable and marginalised populations, including in relation to immunisation programmes and access to essential drugs,[180] 'population groups with pre-existing social, health and economic vulnerabilities' and who are likely to suffer intersectional discriminations,[181] such as irregular migrants, not only should not be forgotten but ought to be prioritised in the vaccine rollout to comply with human rights obligations.

### 3.4.2 *'Firewalls' to Guarantee the Effective Enjoyment of Health Services by Irregular Migrants*

The previous pages demonstrated that it is beyond doubt that a right to health of irregular migrants exists in international and regional human rights law and in many national legal frameworks.[182] Nonetheless, realising a right to health that prioritises vulnerable and disadvantaged people involves considering how to remove existing barriers to the enjoyment of the right to health and access to health care. Indeed, having a right does not just mean to have it codified in a statute, constitution or treaty or interpreted, monitored and adjudicated by a court or tribunal; policies and procedures are equally important for the

---

[177] Joint Guidance Note on [. . .] COVID-19 Vaccines for All Migrants (n 90).
[178] Ibid, 1.
[179] Sharifah Sekalala et al., 'An Intersectional Human Rights Approach to Prioritising Access to COVID-19 Vaccines' (2021) *BMJ Global Health* 6 1.
[180] CESCR, GC14 (n 27, Introduction) paras 43 and 44.
[181] Sekalala (n 178) 1, 6.
[182] Spencer and Hughes (n 2, Introduction).

effective realisation of a right and should include administrative procedures that guarantee access to public services and complaint mechanisms. For instance, the ECHR and the ESC, on a general level, reaffirm that they do not guarantee rights that are 'theoretical or illusory but rights that are practical and effective'.[183]

Irregular migrants face various barriers to the effective enjoyment of their human rights: their 'irregular' immigration status, compounded by poverty, is the major cause of their 'unfreedom'.[184] The implementation of immigration policies aimed at detecting, processing, deporting and often criminalising people who do not comply with immigration requirements has rendered very difficult the enjoyment of human rights, especially when the effective enjoyment of social rights – as in the cases of the right to health and the right to education – requires the fulfilment of state duties through public and private authorities and services. To avoid this erosion of public service provision, academics and international bodies have proposed establishing 'firewalls' between immigration enforcement and social services.[185] As far as health care is concerned, establishing 'firewalls' entails, at least, (1) ensuring that health care providers and administrative staff involved in the health system have no duty to report migrants' irregular status to immigration authorities; (2) preventing immigration authorities from apprehending irregular stayers near health care facilities; and (3) organising health care services, including methods for recouping the cost of services, in a way that guarantees personal data are not disclosed and shared with immigration authorities. These mechanisms do exist in a number of states.[186] For example, in Italy, a statutory provision clearly prohibits health care staff from reporting irregular migrants when they access health services.[187] In Ireland, during the COVID-19 pandemic, firewalls were established to ensure irregular migrants had access to urgent health and social care, including COVID-19 treatment.[188] However, such

---

[183] For example, *Airey* (n 263, Ch 2); *DCI v the Netherlands* (n 218, Ch 1) para 27.

[184] For Sen (n 44, Ch 2), the enjoyment of all (subcategories of) human rights, together with other factors, represents a factor determining the real freedom that people can enjoy.

[185] Joseph Carens, 'The Rights of Irregular Migrants' (2008) *Ethics and International Affairs* 22(2) 163; European Commission against Racism and Intolerance of the Council of Europe (ECRI) 'ECRI General Policy Recommendation No. 16 on Safeguarding Irregularly Present Migrants from Discrimination' (16 March 2016) Ref Doc CRI (2016)16.

[186] François Crépeau and Bethany Hastie, 'The Case for "Firewall" Protections for Irregular Migrants: Safeguarding Fundamental Rights' (2015) *European Journal of Migration and Law* 17 (2–3) 157.

[187] Consolidated Immigration Act (n 81) Article 35(5).

[188] Migrant Rights Centre Ireland (MRCI), 'If You Have Symptoms of Covid-19' (News and Updates MRCI, 18 March 2020) <www.mrci.ie/2020/03/18/if-you-have-symptoms-of-covid19/>;

mechanisms are normally provided through ordinary statutes and administrative measures, which means that they are delicate and at risk of being dismantled in the current political climate of the securitisation of borders, new technologies of control and the general view of (irregular) migrants as a 'danger'.[189]

If the right to health is to be genuinely universal, the establishment of 'firewalls' for the enjoyment of social rights needs to be considered by international and national monitoring mechanisms and to be explicitly recognised by courts and tribunals as a balanced and proportionate solution to guarantee effective social rights in relation to the 'human rights–immigration sovereignty' clash. The use of firewalls has begun to gain international recognition among, for example, the European Commission against Racism and Intolerance of the Council of Europe, the special rapporteur on the right to health and the CRC and CMW Committees.[190] The CESCR has also recently recommended that Germany establish '[a] clear separation (firewall) between public service providers and immigration enforcement authorities, including through repealing section 87(2) of the Residence Act, to ensure that irregular migrant workers can access basic services without fear'.[191] Similar measures have been recommended by the CRC and the CMW Committees in their seminal joint general comments, which urge states to:

> Prohibit the sharing of patients' data between health institutions and immigration authorities as well as immigration enforcement operations on or near public health premises, as these effectively limit or deprive migrant children or children born to migrant parents in an irregular situation of their right to health. Effective firewalls should be put in place in order to ensure their right to health.[192]

Finally, during the COVID-19 pandemic, the CEDAW and CMW Committees, as well as the special rapporteurs on the rights of migrants and on the right to health, have restated that irregular migrants must have access to testing, treatment and social services 'without fear of detection, detention and

---

MRCI, 'Rights of Undocumented Workers to Access Social Welfare Supports During COVID-19' (News and Updates MRCI, 22 April 2019) <www.mrci.ie/2020/04/22/rights-of-undocumented-workers-to-access-social-welfare-supports-during-covid-19/> accessed 21 December 2020.

[189] Didier Bigo, 'Criminalisation of "Migrants": The Side Effect of the Will to Control the Frontiers and the Sovereign Illusion' in Bogusz et al. (n 22, Introduction) 61.

[190] ECRI (n 184); Grover (n 256, Ch 2) paras 5, 41; CMW and CRC Committees, JGC 4/23 (n 175, Ch 1) para 56.

[191] CESCR, COs Germany (n 144) para 27.

[192] CMW and CRC Committees (n 175, Ch 1) para 56.

deportation', and that 'firewalls' should be introduced to support the enjoyment of a real and effective right to health and to help contain the pandemic for the health and well-being of both nationals and non-nationals.[193]

### 3.4.3 *The Most Vulnerable Situations among Vulnerable Migrants*

Certain people, because of their personal circumstances or their socially constructed roles, have been traditionally considered particularly vulnerable to actual or potential human rights abuse and discrimination in human rights. Indeed, outside of the general human rights framework and its antidiscriminatory clauses, several group-specific treaties pursue the elimination of discrimination and require the adoption of positive measures to achieve substantial equality, including in relation to the right to health and its determinants.[194] Furthermore, prohibited or suspect grounds of discrimination may overlap in individual experiences, giving rise to situations of compounded vulnerability and phenomena of multidimensional or intersectional discrimination,[195] as is the case, for example, of poor women of colour living in migrant communities.[196] As far as the right to health is concerned, the special health needs of different groups of people are relevant to human rights law to the extent that conventions and treaty bodies have developed special standards and obligations. Furthermore, framing the denial or restriction of health care services and goods as discrimination based on gender, age or disability may be beneficial for irregular migrants' advocacy, as there is broader state and human rights community consensus on the need to tackle these factors of vulnerability than on eliminating differentiations on the grounds of legal status. While Chapter 5 elaborates on international disability law as applied to mental health, Sections 3.4.3.1 and 3.4.3.2 briefly recall certain special approaches in relation to children's health care and sexual and reproductive health for women, particularly in light of the fact that 'motherhood and childhood are entitled to special care and assistance' under the UDHR and subsequent treaties.[197]

---

[193] CEDAW Committee, 'Guidance Note on CEDAW and COVID-19', 22 April 2020, para 7(3); CMW Committee and special rapporteur on the human rights of migrants (n 158) para 10; Dainius Pūras, 'Final Report of the Special Rapporteur on the Right of Everyone to the Enjoyment of the Highest Attainable Standard of Physical and Mental Health (Focus: Covid-19 Pandemic)' (16 July 2020) A/75/163, para 30.

[194] For example, CEDAW; CRC; CRPD (n 42, Introduction).

[195] CESCR, GC20 (n 100, Ch 1) paras 17 and 27.

[196] CEDAW Committee, 'General Recommendation No. 26 on Women Migrant Workers (5 December 2008) CEDAW/C/2009/WP.1/R, para 14.

[197] UDHR (n 2, Ch 1) Article 25(2).

### 3.4.3.1 The Right to Health Care for All Migrant Children

The CRC is built upon four general principles, namely, the right to non--discrimination (Article 2); the best interest of the child, which must be prioritised in all actions regarding children (Article 3); the right to life, survival and development, with the last intended in its 'broadest sense as a holistic concept, embracing the child's physical, mental, spiritual, moral, psychological and social development'[198] (Article 6); and the right of the child to have his or her views respected (Article 12). These principles are dynamically related to all other provisions of the Convention and highlight the inherent and structural vulnerabilities of children in relation to 'age, physical weakness, immaturity, [presumed] lack of knowledge and experience' and normally reduced opportunities to have their views, autonomy and rights taken seriously.[199] Article 24 CRC on the right of the child to the enjoyment of the highest attainable standard of health spells out health-related obligations of conduct in more detail than other general treaties, such as the ICESCR. This article determines that the state should enjoy a narrower margin of discretion in adopting measures that realise the right to health of children, which notably include ensuring prenatal and postnatal care to mothers, diminishing child mortality, developing preventive health care and 'ensur[ing] the provision of necessary medical assistance and health care to *all* children with emphasis on the development of primary health care'.[200] The CRC Committee has clarified that health care–related 'core obligations' encompass, substantively, 'ensuring universal coverage of quality primary health services, including prevention, health promotion, care and treatment services, and essential drugs' that are 'within the physical and financial reach of all sections of the child population, and acceptable to all' and procedurally, duties of periodic review and monitoring on domestic law and policies regarding the health of children.[201] The realisation of health-supporting environments is another component of 'an adequate response to the underlying determinants of children's health' and is specifically addressed in Chapter 4.

---

[198] CRC Committee, 'General Comment No. 5: General Measures of Implementation of the Convention on the Rights of the Child (Arts. 4, 42 and 44, Para 6)' (November 2003) CRC/GC/2003/527.

[199] Sarah Ida Spronk-van der Meer, The Right to Health of the Child (Intersentia 2014) 32–36.

[200] CRC (n 42, Introduction) Article 24(2).

[201] CRC Committee, GC15 (n 173, Ch 2) paras 25, 73. See also Wenche Barth Eide and Asbjørn Eide, *A Commentary on the United Nations Convention on the Rights of the Child, Article 24: The Right to Health* (Brill/Nijhoff 2006) 21.

The CRC contains several provisions that address the special vulnerability of certain categories of children,[202] and the CRC and CMW Committees have jointly acknowledged the multiple vulnerabilities of migrant children and the offspring of migrants in relation to factors such as age, legal status, nationality, race and socioeconomic status.[203] Considerations regarding the operationalisation of the best interests of children and their multidimensional development needs caused these treaty bodies to state that 'every migrant child should have access to health care *equal* to that of nationals, regardless of their migration status', and that 'migrant children should have access to health services without being required to present a residence permit or asylum registration'.[204]

The spirit of these interpretative statements is that 'primary [...] and paramount consideration'[205] should be given to the best interest of the child by decision-makers and service providers in the sensitive area of health care, and that this should displace any migration policy which reduces the enjoyment of children's rights, including the fact that migratory status and administrative barriers linked to affiliation with the health system may result in a denial of necessary health care. Not only is the right to health of the child pitched at a higher standard with a clearer textual roadmap for its realisation than that relating to adults, but the principle of non-discrimination is also strictly interpreted where children are concerned. The latter not only prevents any differentiations on the grounds of legal status that are detrimental to children's best standards of health but also encompasses the adoption of positive measures able to address 'the implications of [other] multiple [and intersecting] forms of discrimination'.[206] Notably, the principles of the development and best interest of the child led the CRC and CMW Committees to require that states avoid 'restrictions on adult migrants' right to health on the basis of their nationality or migration status' because such restrictions might affect 'their children's right to health, life and development'.[207] This

---

[202] For example, CRC (n 42, Introduction) Articles 22 (refugee children), 23 (children with disabilities), 25 (children placed out-of-home), 30 (children belonging to minority groups), 33–36 (children who are at risk of exploitation, abuse and trafficking) and 38 (children in armed conflict).

[203] CMW and CRC Committees, JGC 3/22 (n 175, Ch 1) para 3.

[204] Ibid, paras 11, 21, 22, 27, 28; CMW and CRC Committees, JGC 4/23 (n 175, Ch 1) paras 55, 56, emphasis added.

[205] CRC Committee, 'General Comment No. 14: The Right of the Child to Have His or Her Best Interests Taken as a Primary Consideration (Art. 3, Para 1)' (29 May 2013) CRC/C/GC/14, paras 38.

[206] CMW and CRC Committees, JGC 4/23 (n 175, Ch 1) para 55.

[207] Ibid, para 58. See also, CMW and CRC Committees, JGC 3/22 (n 175, Ch 1) para 44: 'States parties should ensure that children's development, and their best interests, are taken fully into

argument, read in the light of the standards developed by the CESCR, can benefit at least those irregular migrants who are carers of minors, because providing them with only emergency care in life-saving situations, disregarding any other health needs, is hardly compatible with the creation of adequate living standards for 'the survival, growth and development of their child[ren], including the physical, mental, moral, spiritual and social dimensions of their development'.[208]

### 3.4.3.2 Gender Equality and Sexual and Reproductive Health for Migrant Women and Girls

Placing a gender perspective at the centre of health policies, programmes and service provision means considering that biological differences between men and women, structural inequalities and socioeconomic factors disproportionally affect women's health outcomes.[209] Accordingly, failure to adequately address health issues that specifically concern women would constitute a form of gender-based discrimination, in violation of, *inter alia*, Article 12 CEDAW. If states are to take equality and non-discrimination seriously, they must give special attention to the 'health needs and rights of women belonging to vulnerable and disadvantaged groups, such as migrant women, [...] the girl child and [...] women with physical or mental disabilities'.[210] A particularly exclusive area of women's health is access to and delivery of certain sexual and reproductive health services. From a human rights perspective, this entails a set of freedoms (e.g. the right to make free and informed decisions, without coercion, concerning one's body and health) and entitlements to affordable access to a whole range of services.

Building on the state obligations under Articles 2, 3 and 12 of the ICESCR and the general comments of other treaty bodies,[211] the CESCR's 2016 General Comment No. 22 provides detailed guidance on the scope of

---

account when it comes to policies and decisions aimed at regulating their parents' access to social rights, regardless of their migration status. Similarly, children's right to development, and their best interests, should be taken into consideration when States address, in general or individually, the situation of migrants residing irregular [...]'.

[208] CRC Committee, GC15 (n 173, Ch 2) para 16.
[209] CEDAW Committee, GR24 (n 240, Ch 2) paras 6 and 12.
[210] Ibid, para 6.
[211] Ibid; CEDAW Committee, GR26 (n 195) paras 17, 18.

the right to sexual and reproductive health, including remarks on the limits to differentiation based on legal status regarding access to prevention, promotion, treatment and care.[212] As far as our target group is concerned, the CESCR states that:

> Prisoners, stateless persons, asylum seekers and undocumented migrants, given their additional vulnerability by condition of their detention or legal status, are [...] groups with specific needs that require the State to take particular steps to ensure their access to sexual and reproductive information, goods and health care.[213]

This prioritisation of vulnerable groups, including migrant women in an irregular situation, is confirmed by the assertive vocabulary that the CESCR uses to spell out the 'core obligations' that Article 12 ICESCR generates in this area. Accordingly, states are required:

> (a) To *repeal or eliminate laws*, policies and practices that criminalize, obstruct or undermine access by individuals *or a particular group* to sexual and reproductive health facilities, services, goods and information [...] (c) *To guarantee universal and equitable access* to affordable, acceptable and quality sexual and reproductive health services, goods and facilities, in particular for women and *disadvantaged and marginalized groups*.[214]

In addition, recalling the reflections of the previous pages, migrant children's care 'should [include] full access to age-appropriate sexual and reproductive health information and services'.[215] Indeed, 'all policies and programmes affecting children's health should be grounded in a broad approach to gender equality' to ensure 'social and economic empowerment and [...] the elimination of all forms of sexual and gender-based violence'.[216]

This approach is upheld by the CEDAW Committee, which stated that, in times of pandemic, states must 'ensure that migrant women and girls, including those in an irregular situation and those without health insurance, have adequate access to health care [including sexual and reproductive care] and that health care providers are not under a duty to report them to immigration authorities'.[217]

---

[212] CESCR, GC22 (n 209, Ch 2).
[213] Ibid, para 31.
[214] Ibid, para 49, emphasis added.
[215] CRC and CMW Committee, JGC 4/23 (n 175, Ch 1) para 55.
[216] CRC Committee, GC15 (n 173, Ch 2) para 10.
[217] CEDAW Committee, 'CEDAW and Covid' (n 192) paras 2 and 7(3).

## 3.5 CONCLUSIONS

This chapter showed the different extents to which the right to health care of irregular migrants is protected in European and international human rights law and how the arguments of international human rights law can be further developed to clarify state duties in relation to different levels of accessible health care.

The ECtHR, with its conservative case law vis-à-vis the principle of sovereign immigration management, has expressly avoided the legal qualification of irregular migrants as especially vulnerable, a qualification it has applied to asylum seekers and other selected groups. The scope of the ECHR in relation to civil and political rights has pushed the Court to protect health interests in cases of important violations of the rights to life and freedom from degrading treatment. While the ECtHR has progressively enhanced its jurisprudence around migrant urgent health needs over the last twenty years, it is worth noting that the Court's current approach, which limits the weight of applicable contextual sources of international law, has so far prevented the Court from directly protecting and promoting the human interest of the highest attainable standard of health of irregular migrants, even though a certain dissatisfaction with this approach has increased among individual judges. A partial departure from this emergency logic seems to be evident in the recent quasi-legal jurisprudence of the ECSR, which emphasises that medical assistance should be provided to irregular migrants without stringently adhering to a standard of urgency in terms of their health needs.

Unlike the ECHR, several UN bodies have employed arguments relating to vulnerability, non-discrimination and positive and core obligations to unpack the levels of health care that irregular migrants should enjoy without discrimination. These arguments include not restricting compliance with Article 6 ICCPR (the right to life in dignity) to the provision of emergency treatment only, in line with the HRCtee jurisprudence.

The analysis proceeded to consider the textual and purposive interpretation of Article 12 ICESCR, as jointly read with other key articles; an analysis of the possible and disproportionate interferences with the right to health and non-discrimination in that legal framework; and the operationalisation of the priority granted to irregular migrants as vulnerable people by the CESCR's jurisprudence on core obligations, in the light of a recurrent reference to the PHC paradigm. The findings led me to conclude that, in this context of progressively evolving standards and a certain state discretion, the ICESCR should be interpreted to prioritise preventive and primary care for irregular migrants – together with, rather than in opposition to, emergency and urgent care – as essential elements of PHC to be safeguarded through the use of 'firewall' mechanisms. Additionally, to comply with the key principles of international children's rights and gender equality, states must provide comprehensive health care on an equal basis with nationals to all migrant children and sexual and reproductive health care to migrant women and girls, regardless of migration status. Upholding public health arguments in human rights law exposes inequitable findings in the human rights jurisprudence concerning the health of vulnerable people and could result in states being held accountable when their law and policies are inconsistent and insufficient for targeting irregular migrants' health needs or their capability to be healthy above a healthy and not bare subsistence threshold.

# 4

## The Determinants of the Health of Irregular Migrants

### Between Interrelatedness and Power

Achieving good health outcomes and realising the right to health require a well-functioning health care system and the adoption of intersectoral measures that support, in the form of prevention and promotion, the social determinants of individual and collective health. This is a straightforward maxim of public health; however, a relatively small number of human rights studies have grappled with the realisation of human rights other than the right to health as an aspect of health protection and promotion,[1] especially where undocumented people are concerned.

To comprehensively evaluate how international and European human rights law can be employed to make states accountable for actions targeting health justice for all migrants, the social or underlying determinants of health (SDH or UDH), which are also dimensions of the aforementioned PHC model,[2] cannot be neglected. Indeed, building on an abundance of public health literature, independent and international observers like the WHO and the International Organization for Migration (IOM) have repeatedly noted that poor health among the migrant population in Europe is significantly linked to poor living and working conditions, especially in destination countries.[3]

---

[1] Paul Hunt, 'Missed Opportunities: Human Rights and the Commission on Social Determinants of Health' (2009) *Global Health Promotion* 16 36; Audrey R. Chapman, 'The Social Determinants of Health, Health Equity and Human Rights' (2010) *Health and Human Rights Journal* 12 17; Brigit Toebes and Karien Stronks, 'Closing the Gap: A Human Rights Approach towards Social Determinants of Health' (2016) *European Journal of Health Law* 23 510.

[2] John Macdonald, 'The Social Determinants of Health: New Life for Primary Health Care' (2000) *Primary Health Care Research and Development* 1 195.

[3] WHO European Region/Italian National Institute for Health, Migration and Poverty (INMP), 'Report on the Health of Refugees and Migrants in the WHO European Region' (WHO 2018) <www.euro.who.int/en/media-centre/sections/press-releases/2019/migrants-and-refugees-at-

On a conceptual level, Section 4.1 describes how the determinants of health – employed in research on both public health and human rights – fit within the human rights paradigm, focusing on their relations with the principle of the interrelatedness of rights and the descriptive and normative concept of vulnerability. It also explains the conceptual obstacles to fitting the UDH or SDH within the human rights paradigm where irregular migrants are concerned. It shows why the construct of the welfare state, which targets exclusive forms of social vulnerability, proves to be problematic in relation to precarious forms of immigration and how the empowering function of addressing the determinants of health – an essential component of the PHC approach – can be emasculated by an authoritarian construction of power in international law.

On an applied level, Sections 4.2 and 4.3 test the concepts of the determinants of health – which, by and large, are linked to the scope of several human rights, particularly social rights – against the reality of the European and international human rights jurisprudence on irregular migrants. Attention is given to human rights findings that directly employ the terminology of SDH or UDH and to decisions that remind states of their duty to establish and implement entitlements of a certain quality – which indirectly support the determinants of health – for migrants with irregular status. As the protection of the determinants of health involves addressing several other human rights beyond the right to health care, the extensive analysis of the right to health care in Chapter 3 cannot be reproduced here for each social determinant. The cases referred to in this chapter are examples of a trend which necessitates further research on the relationships between human rights, medicine, public health and social policy as complementary strategies to reduce health inequities and ultimately contribute to good health outcomes, or the capability to be healthy,[4] for everyone. Indeed, by focusing on the right to health – a human right which has, to date, undoubtedly gained a primary position in national and international fora – and by implementing its extensive scope, the overall social position of disadvantaged and marginalised people, as protected under several other interdependent social rights, might be enhanced.

---

higher-risk-of-developing-ill-health-than-host-populations-reveals-first-ever-who-report-on-the-health-of-displaced-people-in-europe> accessed 21 March 2019; IOM, 'Migration: A Social Determinant of the Health of Migrants', background paper, IOM Migration Health Department (2006).

[4]   Venkatapuram (n 67, Ch 2).

## 4.1 CONCEPTUAL ANALYSIS OF THE APPLICABILITY OF THE DETERMINANTS OF HEALTH APPROACH FOR IRREGULAR MIGRANTS IN HUMAN RIGHTS AND PUBLIC HEALTH

### 4.1.1 *Enabling Arguments: (a) The Interdisciplinary Recognition of the Determinants of Health*

The determinants of health are closely associated with the idea that human health outcomes or statuses are not exclusively shaped by biological and medical circumstances but are also the result of extra-medical factors, such as the socioeconomic contexts and conditions in which people live and work and their power to change these conditions. This concept is grounded in public health, social medicine and epidemiology and has gained recognition in ethics and human rights law.[5]

For example, authoritative global recognition of the SDH is contained in a series of WHA resolutions that endorse the 2008 Report of the WHO's Commission on the Social Determinants of Health (CSDH), the 2011 Rio Political Declaration on Social Determinants of Health and the 2018 Declaration of Astana on PHC.[6] These documents, which focus on population health, define the SDH as a combination of the underlying structural determinants of health and the conditions of daily life. The former refer to how political, economic and social contexts affect the social position of people and correspond to a certain distribution of 'power, money, and resources', which are the 'structural drivers of [the] conditions of daily life – globally, nationally, and locally'.[7] The latter constitute the conditions in which people are 'born, grow, live, work, and age' and that shape their well-being and health status and include access to education, housing, work opportunities and health care.[8]

In international human rights law, the CESCR has interpreted Article 12 ICESCR as explicitly encompassing the UDH, although this approach

---

[5]   *Ex multis*, Amory Winslow (n 2, Ch 2) 3; Declaration of Alma-Ata (n 28, Introduction) para VII.3; UNCHR, Submission of the Director of the WHO (n 89, Ch 2) 2; Marmot and Wilkinson (n 103, Ch 2) 79–102; Paula Braveman, 'Social Conditions, Health Equity, and Human Rights' (2010) *Health and Human Rights Journal* 12(2) 31; Toebes and Stronks (n 1).

[6]   WHA Res 62.14 'Reducing Health Inequities through Action on the Social Determinants of Health' (21 May 2009); WHA Res 65.8 'The Outcome of the World Conference on Social Determinants of Health' (26 May 2012); WHA Res 72.2 (n 176, Ch 2).

[7]   CSDH Report (n 111, Ch 2) 1–2, 42–44.

[8]   Ibid.

was also criticised as too expansive vis-à-vis formal textual obligations.[9] Therefore, for the CESCR, the scope of the right to health embraces '[a] wide range of socio-economic factors that promote conditions in which people can lead a healthy life [. . .] such as food and nutrition, housing, access to safe and potable water and adequate sanitation, safe and healthy working conditions, and a healthy environment'.[10] Furthermore, in its General Comment No. 14, the CESCR recognised, albeit in a cursory way, 'resource distribution', 'gender' and 'education' as determinants of health.[11] Former special rapporteur on the right to health, Paul Hunt, insisted upon synergies between public health and human rights arguments, and, in his 2005 report to the UNGA, he recognised that 'there is considerable congruity between the CSDH's mandate and the UDH dimension of the right to health'.[12] The CSDH's final report is the outcome of a study commissioned by the WHO on the social determinants and is a key reference (public health) document for my analysis in this chapter. The final report is divided into 'chapters' corresponding to twelve SDH-related areas of intervention and goals, which overlap significantly with the scope of several human rights issues such as the development of children via adequate living standards and education, decent living and working conditions, social protection, universal health care and gender equality.[13]

The determinants of health can receive legal protection in human rights law if this body of law adequately upholds both the right to health and other human rights that support it, such as the freedom from ill treatment and the rights to life, an adequate standard of living, water, housing and a healthy environment. This highlights the interconnectedness of human rights which can empower people by enhancing their individual and collective enjoyment of healthy living conditions. Furthermore, by holding governments accountable for failing to adopt policies that ensure the social determinants of health, human rights law can offer a useful legal framework to support the achievement of the goals of public health and social justice, thus complementing the strategy for tackling populations' health inequalities and the unfair distribution of social goods and capabilities.[14]

---

9    Tobin (n 1, Ch 2) 108.
10   CESCR, GC14 (n 27, Introduction) para 4.
11   Ibid, paras 10, 16.
12   Paul Hunt, Special Rapporteur on the Right to [. . .] Health (12 September 2005) No A/60/348, para 7.
13   For a table on these 'cross connections' see Toebes and Stronks (n 1) 516–519.
14   Michael Marmot et al., 'WHO European Review of Social Determinants of Health and the Health Divide' (2012) Lancet 380 1011; Karien Stronks et al., Social Justice and Human Rights as

It should be noted, however, that although this chapter often refers to 'the determinants of health' without distinguishing between the SDH and the UDH, these concepts do differ slightly. An examination of the SDH, as embraced by the WHO in its recommendations, sheds light on consistent patterns of inequality and their direct or indirect impact on health outcomes.[15] Therefore, appropriate health measures that target health equity should tackle, *inter alia*, the structural determinants or drivers of social stratification or class division. This programmatic call for a rebalancing of power dynamics is less apparent in human rights law,[16] despite growing interest in the relationship between poverty and human rights.[17] Although socioeconomic rights, in principle, provide a legal source for protecting the rights supporting the UDH, they are focused more on progressive state measures and the immediate realisation of the 'minimum essential level of each right' on a non-discriminatory basis than on addressing the underlying structural causes of inequality.[18]

In the field of public health, the determinants of health are conceptualised as the 'means' to achieve health equity, a fair needs- or capability-based distribution of health inputs. As such, they are included in some of the most authoritative theories of health justice, which also elaborate on human rights as essential means to realise further 'valued features of human lives'.[19] Daniels calls these valued features basic needs, while Sen and Nussbaum speak of human capabilities.[20] Sen's capability approach, which emphasises the real practical possibility of exercising freedom of choice, with regard to individual life and health, is expressly referred to in the report of the CSDH.[21] Indeed, this approach broadens the focus from health care inequalities to inequalities in the distribution of other social determinants of health,[22] although it appears to be neutral regarding the 'how much' of distributive justice policies,

---

a *Framework for Addressing Social Determinants of Health: Final Report of the Task Group on Equity, Equality and Human Rights* (WHO Publishing 2016) 10, 11.

[15] Kristi H. Kenyon, Lisa Forman and Claire E. Brolan, 'Editorial – Deepening the Relationship between Human Rights and the Social Determinants of Health: A Focus on Indivisibility and Power' (2018) *Health and Human Rights Journal* 20(2) 1, 8.

[16] Chapman (n 181, Ch 2) 250–251, 255–257.

[17] For example, see the CESCR, Statement on Poverty and the International Covenant on Economic, Social and Cultural Rights (4 May 2001) E/C.12/2001/10; ECSR, Conclusions 2013 – Statement of interpretation of Article 30 ESC, 2013_163_06/Ob/EN (2013); Yamin (n 5, Introduction) 49–72.

[18] CESCR, GC3 (n 80, Ch 2) para 10.

[19] Van Duffel (n 50, Ch 2) 33.

[20] More details on these authors' philosophies are provided or referenced in Section 2.3.

[21] CSDH Report (n 111, Ch 2) 1.

[22] Venkatapuram (n 67, Ch 2) 19; Stronks et al. (n 14) 19.

including policies that determine the level of social rights to which migrants are entitled.

### 4.1.2 Enabling Arguments: (b) Vulnerability and the Determinants of Health

In human rights, the CESCR has clarified that state obligations in the ICESCR require states to adopt measures to make 'facilities, goods, services, and *conditions* necessary for the realisation of the highest attainable standard of health' available, accessible, acceptable and of good quality for everyone without discrimination, particularly for vulnerable people.[23] In public health, the aforementioned report of the CSDH emphasises the key role of the SDH in 'closing the gap' created by health inequities within and between societies, implying a need to target people who are especially vulnerable to health deterioration because of the ways in which the structural drivers of inequality play out in their circumstances, as in the cases of workers in hazardous environments, children and women.[24]

Accordingly, the concept of vulnerability provides a useful conceptual bridge between the SDH and the human right to health. Indeed, contextual and multilayered risks of harm and human vulnerability to ill health are common targets of both the intersectoral measures that the SDH approach requires to achieve health equity and the contemporary interrelated take on human rights law.[25]

As indicated at the end of Chapter 2, while the descriptive and normative concept of vulnerability is defined in different ways in the social sciences (e.g. inherent or contextual, human or group-based), it is often reconstructed as the result of a relationship of comparison between individuals or groups whereby those people who are deemed especially vulnerable to multidimensional harm because of personal conditions or social stratification should be granted special attention in law, in policy-making and in society at large to avoid discrimination.[26] For instance, to address the socioeconomic vulnerability of disadvantaged groups, including in the field of health, the human rights community employs the concept of substantive equality – which largely coincides with the concept of equity in health and social justice – whereby

---

[23] CESCR, GC14 (n 27, Introduction) paras 9, 12, 18, 43(a), 43(f). Further details at Section 2.3, *supra.*

[24] CSDH Report (n 111, Ch 2) 42, 49, 55, 60, 71, 84, 97, 171, 174.

[25] World Conference on Social Determinants of Health: Rio Political Declaration on Social Determinants of Health (19–21 October 2011) paras 1, 6; on the concept of 'interrelatedness' of human rights see *infra* at Section 4.1.1.3.

[26] For further details, see Sections 2.7.1 and 2.7.2, *supra.*

recognising the special vulnerability of a certain group or individuals corresponds to the need for a certain type of targeted state duty of a positive and preferential nature. In Chapters 2 and 3, I offered examples of how both European and international courts and tribunals have employed vulnerability in a normative way to address instances of substantive discrimination.[27] Similarly, the WHO's report on the SDH has recommended that states adopt 'active intersectoral measures' to tackle substantive discrimination in health and strive to achieve health equity, particularly for the worst off.[28] These cross-disciplinary connections bear witness to the fact that the approaches of human rights and public health can be truly complementary in pushing for the realisation of the highest attainable standards of health for all,[29] also regardless of migration status.

### 4.1.3 *Enabling Arguments: (c) Interrelated Rights and Intersectoral Measures*

The concepts of indivisibility and interrelatedness are integral to human rights law and are tightly linked to the public health idea of intersectoral measures targeting populations' inequalities in the determinants of health.

The term 'indivisibility' in human rights law specifically refers to states' duty to treat all human rights 'globally in a fair and equal manner, on the same footing, and with the same emphasis'.[30] The use of this terminology became necessary to respond to the unequal treatment of civil and socioeconomic rights during the second half the twentieth century.[31] Indivisibility means that all rights are equally important and should be regarded as such in order to respect, protect and fulfil human dignity, freedom and equality. The concepts of interrelatedness and interdependency are often mentioned together with indivisibility in connection with human rights. No human right can be realised in isolation: the enjoyment of each right requires the enjoyment of other rights and often represents a precondition or element of other human rights.[32]

---

[27] See Sections 2.7.3, 2.7.4 and 3.3.3, *supra*.
[28] CSDH Report (n 111, Ch 2) 200–206; WHA 62.14 (n 6).
[29] Gillian MacNaughton and Mariah McGill (n 190, Ch 2) 480.
[30] Vienna Declaration and Programme of Action on Human Rights (n 28, Ch 2) para 5.
[31] Daniel J. Whelan, *Indivisible Human Rights* (University of Pennsylvania Press 2011) 1–10.
[32] The right to water is a particularly instructive example is interdependence of human rights: 'Water is a limited natural resource and a public good fundamental for life and health [...]. The right to water is [...] inextricably related to the right to the highest attainable standard of health [...] and the rights to adequate housing and adequate food [...]. The right should also be seen in conjunction with other rights [...] amongst them the right to life and human dignity' in CESCR, 'General Comment No. 15 (the right to water)' (20 January 2003) E/C.12/

For the WHO, the SDH exemplify the characteristics of interdependence and interrelatedness with regard to certain decent conditions of life – the interests protected by socioeconomic rights – and the underlying power structures that affect health outcomes.[33] Overall, intersectoral or interdependent measures, which protect and promote health beyond health care, should address unhealthy living conditions by also challenging the causes of structural inequality in health.

Against this background, it is worth noting that certain policy choices, as well as societal norms and values vis-à-vis (economic) irregular migration, often have an adverse impact on the social position of irregular migrants. Unless favourable intersectoral measures are taken, this adverse socio-institutional context, together with factors such as gender, occupation, income and ethnicity, will continue to prevent irregular migrants from effectively enjoying their human rights and their health and well-being.[34] In sum, the public health and human rights fields share, explicitly or implicitly, various concepts – vulnerability, substantive equality or equity, interrelatedness or intersectoral measures – which help situate the determinants of health within the human rights conception of the right to health. However, as Sections 4.1.4 to 4.1.6 explain, human rights as a branch of international law and public policy development must also accommodate other state interests which, to date, have undermined efforts to protect the SDH or UDH as essential elements of the human right to health of irregular migrants.

### 4.1.4 *Conceptual Obstacles: (a) Immigration, Policy Models and Welfare Rights*

Building on the arguments of Chapters 1 and 3 on how the clash between sovereignty and migrant rights plays out and threatens irregular migrants' effective enjoyment of rights, this subsection addresses the current failures of traditional welfare state models to genuinely enhance the position of irregular migrants and their enjoyment of rights and access to services.

First, it is worth considering that the implementation of social rights which support the determinants of health, in the Western world, is intimately linked

---

2002/11. On the interconnected nature of the right to health with other human rights, see CESCR, GC14 (n 27, Introduction) para 3.

[33] WHA Res 65.8 (n 6) 1.

[34] CSDH Report (n 111, Ch 2) 42–46; Alessandro Rinaldi et al., 'Salute, Lavoro e Immigrazione: il Ruolo degli Operatori della Salute in una Prospettiva di Sanità Pubblica' in Laura Calafà, Sergio Iavicoli and Benedetta Persechino (eds) *Lavoro Insicuro: Salute, Sicurezza e Tutele Sociali dei Lavoratori Immigrati in Agricoltura* (Il Mulino 2020) 279–311.

to the establishment of a 'welfare' or 'social' state.[35] As Chapter 2 explained, the history of social rights goes hand in hand with that of the Western welfare state, and both phenomena have gained international mainstream recognition since World War II.[36] Public health research, which is grounded in the concept of social justice,[37] has also recognised the need to consider the SDH from a welfare state perspective.[38]

The dominant literature on social policy recognises that immigration represents a threat to a strong welfare state.[39] As such, welfare is essentially and normally framed as a 'protectionist and nationalist' concept according to which limited resources are transferred from the better off to the worse off 'within a given society'.[40] For instance, whereas nationalism and the idea of the welfare state worked in the UK during the years after the end of World War II as a 'social glue' between citizens and non-citizens and helped to rebuild the nation and establish national solidarity, contemporary forms of nationalism operate according to a set of values that run counter to the granting of social benefits to (all) immigrants.[41] Social heterogeneity is even described as a factor that undermines solidarity within nations and that contributes to working-class fragmentation,[42] although an increasing number of studies bear witness to the contributions of migrants to the economies of their host countries.[43] Furthermore, since the 1980s, the rise of neoliberal

---

[35] Katrougalos (n 34, Ch 2) 9.

[36] Toomas Kotkas, 'The Short and Insignificant History of Social Rights Discourse in the Nordic Welfare State' in Toomas Kotkas and Kenneth Veitch (eds) *Social Rights in the Welfare State: Origins and Transformations* (Routledge 2016) 15.

[37] Nancy Krieger and Anne-Emmanuelle Birn, 'A Vision of Social Justice as the Foundation of Public Health: Commemorating 150 Years of the Spirit of 1848' (1998) *American Journal of Public Health* 88(11) 1603–1606.

[38] Clare Bambara, 'Going beyond the Three Worlds of Welfare Capitalism: Regime Theory and Public Health Research' (2007) *Journal of Epidemiology & Community Health* 61(12) 1098.

[39] Diane Sainsbury, *Welfare States and Immigrant Rights: The Politics of Inclusion and Exclusion* (OUP 2012) 1–10.

[40] Gunnar Myrdal, *Beyond the Welfare State: Economic Planning in the Welfare States and Its Economic Implications* (Duckworth 1960) as referred to in Han Entzinger, 'Open Borders and the Welfare State' in Antoine Pécoud and Paul de Guchteneire (eds) *Migration without Borders: Essays on the Free Movement of People* (Berghan/UNESCO 2007) 119.

[41] Gerard Delanty, 'Beyond the Nation-State: National Identity and Citizenship in a Multicultural Society – A Response to Rex' (1996) *Sociological Research Online* 1(3) 1.

[42] Gary P. Freeman, 'Migration and the Political Economy of the Welfare State' (1986) *Annals of the American Academy of Political and Social Science* 485, 51.

[43] Amandine Aubry, Michał Burzynski and Frédéric Docquier, 'The Welfare Impact of Global Migration in OECD Countries' (2016) *Journal of International Economics* 101; Grațiela G. Noja et al., 'Migrants' Role in Enhancing the Economic Development of Host Countries: Empirical Evidence from Europe' (2018) *Sustainability* 10(3); José Iván Rodriguez-Sanchez, 'Undocumented Immigrants in Texas: A Cost–Benefit Assessment' (May 2020, *Rice University's*

ideologies and policies – interlinked with certain constructions of race, poverty and immigration – has fuelled a gradual dismantling of the welfare state and a shift from universal access to residual approaches for socially excluded people.[44]

Granting social rights to migrants would also conceptually destabilise the traditional T. H. Marshall scheme of domestic rights acquisition 'from civil rights to political rights, and from the latter to social rights', because it would mean that, before gaining political rights in a state, migrants would enjoy social rights by virtue of their legally recognised or actual residence rather than on the grounds of their citizenship, nationality or regularised membership.[45] Research in the area of social policy has debated whether it is desirable for the financial sustainability of national systems to extend welfare provisions to migrants and whether different welfare regimes influence the quality and quantity of social benefits available to non-nationals.[46] The influential analysis of welfare state regimes by Gøsta Esping-Andersen also encounters conceptual difficulties where migrants – particularly irregular migrants – are concerned.[47] Esping-Andersen classifies welfare state regimes as liberal, conservative or social democratic. In liberal regimes, welfare is funded by the market and the state, and state provision is minimal and is aimed at poverty reduction for the neediest. Conservative or corporatist regimes regard 'work' as a basis for entitlement to generous welfare provisions and support residual programmes for the non-employed population. In social democratic systems, citizenship or residence is the basis for entitlement and the guarantor of universal access to welfare. Since the second and third systems generally reserve measures relating to 'income maintenance' and 'well-being' (e.g. through health and social assistance systems) for regular workers, regular residents and citizens, it is intuitive that irregular migrants, in principle, fall outside of these welfare systems. Liberal regimes are conceptually a better fit for undocumented

Baker Institute for Public Policy); Mats Tjernberg, 'The Economy of Undocumented Migration: Taxation and Access to Welfare' (2010) European Journal of Migration and Law 12 149.

[44] Katie Bales, 'Asylum Seekers, Social Rights and the Rise of New Nationalism: From an Inclusive to Exclusive British Welfare State?' in Kotkas and Veitch (n 36) 109; Stephen Castles and Carl-Ulrik Schierup, 'Migration and Ethnic Minorities' in Francis G. Castles et al. (eds) The Oxford Handbook of the Welfare State (OUP 2010) 278, 287–288.

[45] Virginie Guiraudon, 'The Marshallian Triptych Reordered: The Role of Courts and Bureaucracy in Furthering Migrants' Social Rights' in Michael Bommes and Andrew Geddes (eds) Immigration and Welfare: Challenging the Borders of the Welfare State (Routledge 2000) 72.

[46] Sainsbury (n 39).

[47] Gøsta Esping-Andersen, The Three Worlds of Welfare Capitalism (Polity Press 1990).

people, although they are less generous in terms of the quality of benefits and more likely to be emergency-oriented, as they target poverty alleviation.[48] It is important to highlight that Mediterranean forms of conservative welfare distinguish between the provision of universal health care and other more restrictive work-related, corporatist social benefits.[49] This distinction tends to limit health justice to equal entitlements to health care, resulting in the neglect of other social provisions as determinants of health.

While human rights scholars cannot overlook these policy-based considerations at the operational level, their entire discipline revolves around certain universal minimum (moral and legal) entitlements for the protection of human dignity, equality and freedom, regardless of people's nationality or immigration status. However, in spite of the declared universal scope of human rights, domestic law and some pieces of international and European law tend to use birth right status, regular presence, prolonged residence or work, as welfare models do, rather than personhood as the main criteria for enjoying socioeconomic rights to their full extent. The teachings of Hannah Arendt are instructive in this regard. She regarded citizenship as legal belonging to a political community and, hence, as the 'right to have rights'.[50] In the same spirit, the writings of some contemporary authors reflect that 'protection and empowerment are inherent to the notion of citizenship' and that a lack of these creates conditions for human insecurity.[51]

This line of argument is supported by a comparison of Sections III and IV of the ICMW, which demonstrates that documented or regular migrant workers should 'enjoy equality of treatment' with nationals in relation to education, housing and social and health services, whereas irregular migrants should enjoy only 'the basic right of access to education' and 'medical care that is urgently required for the preservation of [...] life or the avoidance of irreparable harm'.[52] In the European context, the case law of the ECtHR has begun, with the case of *Gaygusuz* v. *Austria*, to consider that states should put forward 'very weighty reasons' to justify differential treatment in relation to the enjoyment of rights on the grounds of nationality. In the above case, the Strasbourg Court ruled out the denial of social security benefits on the sole ground of nationality to a regular migrant with over ten years' residence in Austria because it was discriminatory and, hence, incompatible with Articles 14 and

[48] Sainsbury (n 39) 7–113.
[49] Maurizio Ferrara, 'The South European Countries' in Castles et al. (n 44) 616, 621.
[50] Hannah Arendt, *The Origins of Totalitarianism* (first published 1950, Harcourt 1968) 177, 278.
[51] Constantin Sokoloff and Richard Lewis (n 108, Ch 1) 38. See also, Kingstone (n 52, Ch 1).
[52] ICMW (n 42, Introduction) Articles 28, 30, 43.

1 Protocol 1 ECHR.[53] However, as the pages that follow show, unlike nationality, which is considered a suspect ground for differentiation,[54] irregular migratory status has not been fully recognised by the ECtHR as an illegitimate criterion for differential treatment where human rights and, in particular, social interests are concerned.[55]

Even though irregular migrants are guaranteed a certain minimum level of protection in all international human rights frameworks, the question of what is meant by the minimum acceptable level of socioeconomic rights that support the determinants of health – whether it is a dignified minimum, a healthy subsistence or a bare survival minimum[56] or a minimal or an adequate provision of social benefits[57] – remains unclearly answered in human rights law.

### 4.1.5 Conceptual Obstacles: (b) The Effects of Power Constructs on the Rights of Irregular Migrants

The aim of addressing the determinants of health on a conceptual level is to enable or empower people to take control of their health and well-being and reach their highest attainable standard of health. This requires both individual and collective and both private and public efforts to target structural and social determinants of health through the adoption of truly intersectoral and interdisciplinary measures. For this reason, indivisibility and power are here used as conceptual angles to examine the SDH.[58] Whereas indivisibility, interrelatedness and interconnectedness, as conceptualised in human rights doctrine, address *relationships between rights*, power relates to *relationships between subjects*, be they individuals, institutions or states.

Power is a contested and interdisciplinary concept. While it is beyond the scope of this chapter to give a full account of the rich literature on this concept, it is necessary to distinguish between 'power over' (authority) and 'power to' (empowerment).[59] The former can be described as 'the probability

---

[53] *Gaygusuz* (n 100, Ch 1) para 42.

[54] For a critical analysis of *Gaygusuz* in the light of subsequent contradicting cases before the ECtHR, see Dembour (n 5, Ch 1) 251–281.

[55] *Anakomba Yula v Belgium* App no 45413/07 (ECHR 2009) para 37; *Ponomaryov* (n 19, Introduction) para 54.

[56] Young (n 140, Ch 2) 113; King (n 140, Ch 2) 29.

[57] David Bilchiz, *Poverty and Fundamental Rights: The Justification and Enforcement of Socio-Economic Rights* (OUP 2007) 187–188.

[58] Kenyon, Forman and Brolan (n 16) 1–8.

[59] Amy Allen, 'Feminist Perspectives on Power' in *The Stanford Encyclopedia of Philosophy* (2005–2016) <https://plato.stanford.edu/entries/feminist-power/> accessed 1 March 2019.

that one actor within a social (and institutional) relationship will be in a position to carry out his own will despite resistance'.[60] The latter represents 'the human ability not just to act but to act in concrete', that is, to be enabled, as suggested by the Latin etymology *potere*, which means to be capable of doing something.[61]

International human rights law incorporates both dimensions of power, which generates frictions between rules and foundational principles within the same legal framework. Power can be synonymous with state authority or sovereignty over people settled in a territory, which – as demonstrated in Chapter 1 – is itself a structural principle of international law. Furthermore, legislative, executive and judicial powers, as they relate to the incorporation and implementation of human rights, are precisely the targets of international human rights law because this normative framework aims to limit or qualify state powers while empowering people vis-à-vis the arbitrary exercise of state regulatory or executive authority.

As far as irregular migrants are concerned, balancing 'sovereignty as power over' borders, people and territories with 'empowerment', as embedded in the human right to the determinants of health, can lead to unpredictable normative consequences that may be difficult to justify under a genuine human rights– and non-discrimination–based approach to law and policy. This impasse was acknowledged by the CESCR which stated that 'lack of documentation frequently makes it impossible for parents to send their children to school, or for migrants to have access to health care, including emergency medical treatment, to take up employment, to apply for social housing or to engage in an economic activity in a self-employed capacity'.[62]

State-designated *illegal* migratory status is one of the most disempowering dimensions of irregular migrants' lives in destination countries, as well as during migration journeys, where people are likely to experience unsafe and even exploitative living and working conditions while hiding from the authorities and mainstream society.[63] It is undeniable that governance processes and norms in Western nation-states – grounded in the perceived costs, dependency and different identities of (undocumented) migrants within a nationalist

[60] Max Weber, *Economy and Society: An Outline of Interpretive Sociology* (University of California Press 1978) 53.
[61] Hannah Arendt, *On Violence* (Harcourt Brace & Co. 1970) 44.
[62] CESCR, Statement on migrant rights (n 174, Ch 1) para 11.
[63] Rinaldi (n 34) 290–294; IOM (n 3).

discourse[64] – as well as systemic and structural discrimination processes,[65] have marginalised and socially excluded irregular migrants and that these, together with the precarious living conditions they cause, constitute unfavourable determinants of health. The struggles of marginalised people to achieve socioeconomic well-being and the recurrent rights violations they experience, which are often the result of unchallenged discriminatory patterns, have been described as true 'pathologies of power'.[66] Against this background, power, in the context of migration, is, in the reality of state practices, often synonymous with the authority to regulate immigration, a sovereign competence that is recognised, although to varying extents, in both international and European human rights law and that can disrupt the full empowering nature of these legal frameworks.[67]

In the fields of public health and social medicine, states' authority to regulate is implied. However, greater attention is drawn to the enabling or empowering function of maintaining certain conditions of life and to the distribution of resources, money and power – corresponding to the concept of empowerment – which features in both the SDH and PHC models. Indeed, the WHO member states have been urged to 'contribute to the empowerment of individuals and groups, especially those who are marginalized, and to take steps to improve the societal conditions that affect their health'.[68] Furthermore, from an SDH perspective, 'it is important to understand exclusion, vulnerability, and resilience as dynamic multidimensional processes operating through relationships of power'.[69] While the public health literature has widely elaborated on the relation between migration and health,[70] it is

---

[64] Baumgartel (n 12, Introduction) 138–139.

[65] 'Structural discrimination' refers to 'both institutional discrimination' and 'also a broader cultural discrimination based upon widely shared social paradigms [. . .] that both constructs and devalues the "other" vis-à-vis "us"', see Tom R. Burns, 'Towards a Theory of Structural Discrimination: Cultural, Institutional and Interactional Mechanisms of the "European Dilemma"' in Gerard Delanty, Ruth Wodak and Paul Jones (eds) Identity, Belonging and Migration (Liverpool University Press 2011) 152–172 Similarly, see the concept of 'systemic discrimination' at CESCR, GC20 (n 100, Ch 1) para 12.

[66] Farmer (n 322, Ch 2) 6–7.

[67] As argued in Chapter 1, see supra.

[68] WHA Res 62.14 (n 6) para 3(7).

[69] Marmot et al. (n 14) 1022.

[70] Ex multis, Kolitha Wickramage et al., 'Migration and Health: A Global Public Health Research Priority' (2018) BMC Public Health 18; Hannah Bradby et al., 'Public Health Aspects of Migrant Health: A Review of the Evidence on Health Status for Refugees and Asylum Seekers in the European Region', Health Evidence Network Synthesis Report 44, WHO Regional Office for Europe (2015); Helena Legido-Quigley and Montserrat Gea-Sánchez (eds) 'Special Issue "The Health and Wellbeing of Migrant Populations"' (2020) International

notable that the report of the CSDH and the WHO's resolutions discussed in this chapter and Chapter 3, which are persuasive instruments of a recommendatory nature, do not elaborate on the special powerlessness and vulnerability of *irregular* migrants. For instance, the CSDH report explicitly mentions irregular migrants only once in relation to their precarious employment and exploitation in the informal economy,[71] and the WHO only refers generally to the priority of progressively tackling the social determinants of refugees' and migrants' health.[72] However, it is worth noting that other studies, authored by some of the leading experts behind the CSDH report, have found that irregular migrants are particularly exposed to 'exclusionary processes' and that this constitutes a form of 'internal migration control' that is likely 'to increase [their] vulnerability to marginalisation, poverty, illness, and exploitation'.[73]

### 4.1.6 *Empowering Irregular Migrants with Indivisible Rights? From Theory to Human Rights Practice*

Although irregular migrants are undeniably in vulnerable or precarious socioeconomic situations in receiving societies and their vulnerability is exacerbated by crises such as the recent COVID-19 pandemic,[74] this section demonstrated that conceptual obstacles to the full incorporation of their determinants of health into human rights, welfare constructs and public policy frameworks still exist. As far as human rights practice is concerned, power, when it refers to the individual empowerment of people who are rights holders although they do not have the right to stay in a certain territory, is antithetical to the dominant doctrine of the power of states to exclude. In contrast, arguments for 'power as the authority to exclude' can be used to justify the maintenance of certain polity outsiders' enjoyment of the human rights and services that support the determinants of health at bare minimum levels in law and policy.

The concepts of the interdependence, interrelatedness and indivisibility of human rights are, in principle, aimed at assigning the same dignity and value to all human rights and at bridging the conceptual gap between traditionally

---

Journal of Environmental Research and Public Health, <www.mdpi.com/journal/ijerph/special_issues/migrant_health_wellbeing> accessed 19 April 2021.

[71] CSDH Report (n 111, Ch 2) 80.

[72] WHO, 'Promoting the Health of Refugees and Migrants – Draft Framework of Priorities and Guiding Principles to Promote the Health of Refugees and Migrants' (doc no A70/24, 17 May 2017) Annex para D.3; WHO, Draft Global Action Plan (n 62, Ch 3) para 33; WHA Res 70.15 (n 62, Ch 3).

[73] Marmot et al. (n 14) 1023.

[74] CMW Committee and SR on the Human Rights of Migrants (n 192, Ch 3) para 1.

enforceable civil and political rights and non-justiciable economic, social and cultural rights. In legal practice, they facilitate the indirect judicial protection of socioeconomic interests through civil rights–related litigation, rather than equalised, parallel or integrated forms of protection.[75] Whereas this jurisprudence on indirect protection is undeniably significant in advancing the socioeconomic judicial protection of people – which would otherwise be impossible to achieve in many legal frameworks[76] – it has also framed the legal protection of the determinants of health in exceptional terms by instrumentally safeguarding life and personal integrity rather than health as a human and social value in itself. As mentioned in Chapter 3, European human rights law has tended to acknowledge violations of irregular migrants' rights only when they are in dire need of socioeconomic protection, as 'a finding to the contrary would place too great a burden on the contracting states'.[77]

In turn, greater support for the implementation of socioeconomic rights in a non-discriminatory way – not only in rhetorical statements – and the genuine incorporation of the determinants of health arguments into human rights jurisprudence would increase international state accountability for laws and policies that perpetuate inequitable practices and that neglect the well-being and health of irregular migrants. As the remainder of this chapter demonstrates, this process of shaping human rights norms in line with public health principles of universal scope is at an initial but promising stage of development. However, in the contentious areas of irregular immigration, welfare and health, international and European human rights law have proposed certain inconsistent solutions, which reveal different ways of accommodating the relation between human rights and state sovereignty and between 'universalism and particularism'.[78]

## 4.2 EUROPEAN HUMAN RIGHTS FRAMEWORKS: FROM CONSTRAINED TO IMPLICIT CONSIDERATION OF THE DETERMINANTS OF HEALTH OF IRREGULAR MIGRANTS

The bodies of the Council of Europe have produced a number of important instruments that are relevant for standard setting and monitoring in relation to

---

[75] For further details, see Sections 2.6.1 and 3.2.1.

[76] Ioana Cismas, 'The Intersection of Economic Social and Cultural Rights and Civil and Political Rights' in Eibe Riedel, Gilles Giacca and Christophe Golay (eds) *Economic Social and Cultural Rights in International Law: Contemporary Issues and Challenges* (OUP 2015) 448; Ingrid Leijten, *Core Socio-Economic Rights and the European Court of Human Rights* (CUP 2018) 259–316.

[77] A.S. (n 42, Ch 3) para 31.

[78] Dembour (n 5, Ch 1) 251.

health, well-being and irregular migration. These include contributions from PACE, the European Commission against Racism and Intolerance, the Commissioner for Human Rights and the Group of Experts on Action against Trafficking in Human Beings.[79] However, in parallel with the analysis in Chapter 3, this section mainly focuses on the ECHR and the ESC, as general Council of Europe's human rights treaties with supervisory bodies capable of monitoring and adjudicating on individual and collective complaints. In relation to these procedures, it is important to recall, once again, that the ECHR and the ESC have limited material or personal scope regarding issues concerning the socioeconomic rights of irregular migrants,[80] and that national immigration powers are often referenced as starting conceptual angles for most European case law.[81] Additionally, although the socioeconomic conditions of people with a precarious or irregular migratory status have been frequently adjudicated before the ECtHR and the ECSR, these human rights bodies have made no explicit mention of the concept of health *determinants*.

### 4.2.1 *The Sovereignty-Constrained Case Law of the ECtHR*

Based on the interrelatedness of civil and political and socioeconomic rights, the Strasbourg Court has, since the 1980s, extended the material scope of the civil rights set out in the ECHR to situations that have implications of a social or economic nature,[82] although the level of 'deprivation and want incompatible with human dignity' that is needed to reach the threshold of applicability of the ECHR in the socioeconomic area is difficult to achieve.[83] State parties have been recognised to have a wide margin of discretion in relation to 'general measures of economic and social strategy', including measures of socioeconomic assistance. As a general rule, only 'manifestly unreasonable' socioeconomic measures are ruled out by the Court.[84] In relation to social support and housing, under Articles 2 (life), 3 (prohibition of inhuman or degrading treatment) and 8 (private and family life) ECHR, only situations of

---

[79] PACE and ECRI (n 18, Introduction); GRETA, 'Human Trafficking for the Purpose of Labour Exploitation' *Chapter of the 7th General Report on GRETA's Activities* (October 2019); Commissioner for Human Rights, 'Positions on the Rights of Migrants in an Irregular Situation', CommDH/PositionPaper(2010)5 (24 June 2010).

[80] See Sections 1.3.2, 1.4.2, 2.6 and 3.2.

[81] Dembour (n 5, Ch 1) 1–6.

[82] *Airey* (n 263, Ch 2) para 26.

[83] *Budina v Russia* App no 45603/05 (Decision ECHR 2009).

[84] For example, *Stec* (n 269, Ch 2) para 52; *Carson and Others v UK* App no 42184/05 (ECHR 2010) para 61.

poverty affecting the most marginalised groups and those who are fully dependent on state support seem to qualify for protection under ECHR.[85]

For example, in a series of cases regarding the conditions of detention of irregular migrants and asylum seekers in Greece, the Court held that the material conditions in those detention centres constituted degrading treatment and failed to respect migrants' human dignity.[86] These findings were linked to particularly unhealthy living conditions in overcrowded detention facilities, characterised by an absence of cleanliness, appalling conditions of hygiene and sanitation, inadequate medical care and a lack of facilities for leisure and meals. In a significant case against Malta, the Court found, *inter alia*, that the threshold for violation of Article 3 was met because the applicant – an irregular migrant woman – was held for a long period in a detention centre in cold conditions, which 'may affect one's well-being and *may in extreme circumstances affect health*', with no female staff and no access to open air for exercise and was provided with an inadequate diet. All of these were found to be circumstances that exacerbated the particular vulnerability of the applicant due to her fragile health and personal emotional circumstances.[87]

The exceptional approach of the Court with regard to the social circumstances and health care of irregular migrants is also illustrated by comparing the arguments used in the case of *M.S.S. v. Belgium and Greece* with those employed in the case of *Hunde v. the Netherlands*.[88] The former was a case concerning the exposure of asylum seekers in Greece to severe socioeconomic deprivation, which left unmet their 'most basic needs: food, hygiene and a place to live'.[89] The latter involved a claim regarding emergency social care, especially access to shelter, for irregular migrants in the Netherlands. Whereas the dire living conditions, special vulnerability and state dependency of asylum seekers led the Court to find a violation of Article 3 ECHR in *M.S.S.*, Mr Hunde's lack of legal status and his situation of 'extreme poverty' did not qualify him as sufficiently 'vulnerable' to fall under the protection of

---

[85] For example, *Ndikumana v the Netherlands* App no 4714/06 (ECHR Decision 2014) para 44; *M.S.S.* (n 132, Ch 1) paras 249–264; *James and others v UK* App no 8793/79 (ECHR 1986) para 47; *Yordanova* (n 351, Ch 2) para 130. For further analysis, see Nicola Napoletano, 'Estensione e Limiti della Dimensione Economica e Sociale della Convenzione Europea dei Diritti Umani in Tempi di Crisi Economico-Finanziaria' (2014) *Diritti Umani e Diritto Internazionale* 8(2) 389, 394–417; Leijten (n 79) 259.

[86] *A.A. v Greece* App no 12186/08 (ECHR 2010) paras 49–65; *C.D. and Others v Greece* App nos 33441/10, 33468/10 and 33476/10 (ECHR 2013) paras 35–37, 47–54; *F.H. v Greece* App no 78456/11 (ECHR 2014) paras 96–102. For further details see Section 1.3.

[87] *Aden Ahmed* (n 273, Ch 2) paras 91–97, emphasis added.

[88] *M.S.S.* (n 132, Ch 1) paras 249–264; *Hunde* (n 48, Ch 3) paras 55, 59.

[89] Ibid (*M.S.S.*) para 254.

the same article. This resulted in his application being deemed manifestly ill-founded and, thus, inadmissible. Similarly, irregular migrants were not considered particularly vulnerable when their conditions of detention were scrutinised in the case of *Khlaifia* v. *Italy*. Indeed, although the Court recognised that the migrant centre in that case 'was not suited to stays of more than a few days', the relative assessment of the level of severity that must be met under Article 3 ECHR resulted in a finding of no violation.[90]

In contrast to the cases of *Hunde* and *Khlaifia*, the Court categorised irregular migrants as vulnerable people in *Chowdury* v. *Greece*, a qualification that triggered a positive obligation on the part of the state party under the ECHR.[91] Here, however, the finding of vulnerability was linked to the specific circumstances of the case – which concerned trafficked irregular migrants who were kept in dire living and working conditions and subjected to forced labour under the threat of armed guards – which were scrutinised for compliance with Article 4(2) of the ECHR (prohibition of slavery and forced labour).[92]

Two further cases elucidate the ECtHR's approach to the right to education and housing and its general approach to the social rights of migrants with either irregular or precarious immigration status. In *Ponomaryovi* v. *Bulgaria*, the Court assessed the state practice of charging regular and irregular migrants different secondary education fees under the lens of Protocol 1, Article 2 on the right to education in combination with the prohibition of discrimination in Article 14. The judgment is interesting because, notwithstanding the finding of a violation on the merits (the case concerned two Russian-born brothers who had been living in Bulgaria since childhood before they became irregular at the age of eighteen), some of its passages reveal a distinct sovereigntist and nationalist stance: '[The] *state may have legitimate reasons for curtailing the use of resource-hungry public services* – such as welfare programmes, public benefits and health care – *by short-term and illegal immigrants, who, as a rule, do not contribute to their funding*.'[93] The Court continues by stating that states 'may also, in certain circumstances, justifiably differentiate between different categories of aliens residing in its territory'.[94] Also, in assessing that proportionality of a differential treatment, the Court 'must confine its attention, as far as possible, to the particular circumstances of the case before it' in which 'the

---

[90] *Khlaifia* (2016) (n 136, Ch 1) para 197.
[91] *Chowdury* (n 19, Introduction), para 97: 'the Court notes that the applicants began working at a time when they were in a situation of vulnerability as irregular migrants without resources and at risk of being arrested, detained and deported [. . .]'.
[92] Ibid, paras 92–101.
[93] *Ponomaryov* (n 19, Introduction) para 54, emphasis added.
[94] Ibid.

applicants were not in the position of individuals arriving in the country unlawfully and then laying claim to the use of its public services, including free schooling'.[95]

Conversely, in the case of *Bah* v. *the UK*, the Court did not find a violation of Articles 14 and 8 ECHR in relation to the denial of social housing to a person who had indefinite leave to remain and who wanted to live with her son who only had conditional leave to remain. The judgment is significant because, although the Court accepted that 'immigration status can amount to a ground of (prohibited) distinction' for the purposes of the non-discrimination clause as per Article 14 ECHR, in this case:

> Given the element of choice involved in immigration status, [. . .] while *differential treatment based on this ground* must still be objectively and reasonably justifiable, the *justification required will not be as weighty as in the case of a distinction based, for example, on nationality*. Furthermore, given that the subject matter of this case – the provision of housing to those in need – is predominantly socio-economic in nature, the margin of appreciation accorded to the Government will be relatively wide.[96]

This case is instructive because the Court links the findings of non-violation to a series of factors, including the preservation of limited welfare resources and the element of 'choice' attached to immigration. Such findings are likely to severely limit the qualification threshold for claims of socioeconomic discrimination where irregular or precarious migrants are concerned. Overall, the ECtHR, lacking a direct competence in socioeconomic affairs, has developed a responsive case-based body of jurisprudence targeting key determinants of health in exceptionally severe circumstances of socioeconomic deprivation concerning migrants. Even though it is difficult to generalise, the Strasbourg Court's failure to qualify irregular migrants as a vulnerable group per se and its emphasis on the immigration sovereignty maxim seem to prevent it from making general declaratory statements on the need to adopt positive, empowering and interrelated measures regarding the right to the determinants of health of irregular migrants and from initiating corresponding interpretive or normative developments.

### 4.2.2 *The Growing Jurisprudence of the ECSR*

Most, if not all, ESC provisions, which protect individual and collective socioeconomic rights, may also be regarded as rights to the social determinants

---

[95] Ibid, paras 59–60.
[96] *Bah v UK* App no 56328/07 (ECHR 2011) paras 45 and 47, emphasis added.

of health. This is particularly true of the rights contained in Articles 2 (just conditions of work), 3 (safe and healthy working conditions), 11 (protection of health), 12 (social security), 13 (social and medical assistance), 14 (benefit from social welfare services), 17 (children and young persons' social, legal and economic protection), 20 (freedom from discrimination in the workplace on the grounds of gender), 30 (protection against poverty and social exclusion) and 31 (housing). In particular, Article 11 requires states to immediately adopt measures of disease prevention and health promotion, and Article 13 imposes the state duty to provide necessary social and medical assistance, in nature or cash, to people without adequate financial resources to meet their basic social and health needs. This interrelation and interdependence between the protection of health and other social rights was recently highlighted by the ECSR, which, during the COVID-19 pandemic, stated that 'historic and ongoing shortcomings in state efforts to secure Charter rights such as the right to housing (Article 31) and the right to freedom from poverty and social exclusion (Article 30) feed directly into the vulnerability of particular social groups in a pandemic'.[97]

The ECSR has upheld a series of decisions on the socioeconomic conditions of irregular migrants. It has 'adjudicated' on the merits of collective complaints in this area despite the limited personal applicability of the norms of the ESC around non-regular migrant health.[98] Although these decisions do not use the term 'determinants of health', they clearly demonstrate the ECSR's reliance on the concept by linking health and socioeconomic conditions to prohibit certain exclusionary state practices.

In *DCI* v. *the Netherlands*, the ECSR held that 'children unlawfully present' are entitled to the right to (temporary) shelter as per Article 31(2) ESC, whereas a lasting right to housing in Article 31(1) ESC 'would run counter to the state's alien policy objective of encouraging persons unlawfully on its territory to return to their countries of origin'.[99] However, human dignity, which is central to the Committee's arguments, requires that 'even temporary shelter must fulfil the demands of safety, health, and hygiene, including basic amenities, i.e. clean water and sufficient lighting and heating'.[100]

In *DCI* v. *Belgium*, the ECSR considered that the failure to provide care and assistance, including adequate reception facilities, to unaccompanied

---

[97] ECSR, 'Statement of the right to [...] health' (n 261, Ch 2) 6.
[98] See Sections 1.4.2 and 3.2.2.
[99] *DCI v the Netherlands* (n 218, Ch 1) paras 41–48.
[100] Ibid, para 62.

minors exposed them to 'serious risks for their lives and health'. In this decision, the Committee held that the state's failure to provide foreign minors with housing and foster homes led to a violation of Article 11 ESC on the right to protection of health, thereby highlighting the interconnected nature of human rights and the impact of the conditions of daily life on individual health.[101]

In *CEC v. the Netherlands*, a collective complaint concerning the right of undocumented adults to emergency social (and medical) assistance as per Article 13(4), the ECSR found that the respondent state, in failing to provide shelter, food, emergency medical care and clothing, which are necessary for protecting human dignity and for the 'basic subsistence of any human being', had not met the irregular migrants' immediate and urgent needs.[102] In justifying the right of everyone, including irregular migrants, to decent living standards, the ECSR made direct reference to the CESCR's concept of core obligations, which include access to 'basic shelter and essential food for everyone' and are 'linked to the dignity of the human person'.[103] With regard to the severity of the situation of socioeconomic deprivation that would trigger the applicability of the Charter, the ECSR clarified that the criteria of 'urgency and seriousness' concerning individual material needs must not be interpreted too narrowly.[104]

The ECSR's decision in the case of *FEANTSA v. the Netherlands* confirmed that states must provide emergency social assistance to everyone to meet their urgent and immediate needs, including shelter, food and clothing.[105] Furthermore, the ECSR considered that the denial of such assistance as a measure to combat irregular migration is not acceptable, as it does not seem necessary to achieve the aims of immigration policy and appears disproportionate.[106] In these last two cases, the dire situation of social emergency in which homeless migrants were living and the risk of irreparable harm led the ECSR to issue two decisions on interim measures while the decisions on the merits were pending.[107]

---

[101] *DCI v Belgium* (n 218, Ch 1) paras 82, 117.
[102] *CEC v the Netherlands* (n 218, Ch 1) paras 105–126.
[103] Ibid, paras 113–115.
[104] Ibid, para 105; *FEANTSA v the Netherlands* (n 221, Ch 1) para 171.
[105] Ibid (FEANTSA) paras 171–173.
[106] Ibid, paras 180–183.
[107] *CEC v the Netherlands* Com no 30/2013 (ECSR decision on immediate measures 2013); *FEANTSA v the Netherlands* Com no 86/2012 (ECSR decision on immediate measures 2013). For further analysis, see Carole Nivard, 'Précisions sur les droits de la Charte sociale Européenne bénéficiant aux étrangers en situation irrégulière' (2014) *La Revue des Droits de*

The last case decided on the merits[108] in this saga is *EUROCEF* v. *France*, where the ECSR held, *inter alia*, that providing inadequate accommodation for unaccompanied foreign minors is likely to make them more vulnerable to homelessness, a factor that runs counter to the right to health set out in Article 11 ESC.[109] In this case, the Committee seemed to regard the quality and capacity of the French reception system as proxies for the determinants of health and delivered similar findings to those it had returned in *DCI* (v. *Belgium*) above. The findings in the case of *EUROCEF* are significant for at least one other reason: the Committee declared that Article 30 ESC (the right to be protected against poverty and social exclusion) is applicable to irregular migrant children. This is in contrast to the decisions in *DCI* (v. *Belgium*) and *FEANTSA*.[110] Until this case, the ECSR had been reluctant to accept that irregular people – who are, in theory, excluded from the ESC's personal scope – could benefit from a 'co-ordinated approach, aimed at preventing and removing obstacles to access the fundamental social rights, in particular employment, housing, training, education, culture, and social and medical assistance', all of which the right to be protected against poverty entails. The reason for such reluctance lies in the tensions between proactive and inclusive measures on the one hand and the threat of social and institutional exclusion and deportation that prevails for non-authorised migrants on the other. This does not mean that the ECSR has abandoned an emergency-oriented approach to the rights of irregular migrants. However, where migrant children are concerned, states are now required to take positive 'measures to prevent and remove obstacles to access fundamental social rights', including the allocation of sufficient resources and the establishment of coordinated, intersectoral and universal anti-poverty policies and corresponding monitoring and enforcement mechanisms.[111] However, having declared the abstract applicability of Article 30 ESC to irregular migrant children, in the case at hand, the ECSR failed to establish a violation of the same due to the disagreement of five Committee members.[112]

*L'Homme – Actualité Droits-Libertés* 1–12 <https://journals.openedition.org/revdh/982> accessed September 2020.

[108] At the time of writing, the ECSR had adopted a decision on admissibility and on immediate measures in the case *International Commission of Jurists and European Council for Refugees and Exiles v Greece*, Com no 173/2018 (ECSR 2019).

[109] *European Committee for Home-Based Priority Action for the Child and the Family (EUROCEF) v France* Com no114/2015 (ECSR 2018) paras 141, 152.

[110] Ibid, paras 57, 180–186; FEANTSA (n 221, Ch 1) para 211.

[111] ECSR, Statement of Interpretation of Article 30 (2013).

[112] *EUROCEF* (n 112) 'Separate Dissenting Opinion of Petros Stangos'.

The ECSR recognises the interconnected nature of human rights and the link between social conditions and health. The relevant case law of the ECSR is relatively progressive, even though the social deprivations that trigger its protection, where adult irregular migrants are concerned, are those that require 'emergency' or 'urgent' medical and social care, at least in relation to Articles 11 and 13 ESC.[113]

### 4.3 INTERNATIONAL STANDARDS AND UN SUPERVISORY BODIES: DEVELOPING AN EXPLICIT RECOGNITION OF THE DETERMINANTS OF HEALTH OF IRREGULAR MIGRANTS AS HUMAN RIGHTS

International human rights law, from its inception to recent interpretative standards, seems to have achieved a greater level of synergy with the technical standards of global health governance than European human rights. An understanding of how socioeconomic conditions can affect health is apparent in the negotiations of the UDHR, and the recent monitoring activities and interpretative statements of the UN treaty bodies and special rapporteurs have, often explicitly, touched upon critical extra-medical determinants of health for irregular migrants.

#### 4.3.1 *The Foundation of the Determinants of Health in Human Rights: The UDHR*

The 'manifesto' of international human rights is the UDHR, which does not include an autonomous right to health. Rather, Article 25(1) UDHR combines medical care with other determinants of health as components of the scope of the right to an adequate standard of living and draws a link between the latter and the right to social security.[114] The drafting history of Article 25 UDHR reflects different trends regarding health as a human right. The first draft drawn up by the Drafting Committee of the UDHR included a right to 'medical care' and a state 'obligation' to promote public health in Article 35, a right to good working conditions in Article 38 and a right to food, housing and healthy living in Article 42.[115] The representatives of the United States and

---

[113] For example, *CEC* (n 218, Ch 1) paras 73, 75; *FEANTSA* (n 221, Ch 1) paras 171, 173, 182–183, 186.

[114] For the full text of Article 25 UDHR, see Section 2.2.

[115] Commission on Human Rights (UNCHR) (n 26, Ch 2).

France submitted proposals for alternative texts which accentuated social measures to promote the 'highest' or 'best' attainable standard of health, beyond the mere provision of medical care.[116] Furthermore, the Commission on Human Rights' (UNCHR) analysis of the applicable provisions of national constitutions concerning health protection contained several references to public health and social security measures.[117]

After the second session of the UNCHR in December 1947, the original focus on medical care gave way to a broader concept of health, which is apparent in the proposed draft:

> Everyone without distinction as to economic and social conditions has the right to the preservation of his health through the highest standard of food, clothing, housing and medical care which the resources of the State or community can provide. The responsibility of the State and community for the health and safety of its people can be fulfilled only by provision of adequate health and social measures.[118]

Subsequent draft texts gradually got closer to the final formulation, which places primary emphasis on the right to an adequate standard of living in close relation to health and social security.[119] This demonstrates that health and socioeconomic well-being have been explicitly bound together since the birth of the post-war universal and international bill of rights. Although this language refers to a personal universality of rights, it should be recalled – from the analysis conducted in Chapter 1 – that the application of human rights to non-nationals or migrants, including the undocumented, was largely absent until the 1970s.

---

[116] See UNCHR – Drafting Committee, 'United States Revised Suggestions for Redrafts of Certain Articles in the Draft Outline' (1 June 1947) E/CN.4/AC.1/8, Article 36: 'Everyone, without distinction as to economic or social condition, has a right to the highest attainable standard of health [which] can be fulfilled only by provision of adequate health and social measures'; UNCHR – Drafting Committee, 'Revised Suggestions Submitted by the Representative of France for Articles of the International Declaration of Rights' (20 June 1947) E/CN.4/AC.1/W.2/REV.2, Article 33: 'Everyone has a right to the best health conditions possible and to assistance to preserve them. The community shall promote public hygiene and the betterment of housing and food conditions.'

[117] UNCHR – Drafting Committee, 'International Bill of Rights Documented Outline' (11 June 1947) E/CN.4/AC.1/3/add.1, 285–289.

[118] UNCHR, Report to the Economic and Social Council on the 2nd Session of the Commission' (2–17 December 1947) E/600(SUPP), 18; 'Report of the Drafting Committee [on an International Bill of Rights] to the Commission on Human Rights' (21 May 1948) E/CN.4/95, 11.

[119] UNCHR, 'Report of the 3rd Session of the Commission on Human Rights' (24 May–18 June 1948) E/800, 13.

### 4.3.2 *Elaborating on UN Human Rights Treaties' Obligations*

While the UDHR has undoubtedly had a significant influence on rights development, the main contemporary source of human rights obligations regarding the right to health care and to the determinants of health in international law is the ICESCR. While a textual analysis of Article 12 ICESCR is provided in Chapter 2, the following evaluation of the determinants of health for irregular migrants is primarily based on the CESCR's COs and general comments considered in the light of other treaty bodies' documents and the reports of a number of Special Procedures of the HRC.

### 4.3.2.1 The Concluding Observations of the CESCR

For this study, all COs between 2009 and 2020 have been scrutinised to identify the latest applicable trends regarding the social rights of irregular migrants. This time frame was chosen as it coincides with a renewed emphasis on the determinants of health in global public health discourse – a trend which, arguably, ought to have been known to the international human rights institutions.[120] In these documents, the terms 'underlying determinants of health' and 'social determinants of health' are not normally mentioned. The Committee preferred to scrutinise the living conditions and access to social and health services of people at large and of vulnerable groups within the scope of other social rights instead of qualifying them as determinants of health and linking them to Article 12 ICESCR.

Regarding irregular migrants, the main areas of concern, addressed in several COs, have been the difficulty these people face in accessing health care and the informal and abusive working conditions to which they are exposed.[121] The former, which the CSDH describes as one of several social determinants of health, is discussed at length in Chapter 3. The latter is arguably one of the most important determinants of health because '[e]mployment and working conditions have powerful effects on health and

---

[120] CSDH Report (n 111, Ch 2) and the Rio Declaration (n 27) are respectively dated 2008 and 2011.

[121] For example, CESCR, COs on Spain (n 143, Ch 3) para 42; Germany (n 144, Ch 3) para 58; The Russian Federation (6 October 2017) E/C.12/RUS/CO/6, para 32; Cyprus (12 June 2009) E/C.12/CYP/CO/5, paras 15, 27, 28, 40; The Netherlands (n 208, Ch 2) paras 39–41; Poland (n 208, Ch 2) para 21; UK (n 203, Ch 2) para 55; Canada (n 201, Ch 2) para 29; Greece (n 201, Ch 2) paras 35, 11; Tajikistan (25 March 2015) E/C.12/TJK/CO/2–3, para 22; Albania (18 December 2013) E/C.12/ALB/CO/2–3, para 13; Norway (n 101, Ch 3) para 21; Denmark (n 125, Ch 3) E/C.12/DNK/CO/5, para 18; Kazakhstan (7 June 2010) E/C.12/KAZ/CO/1, paras 14, 20; Belgium (n 104, Ch 3) paras 22, 23.

health equity. When these are good, they can provide financial security, social status, personal development, social relations and self-esteem, and protection from physical and psychosocial hazards'.[122] The importance of this for people whose social position is predominantly defined by a state-made absence of legal migratory status and who, therefore, must normally work in the informal economy, in a potentially unsafe, hazardous and precarious position, is self-explanatory.[123]

Furthermore, other COs contain important recommendations for establishing a genuinely accessible education system for all, and particularly children, regardless of any irregularity of immigration status which may reduce their ability to enrol.[124] Some recent findings are worth outlining. For example, in the 2017 reporting cycle for the Netherlands, the CESCR found that making 'access to housing, education and welfare benefits [conditional] to legal residency status have contributed to a precarious situation for undocumented migrants and rejected asylum seekers'.[125] Accordingly, the Committee reminded the state of its obligation to 'ensure that all persons in its jurisdiction enjoy the minimum essential levels of each of the rights in the Covenant, including the rights to food, housing, health, water and sanitation' and urged the state to:

> Refrain from making access to food, water and housing conditional on an individual's willingness to return to his or her country of origin; [...] put in place a comprehensive strategy to ensure that everyone, including undocumented migrants, enjoys the minimum essential levels of all Covenant rights and ensure it is supported by adequate funding.[126]

Although it is not completely clear what the required 'level' of social rights – the 'how' of the theories on distributive justice – is, states are required to guarantee 'minimum essential levels' of rights to irregular migrants. This recalls the formulation of General Comment No. 3, which identifies depriving people 'of essential foodstuffs, of essential primary health care, of basic

---

[122] Marmot and Wilkinson (n 103, Ch 2), as referenced in CSDH Report (n 111, Ch 2) 72.

[123] Michele Salvatore et al., 'Work Related Injuries among Immigrant Workers in Italy' (2013) *Journal of Immigrant Minority Health* 15 182–187; Stefano Angeleri, 'The Health, Safety and Associated Rights of Migrant Workers in International and European Human Rights Law' in Angeleri, Calafà and Protopapa (eds) *Promoting the Health and Safety of Migrant Workers: Different Disciplines, A Shared Objective* (Working Papers of the Centre for the Study of European Labour Law 'Massimo d'Antona' 2020) 2, 12–18.

[124] CESCR, COs on South Africa (n 104, Ch 3) paras 72, 73; Canada (n 203, Ch 2) para 55; Latvia (30 March 2021) E/C.12/LVA/CO/2, paras 46, 47(f).

[125] CESCR, COs on the Netherlands (n 208, Ch 2) para 39.

[126] Ibid, para 40.

shelter and housing, or of the most basic forms of education' as a failure on the part of the state to meet its undeferrable obligations under the ICESCR.[127] The COs regarding Germany are similarly significant, because they recommend, for the first time, the establishment of 'firewalls' to allow irregular migrants to access basic services without fear of being reported to immigration authorities and facing potential deportation.[128] Even though firewalls guarantee the actual enjoyment of social rights that would otherwise remain illusory, the level of recommended social benefits for irregular migrants is 'basic', which, without further qualifiers, seems to indicate that irregular migrants either have access to a subset of the available services or can access all available services but only to the extent that their urgent social needs are met. Recent recommendations for Bulgaria employ a different terminology with regard to the levels of entitlement of people living in migrant centres: they should be provided with 'adequate food meeting their specific needs, and with essential non-food items'.[129] The quality of social benefits here seems to exceed bare survival needs. It is finally worth mentioning, in relation to Argentina, the call to lift barriers to immigration status regularisation to ensure greater enjoyment of social rights for all.[130] After all, irregular migrants' legal status (or lack thereof) is the main factor that prevents their treatment from being equalised to that of citizens and regular migrants. Situations of neglect or reduced access to social rights for migrants are often raised in combination with discrimination vis-à-vis state measures concerning other social groups or the general population. Indeed, the CESCR has, for quite a few years, explicitly interpreted immigration status as prohibited or suspect grounds for discrimination.[131]

Finally, it is also interesting to note that 'poverty and inequality' often come under scrutiny as part of the monitoring activities of the CESCR, during which the link between the socioeconomic deprivations of vulnerable people, including irregular migrants, and the enjoyment of rights, including the right to health, is brought to the fore.[132] However, the CESCR, in its analysis of

---

[127] CESCR, GC3 (n 80, Ch 2) para 10.

[128] CESCR, COs on Germany (n 144, Ch 3) paras 26, 27.

[129] CESCR, COs on Bulgaria (29 March 2019) E/C.12/BGR/CO/6, paras 38, 39.

[130] CESCR, COs on Argentina (12 October 2018) E/C.12/ARG/CO/4, para 39.

[131] CESCR, GC20 (n 100, Ch 1) para 30; CESCR, Statement on migrant rights (n 174, Ch 1) para 5; CESCR, COs on Belgium (n 104, Ch 3) 22.

[132] For example, CESCR, COs on Poland (n 208, Ch 2) para 35; Costa Rica (21 October 2016) E/C.12/CRI/CO/5, para 39; Dominican Republic (7 October 2016) E/C.12/DOM/CO/4, para 48; Greece (n 201, Ch 2) paras 29, 30; Kyrgyzstan (7 July 2015) E/C.12/KGZ/CO/2–3, para 20; Vietnam (15 December 2014) E/C.12/VNM/CO/2–4, para 28; Nepal (12 December 2014) E/

multilayered discrimination, tends not to call into question 'established political power structures, including sovereign control of territory'[133] as factors that keep irregular migrants in general situations of socioeconomic deprivation.

### 4.3.2.2 The General Comments of the CESCR

While the aforementioned COs have indirectly elaborated on the determinants of health approach, it is in its general comments where the CESCR has explicitly described and interpreted UDH or SDH as relevant meta-concepts of human rights obligations.

Beginning with General Comment No. 14, having described the UDH as the socioeconomic conditions that affect the enjoyment of the right to health and that are, thus, included in the scope of this right, the CESCR lists measures that address the UDH as immediate core obligations regarding the right to health and prioritises measures involving vulnerable groups, including irregular migrants. These core obligations include ensuring 'access to the minimum essential food which is nutritionally adequate and safe, to ensure freedom from hunger to everyone' and 'access to basic shelter, housing and sanitation, and an adequate supply of safe and potable water'.[134]

The CESCR's general comment is not particularly helpful for identifying the minimum acceptable quality and quantity of the measures targeting the determinants of health: essential food and freedom from hunger, on the one hand, basic housing and shelter, on the other, require different levels of social intervention. Whereas this wording is broad and unspecific regarding the core content of a 'substantive minimum', it can provide differentiated guidance to states at different levels of development. Furthermore, it is also important to pinpoint that state obligations are still qualified by the rule of non-retrogression for realised elements or levels of socioeconomic rights, in particular vis-à-vis vulnerable groups.

In relation to the levels of the UDH, the Declaration of Alma-Ata, referenced in General Comment No. 14, may offer some partial clarification with regard to at least some determinants. Primary health care, to which the CESCR refers, includes, at minimum, 'education concerning prevailing health problems and the methods of preventing and controlling them;

---

C.12/NPL/CO/3, para 25; Lithuania (24 June 2014) E/C.12/LTU/CO/2, para 18; Denmark (n 125, Ch 3) para 16.

[133] Jaya Ramji-Nogales, 'Undocumented Migrants and the Failures of Universal Individualism' (2014) *Vanderbilt Journal of Transnational Law* 47 740.

[134] CESCR, GC14 (n 27, Introduction) para 43.

promotion of food supply and *proper* nutrition; [and] an *adequate supply* of safe water and basic sanitation'.[135] Apart from this limited, exogenous and programmatic guidance, the lack of further qualifiers for most of the social rights that support the determinants of health makes the identification of the immediate or progressive level of protection and fulfilment somewhat unclear.

Although one may argue that 'adequacy' applies to the programmatic and relative standard of achievement of socioeconomic rights and exceeds the immediate realisation of the core,[136] the CESCR recommends, *inter alia*, that states guarantee 'equal access for *all* to the underlying determinants of health'.[137] Recalling the analysis in Chapter 3 of non-discrimination and vulnerability in relation to limiting access to health care, for the CESCR, here too, any detrimental or potentially discriminatory treatment that targets irregular migrants would, in principle, need to pass a legitimacy and proportionality test. Accordingly, as irregular migrants qualify as vulnerable people and, thus, as a target of especially protective measures, social rights should not be excessively or unnecessarily limited.[138]

General Comment No. 19 analyses the right to social security, a technical matter at the 'core' of the welfare system, which requires states, *inter alia*, to '[e]nsure access to a social security scheme that provides a minimum essential level of benefits to all individuals and families that will enable them to acquire at least essential health care, basic shelter and housing, water and sanitation, foodstuffs, and the most basic forms of education'.[139] It also indicates that non-nationals should have access to 'non-contributory schemes for income support, affordable access to health care and family support' and that 'all persons, irrespective of their nationality, residency or immigration status, are entitled to primary and emergency medical care'.[140]

While contributory schemes are, by definition, excluded for workers within the informal economy, including irregular migrants, non-contributory schemes that support those whose income is below the poverty threshold and that are based on a needs assessment should be accessed without discrimination, especially for vulnerable groups.[141] Core obligations similar to those set out in General Comment No. 14 are established here, and while targeted

[135] Declaration of Alma-Ata (n 28, Introduction).
[136] Bilchiz (n 57).
[137] CESCR, GC14 (n 27, Introduction) para 36.
[138] See Section 3.3.1.1; CESCR, Statement on migrant rights (n 174, Ch 1).
[139] CESCR, 'General Comment No. 19, the Right to Social Security (Article 9 ICESCR)' (4 February 2008) E/C.12/GC/19, para 59 (a).
[140] Ibid, para 37, emphasis added.
[141] Ibid, para 59 (b), (e).

steps are formulated to protect vulnerable groups, legal limitations and differentiation (including on the grounds of legal immigration status), though not prohibited, are required to be objective and reasonable.[142]

Regarding exploitative working conditions, General Comment No. 23, on just and favourable working conditions, acknowledges the special vulnerability of irregular migrants 'to exploitation, long working hours, unfair wages and dangerous and unhealthy working environments'.[143] Accordingly, states are required to take, among other steps, the following targeted procedural measures. First, 'labour inspectorates should focus on monitoring the rights of workers and not be used for other purposes, such as checking the migration status of workers'.[144] Second, 'access to effective judicial or other appropriate remedies, including adequate reparation, restitution, compensation, satisfaction or guarantees of non-repetition [. . .] should not be denied on the grounds that the affected person is an irregular migrant'.[145]

General Comment No. 22 on sexual and reproductive health, which was issued sixteen years after General Comment No. 14 on the right to health, captures the current approach of the CESCR and directly elaborates on both the UDH (which refer to conditions of daily life) and the SDH (the underlying structural determinants of health). Regarding the former, the CESCR adds to the above-mentioned list of material living standards the need for 'effective protection from all forms of violence, torture and discrimination and other human rights violations that have a negative impact on the right to sexual and reproductive health'.[146] Furthermore, the Committee makes a direct interdisciplinary reference to those underlying factors that affect the conditions of living:

> The right to sexual and reproductive health is also deeply affected by 'social determinants of health', as defined by the WHO. In all countries, patterns of sexual and reproductive health generally reflect social inequalities in society and unequal distribution of power based on *gender, ethnic origin,* age, disability and other factors. *Poverty, income inequality, systemic discrimination* and marginalization based on grounds identified by the Committee are all social determinants of sexual and reproductive health, which also have an impact on the enjoyment of an array of other rights as well.[147]

[142] Ibid, paras 37–38.
[143] CESCR, 'General Comment no. 23, the Right to Just and Favorable Conditions of Work (Article 7 ICESCR)' (4 March 2016) E/C.12/GC/23, para 47(f).
[144] Ibid, para 54.
[145] Ibid, para 57.
[146] CESCR, GC22 (n 209, Ch 2) para 7.
[147] Ibid, para 8, emphasis added.

These determinants of health – including 'harmful practices and gender-based violence', which need to be eliminated – even feature in the immediate core obligations regarding this dimension of the right to health.[148] Finally, in the same document, refugees, stateless persons, asylum seekers and undocumented migrants are found to have 'additional vulnerability by condition of their detention or legal status'. This requires states to take particular steps to ensure their sexual and reproductive health.[149]

Another applicable reference to the social rights that support the determinants of health is made in the CESCR's 2017 statement regarding migrants and refugees, which establishes, with regard to core obligations, that states have a duty, at least, 'to secure freedom from *hunger*, to guarantee access to water to satisfy *basic needs*, access to essential drugs, access to education, complying with *minimum educational standards*'.[150]

Without detracting from the detailed recommendations of the other general comments in this section, this statement, which is the specific and potentially universal document that restates the socioeconomic standards of all migrants, including irregular migrants, seems to frame social rights other than the right to health care in overall general and minimalist terms.

### 4.3.2.3 Contributions of Other UN Treaty Bodies

As the report of the CSDH – like other WHO documents – makes several references to living conditions during childhood as a central determinant of health during an individual's life course, it seems appropriate to briefly recall here the CRC and the applicable standards developed by its monitoring body. Indeed, some recent general comments of the CRC Committee acknowledge the SDH and the intersectional vulnerability of migrant children.

Chapters 2 and 3 mention that Article 24 CRC identifies PHC, as per the Declaration of Alma-Ata, as the foundational and explicit approach to the right to health of the child and requires state parties to ensure necessary health care and 'the provision of adequate nutritious food and clean drinking-water'.[151] The PHC approach emphasises, *inter alia*, 'the need to eliminate exclusion and reduce social disparities in health; organize health services

---

[148] Ibid, para 49(d).
[149] Ibid, para 31.
[150] CESCR, Statement on migrant rights (n 174, Ch 1) para 9, recalling the mentions to core obligations in several general comments, emphasis added.
[151] CRC (n 42, Introduction) Article 24.2(b) (c).

around people's needs and expectations; [and] integrate health into related sectors'.[152]

Furthermore, the two recent joint general comments of the CRC and CMW Committees clearly recognise that 'structural determinants, such as the global economic and financial situation, poverty, unemployment, migration and population displacements, war and civil unrest, discrimination and marginalization', deeply affect children's health.[153] Migration processes 'can pose risks, including physical harm, psychological trauma, marginalization, discrimination, xenophobia and sexual and economic exploitation, family separation, immigration raids and detention', all of which are important determinants of health.[154]

Regarding the level of social entitlements, these human rights bodies have clearly stated that all migrant children should have access 'to health care *equal* to that of nationals, regardless of their migration status', a 'standard of living *adequate* for their physical, mental, spiritual and moral development', and '*full* access to all levels and all aspects of education'.[155] These rights should be guaranteed by the introduction of 'procedures and standards to establish firewalls between public or private service providers, including public or private housing providers, and immigration enforcement authorities'.[156] Whereas international human rights obligations require that irregular migrant adults, outside of the provision of urgent and essential PHC, have access to at least basic levels of social rights, in the case of children, the enjoyment of social rights that support the determinants of health is generally equalised with country nationals.

Other treaty bodies have emphasised different factors which expose migrants in general, and undocumented people in particular, to social conditions that are detrimental to their health and well-being: the CERD and CEDAW Committees, interpreting state obligation under CEDAW and International Convention on the Elimination of All Forms of Racial Discrimination (ICERD), have highlighted patterns of race- and gender-based discrimination, which are likely to intersect with poverty and non-national status, as serious human rights violations.

The Durban Declaration adopted at the World Conference against Racism defines 'xenophobia against non-nationals, particularly migrants' as 'one of the

---

[152] CRC Committee, GC15 (n 173, Ch 2) para 4.
[153] Ibid, paras 4, 5; CMW and CRC Committees, JGC 4/23 (n 175, Ch 1) para 54.
[154] CMW and CRC Committees, JGC 3/22 (n 175, Ch 1) para 40.
[155] Ibid, paras 49, 55, 59, emphasis added.
[156] Ibid, paras 52, 56, 60.

main sources of contemporary racism' and notes 'human rights violations against members of such groups occur widely in the context of discriminatory, xenophobic and racist practices'.[157] The growth of these phenomena, which are all too often compound with long-lasting discrimination against people with African origins and descent,[158] in multicultural societies led the CERD Committee to interpretively extend the scope of the International Convention on the Elimination of All Forms of Racial Discrimination and refocus its monitoring activities to encompass differentiation on the grounds of nationality and legal status, as suspect forms of discrimination on the grounds of race, the prohibition of which has become customary international law.[159] As racial discrimination – which also intersects with non-national and undocumented status – is closely associated with social exclusion, unfavourable socioeconomic statuses and pervasive forms of private and institutional rights abuse in general, race or ethnicity is itself considered a social determinant of health, also recognised by the CSDH, which intersectoral state actions on public health and human rights are required to address.[160]

Unhealthy social environments and exposure to risks for health can be exponentially worse for people with non-male gender and precarious migratory status. While Chapter 3 indicted that special biological and psychosocial risk factors of ill health must be adequately addressed to avoid gender-based discrimination and health inequity,[161] other social determinants of health are recognised as equally critical for women's well-being and health by the CEDAW Committee. These include unequal power relationships at home or at work, informal work environment and gender stereotyping work opportunities, pay gaps, the feminisation of poverty and gender-based violence, which 'manifests itself on a continuum of multiple, interrelated and recurring forms, in a range of settings',[162] including trafficking for sexual exploitation.[163] While migration can create 'new opportunities for women and may be a means for their economic empowerment through wider participation, it may

---

[157] Durban Declaration (n 91, Ch 1) para 16.

[158] CERD Committee, 'General Recommendation No. 34 on Racial Discrimination against People of African Descent' (3 October 2011) para 6.

[159] ICERD (n 42, Introduction) Article 1; CERD Committee, GR30 (n 105, Ch 1) paras 2–3, 5, 11.

[160] CSDH Report (n 111, Ch 2) 43.

[161] See reflections on access to sexual and reproductive health care at Section 3.4.3.2, *supra*.

[162] CEDAW Committee, 'General Recommendation No. 35 on Gender-Based Violence against Women, Updating General Recommendation No. 19' (26 July 2017) para 6.

[163] CEDAW Committee, GR24 (n 240, Ch 2) paras 12, 15; CEDAW Committee, 'General Recommendation No. 38 (2020) on Trafficking in Women and Girls in the Context of Global Migration' (6 November 2020) para 20; CSDH Report (n 111, Ch 2) 'Gender Equity' 145–155.

also place their human rights and security at risk',[164] particularly if they are 'compelled to travel through irregular channels' or if it results in 'an irregular migration situation'.[165] Failing to address the special vulnerability of women to human rights abuse, regardless of their migration status, constitutes, at minimum, gender-based discrimination, which is radically prohibited in human rights law and a negative determinant of health.

Finally, Article 6 ICCPR (the right to life), as interpreted by the HRCtee, may constitute another normative vehicle for fulfilling the realisation of the right to the determinants of health of irregular migrants in international law because 'the duty to protect life also implies that States parties should take appropriate measures to address the general conditions in society that may give rise to direct threats to life or prevent individuals from enjoying their right to life with dignity'.[166] These include preventive measures concerning work-related accidents, environmental degradation, substance abuse, gender-based violence and, where necessary, measures for ensuring access to 'essential goods and services such as food, water, shelter, health care, electricity and sanitation'.[167] In the aforementioned case of *Toussaint* v. *Canada*, regarding access to urgent health care for an irregular migrant woman, the HRCtee held that everyone, including an irregular migrant, has an 'inherent right to life'. Accordingly, any differentiation regarding access to essential care based on the applicant's migratory status, which 'could result in the author's loss of life or in irreversible negative consequences for the author's health', would hardly be considered reasonable, objective and proportionate to the state interest of preventing irregular migration.[168] This constitutes an important 'precedent' for legal advocacy in other areas linked to socioeconomic rights as determinants of health to challenge the denial of minimum living standards necessary for the protection of life.[169]

### 4.3.2.4 The Special Procedures: An Endorsement for Healthy Living Environments as a Human Rights Issue

Virtually all Special Procedures of the HRC have monitored and studied the impact of human mobility and displacement on human rights, and migration

---

[164] CEDAW Committee, GR26 (n 195, Ch 3) para 2.
[165] CEDAW Committee, GR38 (n 163) para 22.
[166] HRCtee, GC36 (n 193, Ch 1) para 26.
[167] Ibid.
[168] Ibid, paras 11.7 and 11.8, emphasis added.
[169] ECSR-Net, 'Toussaint v. Canada – Significance of the Case', 12 December 2018, <www.escr-net.org/caselaw/2018/toussaint-v-canada-ccprc123d23482014–2018> accessed 12 December 2020.

is considered a cross-cutting issue in their activities.[170] Some of their reports are particularly relevant in terms of recommending human rights–compliant actions that address key determinants of health for irregular migrants, as they focus on several interconnected human rights. For instance, the special rapporteur on the right to food stated that the 'systemic inequality and discrimination' that migrant communities experience 'contribute to severe economic exploitation, social exclusion and political invisibility', which endanger their effective enjoyment of the right to food. This implicitly affirms the CSDH model, according to which socio-institutional contexts can affect people's social positions and eventually bring about unhealthy conditions of living.[171] The rapporteur, endorsing a 'leave no one behind approach' to development and human rights–based policies, recommends that states adopt immediate and long-term social measures and labour-related regulations to ensure that all 'migrants can feed themselves in a dignified matter'.[172]

Gender, migration and social security nets, which are key determinants of health, were examined by the independent expert on the effects of foreign debts, who dedicated an entire thematic report to the adverse effects of economic reforms on women's socioeconomic rights. He recommended that social protection mechanisms should be accessible 'for all throughout their lives, without regard to employment, migration or any other status' and that 'given the number of women in the informal sector and the vast amount of time that women spend on unpaid care work, the introduction of universal non-contributory social protection is essential' for the protection of human rights and for addressing gender inequalities.[173]

Among other special rapporteurs, the mandate holders on the right to housing have produced some significant reports highlighting the special vulnerabilities of irregular migrants with respect to homelessness or crowded and unhealthy living conditions, which are often compounded by these migrants' inability to access the justice system without being exposed to

---

[170] OHCHR, 'Non-exhaustive List of Special Procedures Reports Relevant to Migration' (last update 2020) <www.ohchr.org/Documents/HRBodies/SP/List_SP_Reports_Migration.pdf> accessed 10 February 2021.

[171] Hilal Elver, 'Interim Report of the Special Rapporteur on the Right to Food (Focus: SDGs and the Right to Food)' (15 July 2019) A/74/164, para 43.

[172] Ibid, paras 7–8, 46–47. The rapporteur also highlighted the special 'vulnerability to food insecurity and human rights violations' of agricultural undocumented workers in 'Interim Report of the Special Rapporteur on the Right to Food (Focus: Agricultural Workers)' (16 July 2018) A/73/164.

[173] Juan P. Bohoslavsky, 'Report of the Independent Expert on the Effects of Foreign Debt [. . .] on the Full Enjoyment of All Human Rights (Focus: Impact of Economic Reforms and Austerity Measures on Women's Human Rights)' (18 July 2018) A/73/179, para 90(4).

immigration enforcement authorities.[174] To effectively realise this right, which is critical for the physical and mental health of people, states are urged to ensure that 'laws, strategies and plans of action are implemented in such a way as to address [migrant status] discrimination by public and private actors', that 'housing should not be denied to undocumented migrants' and that 'they must be afforded a minimum level of housing assistance that ensures conditions consistent with human dignity'.[175]

A certain alignment with the positions of the public health movement and their emphasis on the SDH can indeed be found in the arguments and findings of the special rapporteur on the right to health.[176] A former mandate holder, in his report on the health of migrant workers, which recalls a previous report of the IOM, stated that migration itself should be seen as a determinant of health. Indeed, the conditions of pre-departure, transit, arrival and stay in receiving states determine unfavourable health outcomes for migrant workers, including undocumented people.[177] He called for the participation of all migrants – regardless of their status – in trade unions and in the formulation, implementation, monitoring and enforcement of laws and policies concerning their living and labour conditions, including those related to occupational health.[178] Measures that target an enhancement of irregular migrants' working conditions, including labour inspections, are important determinants of health, as many irregular migrants are precariously employed and even exploited in sectors such as construction and agriculture.[179]

Among other references to the UDH with regard to migrant workers, the rapporteur acknowledged that 'fear of detention and deportation renders migrant workers more vulnerable and unable to enjoy the right to health and its underlying determinants', as these are crucial stress factors that are likely to affect undocumented people's mental and physical health.[180] The former mandate holder has gone so far as to define 'discrimination and stigma' as '[s]ocial determinants in the enjoyment of the right to health, as social

---

[174] Leilani Farha, 'Report of the Special Rapporteur on Adequate Housing (Focus: Access to Justice for the Right to Housing)' (15 January 2019) A/HRC/40/61, para 54.

[175] Raquel Rolnik, 'Report of the Special Rapporteur on Adequate Housing (Focus: Migrants)' (9 August 2010) A/65/261, paras V(B), 83, 93.

[176] Hunt (n 12) paras 5–7.

[177] Grover (n 253, Ch 2) para 6; IOM (n 3).

[178] Ibid (Grover) para 14.

[179] Ibid, paras 6, 46, 62; Anand Grover, 'Report of the Special Rapporteur on the Right to [...] Health (Focus: Occupational Health)' (10 April 2012) A/HRC/20/15, paras 38–44; See also, Urmila Bhoola, 'Report of the Special Rapporteur on Contemporary Forms of Slavery [...] Visit to Italy' (25 July 2019) UN Doc. n. A/HRC/42/44/Add.1, part B.

[180] Ibid (Grover) paras 37, 66.

inequalities and exclusion shape health outcomes and contribute to increasing the burden of disease borne by marginalized groups'.[181] The mandate holders on the right to health have made substantial use of the terminology of the CSDH. For example, one of them has recognised that power asymmetries and unbalanced approaches to health policies, both in terms of material priorities and target groups, represent a 'departure from a holistic approach to human rights' and from a paradigm based on 'the need to reduce poverty and inequalities, including those within and between regions and countries'.[182] Additionally, in a recent report on the relationship between migration and the right to health, the rapporteur recognised that a rights-based approach to health requires consideration of the societal and community-level determinants of the mental health of people on the move,[183] including 'conflict, violence and socioeconomic inequalities', which are 'by-products of powerful political structures', and discrimination experienced in host countries, which reflects 'complex social hierarchies and power relations'.[184]

International human rights law integrates, either directly or indirectly, the standards of the global health movement and extends them to irregular migrants. However, the 'level' of social rights to which irregular migrants are entitled, with some notable exceptions, remains to be clarified: the recurrent use of the word 'basic' seems to undermine the emphasis of human rights law on vulnerability and empowerment, while *general* statements expressing concerns for discriminatory practices on the ground of legal status in the enjoyment of social rights may fail to provide operational guidance vis-à-vis the reality of exclusion that irregular migrants experience in law and in practice.

### 4.3.3 *The Global Compact for Migration and the Determinants of Health*

Finally, the Compact for Migration, explicitly drawing on international human rights law,[185] extends to the socioeconomic situation of all migrants, regardless of their legal status.

Objective 15 of the Compact for Migration recommends ensuring that states, *inter alia*, guarantee 'access to basic services for migrants' in a way that 'does not exacerbate vulnerabilities of irregular migrants'. However, as

---

[181] Pūras (n 251, Ch 2) para 22.
[182] Ibid, paras 49, 51, 55.
[183] Pūras (mental health and human mobility) (n 253, Ch 2) paras 49, 50.
[184] Ibid, para 25.
[185] GCM (n 92, Ch 1) paras 2, 4, 15.

indicated in Chapter 3, the word 'firewalls' disappeared from the final version of this recommendation. In terms of the type of 'basic services' that must be accessible to all migrants, the Compact mentions only health care and education, thus failing to 'fully appreciate the interconnected needs and experiences that migrants have, [...] which require access to a broad array of services' and enabling conditions,[186] including housing, employment services and social assistance, among many others. The Compact also adds that service delivery should not be discriminatory, but that different treatment of regular and irregular migrants is legitimate when it is 'based on law, proportionate, [and] pursue[s] a legitimate aim, in accordance with international human rights law'.[187]

A clear indication of the importance of addressing the determinants of health is absent from the final text of the Compact, although they are cited in the WHO guidelines referred to in the Compact.[188] These WHO guidelines on the promotion of health for refugees and migrants include as a priority the need to 'enhance capacity to address the social determinants of health' of migrants.[189] The recommended way forward consists of 'improving basic services such as water, sanitation, housing and education', as well as multisectoral public policy responses.[190]

In other objectives of the Compact, states pledge to address situations that correspond to certain determinants of health, including migrants' working conditions, gender-related vulnerabilities and structural drivers of migration in origin countries.[191] Not unlike some of the human rights instruments already discussed, the Compact identifies as its 'guiding principles' both the enjoyment of human rights by every migrant and the state power to distinguish between regular and irregular migrants and to expel the former. It will be instructive to observe whether the implementation of, and the follow-up to, this cooperative framework will contribute to better health outcomes for irregular migrants through genuine intersectoral measures at the international, regional, domestic and local levels or whether the social rights that support health will be maintained at a bare survival level and without interconnected empowering policy measures.

---

[186] Hastie (n 86, Ch 3).
[187] GCM (n 92, Ch 1) para 31.
[188] Ibid.
[189] WHO, Framework of Priorities and Guiding Principles to Promote the Health of Refugees and Migrants, endorsed by WHA Res 70.15 (n 62, Ch 3) para D.3.
[190] Ibid.
[191] GCM (n 92, Ch 1) paras 18(b), 22(i) and 23(c).

## 4.4 CONCLUSIONS

This chapter employs the concepts of empowerment, interrelatedness, vulnerability and intersectoral actions to ground a truly holistic approach that builds bridges between human rights and public health. Embracing these concepts entails addressing the determinants of health of everyone to establish real opportunities and capabilities to achieve individual well-being and good health outcomes. However, these persuasive concepts tend to clash with – and dissipate in the face of – states' desire to socially exclude non-authorised non-nationals as a means of constructive deportation. This chapter tests this hypothesis against the major findings of European and international human rights law.

With regard to the European human rights system, the ECtHR has adopted a restrictive approach to the rights that support key determinants of health of irregular migrants, based on case-by-case assessments and limited statements of general application. This led to the adoption of protective standards for undocumented people's determinants of health only in cases characterised by particularly severe medical issues, forced labour, appalling socioeconomic deprivation or the right to education in exceptional circumstances. A positive note, in terms of adjudication on the determinants of health, comes from the ECSR, although it still insists – except for the case of children – on urgent measures of social protection. Unfortunately, the fact that the most well-known human rights case-based jurisprudence in Europe emanates from the ECtHR, which holds a civil rights mandate, intensifies the impression that measures addressing health care and the determinants of health are instrumental for safeguarding life and personal integrity rather than for protecting health as a human right and social value in itself.

In international human rights law, the CESCR and the CRC Committee, in their general comments, have incorporated the UDH into the scope of the right to health, and this practice has been accentuated in their most recent general comments, especially on sexual and reproductive health and children's health, including in relation to irregular migrants. A similar trend can be observed in the reports of the special rapporteur on the right to health, who has, since the early 2000s, proved willing to acknowledge the concept of the SDH and has qualified migration itself as a determinant of health. Furthermore, several other human rights bodies, such as the CERD and CEDAW Committees, have recognised the compounding effect of constructs such as race and gender on migrant living standards and health outcomes, which human rights–based state law, policy and practice are required to address to avoid perpetrating multiple or intersectional discrimination.

The more problematic question to answer concerns what exactly the level of social entitlements, among other SDH, for irregular migrants in international human rights law is, as the jurisprudence oscillates between equalised and basic socioeconomic rights while increasingly requiring the provision of holistic and easily accessible service points. Although the principle of non-discrimination and vulnerability should limit the restriction of social rights that support the determinants of health of irregular migrants, the jurisprudence has proved more tentative in this area than in the area of health care, as discussed in Chapter 3, although 'reasonably foreseeable situations' that create irreversible negative consequences for irregular migrants' life and health should be prevented.[192] Furthermore, a brief reference to the negotiations and final text of the Global Compact for Migration demonstrate that where undocumented people are concerned, a selective, minimalist approach to social rights, which largely ignores the interrelated nature of human rights, is preferred as it does not challenge the structural inequalities between and within states. Human rights themselves have often been criticised as individualist claims that overemphasise formal autonomy and overlook the importance of social ties, group-based identities, material conditions of living and actual situations of vulnerability.[193] Furthermore, a selective or atomistic approach reinforces the notion of a hierarchy of rights:

> Ignoring or not adequately addressing one or more rights of a group of the population reinforces cycles of poverty, inequalities, social exclusion, discrimination and violence, and in the longer run has a negative impact on the health and development of society in general.[194]

The problems of applying the current human rights system to irregular migrants are, once again, linked to a Westphalian human rights system, which accepts significant limitations to the rights of these migrants and, at least partially, 'fails to recognize inequities in the global distribution of wealth, power, opportunity, and social goods that render the playing field uneven'.[195]

Therefore, human rights law, in general, seems to currently set the protection of socioeconomic conditions that support the determinants of health for irregular migrants, other than the provision of medical care, at a 'basic' level.[196] This creates a significant imbalance between the standards of social

---

[192] HRCtee, GC36 (n 193, Ch 1) para 7.
[193] Ramji-Nogales (n 133) 703.
[194] Pūras (n 253, Ch 2) para 45.
[195] Ramji-Nogales (n 133) 710, referring to Fineman, 'The Vulnerable Subject and the Responsive State' (2010) *Emory Law Journal* 60 251, 253.
[196] CESCR, Statement on migrant rights (n 174, Ch 1) para 9.

rights that irregular migrants are entitled to and those that country's citizens or settled migrants are granted. The 'empowering' effect of the determinants of health approach is negated by state policies that reduce social rights and exclude irregular migrants from society, a situation which human rights law does not always address. Therefore, it can be concluded that all elements of the right to health are not evenly protected.

Changing direction and genuinely tackling human and social vulnerability to ill health on a non-discriminatory basis requires raising the target level of social rights that support the determinants of health beyond the mere survival level and exceptional measures. This is particularly the case in high- and middle-income countries, where most of the international case law discussed in this chapter originates.[197] This is certainly not easy for human rights law to tackle alone, as it would require paradigmatic changes vis-à-vis irregular migration and social rights implementation. The treatment of irregular migrants is thus a test of the inclusiveness and consistency of social justice paradigms, such as the SDH approach, and human rights law. Exclusionary processes in law and policies need to be addressed both conceptually and practically if debates in the fields of public health and human rights are to be consistent with their 'universal' and 'empowering' aims. In particular, further efforts from the human rights community are required to lay the basis of a consistent practice around the determinants of health of all vulnerable or marginalised populations.

[197] This remark is based on the arguments of Bilchiz (n 57) 188.

# 5

## Mental Health, Irregular Migration and Human Rights
### *Synergising Vulnerability- and Disability-Sensitive Approaches*

This book employs the wording 'right to health' to cover freedoms and entitlements in relation to both 'conditions and services that are conducive to a life of dignity and equality, and non-discrimination in relation to [physical and mental] health'.[1] While there is a general consensus among public health and human rights practitioners that there is 'no health without mental health', the latter remains largely underfunded in state health budgets and is undoubtedly a neglected element of what is included in the scope of the right to health.[2] Nonetheless, human rights scholarship and bodies have, over the last twenty years, increasingly helped to shape the normative content of the right to mental health, which has included harmonising it with newly established international disability law.[3] In reviewing the consistency of the human rights law approach to irregular migrant health – in which authoritative public health and disability standards are embedded – mental health, which exceeds 'the absence of mental disorders', and related disabilities must not be sidelined.

Migration, as mentioned in Chapter 4, is a determinant of health in itself, as it constitutes 'a process of social change where individuals face a degree of

---

[1] Dainius Pūras, 'Report of the Special Rapporteur on the Right to [...] Health (Focus: the Role of the Determinants of Health in Advancing the Right to Mental Health)' (12 April 2019 A/HRC/41/34, para 11.

[2] WHO, 'Mental Health: Strengthening our Response', factsheet (30 March 2018) <www.who.int/news-room/fact-sheets/detail/mental-health-strengthening-our-response> accessed 16 February 2021; a world average of 2 per cent of health expenditure is for mental health, with significant variations between regions of the world, see WHO, 'Mental Health Atlas 2017' (WHO Publishing 2018) 26.

[3] Paul Hunt, 'Report of the Special Rapporteur on the Right to [...] Health (Focus: Mental Disability and the Right to Health)' (11 February 2005) E/CN.4/2005/51, para 6; Dainius Pūras, 'Report of the Special Rapporteur on the Right to [...] Health (Focus: the Right to Mental Health' (28 March 2017) A/HRC/35/21, para 6.

change and [...] adjustment' to new conditions of living.[4] Changing language, leaving behind family and social networks and adjusting to a set of social norms in the new country setting and to a potentially lower socioeconomic status, are among the several factors that can contribute to the stress of 'transculturation'.[5] While many persons in a situation of human mobility have resilience and adequate coping strategies against these challenges, others, who may be exposed to an interplay of particularly unfavourable social, economic and environmental factors, exacerbated by their migratory status (e.g. social exclusion, fear of deportation, poor living conditions, unsafe and informal working environments and restricted access to basic services), may not be able to navigate these challenges and may be at heightened risk of experiencing mild to severe psychological suffering and mental disorders as a result.[6]

Against this background, any regulatory framework, at different levels of governance, may either create oppressive power structures or 'function as [...] personal protector[s] and important vehicle[s] of social justice'.[7] For these reasons, examining the normative potential of human rights law, which is the only source of law that permits international scrutiny of domestic law, policy and practices that positively or negatively affect migrant mental health, is an exercise worth conducting.[8]

Therefore, to clarify what human rights law can offer, in terms of standard setting and avenues for international legal development and protection, to those irregular migrants who experience either mental health difficulties or have a psychosocial disability,[9] this chapter is structured as follows. Section 5.1 aims to clarify certain complex definitional and classification issues that are required when undertaking an analysis of the fields of mental health and disability law. It details how the conceptual framings and normative principles of all previous chapters (including non-discrimination, vulnerability, PHC and the determinants of health) are valid descriptive and prescriptive lenses

---

[4]   Dinesh Bhugra and Susham Gupta (eds) *Migration and Mental Health* (CUP 2010) 337.

[5]   Marco Mazzetti, *Strappare le radici: Psicologia e psicopatologia di donne e di uomini che migrano* (L'Harmattan Italia 1996); Marco Mazzetti, *Il dialogo transculturale: Manuale per operatori sanitari e altre professioni d'aiuto* (Carocci 2003).

[6]   WHO and Calouste Gulbenkian Foundation, *Social Determinants of Mental Health* (WHO Publishing 2014); WHO Regional Office for Europe, *Mental Health Promotion and Mental Health Care in Refugees and Migrants (Technical Guidance)* (WHO Publishing 2018).

[7]   Gostin et al. (n 37, Introduction) Preface, v.

[8]   Gable and Gostin (n 37, Introduction) 104.

[9]   Following the guidance of the OHCHR and CRPD Committee, this chapter mainly employs the term 'psychosocial' disability instead of 'mental' disability. The reasons for this choice are explained in Section 5.1.1.

to apply a more holistic approach to the individual and collective right to the mental health of all migrants. The chapter then explores the human rights model of disability, as is enshrined in the UN CRPD, which represents an empowering and transformative approach to substantive equality and non-discrimination in relation to mental health and disabilities. To smoothly transition from introductory reflections to the core of the chapter, Section 5.2 details how pieces of human rights jurisprudence address the key relationships between mental health and human rights outside of the migrant-specific perspective. Sections 5.3 and 5.4 examine whether European and international human rights law and key human rights bodies consider the impact of human rights violations on migrant mental health and how they elaborate on the standards of mental health care and support for all, regardless of migratory status. Emergency-oriented decisions are examined alongside a human rights jurisprudence that supports preventive and promotional approaches to irregular migrants' mental health that are genuinely non-discriminatory, rights-based, community-oriented, disability-sensitive and equitable.

## 5.1 APPROACHING THE HUMAN RIGHT TO MENTAL HEALTH IN THEORY AND PRACTICE

### 5.1.1 *Definitional Challenges*

The WHO defines mental health as 'a state of well-being in which an individual realizes his or her own abilities, can cope with the normal stresses of life, can work productively and is able to make a contribution to his or her community'.[10] The international right to mental health corresponds to the freedoms and entitlements necessary to achieve the 'highest attainable standard' of this condition, which is influenced by both biological, environmental, social and institutional factors.[11] Defining the scope of the analysis conducted in this chapter on mental health (issues) and psychosocial disabilities, with respect to irregular migration, is a challenge in itself, as different disciplines and schools within the fields of psychiatry, psychology, public health, law, human rights and disability studies do not share common ethical approaches, methodology and definitions.

---

[10] WHO, 'Strengthening our Response' (n 2). This definition has attracted criticism, see Silvana Galderisi et al., 'Toward a New Definition of Mental Health' (2015) *World Psychiatry* 14(2) 231.

[11] See *infra* at Sections 5.2.3 and 5.4.2.

Differences and nuances exist between terms such as mental health, mental disorder and mental disability[12] and although this thematic analysis cannot comprehensively capture these differences, the terminology employed in this chapter is worth explaining. International human rights law, reflecting disability and mental health users advocacy, has gradually shifted from employing words such as 'mental illness' or 'disorders' to describing the conditions of certain mental health service users,[13] which imply pathological processes that necessitate exclusively medical and at times institutionalised cures, to using a less stigmatising vocabulary such as persons with mental health issues and psychosocial disabilities.[14] Persons with mental health issues covers 'both persons having mental health difficulties and persons who are deemed or labelled with mental health difficulties'.[15] Furthermore, the Office of the United Nations High Commissioner for Human Rights (OHCHR) uses 'psychosocial' as an adjective to describe a disability with regard to persons who, 'regardless of self-identification or diagnosis of a mental health condition, face restrictions in the exercise of their rights and barriers to participation on the basis of an actual or perceived impairment'.[16] While this terminology is employed as a synonym of 'mental' disability in human rights law,[17] 'psychosocial' disability has the advantage of emphasising the societal barriers encountered by people with actual or perceived mental health conditions.[18] Furthermore, the term 'mental disability' may generate confusion; first, it is used to refer to 'both persons with intellectual disabilities and persons with mental health conditions', and second, 'in disability literature [of the recent

---

[12] Hunt (n 3) para 4.

[13] Ibid.

[14] Pūras (n 3).

[15] Bo Chen, *Rethinking China's Mental Health Law Reform: Treatment Decision-Making and the UN Convention on the Rights of Persons with Disabilities*, PhD thesis, NUI Galway, August 2019, 12.

[16] OHCHR, 'Report of the United Nations High Commissioner for Human Rights on Mental Health and Human Rights' (31 January 2017) A/HRC/34/32, para 5.

[17] Hunt (n 3); CRPD (n 36, Introduction) Article 1; CRPD Committee, COs on the Report of Denmark (30 October 2014) paras 5, 48–49. Since 2015, the CRPD Committee's COs stopped using 'mental disabilities' and instead started to employ 'psychosocial and intellectual disabilities'.

[18] There may be *overlaps* between categories of irregular migrants who are potential mental health service users, people with mental health conditions and persons with psychosocial disabilities, but *differences of meaning* exist as 'a user of mental health services may not have a mental health condition and some persons with mental health conditions may face no restrictions or barriers to their full participation in society', see OHCHR (n 16) para 5.

past], mental disability is more likely to be perceived as a transitional term after "mental retardation" but before "intellectual disability"'.[19]

A further clarification is required on the use of 'psychosocial'. It is also employed to refer to any non-biomedical intervention, such as the provision of basic services, community support or psychological care in primary care settings, 'that aims to protect or promote psychosocial well-being' outside of psychiatric drugs and care.[20]

While introducing, albeit briefly, a number of concepts, conventional categories and constructs that public health and human rights studies employ, it is worth acknowledging that diversity in terminology may be welcomed to accord people the freedom to 'define their own experience of mental health'.[21] This also has the effect of extending the plethora of human rights standards and arguments to hold states to account for the realisation of the right to mental health of individuals and populations while avoiding discrimination and respecting people's equality, dignity and autonomy.

I will now summarise the diverse approaches that scholars and practitioners in the fields of health, disability and human rights employ when discussing mental health and disability. These include the (bio)medical approach, the social model, the biopsychosocial paradigm and the human rights approach to health, functioning and disabilities.

A purely (bio)medical model of mental health, which dominates mental health services worldwide, emphasises 'neurobiological aspects and processes as the explanation for mental conditions' and, in the case of 'mental disorders', the need to fix chemical imbalances via psychiatric treatment complemented with psychotherapy[22] for the health, security and well-being of the patient and society at large. Furthermore, this model inextricably links impairment and disability, which are considered biological and pathological states[23] to 'be treated, cured, fixed or at least rehabilitated'.[24] Medical paternalism and 'sanism' have dominated this orthodox approach to mental health care and

---

[19] Chen (n 15) 11. This chapter's personal scope, to avoid overgeneralisations, does not cover persons with intellectual disabilities. However, several considerations and arguments developed below may apply to the right to health of persons with both an irregular status and an intellectual disability.

[20] Inter-Agency Standing Committee, 'IASC Guidelines on Mental Health and Psychosocial Support in Emergency Settings' (IASC 2007) 15.

[21] Pūras (n 1) para 10.

[22] Pūras (n 3) para 18.

[23] Mike Bury, 'Defining and Researching Disability: Challenges and Responses' in Colin Barnes and Geof Mercer (eds) *Exploring the Divide: Illness and Disability* (The Disability Press 1996) 17–38.

[24] Theresia Degener, 'Disability in a Human Rights Context' (2016) *Laws* 2016 35(5) 2.

the law.[25] The operationalisation of this model has historically proven particularly problematic in relation to human rights law, as it is grounded on an accepted power imbalance between patient and carer and between disabled person and their substitute decision maker. This can lead to interventions such as involuntary admission to and detention in mental health institutions, involuntary treatment (including overmedicalisation) and deprivation of the legal capacity of people with psychosocial and intellectual disabilities. Therefore, it is incompatible with general human rights principles – such as autonomy and equal dignity, which have informed human rights adjudication – and is in contravention to the object and purpose of the widely ratified CRPD.[26]

The medical model has been harshly criticised by the proponents of the social model of disability, which frames disability as a social construct that facilitates domination and discrimination against persons with disabilities perpetuated by the society of the so-called able-bodied (and able-minded) at the expense of those who do not fit into a model of mainstream socially acceptable life experience.[27] This approach unveiled an oppressive social and institutional order 'which takes no or little account of people who have [physical or mental] impairments and thus excludes them from participation in the mainstream of social activities'.[28] The social model of disability has helped to 'debunk exclusion and denial of rights on the basis of impairment as ideological constructions of disability'[29] by focusing on the role of a prejudiced social environment rather than that of impairment[30] in disabling people from fitting in and contributing to society.

A third possible approach is the biopsychosocial model of mental health, which integrates elements of the above two paradigms and has been embraced by the WHO in the last two decades, in a move away from a purely medical

---

[25] Michael Perlin, *International Human Rights and Mental Disability Law: When the Silenced Are Heard* (OUP 2012) 8. Perlin describes 'sanism' as 'an irrational prejudice against people with mental illness' that affects social perceptions of and legal responses to people who experience mental health conditions, see Michael Perlin, 'On "Sanism"' (1993) *SMU Law Review* 46 373.

[26] See Section 5.1.3, *infra*.

[27] See Michael Oliver, *Understanding Disability: From Theory to Practice* (St. Martin's Press 1996).

[28] Ibid, 32.

[29] Degener (n 24) 19.

[30] For a critical analysis of the unsettled impairment/disability divide, see Mike Oliver 'Defining Impairment and Disability: Issues at Stake' in Colin Barnes and Geof Mercer (eds) *Exploring the Divide* (Disability Press 1996) 39–54; Michael Rembis, 'Challenging the Impairment/ Disability Divide: Disability History and the Social Model of Disability' in Nick Watson and Simo Vehmas (eds) *Routledge Handbook on Disability Studies* (Routledge 2020).

model approach that has historically been in place. Without neglecting the relevance of an impairment in the experience of disability, which may necessitate appropriate health care, this model also emphasises the relationship between the psychological aspects of life experience and the importance of supportive relationships and healthy contexts in the community.[31] The 2001 WHO International Classification of Functioning, Disability and Health generally endorses this model by 'recognising the [dynamic] role of environmental factors in the creation of disability, as well as the role of health conditions'.[32] Like all aspects of health, the determinants of mental health are constituted by a range of biological, psychological, social and environmental factors.[33]

The most recent model is the human rights model of disability, which was built largely on the social model of disability championed by the 2006 CRPD. The stated purpose of the CRPD is 'to promote, protect and ensure the "full" and "equal" enjoyment of all human rights [...] by all persons with disabilities, and to promote respect for their inherent dignity'. People with disabilities, including people with mental disabilities, are now explicitly recognised in the groundbreaking CRPD treaty text as individuals endowed with dignity and full legal capacity and not as passive recipients of care and cures. This treaty is a contemporary ode to equality and non-discrimination on the grounds of disability in the full enjoyment of human rights – although it does not neglect other personal statuses and circumstances which exacerbate stigma and discrimination – that entails the adoption of positive measures to guarantee substantive equality, structural change and contextual adjustments at the group and individual levels.[34] Impairments are not dismissed in this model; in fact, like disability, they should in principle trigger a number of positive state duties in the social sphere without undermining individual

[31] International Federation of Red Cross and Red Crescent Societies, 'Strengthening Resilience: A Global Selection of Psychosocial Interventions' (Centre for Psychosocial Support – IRCRC 2014) <https://pscentre.org/wp-content/uploads/2018/02/Strengthening-Resilience.pdf>; International Network for Education in Emergencies, 'Psychosocial Support and Social and Emotional Learning for Children and Youth in Emergency Settings', Background Paper (2016) <https://reliefweb.int/sites/reliefweb.int/files/resources/INEE.pdf> accessed 1 March 2021.

[32] T. B. Üstün et al., 'The International Classification of Functioning, Disability and Health: A New Tool for Understanding Disability and Health' (2003) *Disability and Rehabilitation* 25 (11–12) 565.

[33] WHO, 'Mental Health Action Plan 2013–2020' (6 January 2013) 7 <www.who.int/publications/i/item/9789241506021> accessed 1 March 2021.

[34] CRPD (n 36, Introduction) Preamble, Articles 1–5.

autonomy. Unlike the social model, this model frames social rights as potentially empowering tools and not merely charity provisions.[35]

Demonstrating its grounding in the social model, the CRPD's Preamble describes disability as an 'evolving concept' that 'results from the interaction between persons with impairments and attitudinal and environmental barriers that hinder their full and effective participation in society on equal basis with others'. The 'definition' is further qualified in Article 1 CRPD, which adds that disabled people '*include* those who have *long-term* physical, mental intellectual or sensory impairments'.[36]

While mental disabilities are explicitly listed and the word 'include' suggests that other types of impairment are covered by the scope of the Convention, mention of the long-lasting duration of the 'impairment' leaves room for discretionary state interpretation in cases of transitory mental conditions.[37] This has caused the UN special rapporteur on the right to health to distinguish between 'users of [mental health] services' and people who have 'psychosocial disabilities'. For him, the former category includes those who 'experience occasional and short-lived psychosocial difficulties or distress that require additional support' and, at minimum, triggers the protection of general human rights law, including reasonable social rights without discrimination. The latter, 'based on the barriers they face' because of their disability, are more likely to be covered by the transformative equality standards of the CRPD.[38] However, such a distinction is more nuanced in practice, and the CRPD, with the purpose of extending its protective material and personal scope as much as possible, does not attempt to provide an exhaustive definition of disability. Indeed, 'including long-term [...] impairments' does not fully exclude short-term impairments and also means that impairment does not have to be permanent to be covered by the CPRD: 'an injury or a psychiatric episode that requires an extended period of rehabilitation but leaves no ongoing impairment would count'.[39]

Health, impairment and disability are dynamic concepts that vary across time, cultures and societies,[40] as well as across individual human experiences and regulatory frameworks.

---

[35] Degener (n 24) 5–7.
[36] CRPD (n 36, Introduction) Preamble, recital (e) and Article 1, emphasis added. The CRPD intentionally does not technically 'define' disability but instead provides a non-exhaustive wide list of those who may be considered disabled.
[37] Peter Bartlett, 'The United Nations Convention on the Rights of Persons with Disabilities and Mental Health Law' (2012) *Modern Law Review* 75(5) 752, 758.
[38] Pūras (n 3) para 4.
[39] Kris Gledhill, 'Disability Law and Mental Health' in Gostin et al. (n 37, Introduction) 923.
[40] Benedicte Ingstad and Susan R. Whyte (eds) *Disability and Culture* (University of California Press 1995).

### 5.1.2 *Theoretical Grounding: The Concepts of Vulnerability and Disability as Tools of Substantive Equality*

This chapter extends the theoretical and legal scope of this book to cover the rights of persons with disabilities. Indeed, international disability law can offer especially protective legal standards while giving explicit weight to different layers of personal and group identities.[41] The purpose of this section is to attempt to harmonise the conceptual filters that this monograph has thus far employed, to support consistent human rights–based positive obligations with regard to the protection and promotion of the highest attainable standard of health of irregular migrants (non-discrimination, substantive equality and vulnerability), with the human rights model of disability, which derived from the social model.

The reason for this exercise is that disability scholars tend to be critical of the concept of vulnerability, as it evokes a spectrum of 'victimhood, deprivation, [social control,] dependency or pathology', which perpetuates the oppressive manufactured image of disabled persons as inherently in need of cures, charity-like attention and substitute decision-makers.[42] Furthermore, the label special vulnerability can have the stigmatising effect of emphasising the otherness of persons with disabilities or framing disability as a deviation from normality.[43]

Although it lacks agreement between and within different disciplines on what vulnerability means and, thus, on who is vulnerable,[44] it is worth noting that the operationalisation of this concept in human rights law – as a heightened risk of a multidimensional harm because of either inherent personal features or the socio-political contexts within which people live – has nonetheless led to an overall tightening of the scrutiny of monitoring bodies in relation to certain people or groups that are depicted as (especially) disadvantaged or marginalised.[45] This practice, in certain legal frameworks, has explicitly included irregular migrants and subgroups of the same,[46]

---

[41] Degener (n 24) 9–12.
[42] Beverly Clough, 'Disability and Vulnerability: Challenging the Capacity/Incapacity Binary' (2017) *Social Policy and Society* 16(3) 469, 475; Kate Brown, 'Questioning the Vulnerability Zeitgeist: Care and Control Practices with "Vulnerable" Young People' (2014) *Social Policy and Society* 13(3) 371, 383.
[43] Jackie Leach Scully, 'Disability and Vulnerability: On Bodies, Dependence and Power' in Mackenzie et al. (n 331, Ch 2) 219.
[44] Jonathon Herring, *Vulnerable Adults and the Law* (OUP 2016) 5. See further details at Section 2.7.
[45] See Section 2.7.
[46] In particular, see Sections 2.7, 3.1.1 and 4.1.2.

facilitating the conceptualisation of irregular migrants as real human rights holder, particularly vis-à-vis the neglect of their basic capabilities and socio-economic rights by state authorities. The special vulnerability of irregular migrants, which human rights law aims to mitigate – although without comprehensively grappling with its underlying causes – is, first and foremost, determined by structural and institutional conditions that deprive undocumented individuals and communities of legal status, thus exposing them to social exclusions and precarious living conditions that are detrimental to their health and well-being. As such, vulnerability, as a descriptive and normative concept, constitutes a 'useful set of tools to interrogate the structures, concepts and institutions that further inclusion or exclusion'.[47]

Irregular migrant vulnerability or precariousness is the result of political choices and can be described as a socially or legally constructed form of majoritarian community oppression over outsiders, whose mere existence or permanence in a state territory is deemed illegal. Thus, irregular migrants with psychosocial disabilities have at least a double layer of socially constructed vulnerability vis-à-vis human rights enjoyment, originating in their legal status and the ways in which migrant and non-migrant communities in society respond to their impairment. Without contradicting the social model of disability, this take on vulnerability emphasises situational risks of harm and social and legal environments as a panacea for discrimination and disempowerment.[48] In human rights practice, vulnerability and disability are transformed from constructs of oppression into powerful considerations and potential weapons of either substantive[49] or transformative equality.[50] They, in principle, require states to adopt a set of affirmative measures to rebalance the opportunities or capabilities of people who are likely to be marginalised, excluded and impoverished, including on the grounds of migratory status, actual or perceived disability or impairment. Furthermore, the state duties required under an international human rights approach to disability, as developed in the CRPD, are designed to lead to structural changes in power relationships between rights holders with disabilities and institutional duty bearers.[51] For irregular migrants with disabilities, including those with psychosocial disabilities, this very detailed and widely ratified Convention adds a

---

[47] Siobhán Mullally, 'Gender Equality, Citizenship Status and the Politics of Belonging' in Martha A. Fineman (ed) *Transcending Boundaries of Law: Generations of Feminism and Legal Theory* (Routledge 2011) 192.

[48] Mackenzie et al. (n 331, Ch 2) 7.

[49] Chapman and Carbonetti (n 320, Ch 2); Peroni and Timmer (n 337, Ch 2).

[50] Degener (n 24) 17 referring to Fredman (n 312, Ch 2).

[51] Ibid.

significant layer of protection because, for instance, the denial of disability-related health care and social support on the grounds of irregular migratory status can constitute a discrimination on the ground of disability.[52] In concrete circumstances, the above context-related vulnerabilities of irregular migrants are compounded by the inherent vulnerability of migrant children and the structural vulnerability of migrant women, inter alia.[53]

According to both the human rights model of disability and vulnerability-based human rights law, which are compatible with a reinterpretation of well-being in terms of the development of human needs and capabilities,[54] state authorities must play a supportive and positive role in rebalancing the actual opportunities available for people to enjoy human rights while also respecting diversity and agency.[55]

## 5.2 MENTAL HEALTH AND HUMAN RIGHTS LAW

To comprehensively understand whether human rights law has reached a satisfactory stage of standard setting regarding the rights of irregular migrants with mental health conditions, it is worth summarising briefly how this branch of international and European law has developed freedoms and entitlements by elaborating on the relationships between human rights and mental health in general (i.e. from a non-group–specific perspective). Borrowing from authoritative scholarship on health and human rights, three important relationships between mental health and human rights can be identified: (1) mental health laws and policies can affect human rights; (2) human rights violations can affect people's mental health; and (3) human rights law and mental health policies can be shaped as reinforcing promotional strategies for

---

[52] See Section 5.4, *infra*.

[53] See Sections 3.4.3 and 4.3.2, *supra* and 5.4.2.2, *infra*.

[54] See Section 2.3.

[55] Nussbaum (n 68, Ch 2) 70 (on capabilities, human rights and institutional support); Caroline Harnacke, 'Disability and Capability: Exploring the Usefulness of Martha Nussbaum's Capabilities Approach for the UN Disability Rights Convention' (2013) *Journal of Law, Medicine and Ethics* 41(4) 768 (on the synergies between capability and disability approaches); Degener (n 24) 5–6 (on the role of socio-economic rights in the human rights model of disability); Fineman (n 195, Ch 4) 269 (on the active role of social institutions in building resilience and target human vulnerability); Mikaela Heikkilä, Hisayo Katsui and Maija Mustaniemi-Laakso. 'Disability and Vulnerability: A Human Rights Reading of the Responsive State' (2020) *International Journal of Human Rights* 24(8) 1180 (on the obligations of responsive states to 'materialising substantive equality for persons with disabilities as vulnerable legal subjects').

enhancing individual and collective (mental and physical) health and well-being.[56]

### 5.2.1 *Mental Health Regulation on Human Rights*

The first relationship can be captured, for example, by human rights standards associated with involuntary admissions to and living conditions in mental health institutions. Since the 1970s, states and international human rights bodies have established hard and soft law,[57] as well as judicial or quasi-judicial precedents, on the human rights of people with mental disabilities who are deprived of their liberty. For instance, the ECHR has been employed to establish safeguards to prevent arbitrary forced confinement within an institution, requiring that the law must 'clearly define' the conditions under which confinement is permitted and that the constrained environment must be therapeutical.[58] Three conditions are required to lawfully 'detain' a person with mental health issues under Article 5 ECHR, outside of 'emergency' cases.[59] The first is that a 'true mental disorder' must be established by a competent authority on the basis of 'objective medical evidence'. Second, the mental health condition must be of 'a kind or degree that warrants compulsory confinement', and third, the severe disorder must persist to justify the detention.[60] Furthermore, the conditions of residents in mental health institutions or inmates in psychiatric wards of prisons may violate the right to freedom from inhuman and degrading treatment (Article 3 ECHR). However, the European Court considers a treatment to be inhuman only if it reaches a level of gravity 'involving considerable mental or physical suffering' and degrading if the person has undergone 'humiliation or debasement involving a minimum level of severity'.[61] The case law of the ECtHR has traditionally

---

[56] Lance Gable and Lawrence Gostin (n 37, Introduction) 105, referring to Mann et al. (n 33, Introduction).

[57] UNGA, 'Principles for the Protection of Persons with Mental Illness and the Improvement of Mental Health Care' Res 46/119 (17 December 1991); UNGA 'The Standard Rules on the Equalization of Opportunities for Persons with Disabilities', Res No 48/96, annex (20 December 1993); CRPD (n 17, Introduction).

[58] *Kawka v Poland* App no 25874/94 (ECHR 2001) para 49, See also *Aerts v Belgium* App no 25357/94 (ECHR 1998); *L.B. v Belgium* (n 274, Ch 2).

[59] *Hertz v Germany* App no 44672/98 (ECHR 2003) describes as emergencies those circumstances where public safety or patients' best interest are deemed at risk. However, the Court held that appropriate medical examination must occur immediately after emergency admission.

[60] *Winterwerp v the Netherlands* App no 6301/73 (ECHR 1979) para 39; *Stanev v Bulgaria* App no 36760/06 (ECHR 2012) para 145.

[61] Council of Europe, 'ECHR Toolkit', <www.coe.int/en/web/echr-toolkit/definitions> accessed 1 March 2021.

proved to be 'highly deferential to mental health authorities';[62] however, highly abusive circumstances (e.g. severe overcrowding, considerable length of detention, handcuffing in solitary confinement, extremely poor living conditions in institutions) in a number of cases in recent years have caused the Court to increasingly decide in favour of applicants.[63] Among other sensitive areas, Article 8 ECHR (respect for private life) has grounded a number of judgments that have restating the right to freedom of correspondence and the right to be ensured appropriate procedural safeguards against forced medication in mental health institutions.[64] Despite the trend towards more protective human rights standards, the case law of the ECtHR rests on the idea that certain interferences with the rights to liberty and physical and mental integrity, deriving from the implementation of mental health policy and legislation, may be permissible, subject to a test of legality, legitimacy and proportionality, if they are in the interest of the human rights holder with a mental health condition or of the safety of society at large. The 2006 CRPD 'radically departs from this approach' in considering as discriminatory and prohibiting any deprivation of liberty based on physical or mental disability, such as forced institutionalisation, without free and informed consent.[65] Moving away from the practice of institutionalisation entails the adoption of special measures to protect the life in dignity of people with psychosocial disabilities, including making available adequate community-based or alternative social care services as a less intrusive alternative to confinement.[66]

### 5.2.2 *Human Rights Violations on Mental Health*

The second relationship concerns the effects on mental health that human rights violations may cause. Human rights bodies have highlighted this relationship in an extremely wide-ranging body of jurisprudence, of which only

---

[62] Gable and Gostin (n 37, Introduction) 143.

[63] For example, *Romanov v Russia* App no 63993/00 (ECHR 2005); *Kucheruk v Ukraine* App no 2570/04 (ECHR 2007); *Stanev* (n 60).

[64] *Herczegfalvy v Austria* App. No. 10533/83 (ECHR 1992); *X v Finland* App no 34806/04 (ECHR 2012) para 220.

[65] CRPD (n 36, Introduction) Article 14; OHCHR, 'Annual Report of the UN High Commissioner for Human Rights [...] Thematic Study [...] on Enhancing Awareness and Understanding of the CRPD' (26 January 2009) A/HRC/10/48 para 48; CRPD Committee, 'General Comment No. 1: Equal Recognition before the Law' (19 May 2014) para 14; CRPD Committee, 'General Comment No. 6: Equality and Non-discrimination' (26 April 2018) para 30.

[66] HRCtee, GC36 (n 193, Ch 1) para 24; HRCtee, 'General Comment no. 35 – Liberty and Security of Person' (16 December 2014) para 11.

four examples are provided here. Gender-based violence is a form of discrimination that inflicts emotional and mental suffering[67] and that requires state agencies to activate targeted psychological support.[68] The denial of appropriate sexual and reproductive health care services, such as therapeutic abortion, may affect psychological integrity by creating mental anguish and constituting gender-based violence and ill treatment.[69] Furthermore, the psychosocial risks factors of work have been attentively considered by human rights bodies to interpret and monitor the right to fair and decent working conditions and occupational safety.[70] Finally, it is worth mentioning the case of children living in homelessness who are exposed to particularly poor and unhealthy living conditions. This situation raises human rights concerns regarding the responsiveness of housing and other targeted social services in protecting children from potentially severe consequences of homelessness on their 'physical, mental, spiritual, moral and social development' and mental health.[71]

### 5.2.3 *Synergies between Public Health and Human Rights in Right to Mental Health*

The third relationship is that public mental health and human rights can be mutually reinforcing in terms of the protection and promotion of mental health 'to the betterment of [all] human beings'.[72] This inextricable link is exemplified by the international conceptualisation of the right to 'the highest attainable standard' of health, the implementation of which means adopting intersectoral measures regarding, *inter alia*, the prevention of suffering, the promotion of mental health and access to health services while also respecting everyone's freedom and legal capacity to control one's life, health and body.[73] For instance, Article 12 ICESCR, Article 24 CRC and Article 11 ESC, as interpreted by the monitoring bodies of these treaties, require states to enhance the standards of health protection for individuals and communities.

---

[67] CEDAW Committee, GR35 (n 162, Ch 4) para 29.
[68] R.P.B. *v The Philippines* Com no 34/2011 (CEDAW Committee 2014).
[69] L.C. *v Peru* (n 243, Ch 2) para 7.2; *Siobhán Whelan v Ireland* App no 2425/2014 (HRCtee 2017).
[70] ECSR, Conclusions 2013 – Statement of interpretation of Article 3; ECSR, 'Conclusions 2017' (January 2018) <https://rm.coe.int/compilation-of-conclusions-2017-by-country/1680786061> accessed 25 February 2021; Grover (n 182, Ch 4) para 44.
[71] CRC (n 42, Introduction) Article 27; CRC Committee, 'General Comment No. 21 – Children in Street Situations (21 June 2017) para 53; ECSR, *DCI v Belgium* (n 216, Ch 1) paras 81, 97, 121, 128–129.
[72] Gable and Gostin (n 37, Introduction) 107.
[73] See Section 2.4, based on CESCR, GC14 (n 27, Introduction).

As public health aims to create 'conditions for populations to be healthy',[74] mental health policies should, for example, catalyse public and private actors' efforts to realise positive social and underlying determinants of mental health, by focusing on creating healthy and supportive contexts and non-violent relationships.[75] The discourses of human rights and the social determinants of health should therefore converge to advance mental health standards that target enabling environments and structural causes, as well as essential care and support, rather than engaging exclusively with a biological approach to mental health and disability, which overemphasises treatment of mental illness.[76] The realisation of obligations to secure social determinants to promote mental health requires both 'cross-sectoral action'[77] and the enjoyment by all members of society of a broad array of interconnected human rights, including those that directly target material needs (socioeconomic rights), and the eradication of structural violence towards certain groups (people with disabilities and victims of gender-based violence). Indeed, failure to target the above structural determinants of health may bring about situations of multidimensional poverty and discrimination that are disproportionately associated with mental health conditions, and that prevent people with psychosocial disabilities from accessing equal care and support services.[78]

As far as mental health care and treatment within the scope of the right to health are concerned, it is worth recalling that for health policies and service provision to be human rights compliant, they must conform to the AAAQ framework,[79] and, in particular, they should be equity-oriented, non-discriminatory and affordable. State obligations stemming from the right to health care, which also include the progressive development of a comprehensive health care system that covers preventive, curative, rehabilitative and palliative services, overlap with those related to the implementation of the right to life and freedom from ill treatment which require states to provide urgent and emergency health care.[80]

---

[74] Institute of Medicine, *The Future of Public Health* (National Academies Press 1988) 19.

[75] Pūras (n 1) paras 3, 4, 47.

[76] Audrey Chapman et al., 'Editorial: Reimagining the Mental Health Paradigm for Our Collective Well-Being' (2020) *Health and Human Rights Journal* 22(1) 1, 3. See also, Gable and Gostin (n 37, Introduction) 160–162. The realisation of supportive social determinants of mental health is one of five key objectives of the WHO Mental Health Action Plan (n 33).

[77] Pūras (n 3) para 71.

[78] Pūras (n 1) paras H, 36, 84; Jonathan Kenneth Burns, 'Mental Health and Inequity: A Human Rights Approach to Inequality, Discrimination and Mental Disability' (2009) *Health and Human Rights Journal* 11(2) 19, 22.

[79] See Section 2.4.2.3.

[80] See Sections 3.3.1 and 3.3.2.

As noted previously, the classification of health-related obligations in General Comment No. 14 has been strongly influenced by a public health–based PHC paradigm, which strongly emphasises primary care as an essential level of care, as well as measures regarding health promotion.[81] As mental health is one widely accepted dimension of health,[82] the PHC approach, which includes primary care, cannot disregard people's mental health needs. Indeed, integrating mental health services into PHC is one of the WHO's most fundamental health care recommendations,[83] and primary and community care occupy a foundational position among the formal services in the (mental) health care pyramid of the WHO.[84] Primary care, together with other levels of care, can significantly contribute to human rights protection by helping to reduce stigma and discrimination towards people with mental health conditions, improve access to and continuity of care, enhance their social integration and 'prevent people from being admitted into psychiatric institutions [which are] often associated with human rights violations'.[85]

Finally, to ensure a beneficial relationship between mental health policies and human rights, it must be considered that the right to health is also conceptualised within the framework of the CRPD. Article 25 CRPD establishes that people with disabilities, including those with psychosocial disabilities, must have non-discriminatory access to general health care and to specialised services required by their impairment, both of which should be located 'as close as possible to people's own community'.[86] Furthermore, the text of the CRPD explicitly expands the 'broader social matrix'[87] of the right to health by adding a right to 'habilitation and rehabilitation' (Article 26), which is interlinked with other key provisions such as the right to independent living (Article 19). Indeed, 'poor physical and social environments can aggravate primary conditions and exacerbate secondary [co-morbid] consequences of primary conditions'.[88] These obligations, which together are a genuine

---

[81] See Section 2.4.2.

[82] WHO Constitution (n 22, Introduction) Preamble; ICESCR (n 23, Introduction) Article 12.

[83] WHO, *The World Health Report 2001: Mental Health: New Understanding, New Hope* (WHO 2001).

[84] WHO and WONCA, *Integrating Mental Health into Primary Care: A Global Perspective* (WHO 2008) 16.

[85] Ibid, 3.

[86] CRPD (n 36, Introduction) Article 25(a)(b)(c).

[87] Sylvia Bell, 'What Does the Right to Health Have to Offer Mental Health Patients?' (2005) *International Journal of Law and Psychiatry* 28 141, 142.

[88] Catalina Devandas Aguilar, 'Report of the Special Rapporteur on the Rights of Persons with Disabilities (Focus: Right to Health of Persons with Disabilities)' (16 July 2018) A/73/161, paras 4–5.

expression of the interdependence of human rights, entail the implementation of support services and programmes in the community, including 'peer-support' and 'particularly in the areas of health, employment, education and social services'.[89] This moves beyond the practice of institutionalisation and also addresses the 'revolving door phenomenon', whereby mental health service users who are left without adequate community care are more likely to require repeat specialised mental health care.[90] Finally, to create synergies between mental health regulations and international human rights law for people with disabilities, and build healthy and non-discriminatory communities of people, 'immediate action is required to radically reduce medical coercion and facilitate the move towards an end to all forced psychiatric treatment and confinement'[91] by funding 'community-based and non-coercive psychosocial services'.[92] Building on this prioritisation of community-based primary care and supportive environments for mental health, the following sections analyse whether these paradigms are actually endorsed in international law and jurisprudence concerning service users or right holders who are irregular migrants and who, by virtue of their immigration status, are often the target of exclusionary policies and immigration law enforcement.

## 5.3 EUROPEAN HUMAN RIGHTS: QUALIFIED RISKS FOR MENTAL HEALTH AND EMERGENCY APPROACHES

Previous sections of this book have generally depicted the European human rights approach to the health needs of irregular migrants as guided by principles of emergency care and exceptional interventions.[93] Overall, the sophisticated case law of the ECtHR is severely constrained in the field of social entitlements, which are beyond the material scope of the text of the ECHR. Furthermore, the fact that irregular migrants are not labelled by the ECtHR an 'especially vulnerable group' per se has prevented the liberal use of positive obligations to concretely realise their human rights in this legal frame. By contrast, the ECSR has combined several principles of interpretation of international human rights law to successfully adjudicate on the social rights of irregular migrants, thereby overcoming the textual limitations of the ESC, which exclude this group from the treaty's scope of application.

---

[89] CRPD (n 36, Introduction) Article 26.
[90] Antoinette Daly, Donna Tedstone Doherty and Dermot Walsh, 'Reducing the Revolving Door Phenomenon' (2010) *Irish Journal of Psychological Medicine* 27(1) 27.
[91] Pūras (n 3) 65. See also, CRPD Committee, GC6 (n 65) para 30.
[92] Aguilar (n 90) para 29.
[93] See Sections 3.2 and 4.2.

While this section's findings do not significantly depart from these paradigms, European judgments and decisions that were specifically focused on the mental health of irregular migrants add interesting nuances. These are mainly examples of the second of the aforementioned relationships between mental health and human rights (human rights violations affect mental health) and are instructive in demonstrating how the deportation and detention of irregular migrants and their access to social and medical assistance can be minimally regulated to avoid levels of mental health distress that could constitute human rights violations.

### 5.3.1 Deportation Measures and Mental Health

During the last twenty years, the ECtHR has had several opportunities to clarify the circumstances in which the removal of illegally staying individuals with severe health conditions to their country of origin or provenance would constitute refoulement, which constitutes a breach of Article 3 ECHR. The rationale is that 'the suffering which flows from naturally occurring illness may be covered by Article 3 where it is, or risks being, exacerbated by ill treatment [. . .] flowing from [. . .] expulsion or other measure, for which the authorities can be held responsible'.[94]

Early judgments established that the prospect of ill treatment should prevent deportations on health grounds if there are 'substantive grounds to believe' that, if deported, a 'critically ill' person would be at 'imminent risk of dying'.[95] Affected by this restrictive approach, the ECtHR set a seminal precedent with *Bensaid v. United Kingdom* regarding the relevance of a mental health condition (in the words of the Court, a 'schizophrenic [person] suffering from a psychotic illness') as a human rights issue in deportation procedures. The applicant in this case was an Algerian national who had lived for ten years in the UK and who suffered from schizophrenia and was in receipt of mental health care that kept his condition under control. Mr Bensaid held that his deportation to Algeria, in consideration of his diagnosis of mental illness and the limited access in the receiving country to the drugs that helped him to avoid psychotic episodes and enhance his social functioning, would expose him to a risk of inhuman and degrading treatment and jeopardise his physical and moral integrity, which can be considered elements of the right to private life. This claim was based on the fact that

---

[94] *Savran* (n 44, Ch 3) para 44.
[95] D. v UK (n 122, Ch 1) paras 43, 52–53; N. v UK (n 122, Ch 1) paras 42–51.

his hometown in Algeria was 70 km away from the closest hospital in which the necessary treatment was only available on an inpatient basis.

Deportation-related stress and environmental conditions in Algeria, including the practical difficulties in accessing the treatment Mr Bensaid required because of his condition, would have exacerbated – according to his psychiatrist – the risk of recurring psychotic episodes, and would have led to a significant deterioration of the applicant's mental health to the extent that he 'would be at risk of acting in obedience to the hallucinations telling himself to harm himself or others'.[96]

On the merits of the case, the Court started its assessment by highlighting the sovereign state power to control immigration. It then held that, although the severity and the long-term nature of the applicant's mental illness was beyond discussion in that it had been under observation and treatment for years in the UK, the claims of the applicant (e.g. the adverse consequences of the deportation on his mental health, the reduced access to treatment in Algeria and the unsafe nature of the trips to and from the hospital) were largely 'speculative'.[97] In other words, the applicant failed to discharge his burden and standard of proof: the ill treatment of a particular severity resulting from all the circumstances of the case was not proved beyond any reasonable doubts. At that time, the threshold of severity of human suffering necessary to trigger the applicability of Article 3 ECHR in exceptional health-related return cases was extremely high; the criteria employed in *D. v. UK* coincided with 'subjecting [the applicant] to acute mental and physical suffering' to an extent that constituted a risk of death.[98]

Even though the Court left a door open to severe mental health conditions as circumstances that may prevent the removal of a migrant, the 'terminal illness' or 'risk of death' criterion, together with a high standard of proof, seemed ill-fitted to the specific characteristics of mental health conditions, which, while they may greatly impair the overall health and standard of living of people with mental disabilities, are not 'lethal' per se.

Furthermore, although the 'preservation of mental stability is [considered] an indispensable precondition to effective enjoyment of the right to respect for private life' (Article 8), the scope of which extends to the development of 'relationships with other human beings and the outside world', the Court found no violation of this right. Once again, evidentiary problems played a central role, as well as a state-biased approach according to which the

---

[96] *Bensaid v UK* (n 271, Ch 2) paras 21 and 16.
[97] Ibid, para 39.
[98] Ibid, para 40.

'protection of the economic well-being of the country' – an argument raised by the government to deny the applicant leave to remain because of the cost of his mental health care and the cost of generalising such a human rights standard – was hurriedly indicated by the Court as a legitimate interference with the right to private life of a returnee.[99]

While uncertainty regarding the existence of sufficiently severe risks regarding his mental health played against Mr Bensaid in the above case, in the *Aswat* case, uncertainty regarding the type of detention conditions and mental health care that the applicant would encounter in a detention facility in the USA contributed to a finding that the extradition of the applicant – a person with schizophrenia – to the USA would constitute a violation of Article 3 ECHR.[100] Although this case did not technically entail the deportation of an irregular migrant, as it concerned the extradition of a person whose 'nationality [was] not known', it is worth considering as an example of a series of circumstances that can cumulatively play a role in successfully triggering the applicability of Article 3 ECHR. A person with a 'severe' mental disorder (schizophrenia, the same condition that Mr Bensaid suffered from) was to be extradited to a 'country where he had no [family] ties and where he [...] face [d] an uncertain future in an as yet undetermined [detention] institution'.[101] The latter two circumstances were not present in the case of *Bensaid*, and, in light of these and medical evidence, the Court found 'that there was a real risk that the applicant's extradition to a different country and to a potentially very hostile prison environment would result in a significant deterioration in his mental and physical health, and that such a deterioration would be capable of reaching the Article 3 threshold'.[102]

The threshold of severity to trigger Article 3 ECHR was, in consideration of all the circumstances of the case, lowered from the 'risk of dying in distress' to a 'significant deterioration of physical and mental health'. This approach was crystallised, for health-related deportation cases, in the 2016 *Paposhvili* case, where the Court stated that a removal would constitute a violation of Article 3 ECHR whereas it brings about a '[r]eal risk, on account of the absence of appropriate treatment in the receiving country or the lack of access to such treatment, of being exposed to a *serious, rapid and irreversible* decline in [...] health [status] resulting in intense suffering *or* to a significant reduction in life

---

[99] Ibid, paras 44–49.
[100] *Aswat v UK* (n 271, Ch 2) para 52.
[101] Ibid, para 56.
[102] Ibid, para 57.

expectancy'.[103] The latest additions to this saga are the ECtHR's Chamber and Grand Chamber judgments in *Savran v. Denmark*, which adjudicated on the application of the principle of non-refoulement under Articles 3 and 8 to a proposed deportation of a person with paranoid schizophrenia.[104] On the merits of this case, the seven-judge Chamber of the ECtHR, while acknowledging the high threshold of Article 3 ECHR and the state power to regulate border and immigration control, applied some elements of the *Paposhvili* test. This test was used to ascertain whether the removal of a person suffering from mental health conditions constituted prohibited ill treatment and required the state to perform a case-by-case assessment on the availability of treatment and the actual accessibility of care in the country of deportation. For the Court, the accessibility test entails examining the cost of medicines – which must be affordable – the existence of social and family networks of the applicant, and the distance between the applicant's domicile and the place where care, cure and rehabilitation services are provided.[105] If doubts remain on whether the applicant would have a real possibility of accessing necessary care and support services, individual and sufficient assurances must be sought by the deporting state and must be received from the receiving state.[106]

From a human rights and disability perspective, this case is significant because both the application and the judgment include supportive environmental factors (e.g. 'regular contact person supervision, [. . .] follow up scheme [. . .] assistance from social worker [. . .] occupation' and 'family network'), not just medication and psychiatric intensive care, as part of the care necessary to prevent disabling mental suffering, the lack of which would heighten the risk of relapse and suffering.[107] The lack of such care would, therefore, likely to be in breach of Article 3 ECHR.

The Chamber judgment is accompanied by two dissenting opinions from three of the seven judges who sat on the panel. These contain interesting as well as concerning remarks on their views on mental health, which they regarded as inherently different from physical health. They believed that the difference should not warrant any special assessment of the threshold criteria of Article 3 ECHR and cast doubt on the qualification of mental health conditions as serious illnesses able to meet the *Paposhvili* test.[108] The three dissenting judges criticised the Chamber's findings, which mainly relied on

---

[103] *Paposhvili* (n 122, Ch 1) para 183, emphasis added.
[104] *Savran* (2019) (n 45, Ch 3) and *Savran* (2021) (n 44, Ch 3).
[105] *Savran* (n 44, Ch 3) paras 43–47.
[106] Ibid, referring to *Tarakhel* (n 134, Ch 1) para 120.
[107] Ibid, paras 37, 58–63.
[108] Ibid, dissenting opinion of Judges Kjolbro, Motoc and Mourou-Vikstrom, paras 11, 13 and 21.

the appropriateness of available care options and assurance tests, rather than scrutinising attentively whether deportation would expose the applicant to 'a serious, rapid and irreversible decline in his or her state of health resulting in intense suffering or to a significant reduction in life expectancy'.[109] One of the judges went even further in stating the following: 'Mental illness is more "volatile" and open to question. It cannot therefore constitute an obstacle to removal in the light of the criteria established in *Paposhvili* and requires [...] a higher threshold for finding a violation of Article 3."[110]

The recent Grand Chamber judgment in this case reversed the Chamber findings on both Articles 3 and 8 ECHR. Emphasising the state sovereign powers in the field of immigration,[111] the Court found that the Court Chamber had departed from applying the full *Paposhvili* 'threshold test' to engage Article 3 ECHR which requires the seriously ill applicant to demonstrate that his expulsion to Turkey would determine exposure to a 'serious, rapid and irreversible decline in his state of health resulting in intense suffering'.[112] Only after preliminary evidence of this qualified risk is adduced by the applicant does the returning state have a duty to verify that specialised and targeted care is available and accessible in the state of deportation, including by obtaining assurances by the the latter state authorities.[113] The Court found that while Article 3 and the *Paposhvili* test in principle apply to mental health cases,[114] the applicant failed to provide sufficient evidence that his individual situation in the country of deportation was suitable to meet all the 'qualifications' of the risk of his prospective decline in health and suffering, required by the high threshold of this provision as interpreted by the Court.[115]

While accepting that a 'physical medical condition relies more on objective elements than mental illness, which can sometimes be assessed subjectively',[116] it can be argued that it is precisely the knowledge and funding divide between physical and mental health care vis-à-vis real experiences of intense suffering that would constitute a good reason to depart from overly strict rights interpretation or at least require a certain argument adjustment to make freedom from ill treatment effective,[117] even within the already strict criteria

---

[109] Ibid.
[110] Ibid, dissent of Judge Mourou-Vikstrom, para 29.
[111] *Savran* (n 44, Ch 3) paras 124, 133 and 181.
[112] Ibid, para 134.
[113] Ibid, para 135.
[114] Ibid, paras 137 and 14.
[115] Ibid, para 143.
[116] Dissent of J. Kjolbro, Motoc and Mourou-Vikstrom (n 107) para 21.
[117] Ibid, Partly Concurring and Partly Dissenting Opinion of Judge Serghides, paras 13–41.

for the application of Article 3, to avoid neglecting mental health as an undisputed component of human health. Indeed, as Judge Serghides holds in his dissenting opinion, 'a rapid and irreversible' health decline threshold is hardly compatible with the nature of certain mental illnesses such as schizophrenia which is characterised by 'fluctuations and by the fact that any attempt to stabilise it depends on regular supervision of the patient'.[118] Furthermore, the Grand Chamber judgment, unlike that of the Chamber, failed to consider the combined nature of the treatment for the mental health condition of a person with a mild intellectual disability,[119] which according to medical evidence should include a follow-up scheme, outpatient treatment and supervision. This could have required a different argument modulation and evidence assessment to ascertain the risk of ill treatment outlawed by Article 3 ECHR in cases of deportation of people severe mental health issues.

As previously observed,[120] considering that the application of the principle of non-refoulement may directly restrict the sovereign state power to control immigration, the ECtHR has developed very strict criteria for successfully claiming a human rights violation under Article 3 in removal cases linked to the quality of health care provided in a third country. In the cases recalled here, mental impairments and a lack of appropriate health care are key factors that may exceptionally prevent deportation, while disabling environments appear to play a more marginal role.

This Grand Chamber judgment also offers interesting clarifications regarding the factors that must be considered in a proportionality test for permissible and necessary rights limitations under Article 8 ECHR (the right to protection of private life) and that should be balanced against those favouring a decision not to lift expulsion orders with regard to people with mental health issues. The Court, citing *Bensaid*, recalled that 'mental health is a crucial part of private life' and that 'preservation of mental stability' is necessary to realise a right to 'personal development, and the right to establish and develop relationships with other human beings'.[121] While Article 8 is a provision that had not been successfully adjudicated in cases of deportation of unhealthy people, in this judgment the Court observed that, 'on account of his mental condition, the applicant was more vulnerable than an average "settled migrant" facing expulsion' and, as such, medical factors should be thoroughly assessed by domestic jurisdictions in interests balancing

---

[118] Ibid, dissenting opinion, para 21.
[119] Ibid, dissenting opinion, para 13.
[120] See Section 3.2.1.
[121] *Savran* (n 44, Ch 3) para 172, citing *Bensaid*).

exercises.[122] While these medical factors were found to be adequately assessed in this case, the Court concluded that other extra-medical factors were not sufficiently taken into consideration in determining whether expulsion and re-entry bans were proportionate interferences with the applicant's private life. These included: (1) that the commission of the criminal offence while the applicant had most likely been suffering from a mental disorder should have limited the extent to which the respondent state could legitimately rely on the serious nature of the criminal offence to justify his expulsion; (2) a reduced risk of reoffending, given the applicant's overall good conduct for years, before the final decision in the revocation of the expulsion order was held; (3) the different intensity of social, cultural and family ties with the host country vis-à-vis those existing in the country of destination.[123]

Family ties were particularly emphasised by Judge Jelic to criticise the fact that the rest of the Court decided to assess compliance with Article 8 ECHR by conducting an analysis of any interference with 'private life' instead of 'family life'. Indeed, 'the applicant's vulnerability caused by his serious mental illness may result in even stronger emotional bonds with the parents than in regular circumstances not characterised by vulnerability'. On that account, 'his emotional and social dependence on those whom he understood as his family' should have led the court to an extended notion and broad interpretation of the concept of family and family life.'[124]

Overall, it is worth highlighting that the quality of environments, support services and relationships are gradually gaining weight in Court and concurring and dissenting opinion findings. This initial line of argument, if supported in the future, may contribute to developing a social determinants of health-sensitive jurisprudential trend that would helps discrediting a purely biological approach to severe mental health impairments.

### 5.3.2 *Immigration Detention and Psychological Suffering*

Immigration detention is the practice of depriving migrants of their personal liberty when these people are, for example, suspected of irregular entry into a state or held while arrangements are (or 'should' be) being made for their deportation. Health scholars have reached a certain consensus on the fact that 'loss of liberty, [. . .] the threat of forced return to the country of origin' and the length of stay and exposure to poor material conditions in detention centres

---

[122] Ibid, paras 191, 192.
[123] Ibid, paras 195–199.
[124] Ibid, Concurring Opinion of Judge Jelić, paras 4–5.

constitute significant stressors that can cause the onset or worsening of personal mental health difficulties.[125] The case law of the ECtHR has considered psychological health problems of applicants as factors to take into consideration when determining whether immigration detention constitutes a human rights violation. However, their legal appreciation, as indicated later in this section, varies from case to case, and generally only contributes to a finding of violation in cases of dire deprivation.

It must be restated that immigration control is one of the justifications for the deprivation of adults' liberty in Article 5(1)(f) ECHR, and states are not required to justify the necessity of the measure in this legal framework,[126] unlike, for example, in the context of the ICCPR.[127] Nonetheless, immigration detention must not be arbitrary, and the assessment to determine this must take into account, *inter alia*, the appropriateness of detention conditions in relation to the health status of the applicant.[128] Unlike cases of people suffering from degenerative physical diseases,[129] the situation of a migrant who has a diagnosis of mental illness and who is placed in a detention centre with medical attention and psychological support is considered prima facie non-arbitrary under Article 5(1) ECHR.[130]

The poor material conditions in detention centres and their effects on mental health have also been assessed for their compliance with freedom from inhuman and degrading treatment. Indeed, the Court has consistently held that detention conditions must be compatible with 'human dignity', which necessitates that 'the manner and method of the execution of the measure do not subject [the detained person] to distress or hardship of an intensity exceeding the unavoidable level of suffering inherent in detention and that [...] health and well-being are adequately secured by, among other things, providing [...] medical assistance'.[131] For example, in the case of a victim of torture who had irregularly crossed the Turkish/Greek border and was detained in a facility next to a border guard station, pre-existing psychological trauma, compounded by severe limitations of personal liberty and unhealthy living conditions, contributed to the ECtHR ruled that the

---

[125] Martha Von Werthern et al., 'The Impact of Immigration Detention on Mental Health: A Systematic Review (2018) *BMC Psychiatry* 18, 382.

[126] See *Saadi* (n 117, Ch 1) and Section 1.3.1.2.

[127] See Section 1.3.1.2.

[128] *Saadi* (n 117, Ch 1) para 74.

[129] *Yoh–Ekale Mwanje* (n 42, Ch 3) para 124.

[130] *Thimothawes v Belgium* App no 39061/11 (ECHR 2017) para 79; *K.G. v Belgium* App no 52548/15 (ECHR 2018) para 88.

[131] *Kudła* (n 37, Ch 3) para 94.

applicant's detention conditions had attained a sufficient level of severity to qualify as ill treatment and fell within the scope of Article 3 ECHR.[132] The appreciation of this minimum level of severity, as frequently stated throughout this book, is relative and depends on, *inter alia*, 'the nature and context of the treatment, as well as its methods of execution, its duration, its physical or mental effects, as well as, sometimes, the sex, the age and state of health of the victim'.[133] For irregular migrant adults, the case law suggests that a violation of Article 3 is likely to be found only where evidence indicates exceptionally abusive detention conditions, entailing dire physical and mental suffering.[134] Although they are not recognised as a particular vulnerable group per se by the Court, the provision of health care and psychological support in detention constitute the content of a positive obligation,[135] which however does not apply outside cases of deprivation of personal liberty.[136]

As far as children are concerned, the ECtHR has developed a consistent body of jurisprudence according to which their immigration detention is deemed a traumatising experience, which prima facie raises several human rights issues in terms of lawfulness and necessity of the measures (Article 5.1), ill treatment (Article 3) and physical and mental integrity (Article 8), as interpreted in relation to the key principles of the CRC (e.g. the best interests of the child and children's development).[137]

The starting point of the ECtHR's reasoning in such cases is that the 'extreme vulnerability of children' should take 'precedence over other considerations relating to [. . .] the status as illegal immigrants'.[138] From this stems positive obligations of care and protection on the part of states to prevent children from experiencing unbearable living conditions and being deprived of their personal liberty, which cause them considerable distress.[139] During analysis of their age-related and immigrant contextual vulnerability, the Court has repeatedly described the placement of accompanied and unaccompanied migrant children in transit or detention centres as an experience of 'stress and anxiety, with particularly traumatic repercussions for their mental state',

---

[132] *S.D.* (n 150, Ch 1) para 52.

[133] *Moustahi v France* App no 9347/14 (ECHR 2020) para 53.

[134] *J.R. and others v Greece* App no 22696/16 (ECHR 2018); *Kaak and others v Greece* App no 34215/16 (ECHR 2019); *Aden Ahmed* (n 273, Ch 2).

[135] Ibid.

[136] There is no fully-fledged right to health in the ECHR. See Section 2.6.1.

[137] *Mayeka and Mitunga* (n 154, Ch 1); *Muskhadzhiyeva and others v Belgium* App no 41442/07 (ECHR 2010); *Moustahi* (n 121); *Kanagaratnam v Belgium* App no 15297/09 (ECHR 2011); *Popov* (n 153, Ch 1); *Rahimi* (n 148, Ch 1).

[138] *Mayeka and Mitunga* (ibid) para 55.

[139] Ibid 58.

demonstrating 'a lack of humanity to such a degree that it amounted to inhuman treatment'.[140] The ECtHR recognises that the detention of young children in conditions ill-suited to their special needs is likely to have serious psychological effects on their mental and emotional development, and this has significantly contributed to the Court tightening its scrutiny by lowering the high threshold of Article 3[141] and reducing the state margin of discretion in adopting measures affecting their personal liberty or private and family life.[142]

### 5.3.3 *Social Entitlements and Mental Health*

The jurisprudence of the ECSR has interpretatively extended the personal scope of application of the ESC, which is set out in the Appendix, to cover 'emergency' social and medical assistance for irregular migrant adults.[143] These types of assistance that states are required to provide under Article 13 ESC include the necessary 'accommodation, food, emergency care and clothing' to address an 'urgent' and 'serious' state of need. The ESC also indicates that these criteria of urgency and seriousness should not be interpreted 'too narrowly'.[144] In the absence of applicable jurisprudence, as far as mental health services are concerned, the subsidised provision of counselling and psychological care at the primary or community level seems to exceed the 'emergency' requirement set by the ECSR for irregular migrant adults. While the extent to which social contexts and living conditions affect mental health has already been clarified,[145] it must be noted that the provision of 'emergency social assistance' – the standard required by the ECSR to target the special needs of irregular migrants – at least contributes to creating a minimal social baseline that targets the most basic material needs, the lack of which may seriously endanger people's mental health.

More generous standards emerge from the jurisprudence on the social entitlements of migrant children, including those with an irregular migratory status. The decision of *DCI* v. *Belgium* operationalised the concept of the interdependence of human rights to hold that the failure to provide accommodation, care and assistance to (irregular) migrant children violated the ESC, as it exposed them to the risk of being victim to violence or exploitation in the street environment, 'thereby posing a serious threat to the enjoyment of

---

[140] Ibid, para 58; *Moustahi* (n 121) para 66.
[141] *Kanagaratnam* (n 125) paras 67–69.
[142] Ibid 89–95; *Muskhadzhiyeva* (n 125) paras 69–75; *Mayeka* (n 154, Ch1) para 75–87.
[143] See Sections 1.4.2, 3.2.2 and 4.2.2.
[144] *FEANTSA* (n 221, Ch 1) and *CEC* (n 218, Ch 1).
[145] Pūras (n 1); See Section 5.2.3, *supra*.

their most basic rights, such as the rights to life, to psychological and physical integrity [...] and health'.[146] Furthermore, the ECSR affirmed 'the right of migrant minors unlawfully in a country to receive health care extending beyond urgent medical assistance and including primary and secondary care, as well as *psychological assistance*'.[147] In the European human rights system, the inherent vulnerability of all migrant children enhances the right standards for this group, including social rights standards, while the normative role of disability linked to a mental impairment has not yet been explicitly employed in relation to irregular migrants in these legal frameworks.

## 5.4 INTERNATIONAL HUMAN RIGHTS BODIES: EMPHASISING MENTAL HEALTH IN PRIMARY CARE AND SUPPORT SERVICES

Unlike the constrained interpretation of European human rights law, international human rights bodies have not only considered 'impact on mental health' as an element or consequence of human rights violations but also created a number of powerful normative and argumentative tools to establish a non-discriminatory right to health care beyond situations of clinical emergency and extending to the determinants of health, which can be applied to protect the mental health of irregular migrants. First, this section explores how a number of treaty provisions, as interpreted by several UN treaty bodies, can positively address the mental health of people who are about to be expelled and are being held in immigration detention centres. Second, based on a triangulation of arguments, consisting of those of the UN human rights bodies on non-discrimination and vulnerability, the contribution of the WHO's recommendations and studies commissioned by this organisation and the human rights treaty-based approach to disability, I present a number of human rights–based reasons to expansively define the scope of the right of irregular migrants to access mental health care and support.

### 5.4.1 *Mental Health Considerations in Human Rights Violations*

Like in the case of the ECtHR, most of the jurisprudence of UN treaty bodies directly concerning the protection of the mental health of undocumented people to avoid human rights violations is related to the contexts of deportation and detention as irregular migration containment measures.

Article 7 of the ICCPR (freedom from cruel, inhuman or degrading treatment or punishment) is arguably one of the most invoked human rights

---

[146] *DCI v Belgium* (n 218, Ch 1) 82.
[147] Ibid, para 128, emphasis added.

provisions in cases of deportations that may constitute refoulement, where the mental health consequences for the returnee are deemed ill treatment. In such cases, the HRCtee assesses whether the removal of a migrant from a state territory would expose them to a personal risk of an irreparable harm.[148] In the case of *C. v. Australia*, the Committee considered that the removal of the complainant to Iran, where the necessary 'medication and back up treatment' for his mental health condition were likely to be unavailable, constituted a violation of Article 7 ICCPR.[149] In *A.H.G. v. Canada*, the Committee considered the author of the communication, a person diagnosed with a severe mental illness and with a criminal record who had lived for several years in Canada and was deported to Jamaica, as a particularly vulnerable person because of his mental impairment. In the circumstances of the case, the expulsion constituted an 'abrupt withdrawal of the medical and family support on which a person in his vulnerable position is necessarily dependent' and was deemed a form of ill treatment and refoulement.[150] The case *Monge Contreras v. Canada*, concerning the removal of a failed asylum seeker, shed light on the steps that states are required to take to avoid breaching Article 7 ICCPR. The Committee ruled that adequate weight be given to the fact that the complainant had a 'medical certificate, according to which the [complainant] suffered from chronic post-traumatic stress disorder and that he would be highly vulnerable to psychological collapse in case of return' to his origin country where he would face other threats to his psychical and mental integrity.[151]

Other problematic circumstances have arisen in cases where migrants who had been witnesses in criminal proceedings were (about to be) deported to countries where they would be exposed to a highly probable risk of irreparable harm to their human rights to life and physical and mental integrity at the hands of non-state actors.[152] In one such case, *A.H. v. Denmark*, the author of the communication, in support of his claims, provided evidence of his 'unstable state of [...] mental health', which the Committee considered a determining factor that made him 'particularly vulnerable [and] disclose[d] a real risk [...] of treatment contrary to the requirements of Article 7 of the Covenant as a consequence of his removal' from the respondent state territory to the origin country.[153]

---

[148] For further details see Section 2.3.3.
[149] *C. v Australia* Com no 900/1999 (HRCtee 2002) para 8.5.
[150] *A.H.G. v Canada* Com no 2091/2011 (HRCtee 2015) para 10.4.
[151] *Jose Henry Monge Contreras v Canada* Com no 2613/2015 (HRCtee 2017) para 8.9.
[152] *Osayi Omo-Amenaghawon v Denmark* Com no 2288/2013 (HRCtee 2015); *A.H. v Denmark* Com no 2370/2014 (HRCtee 2015).
[153] Ibid (*A.H.*), para 8.8, emphasis added.

Furthermore, a comparison of the findings in A.N. and J.B., two recent 'Dublin' cases against Switzerland before the CAT Committee, demonstrates that the combination of evidence of being a victim of torture and experiencing serious mental health problems is critical in preventing the removal of a migrant to a country where the necessary specialised care is not easily accessible to migrants. In A.N., the Committee found that the ill treatment to which the non-European complainant would be exposed upon return to Italy (his first country of asylum), where shelter, food and basic needs are not always guaranteed, would entail the risk of his depression worsening 'to the extent that he would be likely to commit suicide and that, in the circumstances of this case, this ill treatment could reach a level comparable to torture'.[154] Such 'a precarious situation endangering the life of the complainant would leave him no reasonable choice but to seek protection elsewhere, exposing him to a risk of chain refoulement to his home country'.[155] By contrast, in J.B., the lack of sufficient medical proof of a situation of particular vulnerability, considered in the context of a return to Bulgaria, led the Committee to hold that there were not substantial grounds to believe that the complainant would be at risk of torture if returned.[156]

The CAT Committee's most recent general comment specifically concerned migrant victims of torture in deportation procedures. According to this authoritative document, all people who claim to be victims of torture should be able to access medical and psychological examinations before the deportation is enforced,[157] and migrants who are confirmed as victims of torture should not be expelled to countries where these services are non-existent.[158] Furthermore, in their credibility assessment regarding factual circumstances to validate the refoulement claim, state parties should 'appreciate that complete accuracy can seldom be expected from [those] victims of torture' who experience post-traumatic stress disorder.[159]

In relation to immigration detention, unlike the ECtHR, the HRCtee considers that whereas 'detention of unauthorised arrivals is not arbitrary per se, [. . .] remand in custody could be considered arbitrary if it is *not necessary* given all the circumstances of the case: the element of proportionality

---

[154] A.N. *v Switzerland* (n 181, Ch 1) para 8.10.
[155] Ibid, para 8.5.
[156] J.B. *v Switzerland* (n 181, Ch 1).
[157] CAT Committee, GC4 (n 178, Ch 1) para 41.
[158] Ibid, para 22.
[159] Ibid, para 42.

becomes relevant'.[160] Detention is not an automatic corollary of the state power to enforce immigration law; it must be justified,[161] and the mental health status of irregular migrants upon arrival at a detention centre is key in determining the proportionality and necessity of the restriction of their personal liberty according to Article 9 ICCPR (the right to liberty and security).[162] Prolonged detention can give rise to a finding of violation of Article 10 ICCPR (the right to be treated with humanity in detention) if the conditions are not dignified or the type of detention is not based on 'a proper assessment of the circumstances of the case' but is, as such, 'disproportionate'. This was found to be so in the case of *Madafferi* v. *Australia*, the complainant of which was a person with irregular migration status who was placed and kept in a detention centre against the advice of various doctors and psychiatrists and who, as a consequence, experienced a deterioration of his mental health situation.[163] These maxims are generalised and restated in General Comment No. 35, in which the HRCtee clarified that immigration detention 'must be justified as reasonable, necessary and proportionate in the light of the circumstances and [periodically] reassessed'. The decision must but be 'necessary' and 'proportionate' in that it must consider, *inter alia*, 'less invasive means of achieving the same ends' and 'the effect of the detention on the [. . .] physical or mental health' of migrants.[164]

Health deprivation in detention may also trigger the applicability of Article 7 ICCPR (the prohibition of torture and ill treatment). In *C.* v. *Australia*, where the state party's courts and tribunals had accepted that the worsening of the complainant's mental health was a consequence of the protracted immigration detention, the HRCtee found a violation of this provision on the basis that the state party 'was aware of the author's mental condition and failed to take the steps necessary to ameliorate the author's mental deterioration'.[165] Furthermore, in two other cases against Australia, the HRCtee considered that the prolonged and indefinite detention of migrants and asylum seekers in Australian off-shore migrant camps inflicted 'serious psychological harm upon them [to such an extent to] constitute treatment contrary to Article 7 of the Covenant'.[166] Although medical treatment was available during detention, the Committee, in its decisions, confirmed that respect for human rights should

---

[160] *Madafferi* (n 189, Ch 1) para 9, emphasis added.
[161] *C.* (n 137) paras 8.2 and 8.3.
[162] *F.K.A.G.* (n 239, Ch 2) para 9.3; *Madafferi* (n 189, Ch 1) para 9.
[163] Ibid (*Madafferi*) para 9.3.
[164] HRCtee, GC35 (n 67) para 18; See also *C.* (n 137) paras 8.2. and 8.3.
[165] Ibid (*C.*) para 8.4.
[166] *F.K.A.G.* (n 239, Ch 2) para 9.8; *M.M.M.* (n 239, Ch 2) para 10.7.

take precedence over the enforcement of immigration measures such as detention in cases where medical treatment and psychological support are insufficient to mitigate the inhuman psychological consequences of indefinite detention.

### 5.4.2 Irregular Migrants' Right to Mental Health: Non-discrimination, Vulnerability and Disability Arguments

To appreciate the extent to which international human rights law, drawing on interdisciplinary sources, has contributed to delineating the scope of the right to mental health of irregular migrants, which may resonate and be implemented in other normative frameworks, this section presents a staged analysis. First, it examines significant examples of the jurisprudence of the UN human rights bodies on mental health care and the determinants of mental health of migrants in precarious situations and with irregular migratory status, in light of the findings of Chapters 3 and 4 regarding a vulnerability- and PHC-based approach to the right to health. Second, adding to these general remarks, it elaborates on a number of layers of identity or factors of inherent and social vulnerability that have contributed to the development of a differentiated human rights approach. Finally, it examines the consequences of using the new CRPD model of equality, which has the potential to cement international law's normative favour for establishing a supportive environment for mental health and for reducing discrimination, social exclusion and disablement for all, including for irregular migrants.

#### 5.4.2.1 Mental Health in the PHC Model for Irregular Migrants

Chapter 2 stressed the validity of the PHC approach, which includes consideration of the social determinants of health, as an influential model for the normative development of an equity-oriented right to physical and mental health in international human rights law. Indeed, this paradigm targets social and health vulnerabilities while granting states a certain margin of appreciation regarding the programmatic realisation, organisation and actual provision of health and social services.[167] Authoritative international public health declarations, backed by the WHO, have defined PHC as a 'strategy' for eliminating health inequity and realising the right to health by prioritising the 'levels' of primary and preventive health care and adopting intersectoral

---

[167] See Sections 2.4.2.4 and 2.4.2.5.

measures that target the social determinants of health.[168] Thus, for instance, the CESCR established a number of PHC-inspired core obligations relating to the right to health with immediate operational force. These included the duty to secure equitable access to 'health facilities, goods and services on a non-discriminatory basis, especially for vulnerable and marginalised groups' and the provision of essential drugs and food, basic housing and adequate water supply for all.[169]

The normative priority accorded to PHC in the conceptualisation and operationalisation of the right to health, including via vulnerability-oriented core obligations in the context of the ICESCR, were explained in Chapters 2 and 3 to ground a human rights–based theory that limited the margin of discretion afforded to states for interpreting and implementing health rights for irregular migrants. In particular, the rules of interpretation of international law, the qualification of irregular migrants as vulnerable people, the applicability of the non-discrimination principle on the grounds of migratory status in relation to the core elements of this right and the substantive notion of equality that qualifies state obligations have all contributed to establishing that the international right to health of irregular migrants cannot be restricted to a right to emergency medical treatment only.[170]

As Article 12 ICESCR explicitly applies to both physical and mental health, mental health services and psychosocial interventions should be offered in a consistent way with the PHC approach and the core obligations in General Comment No. 14. Accordingly, following their non-discriminatory and equity-oriented guidance, these services should be at least partially integrated into primary or community care, complemented with other levels of services and made accessible for irregular migrants as persons who experience contextual vulnerability and who should not be discriminated against.[171] This is generally synchronised with the recommendatory approach of the WHO on this subject. Indeed, if mental health care were to be provided only in specialised care settings, the migratory and socioeconomic status of some prospective service users may prevent them from being able to have equal and affordable access this care.[172] Additionally, primary care, as formerly indicated, might reduce the stigma and discrimination associated with the use of psychiatric care – which, for irregular migrants, is often compounded by the discriminatory

---

[168] Declaration of Alma-Ata (n 28, Introduction); Declaration of Astana (n 174, Ch 2); WHO/UNICEF (n 1, Ch 3).
[169] CESCR, GC14 (n 27, Introduction) para 43.
[170] See, in particular, Section 3.3.
[171] CESCR, GC14 (n 27, Introduction) paras 17, 36 and 43. Bell (n 89) 141–153.
[172] WHO Europe (n 6) 14.

labelling they experience as non-nationals with no legal status – and minimise the potential for violations of human rights to occur behind the closed doors of institutions.[173]

In contrast, urgent care, such as that required in cases of relapse of certain psychotic episodes, should be accessible for irregular migrants as an ICCPR-related obligation concerning the right to life in dignity, which entails the right 'to receive any [mental health] care that is "urgently" required for the preservation of their life or the avoidance of irreparable harm to their health'.[174] Essential psychotropic drugs, as periodically listed by the WHO, should be available on a universal basis as a right-to-health core obligation,[175] although their inclusion should be periodically reviewed in accordance with a risk–benefit analysis.[176] For any 'mental health system to be compliant with the right to health', the biomedical or pharmacological approach to mental health must be appropriately balanced with psychosocial interventions, 'the arbitrary assumption' that biomedical interventions are the most effective strategy for addressing mental health conditions should be avoided[177] and 'diversity of care' should be pursued.[178]

At several points in this book, it is specified that the scope of the right to the highest attainable standard of physical and mental health not only entails ensuring access to appropriate health care services but also embraces under-lying or social determinants of health. The SDH model, as incorporated in human rights law, applies to both physical and mental health and explains inequalities in health outcomes at population and individual levels.[179] Public health and social medicine studies have often associated inadequate income, substandard housing and status inequality with the prevalence of mental disorders.[180] In addition, the onset of mental health conditions have been associated with, among other factors, low levels of social trust and cohesion,[181]

---

[173] WHO and WONCA (n 84).
[174] HRCtee, GC36 (n 193, Ch 1); *Toussaint* (n 190, Ch 1) para 11. Similarly, ICMW (n 42, Introduction) Article 28.
[175] CESCR, GC14 (n 27, Introduction).
[176] Dainius Pūras, 'Report of the Special Rapporteur on the Right to [...] Health (Focus: Mental Health and Human Rights: Setting a Rights-based Global Agenda' (15 April 2020) A/HRC/44/48, paras 40 and 43.
[177] Pūras (n 3) para 20.
[178] Pūras (n 164) paras 61–66.
[179] See Section 4.1.
[180] Kate Pickett, Oliver James and Richard Wilkinson, 'Income Inequality and the Prevalence of Mental Illness: A Preliminary International Analysis' (2006) *Journal of Epidemiology and Community Health* 60 646–647.
[181] Richard Wilkinson, *The Impact of Inequality: How to Make Sick Societies Healthier* (New Press 2005).

negative views of self-status and self-worth,[182] and a perceived lack of control over one's work and life.[183] All of these are stressful circumstances that unprivileged migrant populations are likely to experience in the xenophobic climates of modern Western societies.[184] Irregular or undocumented migrants, as a direct or indirect consequence of their precarious migratory status in receiving countries, 'are vulnerable to exploitation, long working hours, unfair wages and dangerous and unhealthy working environments' that affect their material living conditions and health status.[185] These circumstances, together with social isolation, fear of being returned to their origin country and difficulties obtaining entitlements,[186] are considered by the WHO to be stressors or risk factors for mental health problems.[187] Against this background, the current COVID-19 pandemic and widespread public health responses are reported to have 'worsened pre-existing mental health conditions and [. . .] created new vulnerabilities' for migrant populations with a precarious migratory and socio-economic status.[188]

The UN special rapporteur on the right to health has been particularly vocal regarding the need to support the social determinants of mental health of people in situations of human mobility, including irregular migrants, via collective and individualised measures at both the preventive and assistance levels. At the macro level, the special rapporteur has recommended decriminalising irregular migration and taking steps to prevent the fuelling of intolerance and xenophobia towards people on the move, which are manifestations of structural violence and discrimination that directly impact the context in which people live and affect their mental health.[189] While the UN rapporteur has emphasised the importance of supportive environments and relationships for preventing critical mental distress and meeting the right to public mental health of migrant populations, this goal can only be facilitated by regulating

---

[182] Simon Charlesworth, Paul Gilfillan and Richard Wilkinson, 'Living Inferiority' (2004) *British Medical Bulletin* 60(1) 49.

[183] Michael Marmot, *Status Syndrome: How Your Social Standing Directly Affects Your Health and Life Expectancy* (Bloomsbury 2004).

[184] Achiume E. Tendayi, 'Report of the Special Rapporteur on Contemporary Forms of Racism (Focus: Xenophobia)' (13 May 2016) A/HRC/32/50; Tendayi (2018) (n 26, Ch 3).

[185] CESCR, GC23 (n 143, Ch 4) para 47. For further details, see Section 4.3.

[186] Christa Straßmayr et al., 'Mental Health Care for Irregular Migrants in Europe: Barriers and How They Are Overcome' (2012) *BMC Public Health* 367; Lena Andersson, Anders Hjern and Henry Ascher, 'Undocumented Adult Migrants in Sweden: Mental Health and Associated Factors' (2018) *BMC Public Health* 18.

[187] WHO Europe (n 6) 4.

[188] Justo Pinzón-Espinosa, 'The COVID-19 Pandemic and Mental Health of Refugees, Asylum Seekers, and Migrants' (2021) *Journal of Affective Disorders* 280 407.

[189] Pūras (n 253, Ch 2) paras 30–32, 78, 79, 83.

socioeconomic rights for all migrants and, in particular, by providing psychosocial services for migrants with mental health issues without discrimination.[190]

This would require national, regional and local government departments to pay greater attention to irregular migration and adopt intersectoral measures and services targeted at achieving at least a minimum level of social integration and meeting the basic needs of all migrants,[191] in accordance with the principles of indivisibility and interdependence of all human rights. Although this would represent the optimum from both a human rights and a health promotion perspective, Chapter 4 explained how difficult it may be to fully implement these general standards in the context of irregular migration. Indeed, the exercise of sovereign governmental powers in the fields of immigration policy and social welfare, and the still uneven playing field where civil and political rights tend to obscure socioeconomic rights in human rights, in practice create regulatory barriers to holistic and inclusionary care as a human rights issue.[192]

However, I would argue that if the services included in psychosocial support were qualified as a valid and necessary alternative or as essential supplementary 'care' to psychiatric treatment,[193] in particular for anxiety and depression, this would place them in the realm of 'essential health care' and they should, therefore, be covered by the combined scope of the aforementioned right to primary and community health care, as well as by the scope of the right to a life in dignity with no discrimination. Finally, it must once again be reiterated that to make these entitlements real in practice, 'firewalls' must be established in relation to all public services to ensure that irregular migrants enjoy mental health care and support services for mental health without factual barriers based on immigration status.[194]

To conclude this human rights analysis, which applies the arguments developed throughout the book to the neglected area of mental health, it can be asserted that general international human rights law offers compelling normative and argumentative reasons to include non-discriminatory preventive and primary health care, as well as urgent health and social care, within the levels of health care and material conditions that meet the 'right to mental health' obligations of irregular migrant adults. In relation to certain

[190] Ibid, paras 2, 30, 36, 39, 53, 57, 63, 72, emphasis added.
[191] Social integration is one of the four critical areas of intervention to promote mental health of all migrants according to WHO Europe (n 6).
[192] See Section 4.1.4.
[193] Pūras (n 1) paras 36, 50–52.
[194] Ibid, para 56.

subcategories of irregular migrants, age-, gender- and disability-related considerations in human rights law support the equalisation of standards in relation to the care provided to citizens and regular migrants.

### 5.4.2.2 Age- and Gender-Related Considerations

The multidimensional development needs of children – which are proxies for inherent vulnerability to physical and psychological harms, with potentially long-lasting consequences on health and well-being in adult life – have played a key role in enhancing the protective scope of international law regarding the quality of state obligations vis-à-vis children rights.

Accordingly, the most prominent of the applicable human rights treaties in this area, the CRC, contains much more detailed textual treaty obligations than general human rights law, which reduce the state margin of discretion in discharging human rights treaty obligations regarding, for example, the provision of 'necessary medical assistance' and the development of social determinants–sensitive PHC policies.[195] For instance, the CRC Committee has acknowledged that 'mental health and psychosocial problems [...] are primary causes of ill health, morbidity and mortality among adolescents, particularly among those in vulnerable groups' and has urged states to adopt, within the context of a comprehensive multisectoral response, 'an approach based on public health and psychosocial support rather than overmedicalization and institutionalization'.[196] The international jurisprudence recognises that human rights–compliant state actions should dedicate 'increased attention for behavioural and social issues that undermine children's mental health, psychosocial well-being and emotional development'.[197] Child-focused human rights law is premised on the fact that the 'best interests of the child' are a primary consideration in all decisions that concern children and may displace other state interests,[198] such as immigration control or the related state interest of reducing access to services by irregular migrants for the protection of the economic well-being of a country.

In the same spirit, the CRC and CMW Committees have stated outright that reduced access to social and health services, which is normally associated with irregular migration status, 'can negatively affect the physical, spiritual,

---

[195] CRC (n 42, Introduction) Article 24. See also Articles 25–29.
[196] CRC Committee, 'General Comment No. 20 on the Implementation of the Rights of the Child During Adolescence' (6 December 2016) para 58; See also CRC, Committee, GC15 (n 173, Ch 2) para 38.
[197] Ibid.
[198] CRC (n 42, Introduction), Article 3; CRC Committee, GC14 (n 204, Ch 3).

mental and social development of migrant children'.[199] In the light of this, the Committees held that:

> Every migrant child should have access to health care 'equal' to that of nationals, regardless of their migration status. This includes all health services, whether preventive or curative, and mental, physical or psychosocial care, provided in the community or in health-care institutions.[200]

These human rights treaty bodies embrace a strict approach to the principle of non-discrimination on the grounds of nationality and legal status to the extent that no degree of differentiated treatment is acceptable, as 'states have an obligation to ensure that children's health is not undermined as a result of discrimination, which is a significant factor contributing to vulnerability'.[201]

The right to health of migrant children, like that of adults, goes beyond access to mental health care, psychological support and rehabilitation services but also extends to the adoption of coherent intersectoral measures that address 'a variety of factors, including structural determinants such as poverty, unemployment, [...] violence, discrimination and marginalization'.[202] Furthermore, given that the maintenance of stable support networks and family relationships are especially critical determinants of children's mental health, regulations and decisions concerning deportations and family reunification should adequately consider the effects on the mental health and development of every child.[203]

In addition to age, gender is a social determinant of physical and mental health[204] and a prominent ground of non-discrimination.[205] A gender-sensitive approach to the human right to health must consider and address those biological, socially constructed and environmental factors that disproportionally affect the achievement of the highest attainable physical and mental health standards by women, as interrelated with other human rights.[206] For instance, the right to sexual and reproductive health has a broad scope that applies to all, but some of its dimensions are especially critical for or exclusively relate to the health and well-being of women because of their

---

[199] CMW and CRC Committees, JGC 3/22 (n 175, Ch 1) para 40.

[200] CMW and CRC Committees, JGC 4/23 (n 175, Ch 1) para 55, emphasis added.

[201] Ibid.

[202] Ibid, para 54.

[203] Pūras (n 253, Ch 2) paras 69–70.

[204] CSDH Report (n 109, Ch 2) 145–155.

[205] For example, ICCPR and ICESCR (n 42, Introduction) Articles 2(2) and 3; CEDAW (n 42, Introduction).

[206] CEDAW Committee, GR24 (n 240, Ch 2) paras 6 and 12.

reproductive capacity.[207] Therefore, included in the right to health are state obligations to provide access to antenatal, perinatal and postnatal care, 'safe abortion services and quality post-abortion care [...] and to respect the right of women to make autonomous decisions about their sexual and reproductive health'.[208]

To avoid gender-based discrimination, all women, particularly women belonging to lower social classes and vulnerable groups such as irregular migrants, should have access to comprehensive sexual and reproductive care.[209] A WHO review of relevant literature on this topic demonstrates a strong causal relationship 'between psychological distress, depression and anxiety disorders, and aspects of reproductive health', such as childbirth, sexual violence and adverse maternal outcome.[210]

A growing body of international jurisprudence has found that the denial of access or limitations to appropriate sexual and reproductive health services that specifically address women's health, such as therapeutic abortion or post-abortion counselling and mental health services, can affect psychological integrity by creating mental anguish and can constitute forms of gender-based violence, ill treatment and violation of the right to health.[211] In the light of the reinforced protection of the principle of gender equality in human rights law – to be achieved via formal and substantive anti-discriminatory measures – and considering the entrenched relationships between reproductive health and mental health, all women, regardless of their migration status, should have comprehensive access to mental health and support services, at least in relation to their sexual and reproductive health.

Limiting irregular migrant women's access to sexual and reproductive health care and related psychological care constitutes discrimination on multiple grounds. It directly differentiates their enjoyment of the right to health and interrelated rights on the grounds of legal status vis-à-vis citizens and regular migrants, which should remain proportionate to its aim and, by disproportionately affecting women, it constitutes indirect gender-based discrimination between irregular migrant women and migrant and non-migrant men. The seriousness of the bundle of rights at stake, the enjoyment of which affects women and men differently, and the variable breath of socially

---

[207] CESCR, GC22 (n 209, Ch 2) para 25.
[208] Ibid, para 28.
[209] See Sections 3.4.3.2 and 4.3.2.
[210] WHO and UNFPA, *Mental Health Aspects of Women's Reproductive Health: A Global Review of the Literature* (WHO 2009) 159.
[211] *R.P.B.* (n 68); *L.C.* (n 243, Ch 2) para 7.2; *Siobhán Whelan v Ireland* (n 69); CESCR, GC22 (n 209, Ch 2).

constructed 'disadvantages, discrimination and subordination suffered by women' in all societies, especially in the context of migration, requires strict human rights scrutiny.[212]

Furthermore, as poor mental health suffered by women in the context of sexual and reproductive health is often associated with disadvantaged socio-economic conditions[213] and aggravated by structural inequalities in the work environment and in relation to household responsibilities,[214] pursuing gender equality – which is a key human rights principle – would require making psychosocial services that target the underlying structural determinants of health accessible to all women, including irregular migrants.

### 5.4.2.3 The CRPD: A Transformative Tool for Combating Multiple Sources of Discrimination and Health-Related Rights Violations

The CRPD – which builds on the social model of disability, according to which disability is an oppressive social construct – is a young human rights treaty system that aims to 'promote, protect and ensure the full and equal enjoyment of all human rights and fundamental freedoms by all persons with disabilities'.[215] It establishes a number of detailed positive obligations regarding civil, political, economic, social and cultural rights. By ratifying the CRPD, states commit to reverse discriminatory attitudes and enable people with disabilities to live as equal rights bearers and achieve their full potential in society on an equal basis with others.[216]

Article 5(2) of this treaty stipulates that 'state parties shall prohibit all discrimination on the basis of disability, and guarantee to persons with disabilities equal and effective legal protection against discriminations *on all grounds*',[217] which includes the provision of reasonable accommodation in particular cases.[218] This provision establishes far-reaching positive duties and stipulates that 'discriminations on all grounds' should be interpreted as

---

[212] Bantekas (n 32, Ch 1) 508.
[213] WHO and UNFPA (n 199) 25.
[214] CSDH Report (n 111, Ch 2) 145.
[215] CRPD (n 18, Introduction) Article 1.
[216] Ibid, Article 3.
[217] Ibid, Article 5(2).
[218] According to Article 2 CRPD, 'reasonable accommodation means necessary and appropriate modification and adjustments not imposing a disproportionate or undue burden, where needed *in a particular case*' to allow the enjoyment of human rights by people with disabilities, emphasis added.

including 'migrant [...] status', as well as multiple and intersectional discriminations.[219]

In the CRPD, equality and non-discrimination 'are principles and rights' and constitute 'an interpretative tool for all the other principles and rights enshrined in the Convention', which demand the adoption of transformative 'cross-cutting obligations of immediate realisation'.[220]

Therefore, Article 25 CRPD on the right to health of people with disabilities is equally applicable to all migrants with mental or psychosocial disabilities. Denying or restricting access to the 'specific health services needed' because of a mental impairment to an irregular migrant can constitute a multiple discrimination on the grounds of disability, health and migration status. Indeed, it is worth noting that 'discrimination on any ground [...] is both a cause and a consequence of poor mental health'.[221] In contrast to the aims and principles of the Convention and to the specific purpose of this article – which includes 'minimis[ing] and prevent[ing] further disabilities' – reduced access to care, combined with the suffering associated with mental impairment and the social response to the same, is likely to result in disabling and discriminatory outcomes. In this course of action, the specific needs, in terms of psychosocial care and support, of irregular migrants with mental health issues, would be treated like those of other people on the move, or citizens who do not have any psychosocial impairment or disability.[222] Further textual qualifiers of this right include that health services should be located as close as possible to people's own communities, which reinforces the CRPD's duty to deinstitutionalise care.[223]

As far as access to 'general' health care that does not precisely target the impairment of the disabled person, irregular migrants with psychosocial

---

[219] CRPD Committee, GC6 (n 65) paras 19 and 21: 'Protection against "discrimination on all grounds" means that all possible grounds of discrimination and their intersections must be taken into account. Possible grounds include but are not limited to: disability; health status; genetic or other predisposition towards illness; race; colour; descent; sex; pregnancy and maternity/paternity; civil; family or career status; gender expression; sex; language; religion; political or other opinion; national, ethnic, indigenous or social origin; migrant, refugee or asylum status; belonging to a national minority; economic or property status; birth; and age, or a combination of any of those grounds or characteristics associated with any of those grounds.' On the need to address multiple or intersectional discrimination, including on the ground of migratory status, see CRPD Committee, COs on the Report of Norway (7 May 2019) CRPD/C/NOR/CO/1, para 8; Slovenia (16 April 2018) CRPD/C/SLV/CO/1, para 7, Morocco (25 September 2017) CRPD/C/MOR/CO/1, para 13.

[220] Ibid, para 12.

[221] Pūras (n 1) para 36.

[222] CRPD (n 36, Introduction) Article 25(b).

[223] Ibid, Article 25(c).

disabilities should have access to the 'same range, quality and standards of free and affordable health care and programmes as provided to other persons'.[224] This provision may require further interpretative clarifications, as the meaning of the comparator 'other persons' is fundamental for understanding the scope of the applicable principle of non-discrimination. If we qualify the position of irregular migrants with disabilities according to their migratory legal status, the latter may justify differentiated or restricted access to non-disability–specific care under the several legal frameworks discussed in Chapters 3 and 4. Accordingly, the non-disability–specific health care that they should be able to access would be the same as that provided to all irregular migrants in that particular country, and in any case, as formerly argued, should include access to affordable primary services and preventive care and essential drugs, as well as urgent and emergency care.[225] On the other hand, if 'other persons' is interpreted as 'other persons without disability regardless of their migration status', irregular migrants with psychosocial disabilities should be offered comprehensive and affordable health care on an equal basis with an abstract non-disabled person in the country. While the latter may appear more in line with the inclusionary and precautionary object, purpose and text of the treaty, particularly considering that mental disabilities contribute to significant physical morbidity,[226] only the development of international practice will indicate whether this is the case. Indeed, this exposes the unresolved tension in international law between the exclusionary state powers regarding immigration and the prima facie inclusive scope of human rights law, frequently mentioned throughout this book.

Reinforcing the considerations above, in its 2016's COs on Italy, regarding Article 11 CRPD on 'situations of risks and humanitarian emergencies', the CRPD Committee recommended that states 'ensure that *all persons* with disabilities arriving in the State party are able to access facilities on an *equal basis* with others and that those with psychosocial disabilities are given appropriate [mental health] support and rehabilitation through strengthened systems'.[227] Furthermore, 'psychosocial and legal counselling, support and rehabilitation' to be provided for all migrants with psychosocial

---

[224] Ibid, Article 25(a).

[225] See Sections 3.3.1 and 3.3.2.

[226] Samantha Battams and Julie Henderson, 'The Physical Health of People with Mental Illness and "The Right to Health"' (2010) *Advances in Mental Health* 9(2) 117; Javed Latoo, Minal Mistry and Francis J. Dunne, 'Physical Morbidity and Mortality in People with Mental Illness' (2013) *British Journal of Medical Practitioners* 6 3.

[227] CRPD Committee, COs on the Report of Italy (6 October 2016) CRPD/C/ITA/CO/1, para 25, emphasis added.

disabilities should be 'disability-, age- and gender-sensitive and culturally appropriate'.[228]

The indivisibility and interdependence of all human rights are intentional structural features of the provisions of the CRPD. For example, the right to independent living in Article 19 CRPD is an autonomy-based civil right with a strong social matrix because of the public support and funding that are needed to materialise it as an alternative to institutionalisation.[229] It is crucial for this analysis that the CRPD provisions target the underlying structural and inter-mediate determinants of disability and health in a holistic way. Enabling relationships and social contexts, which are impairment-cognisant but non-discriminatory, play a key role in enhancing people's dignity and health in the human rights–based approach to disability and health.[230]

Article 26 CRPD (habilitation and rehabilitation) is an integral element of this strategy for minimising the impact of disability, including intellectual and psychosocial disabilities. It requires states to offer, *inter alia*, 'comprehensive habilitation and rehabilitation services and programmes, particularly in the areas of health, employment, education, [and] social services', including via peer support, 'to enable people with disability to attain and maintain [. . .] full physical, mental, social and vocational ability'.

The precise scope of this article, read in the context of the treaty, clearly militates against episodic health interventions and emergency social assistance and is premised on the fact that all persons with disabilities, which 'include those who have long term impairment', may require continuity of care and support. The special rapporteur on the rights of persons with disabilities considered the provision of these services to be core obligations, thus high-lighting their primary importance and the immediate nature of the measures that states should take to implement them.[231] Given the transversal applicabil-ity of Article 5 on equality and non-discrimination on 'all grounds', the absence of limitation clauses within the treaty, and the transformative and inclusive purpose of the CRPD in general and of Article 26 in particular, there is no reason why this provision should not apply to irregular migrants with disabilities, including those of a psychosocial nature. This is also endorsed by actors outside the CRPD treaty monitoring system: for instance, the special rapporteur on the right to health also recognised that 'mental health care and

---

[228] CRPD Committee, GC6 (n 65) para 73(p).
[229] Degener (n 24); CRPD (n 36, Introduction) Article 19.
[230] Pūras (n 1) para 4.
[231] Aguilar (n 90) para 18.

support services should be accessible to people on the move with disabilities on an *equal* basis with others'.[232]

The fact that the CRPD aims to achieve structural changes vis-à-vis mainstream perceptions of disability, thereby unveiling disabling social constructs to be addressed, constitutes a paradigmatic change in grappling with the human rights of traditionally marginalised groups in society. Irregular migrants with psychosocial disabilities have been subject to a number of disabling and disempowering labels: they are institutionally or socially considered immigration law breakers or even criminals, as well as 'sick or mad people'. While the latter may even go unnoticed or be absorbed within the narrative of the 'illegal migrant', the combination of these labels, compounded by other critical factors such as gender, race and poverty, is a perfect recipe for exclusionary and discriminatory patterns that, in practice, can prevent the enjoyment of human rights on an equal basis with others.[233] The CRPD's approach to equality, which also targets intersectional discrimination, seeks to 'address the socially constructed barriers, stereotypes, negative customs and practices which hinder the full enjoyment of rights by marginalized groups'.[234]

In the spirit of the CRPD and according to its text, all migrants with disabilities should be the target of truly inclusionary and intersectoral measures. Indeed, the general principles or goals of this treaty include a fully rounded approach to non-discrimination and participation in society on an equal basis with others. As such, the CRPD's transformative approach, which entails the adoption of a broad array of 'positive measures that change structures and systems',[235] if fully embraced, may have the ability to shake the foundations of social policies that are exclusionary towards irregular migrants.

Although the 'unreserved' letter[236] of this treaty and the early jurisprudence of the CRPD Committee, respectively, urge and recommend the need to implement non-episodic health care and support services for *all* non-nationals with disabilities, regardless of their 'migrant status', it is worth making a few remarks on the inclusiveness and operationalisation of this legal instrument and its key principles, while bearing mind that the concerns raised later in this

---

[232] Pūras (n 253, Ch 2) para 57, emphasis added.

[233] Pūras (n 1) para 27.

[234] Andrea Broderick, 'The Long and Winding Road to Equality and Inclusion for Persons with Disabilities', PhD thesis, Maastricht University, the Netherlands, 20 November 2015, 36.

[235] Degener (n 24) 17.

[236] No state added any reservations to the treaty articles that are of relevance here (Articles 5, 25, 26 CRPD) to limit the scope of the rights of the Convention to certain migrants only.

section may dissipate vis-à-vis the development of new jurisprudence on the interpretation and implementation of the CRPD.

First, while the jurisprudence of the CRPD Committee has been generally inclusive (referring to 'all migrants' or 'non-discrimination on the ground migrant status'), it has thus far failed to recommend a certain course of action with specific regard to *irregular* migrants with disabilities. The impression that the CRPD Committee avoids the politically sensitive wording of 'irregularity' is supported by the fact that asylum seekers' and refugees' situations, unlike those of irregular migrants, are explicitly mentioned in the monitoring of the CRPD's rights.[237] Second, it would be useful for the CRPD to clarify in its jurisprudence what the general principle of 'participation' might mean with regard to the rights of irregular migrants with disabilities. Considering that it is antithetical to the widely recognised 'sovereign immigration policy' principle, its operationalisation may either require true structural changes to the way states approach irregular migration in the field of disability or remain an empty promise. Finally, the concrete and non-illusory realisation of the ambitious human rights programme to disability in the context of human mobility must include the recommendation and adoption of intersectoral and reinforced firewall mechanisms (which prevent information sharing between service provision departments and immigration authorities) to allow safe and unreported access to mental health care and support services by irregular migrants with disabilities.[238]

## 5.5 CONCLUSIONS

Feeding into the overall objective of this monograph, this chapter offers an analysis of the legal and interpretative trends that specifically concern the international and European right to care and support of people with mental health issues and psychosocial disabilities, in the context of irregular migration, and the different levels of protection they offer. Indeed, the responsiveness of human rights law in this area constitutes a critical inclusiveness and consistency test for a truly universal and holistic rights-based theory and practice.

To adequately approach this topic, Section 5.1 summarises the contentious definitional and conceptual challenges that discussing mental health and

---

[237] CRPD Committee, COs on the Report of Slovenia (n 206) para 30; Montenegro (22 September 2017) CRPD/C/MNE/CO/1, para 10; and Cyprus (8 May 2017) CRPD/C/CYP/CO/1, para 15.

[238] See Section 3.4.2.

disability entails. In particular, it clarifies that contemporary human rights and public health tend to agree that mental ill health or disability is the result of a combination of biological and environmental factors. The 'social environment, and in particular social affiliations and social status, may be important risk factors [or vulnerability factors] in relation to psychosocial health' or disability.[239] This consideration has indeed affected the scope of the right to health care and to the social determinants of mental health in terms of prevention, promotion and care and shaped the duties that states should adopt to avoid discrimination on the grounds of disability and to minimise further disability. Furthermore, vulnerability and disability are presented as potentially synergetic protective arguments, born from constructs of oppression, that ground positive human rights duties in relation to mental health care and promotion for irregular migrants.

While Section 5.2 clarifies the conceptual and normative boundaries, which includes unpacking the different relations between mental health and human rights, Section 5.3 examines the applicable jurisprudence of the ECtHR and the ECSR. While both monitoring bodies consider the impact of human rights violations on the mental health of people as a relevant factor in their human rights examination, they are constrained by the material and personal scope of the ECHR and ESC, respectively, and have developed an 'urgent health-related' human rights jurisprudence regarding irregular migrant adults. Thus, violations of rights are likely to be found only where particularly qualified rights deprivation exposes people to a real risk of severe consequences on their mental health in the context of detention or deportation. Nonetheless, the jurisprudence of these bodies has gradually attributed greater weight to the quality of environments, support services and relationships as factors that contribute to human rights verdicts in cases concerning migrants with mental health problems, rather than exclusively focusing on the provision of medical care. Furthermore, arguments related to vulnerability and psychological development have generated an especially protective European body of jurisprudence on the rights of migrant children to mental health and well-being, which should be prioritised over the enforcement of migration policies.

Finally, Section 5.4 offers four main lines of argument, grounded in the vulnerability- and disability-sensitive international human rights law. First, key cases and general comments of the HRCtee and the CAT Committee demonstrate the extent to which the deportations and immigration detention of

---

[239] Richard G. Wilkinson, 'Ourselves and Others – For Better or Worse: Social Vulnerability and Inequality' in Marmot and Wilkinson (n 101, Ch 2) 341, 344.

people with mental health difficulties can negatively affect mental health and are, therefore, not considered necessary and proportionate (which is a test that the ECtHR does not fully perform in the case of immigration detention). Second, a general right to mental health care for irregular migrants can be derived from the approach developed in Chapters 3 and 4. This is based on the combination of the recommended standards of global public health (including PHC and SDH) with the preceptive human rights principle of non-discrimination read in conjunction with the scope of human rights as developed by the treaty bodies. These standards are influenced by the application of the conceptual and normative lens of contextual vulnerability: limitations of preventive, promotional and curative measures vis-à-vis those offered to other community members should not be excessive in consideration that undocumented immigrants because, given the constraining effect of their legal status, they are exposed to unhealthy socioeconomic conditions that constitute particularly unfavourable determinants of physical and mental health. Therefore, the obligations under the ICESCR and ICCPR require states to make the right to life in dignity, and the right to health care effective and accessible by at least providing, without differentiation on the grounds of legal status, essential drugs, community mental health care and basic support, as well as urgent and emergency care.

Several human rights bodies have also employed age- and gender-related factors to extend health rights standards. Mental health care and measures to ensure healthy environments for regular migrant and national children should be comprehensive and should 'equally' extend to irregular migrant children as a result of the operationalisation of the principles of non-discrimination, the 'best interest of the child' and 'children's development needs'. Mental health care and support, which are a necessary component of women's reproductive care, should also be equalised between migrants and all non-migrant populations to avoid discrimination of people on the grounds of gender. Preventing or restricting access to such care would treat men and women the same despite different objective needs and would not address substantive and structural discrimination on the grounds of gender.

Finally, the CRPD is arguably a true game changer with regard to the human rights of traditionally marginalised groups, as it requires states to make structural changes in the form of collective and individualised positive duties targeting discrimination on the grounds of disability, as compounded, by other grounds of discrimination and marginalisation. The scope of application of the CRPD and its definition of persons with disabilities are intended to be sufficiently broad to include those who experience disability as a result of the interaction between impairments and social barriers. As far as irregular migrants with psychosocial disabilities are concerned, their disabling experience is, at the bare minimum, the result of unaddressed social or institutional discriminatory practices on the grounds of disability and migratory status. Article 5 CRPD outlaws any law, policy or practice which contribute to this 'status quo' specifying that all persons with disabilities must have 'equal and effective legal protection against discrimination on all grounds'. With respect to health care and support services, disability-specific services should be enjoyed by all persons with disability, as any status-based restrictive practice would indirectly result in discrimination on the grounds of disability between those who experience impairment and disability and those who do not.

The CRPD is also a treaty that 'textually' realises the principle of indivisibility and interdependence of human rights. The right to community-based health care, the right to 'habilitation and rehabilitation' and the right to independent living are strongly related and mutually reinforcing, including in relation to disease prevention and health promotion targets. As related state duties must target all people with disabilities, this approach offers truly holistic, comprehensive and textual human rights protection for all migrants with psychosocial disabilities, which is not as fully fledged in other legal frameworks. The CRPD is conceived as a truly transformative convention insofar as its scope of application exceeds disability policies and requires the adoption of intersectoral measures and reforms that embrace, *inter alia*, health, social and immigration law and policies. However, its potential is yet to be operationalised, via the jurisprudence of the CRPD Committee, with respect to the rights and needs of irregular migrants. These normative developments and state responses to detailed obligations will be a critical test of the real transformative and inclusive nature of the ambitious human rights approach to (psychosocial) disabilities.

# Conclusion

In 2018, three years into the ongoing Venezuelan migrant crisis, photographer Paddy Dowling powerfully documented the life of migrants in the streets of Colombia.[1] One of the pictures that struck me most delved into the emotions of a young migrant in an irregular situation in his twenties. His name was John, and he was sleeping on the streets of Bogotá at that time. He was wearing a facemask and appeared visibly desperate and vulnerable, and the narrative accompanying the photograph explained that he was feeling unwell and had had a temperature for a few days but was unable to see a doctor. This story dramatically captures several interlinked aspects of irregular migration that the present book examines from the perspective of human rights law: the significance of legal status in gaining access to human rights; the concerns associated with a management of migration and health policies within a state sovereign paradigm, with diluted human rights considerations; the contested trend of treating the human right to health care for polity outsiders as an emergency medical issue; and the need to approach the right to the highest attainable standards of physical and mental health of everyone, including all migrants, from a primary health perspective that integrates disease prevention, essential treatment and health promotion via intersectoral measures and social rights while respecting personal autonomy and recognising oppressive man-made laws and practices.

Since the end of World War II, international and European human rights law has played a significant role in shaping domestic legal orders, rights and policies. This is why I chose it as a legal framework of reference to challenge the barriers that irregular migrants, as human beings, encounter in accessing

---

[1] Paddy Dowling collaboration for CARE, 'Venezuelan Refugee Crisis, an Exodus in Photos' (2 April 2019) <www.care.org/news-and-stories/news/venezuelan-refugee-crisis-an-exodus-in-photos/> accessed 10 March 2021.

enabling services and conditions due to state choices to exclude or ignore their health needs. However, the analysis navigated a number of normative tensions that led to the current state of the art of international and European law, which is characterised by an accumulation of standards, decisions and interpretative documents (either binding, authoritative, persuasive or of a guiding nature) that contain certain inconsistencies within and across legal frameworks. This book discuss controversial issues relating to the relationships between irregular migration and health as human rights issues (e.g. core obligations, primary care, the social determinants of health and mental health) to offer interpretative proposals grounded in international law, which, while acknowledging the normative limits of the legal frames of reference, are compatible with the foundational and interpretative principles of human rights (e.g. equality, non-discrimination and indivisibility) and are cognisant of the priorities of widely embraced and relevant public health and disability models that an increasingly interdisciplinary human rights practice and scholarship cannot overlook. Overall, it shows that technical standards, theoretical approaches and legal arguments that enhance the right to health of irregular migrants as human beings in international and European law do exist, but that greater internal and relational consistency is needed within these legal frameworks.

The purposes of this concluding chapter are to summarise each chapter's findings, highlight progressive developments and point to fruitful questions for future research that might strengthen the findings of this study.

## C.1 MAIN FINDINGS: FROM FRAMEWORK LIMITATIONS TO EXPANSIVE HUMAN RIGHTS STANDARDS

Chapters 1 and 2 identified the structural hurdles that international and European human rights law encounter in normatively shaping the areas of irregular migration and health. The subsequent chapters examined how 'thick' the rights to physical and mental health care and to other social determinants of health for irregular migrants are. All chapters presented enabling and constraining legal and extra-legal factors against a background of progressively more supporting human rights law developments.

### C.1.1 Chapter 1 – 'Sovereignty and the Human Rights of Irregular Migrants'

This chapter addressed the subquestion of how the clash between the principle of sovereignty in the area of immigration – which is internationally recognised – and the development of universal human rights has shaped the conceptualisation of the rights to which irregular migrants are entitled in international and European human rights law.

An analysis of the texts of the fathers of international law, such as Hugo Grotius and Emer de Vattel, reveals that they did not regard *jus gentium* as a legal system for limiting migration flows. On the contrary, individual freedom of movement and the freedom to establish at least a temporary residence outside one's country of nationality were not considered excessively controversial issues prior to the end of the nineteenth century when economic migration served the interests of the Western world. Therefore, the doctrine of absolute sovereignty in relation to immigration is not a natural feature of the international concept of state sovereignty.

At the end of the nineteenth century, common law jurisprudence began erroneously to attribute highly discretional state sovereignty to regulate the entry, stay and rights of 'foreigners' to the teachings of international law, and this 'rule' has since been legally recognised as a maxim of (contemporary) international law, which includes human rights law.

However, the state power to determine the right to entry and the treatment of migrants is not absolute because it has been internationally limited by the development of universal human rights law and refugee law. Since the second half of the twentieth century, everyone, including those living outside their state of nationality, has been entitled to the provisions of the human rights law ratified by the state in which they reside. The mutual impact of sovereignty and the idea of human rights has led to a situation where irregular migrants enjoy legal human rights to a lesser extent than country nationals. This trend is reflected in certain treaties and in the findings of some important international and European human rights adjudicators.

Overall, in relation to irregular migrants, European human rights case law tends to be somewhat deferential to states and relies heavily on the concept of sovereign power over immigration as a maxim of international law to condone differential or even detrimental treatment. International and the briefly mentioned inter-American human rights law provide more generous rights for irregular migrants, and the related case law tends to refer less to immigration control as a state prerogative required by international law.

## C.1.2 *Chapter 2 – 'The Normative Contours of a Vulnerability- and Equity-Oriented Right to Health'*

This chapter outlined and assessed the development of the right to health in international and European human rights law, which in operative terms is relatively new. The analysis is underpinned by the fact that health is a technical and intersectional field and one over which states have maintained high levels of discretion or sovereignty vis-à-vis the development of international standards. To understand whether human rights law can help enhance the protection and promotion of the right to health of irregular migrants, as vulnerable people, it was essential to clarify what having a right to health means in these legal frameworks.

The origins of the right to health, conceived as the right to the highest attainable standard of health, lie in the twentieth century, and the development of this right has been strongly inspired by the principles of public health governance. Indeed, its scope extends to both health care and the determinants of health, which can be addressed by intersectoral measures to support disease prevention, health promotion and treatment.[2] The PHC approach of the international Declaration of Alma-Ata of 1978, the so-called Magna Carta of health,[3] remains an internationally endorsed authoritative reference for determining the priorities of health policies. This was confirmed in the 2030 Agenda for Sustainable Development, the 2018 Declaration of Astana and several other global health and human rights documents discussed in the chapter, which emphasise equity in regulatory frameworks and its operationalisation.

Since the 1990s, international human rights law has developed several conceptual frameworks to implement the complex state obligations in the area of social rights, including the right to health. All of them, especially the AAAQ framework and core obligations, revolve around the concepts of non-discrimination and vulnerability. Indeed, social rights are extremely important for people who find themselves in situations of vulnerability or socioeconomic precariousness.

Vis-à-vis positive developments, socioeconomic rights have traditionally been conceptualised as rights or interests to be realised progressively. This has led to a situation in which the right to health, among other social rights, has often not been considered a real legal right and has, therefore, been deemed unsuitable for international adjudication. This has enabled states to partially avoid international accountability and has afforded them wide margins for 'manoeuvre' when dealing with resource-demanding public interests or social rights. In the midst of such an impasse, which has not been completely resolved to this day, health interests have often been addressed in international and European human rights law through case-based litigation on civil rights. However, the resulting jurisprudence on health care does not fully

[2]    CESCR, GC14 (n 27, Introduction) para 8.
[3]    Parran (n 17, Ch 2) on the Declaration of Alma Ata (n 28, Introduction).

cover the scope of the right to the highest attainable standard of health because it generally frames human health in medical terms and often only offers protection in very critical or life-saving situations.

Today, this gap in international accountability has been partly bridged, at least conceptually, and the provision of the right to health is recognised as a state obligation of both a progressive and an immediate nature. Most notably, the right to the highest attainable standard of health gives rise to an obligation to ensure non-discrimination with immediate normative force.[4] Non-discrimination and vulnerability are solid and multifaceted notions present in all human rights frameworks and are directly or indirectly acknowledged by a series of WHO standards on PHC, SDH and UHC. The reliance on these standards in human rights law pushes states towards more genuine forms of substantive equality, including positive duties that benefit the worst off.[5] However, there is disagreement between different international and European legal frameworks on the identification of deserving vulnerable people and, in particular, on the inclusion of irregular migrants in that category.

### C.1.3 *Chapter 3 – 'The Right to Health Care of Irregular Migrants: Between Primary Care and Emergency Treatment'*

This chapter uncovered several inconstancies across different legal frameworks in relation to the legal recognition of irregular migrants' vulnerability and, accordingly, what discriminatory practices consist of and how thick irregular migrants' health rights and correlative state obligations should be. Although this chapter's interdisciplinary human rights analysis is dense, the findings and recommendations can be summarised as follows.

The European human rights system is generally constrained by the limitations of its personal and material scope in the matter at hand. The ECtHR, which is at the heart of the European system and adjudicates on a treaty that is civil and political in nature, has not provided for the health and well-being of irregular migrants beyond situations of severe material and health deprivation. The ECSR, although it extended the limited personal scope of the ESC to irregular migrants, has also proved incapable of affirming the right to health care for this group beyond health care that addresses urgent health needs. These findings reflect a European trend whereby states maintain high levels of sovereignty in these areas. Although slightly different conclusions can be

---

4  ICESCR (n 23, Introduction) Artcile 2(2); CESCR (n 27, Introducion) para 43.
5  See Section 2.7.

drawn from the case law of various bodies, European human rights law generally draws on the value of human dignity, but it does so only to rule out the most severe deprivations of health.[6] It must be acknowledged that caring for people's health only in emergency situations coincides with the right to life and the right to freedom from degrading treatment but does not directly relate to the concept of health.

In contrast, the international human rights system, which recognises irregular migrants as especially vulnerable people, is more inclined to grant greater protection of their health needs. The HRCtee, employing the positive scope of the right to life in dignity, established that irregular migrants should enjoy urgent care that exceeds life-saving treatment, as the sole provision of the latter would entail an illegitimate and disproportional differentiation between irregular migrants and the rest of the population.[7]

In particular, the jurisprudence of the CESCR identifies as a core obligation of an immediate nature the duty 'to ensure the right of access to health facilities, goods, and services on a non-discriminatory basis, especially for vulnerable or marginalised groups'.[8] It does so by identifying access to essential PHC as one element of the minimum core content, under the compelling guidance of the Alma-Ata Declaration. This chapter explored in depth the relations between preventive and primary care and the human rights concepts of vulnerability and non-discrimination towards the normative goal of building a bridge between the notions of non-discrimination as a core obligation of process and outcome and the substantive requirements of the PHC approach, which rejects the notion that irregular migrants should be entitled only to 'urgent' or 'life-saving' treatment.

However, international human rights law does not always employ consistent terminology in describing the level of minimum acceptable health care for irregular migrants, and this lack of clarity in monitoring practice may jeopardise the normative positive effects of the Committee's jurisprudence in granting priority to vulnerable people. Therefore, this chapter recommended a more consistent use of human rights arguments by explicitly elaborating on the rules of interpretation of international law to hold that pursuing the purpose of Article 12 ICESCR, for everyone, cannot be achieved by depriving irregular migrants of preventive and primary care.

---

[6] See Section 3.2.

[7] HRCtee, *Toussaint* (n 190, Ch 1).

[8] CESCR, GC14 (n 27, Introduction) para 43(a).

Finally, the chapter considered some recent interpretive developments.[9] These include urging states to equalise the position of irregular migrant children and women in need of reproductive care to that of citizens and establishing 'firewalls' between public services providers and immigration enforcement, which has the potential to transform human rights into practicable and non-illusory entitlements.

### C.1.4 *Chapter 4 – 'The Determinants of the Health of Irregular Migrants: Between Interrelatedness and Power'*

This chapter explored how seriously committed European and international law are to the underlying or social determinants of health of irregular migrants, which constitute a dimension of the scope of the international right to health.

State measures that address the determinants of health are necessary for a genuine equity-oriented realisation of the right to health. This paradigm focuses on the relations between people's living and working conditions and health outcomes, as well as on power, money and resources as structural drivers of health (in)equity.[10] The concept of the determinants of health encompasses the interrelatedness and interdependence of all human rights and the multilayered vulnerability of human beings. To address the determinants of health, states should adopt measures of substantive equality that target differentiated but essentially human vulnerabilities to socioeconomic deprivation and ill health.

In the context of human rights law, due consideration of the determinants of health requires, at the bare minimum, a conceptualisation and monitoring of human rights, and in particular social rights, that accounts for their impact on human health. However, as many of these rights are normally operationalised domestically by welfare state agencies, the health and social needs of irregular migrants – who do not fit within the nationalist and protectionist principles of the welfare system – are often unmet. Once again, the institutional sovereign power to exclude and expel irregular migrants, entering the realm of other state policies, can nullify or dilute any real empowering function of indivisible and interrelated human rights.

On a more applied level, the second part of the chapter investigated how these concepts feature in the human rights jurisprudence regarding irregular

---

[9] See Section 3.4.
[10] CSDH Report (111, Ch 2).

migrant rights that support the determinants of health. European human rights law encounters similar difficulties to those mentioned in Chapter 3. The ECHR, while it may protect social interests through its civil and political rights, allows states a broad margin of appreciation and sets high thresholds for human rights violations. These circumstances, together with a sovereignty-oriented approach and the clear statement that states 'may have legitimate reasons for curtailing the use of resource-hungry public services by short-term and illegal immigrants, who, as a rule, do not contribute to their funding',[11] make the ECHR a generally unsuitable legal framework for the protection of the socioeconomic determinants of health of undocumented people, beyond very exceptional circumstances. The ECSR, notwithstanding the significant textual limitation of the ESC, does appear to appreciate the interdependence between health outcomes for irregular migrants and the socioeconomic determinants of health, such as housing and social assistance, although the recommended measures tend to focus on people's *urgent needs*, at least where adults are concerned.[12]

International human rights law, although it appears to be more receptive than the European systems to a concept that is explicitly its own, sets somewhat unclear standards. Although some examples of recommendations for greater equality in relation to the level of social benefits granted to nationals and regular and irregular migrant workers can be found, the recommended standards of social rights that support the determinants of health of irregular migrants are often *basic* and seem to provide for only a subset of empowering socioeconomic conditions.

Overall, where irregular migrants are concerned, an 'atomistic' approach that largely ignores the interrelated nature of human rights appears to be preferred, as it does not strongly challenge structural inequalities within (and between) countries. To genuinely tackle human and social vulnerability to ill health and truly commit to the universal empowerment that human rights and health promotion entail would require improving the protection of social rights that support the determinants of health, if not to the extent of equalising irregular migrants' enjoyment of those rights to the level of their enjoyment by vulnerable nationals, then, at least to a level of truly accessible protection beyond mere survival level, particularly in high- and middle-income countries.

---

[11] For example, *Ponomaryov* (n 19, Introduction).
[12] For example, *DCI v Belgium* (n 218, Ch 1).

C.1.5 *Chapter 5 – 'Mental Health, Irregular Migration and Human Rights: Synergising Vulnerability- and Disability-Sensitive Approaches'*

Chapter 5 unveiled how international and European human rights law have begun to address mental health care and supportive social determinants in the context of irregular migration. This chapter combined the arguments of the previous chapters and applied them to the contentious area of mental health and added a theoretical and international legal frame of reference: international disability law as based on the social model of disability.

Indeed, vulnerability and disability, rather than paternalistic, disabling and oppressive concepts, are presented here as protective arguments with certain synergies. Their recognition at the individual and group levels can ground positive human rights duties in relation to mental health care and promotion for irregular migrants. As such, the source of the oppressive power structures that the social model of disability criticises and the source of the special contextual and state-made vulnerability of irregular migrants partly coincide and stem from exclusionary approaches to diversity and otherness recognised in law and society that human rights law, at least in principle, should contribute to redress. In European human rights law, where the human rights model of disability is less influential, rights violations tend to be found only where particularly abusive deprivation exposes people to a real risk of severe consequences for their mental health in the context of detention or deportation. Nonetheless, certain pieces of the ECtHR's jurisprudence have gradually attributed greater weight to the quality of environments, support services and relationships as factors that contribute to verdicts in cases concerning migrants with mental health issues.[13]

In international human rights law, the articulation of human rights arguments and their interpretation in different treaty systems led to the identification of numerous protective findings. Among them, the ICCPR's right to life in dignity establishes a non-discriminatory entitlement to urgent mental health care for people experiencing a mental health crisis. Furthermore, combining the preceptive human rights principle of non-discrimination with the scope of the ICESCR's right to mental health – as influenced by global public health standards, including PHC and the SDH – which should not be unreasonably restricted, including on the ground of legal status, led me to conclude that irregular migrants should have access to essential drugs, community mental health care and basic social support.[14]

---

[13] For example, *Savran* (n 44, Ch 3).
[14] See Section 5.4.

However, the real game changer was the CRPD, which is a treaty that textually aims to achieve a transformative change of regulatory frameworks and eliminate oppressive constructs in law, policy and practice. For those migrants who identify as people with psychosocial disabilities, this treaty contains sufficiently clear provisions stating that they must enjoy equal specialised and general health care without discrimination on any grounds, to avoid their disabilities, alone or in conjunction with other conditions, resulting in disabling effects.[15]

## C.2 TAKING A 'FINAL' SNAPSHOT? MAJOR ADVANCES AND UNADDRESSED ISSUES IN RELATION TO ENSURING COMPREHENSIVE PROTECTION OF ALL MIGRANTS' HEALTH RIGHTS

Having offered a bird's eye view of the findings of this book, I now conclude by restating core examples of how international standards are being progressively raised towards a genuinely universal and holistic rights-based environment, which encompasses the protection of the right to health of irregular migrants. I also raise some unaddressed questions to which future human rights scholarship and practice might respond.

Two global initiatives that have recently brought renewed attention to migration and health inequities, respectively, are the above-mentioned Global Compact for Migration and the Declaration of Astana on Primary Health Care, both of which were adopted in late 2018.[16] These political commitments, which are not formally legally binding on state norm-making mechanisms, have involved a broad array of stakeholders in the areas of immigration and health and have set out technical principles, vulnerability-oriented priorities and political frameworks according to which the human right to health of all migrants should be nationally operationalised by states and internationally monitored.

As far as European human rights law is concerned, the ECSR's 2018 decision on the merits of *EUROCEF* demonstrated that a truly interrelated rights approach to the health of irregular migrant children is possible. Indeed, the violation of Article 11 ESC on the right to the protection of health was, in that case, directly due to situations of systematic homelessness.[17] This case constitutes an operationalisation of the SDH approach, which the Council of Europe, against the current COVID-19 pandemic scenario, is increasingly

---

[15] On the analysis of the joint reading of Articles 5, 25 and 26 CRPD, see Section 5.4.2.3.
[16] Declaration of Astana (n 174, Ch 2); GCM (n 92, Ch 1).
[17] *Eurocef* (n 112, Ch 4) para 211.

supporting to recommend human rights–compliant measures that target health inequities.[18] For its part, the ECtHR, even while upholding a restrictive approach to protecting the health of irregular migrants, clarified and eased its approach regarding the threshold of human rights–relevant health deprivation in its judgment in the case of *Paposhvili*. Part of this judgment reads as an injunction to prevent the deportation of irregular migrants to countries that fail to make available appropriate treatment necessary to avoid 'a serious, rapid and irreversible decline in [the person] state of health'.[19]

At the UN human rights level, in less than a decade, many human rights bodies have developed jurisprudence that is particularly favourable to the expansion of the human rights of migrants around health and social issues and have even issued recommendations on equalising standards with citizens to fully comply with human rights obligations. Examples, which are widely analysed in this book for their vulnerability-grounded approach, include the 2017 CESCR statement on core obligations and the 'special' vulnerability of undocumented migrants in relation to their enjoyment of socioeconomic rights;[20] two joint general comments of the CRC and CMW Committees on equalised human rights with minor country nationals; several recommendations on the creation of firewalls between public service providers and immigration authorities;[21] and the first decision on the merits of the HRCtee Committee on the right to health and life of irregular migrants, which, *inter alia*, labelled any differentiation on the grounds of irregular status as a consequence of immigration policy that could 'result in the author's loss of life or in irreversible negative consequences for the author's health' as unreasonable and thus discriminatory.[22] It is worth adding that the implementation of the CPRD may constitute a paradigmatic shift for the all human rights of *all* persons with *any* disabilities, not only for irregular migrants with psychosocial disabilities. Articles 5 and 25 CRPD can be employed to equalise the health rights of irregular migrants with chronic or continuous health needs due to impairment with those of citizens. If affordable specialised care is not accessible to irregular migrants with these needs, impairments, in consideration of adverse or oppressive social contexts where they live, may become a disabling factor that constitutes a discriminatory practice against the text, object and purpose of the treaty.

---

[18] Commissioner for Human Rights (CoE) (n 261, Ch 2) 41–46.
[19] *Paposhvili* (n 122, Ch 1) 141–142, emphasis added.
[20] CESCR, Statement on migrant rights (n 174, Ch 1).
[21] ECRI (n 128, Ch 3); CESCR, COs Germany (n 144, Ch 3), CRC and CMW Committees (n 175, Ch 1).
[22] *Toussaint* (n 190, Ch 1).

Whereas the above remarks bear witness to an increasingly supportive regulatory framework for the protection of migrant health at the international level, the findings of this study also reveal a number of inconsistencies between the solutions offered in different legal frameworks. It is undeniable that distance exists between international and European human rights law in relation to impermissible grounds for discrimination, the test of proportionality for differentiating measures and the *levels of social and health benefits* to which irregular migrants are entitled. This is problematic, particularly because the decisions of the ECtHR, which is a court of law, are legally binding, while those of other more progressive human rights bodies – albeit authoritative – are not. To fill the gap between rhetorical support for the principles of indivisibility, interrelatedness and universality and certain restrictive migration-related pieces of human rights law and jurisprudence, I argue that a 'healthy minimum', but not 'minimal survival', should be considered a starting point towards the progressive equalisation of human rights. This is based on an interpretation of process and outcome core and positive obligations, the principle of non-discrimination and the concepts of substantive equality and multidimensional vulnerability, all of which ought to comply with basic public health principles, the rules of interpretation of international law and the new human rights approach to disability. These cross-disciplinary references have proved very useful because, as indicated in the Introduction, law, no matter how sophisticated it is, does not exist in a social vacuum,[23] and this extends to human rights law,[24] the underlying principles of which are embedded with moral and social considerations.

While my conclusions on access to health care are relatively detailed, those concerning the right to the social determinants of health of irregular migrants, against an as yet underdeveloped applicable human rights practice, reflect a struggle to depart from an emergency care-oriented model, although alternatives – particular disability-based and preventive approaches – have been identified. If the human rights model of disability and an SDH approach were genuinely endorsed regardless of migrant status and nationality, across human rights frameworks, they could contribute to the realisation of structural shifts towards real universal enjoyment of health and social rights to their full extent and for every human being.

However, *several questions* still remain, at least partially, unaddressed in human rights law and scholarship with regard to the topic at hand. While several of them will require structural changes and interpretative shifts in

---

[23] Ibbetson (n 40, Introduction).
[24] Freeman (n 34, Introduction).

human rights law, I like the idea of concluding this book by posing them, as they point at 'variables' for future developments. Indeed, reflecting on these questions helps to situate this research within a broader normative context and may significantly contribute to further developing and using the findings towards the development of a dynamic, interdisciplinary and truly non-discriminatory human rights practice.

Will the CESCR – which, to date, offers the most protective general conceptualisation and frequent monitoring on the right to health of all migrants – rely more consistently on its conceptualisations of core obligations and the determinants of health and, more specifically, on the rules of inter-pretation of international law? This would arguably increase its legitimacy in international and national law and practices.

Will European human rights law – perhaps in the light of the current pandemic and its mid- and long-term effects on economies, state priorities, individual health and disability – more seriously consider the social rights of all vulnerable people in all its treaty systems? Will the ECtHR genuinely embrace the indivisibility of all human rights for every person by perhaps resorting to a stronger contextual and purposive interpretation of the ECHR?

Is it likely that the international *corpus juris*, which encompasses inter-national instruments of different natures and legal frameworks,[25] will resonate more strongly with the jurisprudence of the European Court? This occurred in the inter-American system of human rights and helped to make the social and health rights of vulnerable people justiciable in that legal framework, which is primarily a civil and political rights treaty.[26]

When will human rights bodies clarify the minimum core of all social rights that support key determinants of health for irregular migrants? As I have indicated in this book, this could contribute to radical changes in the way human rights law targets social disadvantage, health disparities and non-discrimination.

Will the right to health, as a 'basic right'[27] with a complex and expansive social scope, become a central post-pandemic tool for enhancing jurisprudence targeting the physical and mental health and social inequalities of all migrants?

---

[25] This concept originated in Inter-American human rights law to highlight the dynamic and evolutive interpretation of human rights law, in the light of the contribution of various treaties and human rights bodies with respect to a certain issue. For example, IACtHR, *The Right to Information on Consular Assistance*, Advisory Opinion OC-16/99, para 114.

[26] *Poblete Vilches et al. v Chile* (IACtHR 2018) Series C No. 349, paras 108–127; *Hernández v. Argentina* (IACtHR 2019) Series C No. 395, para 78; *Cuscul Pivaral et al. v. Guatemala* (IACtHR 2018) Series C No. 359, paras 72, 109.

[27] Shue (n 115, Ch 2).

Will the monitoring and implementation of the CRPD contribute to radically outlawing disabling differentiations, including on the grounds of psychosocial disability and legal status, as the initial jurisprudence of the CRPD Committee suggests?

Clarifying these issues to the greatest possible extent will increase the internal and relational consistency of human rights legal frameworks and positively contribute human rights–based approaches to development and policy-making. This book constitutes a first step in this process of normative clarification at the interpretative level, which is essential for shaping the operationalisation or realisation of rights beyond the realm of law, that is, on the ground where irregular migrants live, between constraining and enabling environments, shaped by a multitude of state and non-state actors.

# Select Bibliography

Achiume TE, 'Reimagining International Law for Global Migration: Migration as Decolonization?' (2017) 111 *American Journal of International Law* 142.

Agamben G, *Homo Sacer: Sovereign Power and Bare Life* (Stanford University Press 1998).

Alexy R, *A Theory of Constitutional Rights* (first published 1994, OUP 2002).

Allen A, 'Feminist Perspectives on Power', *Stanford Encyclopedia of Philosophy* (2005–2016).

Alvarez J, 'State Sovereignty in Not Withering Away: A Few Lessons from the Future' in Cassese A (ed) *Realizing Utopia* (OUP 2012) 26.

Andersson L, Hjern A and Ascher E, 'Undocumented Adult Migrants in Sweden: Mental Health and Associated Factors' (2018) *BMC Public Health* 18.

Andreassen B, et al., 'Assessing Human Rights Performance in Developing Countries: The Case for a Minimal Threshold Approach to the Economic and Social Rights' in Andreassen B and Eide A (eds) *Human Rights in Developing Countries* (Academic Press 1987) 333.

'Article 22' in Alfredsson G and Eide A (eds) *The Universal Declaration of Human Rights: A Common Standard of Achievement* (Martinus Nijhoff Publishers 1999) 453.

Angeleri S, 'The Impact of the Economic Crisis on the Right to Health of Irregular Migrants, as Reflected in the Jurisprudence of the UN Committee on Economic, Social and Cultural Rights' (2017) 19(2) *European Journal of Migration and Law* 165.

'Healthcare of Undocumented Migrants Framed as a Right to Emergency Treatment? The State of the Art in European and International Law' in Nesi G (ed) *Migrazioni e Diritto Internazionale: Verso il Superamento dell'Emergenza?* (Editoriale Scientifica 2018) 467.

'The Health, Safety and Associated Rights of Migrant Workers in International and European Human Rights Law' in Angeleri S, Calafà L and Protopapa V (eds) *Promoting the Health and Safety of Migrant Workers: Different Disciplines, a Shared Objective* (Working Papers of the Centre for the Study of European Labour Law 'Massimo d'Antona' 2020) 2.

Anghie A, 'The Evolution of International Law: Colonial and Postcolonial Realities' (2007) 27(5) *Third World Quarterly* 739.

Anghie A and McCormack W, 'The Rights of Aliens: Legal Regimes and Historical Perspectives' in Maloney T and Korinek K (eds) *Migration in the 21st Century: Rights, Outcomes and Policy* (Routledge 2010) 23.

Arendt H, *The Origins of Totalitarianism* (first published 1950, Harcourt 1968).
  *On Violence* (Harcourt Brace & Co. 1970).

Atak I, 'GCM Commentary: Objective 7 – Address and Reduce Vulnerabilities in Migration' (Refugee Law Initiative Blog, 30 October 2018).

Atak I, Nakache D, Guild E and Crépeau F, '"Migrants in Vulnerable Situations" and the Global Compact for Safe Orderly and Regular Migration' (Queen Mary School of Law Legal Studies Research Paper No. 273/2018, 15 February 2018).

Aubry A, Burzynski M and Docquier F, 'The Welfare Impact of Global Migration in OECD Countries' (2016) *Journal of International Economics* 101.

Bales K, 'Asylum Seekers, Social Rights and the Rise of New Nationalism: From an Inclusive to Exclusive British Welfare State?' in Kotkas T and Veitch K (eds) *Social Rights in the Welfare State: Origins and Transformations* (Routledge 2016) 109.

Bambara C, 'Going beyond the Three Worlds of Welfare Capitalism: Regime Theory and Public Health Research' (2007) 61(12) *Journal of Epidemiology & Community Health* 1098.

Bantekas I and Oette L, *International Human Rights Law and Practice* (3rd edn, CUP 2020).

Barnes D et al., 'Primary Health Care and Primary Care: A Confusion of Philosophies' (1995) 43(1) *Nursing Outlook* 7.

Bartlett P, 'The United Nations Convention on the Rights of Persons with Disabilities and Mental Health Law' (2012) 75(5) *Modern Law Review* 752.

Battams S and Henderson J, 'The Physical Health of People with Mental Illness and "The Right to Health"' (2010) 9(2) *Advances in Mental Health* 117.

Baumgärtel M, *Demanding Rights: Europe's Supranational Courts and the Dilemma of Migrant Vulnerability* (CUP 2019).

Bell M, 'The Right to Equality and Non-discrimination' in Hervey T and Kenner J (eds) *Economic and Social Rights under the EU Charter of Fundamental Rights: A Legal Perspective* (Hart Publishing 2003) 95.

Bell S, 'What Does the Right to Health Have to Offer Mental Health Patients?' (2005) 28 *International Journal of Law and Psychiatry* 141.

Benhabib S, *The Rights of Others: Aliens, Residents and Citizens* (CUP 2004).

Besson S, 'Sovereignty' in Peters A (ed) *Max Planck Encyclopaedia of Public International Law* (OUP 2011).

Betts A, 'Towards a "Soft Law" Framework for the Protection of Vulnerable Irregular Migrants' (2010) 22(2) *International Journal of Refugee Law* 209.

Bhugra D and Gupta S (eds) *Migration and Mental Health* (CUP 2010).

Bilchiz D, *Poverty and Fundamental Rights: The Justification and Enforcement of Socio-economic Rights* (OUP 2007).

Björgvinsson D, *The Intersection of International Law and Domestic Law: A Theoretical and Practical Analysis* (Edward Elgar 2015).

Bodin J, *Les Six Livres de la République* (first published 1579, Alden Press 1955).

Boeles P et al., *European Migration Law* (2nd edn, Intersentia 2014).

Bosniak, L, 'Human Rights, State Sovereignty and the Protection of Undocumented Migrants under the International Migrant Workers Convention' in Bogusz B et al. (eds) *Irregular Migration and Human Rights: Theoretical, European and International Perspectives (Immigration and Asylum Law and Policy in Europe)* (Martinus Nijhoff Publishers 2004) 311.

Boso A and Vancea M, 'Should Irregular Migrants Have the Right to Healthcare? Lessons Learnt from the Spanish Case' (2016) 36(2) *Critical Social Policy* 225.

Bradby H et al., 'Public Health Aspects of Migrant Health: A Review of the Evidence on Health Status for Refugees and Asylum Seekers in the European Region', *Health Evidence Network Synthesis Report* 44 (WHO Regional Office for Europe 2015).

Braveman P, 'Social Conditions, Health Equity, and Human Rights' (2010) 12(2) *Health and Human Rights Journal* 31.

Braveman P and Gruskin S, 'Defining Equity in Health' (2003) 57 *Journal of Epidemiology and Community Health* 254.

Brillat R, 'The Supervisory Machinery of the European Social Charter: Recent Developments and Their Impact' in De Búrca G and De Witte B (eds) *Social Rights in Europe* (OUP 2005) 31.

Brown K, 'Questioning the Vulnerability Zeitgeist: Care and Control Practices with "Vulnerable" Young People' (2014) 13 *Social Policy and Society* 3 371.

Brown K, Ecclestone K and Emmel N, 'The Many Faces of Vulnerability' (2017) 16(3) *Social Policy and Society* 497.

Bueno De Mesquita J, 'The Universal Periodic Review: A Valuable New Procedure for the Right to Health?' (2019) 21(2) *Health and Human Rights Journal* 263.

Burns JK, 'Mental Health and Inequity: A Human Rights Approach to Inequality, Discrimination and Mental Disability' (2009) 11 *Health and Human Rights Journal* 2.

Burns T, 'Towards a Theory of Structural Discrimination: Cultural, Institutional and Interactional Mechanisms of the European Dilemma' in Delanty G, Wodak R and Jones P (eds) *Identity, Belonging and Migration* (Liverpool University Press 2011) 152.

Bustamante JA, 'Immigrants' Vulnerability as Subjects of Human Rights' (2002) 36(2) *International Migration Review* 339.

Butler J, 'Rethinking Vulnerability and Resistance' in Butler J, Gambetti Z and Sabsay L (eds) *Vulnerability in Resistance* (Duke University Press 2016) 12.

Calafà L, Iavicoli S and Persechino B (eds) *Lavoro insicuro: salute, sicurezza e tutele sociali dei lavoratori immigrati in agricoltura* (Il Mulino 2020).

Carens J, 'The Rights of Irregular Migrants' (2008) 22(2) *Ethics and International Affairs* 163.

Carozza P G, 'Subsidiarity as a Structural Principle of International Human Rights Law' (2003) 97 *American Journal of International Law* 38.

Cassese A, *International Law* (2nd edn, OUP 2003).

Castles S and Schierup C U, 'Migration and Ethnic Minorities' in Castles FG et al. (eds) *The Oxford Handbook of the Welfare State* (OUP 2010) 278.

Chambers R, 'Vulnerability, Coping and Policy' (2006) 37(4) *Institute of Development Studies Bulletin* 33.

Chapman A, 'Conceptualizing the Right to Health: A Violation Approach' (1998) 65 *Tennessee Law Review* 389.

'Core Obligations Related to the Right to Health' in Chapman A and Russell S (eds) *Core Obligations: Building a Framework for Economic, Social and Cultural Rights* (Intersentia 2002) 185.

'The Foundations of a Human Right to Health: Human Rights and Bioethics in a Dialogue' (2015) 17(1) *Health and Human Rights Journal* 6.

*Global Health, Human Rights, and the Challenge of Neoliberal Policies* (CUP 2016).

et al., 'Editorial: Reimagining the Mental Health Paradigm for Our Collective Well-being' (2020) 22 *Health and Human Rights Journal* 1.

Chapman A, and Carbonetti B, 'Human Rights Protections for Vulnerable and Disadvantaged Groups: The Contributions of the UN Committee on Economic, Social and Cultural Rights' (2011) 33 *Human Rights Quarterly* 682.

Chapman A, and Carbonetti B, Forman L and Lamprea E, 'Evaluating Essential Health Packages from a Human Rights Perspective' (2017) 16(2) *Journal of Human Rights* 141.

Charlesworth H, 'Concepts of Equality in International Law' in Huscroft G and Rishworth P (eds) *Litigating Rights: Perspectives from Domestic and International Law* (Hart Publishing 2002) 137.

Chen B, 'Rethinking China's Mental Health Law Reform: Treatment Decision-Making and the UN Convention on the Rights of Persons with Disabilities' (PhD thesis, NUI Galway 2019).

Chetail V, 'The Human Rights of Migrants in General International Law: From Minimum Standards to Fundamental Rights' (2014) 28 *Georgetown Immigration Law Journal* 225.

Chimienti M and Solomos J, 'How Do International Human Rights Influence National Healthcare Provisions for Irregular Migrants? A Case Study in France and the United Kingdom' (2015) 15(2) *Journal of Human Rights* 1.

Cismas I, 'The Intersection of Economic Social and Cultural Rights and Civil and Political Rights' in Riedel E, Giacca G and Golay C (eds) *Economic Social and Cultural Rights in International Law: Contemporary Issues and Challenges* (OUP 2015) 448.

Clapham A, et al. (eds) *Realizing the Right to Health* (Rüffer und Rub 2009).

Clifford J, 'Equality' in Shelton D (ed) *The Oxford Handbook of International Human Rights Law* (OUP 2013) 420.

Clough B, 'Disability and Vulnerability: Challenging the Capacity/Incapacity Binary' (2017) 16(3) *Social Policy and Society* 469.

Colleen M. Flood and Aeyal Gross, 'Litigating the Right to Health: What Can We Learn from a Comparative Law and Health Care Systems Approach' (2014) 16(2) *Health and Human Rights Journal* 62.

Coomans F, 'In Search of the Core Content of the Right to Education' in Chapman A and Russell S (eds) *Core Obligations: Building a Framework for Economic, Social and Cultural Rights* (Intersentia 2002) 217.

Cornelisse G, 'A New Articulation of Human Rights, or Why the European Court of Human Rights Should Think beyond Westphalian Sovereignty' in Dembour M and Kelly T, (eds) *Are Human Rights for Migrants? Critical Reflections on the Status of Irregular Migrants in Europe and the United States* (Routledge, 2011) 99.

Craven M, *The International Covenant on Economic, Social, and Cultural Rights: A Perspective on Its Development* (Clarendon Press 1995).

Crawford J and Koskenniemi M (eds) *The Cambridge Companion to International Law* (CUP 2012).

Crépeau F and Hastie B, 'The Case for "Firewall" Protections for Irregular Migrants: Safeguarding Fundamental Rights' (2015) 17(2–3) *European Journal of Migration and Law* 157.

Cruft R, Liao S. and Renzo M (eds) *'The Philosophical Foundations of Human Rights* (OUP 2015).

Cryer R et al., *Research Methodologies in EU and International Law* (Hart Publishing 2011).

Cueto M, 'The Origins of Primary Health Care and Selective Primary Health Care' (2004) 94(11) *American Journal of Public Health* 1864.

Da Lomba S, 'Immigration Status and Basic Social Human Rights: A Comparative Study of Irregular Migrants' Right to Health Care in France, The UK and Canada' (2010) 28(1) *The Netherlands Quarterly of Human Rights* 6.

Dailler P and Pellet A, *Droit International Public* (7th edn, LGDJ 2002).

Daly MA, Tedstone Doherty D and Walsh D, 'Reducing the Revolving Door Phenomenon' (2010) 27(1) *Irish Journal of Psychological Medicine* 27.

Daniels N, *Just Health Care* (CUP 1985).

*Just Health: Meeting Health Needs Fairly* (CUP 2007).

Dauvergne C, 'Sovereignty, Migration and the Rule of Law in Global Times' (2004) 67 (4) *The Modern Law Review* 588.

Davies A, Basten A and Frattini C, 'Migration: A Social Determinant of the Health of Migrants' (International Organization for Migration Background Paper, 2006).

Davy U, 'Social Citizenship Going International: Changes in the Reading of UN-Sponsored Economic and Social Rights' (2013) 22(Suppl. 1) *International Journal of Social Welfare* S15.

De Jesús Butler I, *Unravelling Sovereignty: Human Rights Actors and the Structure of International Law* (Intersentia 2007).

De Vattel E, *The Law of Nations* (first published 1787, Liberty Fund 2009).

De Vitoria F, 'On the American Indians' in Pagden A and Lawrance J (eds) *Vitoria: Political Writings* (CUP 1991) 250.

De Wet E, '*Jus Cogens* and Obligations *Erga Omnes*' in Shelton D (ed) *The Oxford Handbook of International Human Rights Law* (OUP 2013) 541.

Degener T, 'Disability in a Human Rights Context' (2016) 35 *Laws* 5.

Delanty G, 'Beyond the Nation-State: National Identity and Citizenship in a Multicultural Society – A Response to Rex' (1996) 1(3) *Sociological Research Online* 1.

Dembour M, *When Humans Become Migrants: Study of the European Court of Human Rights with an Inter-American Counterpoint* (OUP 2015).

Dembour M and Kelly T (eds) *Are Human Rights for Migrants? Critical Reflections on the Status of Irregular Migrants in Europe and the United States* (Routledge, 2011).

Den Heijer M, 'Whose Rights and Which Rights? The Continuing Story of Non-refoulement under the European Convention on Human Rights' (2008) 10(3) *European Journal of Migration and Law* 277.

Detels R et al., *Oxford Textbook of Public Health* (OUP 2009).

Eide A and Eide W, 'Article 25' in Alfredsson G and Eide A (eds) *The Universal Declaration of Human Rights: A Common Standard of Achievement* (Martinus Nijhoff Publishers 1999) 523.

Eide E and Eide A, *A Commentary on the United Nations Convention on the Rights of the Child, Article 24: The Right to Health* (Brill/Nijhoff 2006).

Engbersen G and Broeders D, 'The State versus the Alien: Immigration Control and Strategies of Irregular Immigrants' (2009) 32 *West European Politics* 867.

Entzinger H, 'Open Borders and the Welfare State' in Pécoud A and De Guchteneire P (eds) *Migration without Borders: Essays on the Free Movement of People* (Berghan/UNESCO 2007) 119.

Esping-Andersen G, *The Three Worlds of Welfare Capitalism* (Polity Press 1990).

European Union Agency for Fundamental Rights (FRA), 'Migrants in an Irregular Situation: Access to Healthcare in 10 European Union Member States' (2011).

'Cost of Exclusion from Healthcare: The Case of Migrants in an Irregular Situation' (2015).

Evans D and Price M, 'Measure for Measure: Utilizing Legal Norms and Health Data in Measuring the Right to Health' in Coomans F, Grünfeld F and Kamminga M (eds) *Methods of Human Rights Research* (Intersentia 2009) 111.

Evju S, 'Application by Domestic Courts of the European Social Charter' (2010) 28(3–4) *Nordic Journal of Human Rights* 401.

Farmer P, *Pathologies of Power: Health, Human Rights, and the New War on the Poor* (University of California Press 2003).

Ferrara M, 'Towards an "Open" Social Citizenship? The New Boundaries of Welfare in the European Union' in De Búrca G (ed) *EU Law and the Welfare State: In Search of Solidarity* (OUP 2005) 11.

'The South European Countries' in Castles FG et al. (eds) *The Oxford Handbook of the Welfare State* (OUP 2010) 616.

Fineman M, 'The Vulnerable Subject: Anchoring Equality in the Human Condition' (2008) 20(1) *Yale Journal of Law and Feminism* 1.

'The Vulnerable Subject and the Responsive State' (2010) 60 *Emory Law Journal* 251.

Footer K and Rubenstein L, 'A Human Rights Approach to Health Care in Conflict' (2013) 95(889) *International Review of the Red Cross* 167.

Forman L et al., 'Conceptualizing Minimum Core Obligations under the Right to Health: How Should We Define and Implement the "Morality of the Depths"' (2016) 20(4) *The International Journal of Human Rights* 531.

et al., 'What Do Core Obligations under the Right to Health Bring to Universal Health Coverage?' (2016) 18(2) *Health and Human Rights Journal* 23.

Francioni F, 'Sovranità Statale e Tutela della Salute come Bene Pubblico Globale' in Pineschi L (ed) *La Tutela della Salute nel Diritto Internazionale ed Europeo tra Interessi Globali e Interessi Particolari* (Editoriale Scientifica 2017) 51.

Fredman S, *Discrimination Law* (2nd edn, OUP 2011).

'Substantive Equality Revisited' (2016) 14 *International Journal of Constitutional Law* 712.

Fredman S and Campbell M, (eds) *Social and Economic Rights and Constitutional Law* (Edward Elgar 2016).

Freeman GP, 'Migration and the Political Economy of the Welfare State' (1986) 485 *Annals of the American Academy of Political and Social Science* 51.

Freeman M, *Human Rights: An Interdisciplinary Approach* (2nd edn, Polity Press 2011).

Galderisi S et al., 'Toward a New Definition of Mental Health' (2015) 14(2) *World Psychiatry* 231.

Giannone D, 'Measuring and Monitoring Social Rights in a Neoliberal Age: Between the United Nations' Rhetoric and States' Practice' (2015) 27(2) *Global Change, Peace & Security* 173.

Glendon M, 'The Forgotten Crucible: The Latin American Influence on the Universal Human Rights Idea' (2003) 16 *Harvard Human Rights Journal* 27.

Gostin L and Mason Meier B (eds) *Foundations of Global Health & Human Rights* (OUP 2020).

Gostin L et al. (eds) *Principles of Mental Health Law and Policy* (OUP 2010).

Grabovschi C, Loignon C and Fortin M, 'Mapping the Concept of Vulnerability Related to Health Care Disparities: A Scoping Review' (2013) 13 *BMC Health Services Research* 94.

Greenwood C, 'Sovereignty: A View from the International Bench' in Rawlings R, Leyland P and Young A (eds) *Sovereignty and the Law* (OUP 2013) 251.

Gregg B, *The Human Rights State: Justice within and beyond Sovereign Nations* (Penn Press 2016).

Griffin J, 'Discrepancies between the Best Philosophical Account of Human Rights and the International Law of Human Rights' (2001) 101(1) *Proceedings of the Aristotelian Society* 7.

*On Human Rights* (OUP 2008).

Grotius H, *De Jure Belli ac Pacis Libri Tres* (first published 1646, Clarendon Press 1925).

*De Jure Praedae Commentarius* (first published 1604, Clarendon Press 1950).

Gruskin S and Ferguson L, et al. (eds) *Perspective on Health and Human Rights* (Routledge 2005).

'Using Indicators to Determine the Contribution of Human Rights to Public Health Efforts' (2009) 87 *Bulletin of the World Health Organization* 714.

Guild E, 'Who Is an Irregular Migrant?' in Bogusz B et al. (eds) *Irregular Migration and Human Rights: Theoretical, European and International Perspectives (Immigration and Asylum Law and Policy in Europe)* (Martinus Nijhoff Publishers 2004) 3.

Guiraudon V, 'The Marshallian Triptych Reordered: The Role of Courts and Bureaucracy in Furthering Migrants' Social Rights' in Bommes M and Geddes A (eds) *Immigration and Welfare: Challenging the Borders of the Welfare State* (Routledge 2000) 72.

Habermas J, *Between Facts and Norms* (MIT Press 1997).

Harnacke C, 'Disability and Capability: Exploring the Usefulness of Martha Nussbaum's Capabilities Approach for the UN Disability Rights Convention' (2013) 4 *Journal of Law, Medicine and Ethics* 768.

Harrington J and Stuttaford M, *Global Health and Human Rights: Philosophical and Legal Perspectives* (Routledge 2010).

Hastie B, 'GCM Commentary: Objective 15: Provide Access to Basic Services for Migrants' (Refugee Law Initiative Blog, 15 October 2018).

Heikkilä M, Katsui H and Mustaniemi-Laakso M, 'Disability and Vulnerability: A Human Rights Reading of the Responsive State' (2020) 24 *International Journal of Human Rights* (8) 1180.

Herzog D, *Sovereignty: RIP* (Yale University Press 2020).

Hessler K and Buchanan A, 'Specifying the Content of the Human Right to Health Care' in Rhodes R, Battin M and Silvers A (eds) *Medicine and Social Justice: Essays on the Distribution of Health Care* (OUP 2002) 84.

Hiam L and McKee M, 'Making a Fair Contribution: Is Charging Migrants for Healthcare in Line with NHS Principles?' (2016) 109(6) *Journal of the Royal Society of Medicine* 226.

Hobbes T, *Leviathan* (first published 1651, OUP 2008).

Hunt P, 'Missed Opportunities: Human Rights and the Commission on Social Determinants of Health' (2009) 16 *Global Health Promotion* 36.

'Configuring the UN Human Rights System in the "Era of Implementation": Mainland and Archipelago' (2017) 39 *Human Rights Quarterly* 489.

Hunt P and Leader S, 'Developing and Applying the Right to the Highest Attainable Standard of Health: The Role of the UN Special Rapporteur' in Harrington J and Stuttaford M, *Global Health and Human Rights: Philosophical and Legal Perspectives* (Routledge 2010) 28.

Hunt P and Leader S, and MacNaughton G, 'A Human Rights–Based Approach to Health Indicators' in Baderin M and McCorquodale R (eds) *Economic, Social, and Cultural Rights in Action* (OUP 2007) 303.

Ingleby D and Petrova-Benedict R, *Recommendations on Access to Health Services for Migrants in an Irregular Situation: An Expert Consensus* (International Organization for Migration, 2016).

International Commission of Jurists, 'Fragmentation of International Law: Difficulties arising from the Diversification and Expansion of International Law', Study Group Report, finalized by Martti Koskenniemi, A/CN.4/L.682 (13 April 2006).

'Draft Articles on the Expulsion of Aliens, Yearbook of the International Law Commission' 2(II) (2014).

International Organization for Migration (IOM), 'Migration: A Social Determinant of the Health of Migrants', Background paper, IOM Migration Health Department (2006).

'World Migration Report 2020' (IOM 2020).

Ippolito F and Iglesias Sánchez S (eds) *Protecting Vulnerable Groups: The European Human Rights Framework* (Bloomsbury-Hart 2015).

Ippolito F, 'La Vulnerabilità come Criterio Emergente per una Maggiore Tutela del Migrante nel contesto Internazionale' in Nesi G (ed) *Migrazioni e Diritto Internazionale: Verso il Superamento dell'Emergenza?* (Editoriale Scientifica 2018) 447.

Jaeger M, 'The Additional Protocol to the ESC Providing for a System of Collective Complaints' (1997) 10(1) *Leiden Journal of International Law* 69.

Jayawickrama N, *The Judicial Application of Human Rights Law* (CUP 2002).

Jouannet E, *The Liberal-Welfarist Law of Nations: A History of International Law* (CUP 2012).

Jung C, Hirschl R and Rosevear E, 'Economic and Social Rights in National Constitutions' (2014) 62 *American Journal of Comparative Law* 1043.

Katrougalos G, 'The (Dim) Perspectives of the European Social Citizenship' (2012) 5 (7) *Jean Monnet Working Paper NYU School of Law* 1.

Keleher H, 'Why Primary Health Care Offers a More Comprehensive Approach for Tackling Health Inequalities than Primary Care' (2001) 7(2) *Australian Journal of Primary Health* 57.

Keller H and Ulfstein G (eds) *UN Human Rights Treaty Bodies: Law and Legitimacy* (CUP 2012).

Kelly D, *A Life of One's Own: Individual Rights and the Welfare State* (Cato Institute 1998).

Kendrick A, 'Measuring Compliance: Social Rights and the Maximum Available Resources Dilemma' (2017) 39(3) *Human Rights Quarterly* 657.

Kenyon KH, Forman L and Brolan CE 'Editorial – Deepening the Relationship between Human Rights and the Social Determinants of Health: A Focus on Indivisibility and Power' (2018) 20(2) *Health and Human Rights Journal* 1.

Khan I, *The Unheard Truth: Poverty and Human Rights* (W.W. Norton & Company 2009).

King J, *Judging Social Rights* (CUP 2012).

Kingston LN, *Fully Human: Personhood, Citizenship, and Rights* (OUP 2019).

Kinney E and Clark B, 'Provisions for Health and Health Care in the Constitutions of the Countries of the World' (2004) 37(2) *Cornell International Law Journal* 285.

Kirby P, *Vulnerability and Violence* (Pluto Press 2005).

Klaassen M, 'A New Chapter on the Deportation of Ill Persons and Article 3 ECHR: The European Court of Human Rights Judgment in Savran V. Denmark' (Strasbourg Observers, 19 October 2019).

Kostakopoulou D, 'Irregular Migration and Migration Theory: Making State Authorisation less Relevant' in Bogusz B et al. (eds) *Irregular Migration and Human Rights: Theoretical, European and International Perspectives (Immigration and Asylum Law and Policy in Europe)* (Martinus Nijhoff Publishers 2004) 41.

Kotkas T, 'The Short and Insignificant History of Social Rights Discourse in the Nordic Welfare State' in Kotkas T and Veitch K (eds) *Social Rights in the Welfare State: Origins and Transformations* (Routledge 2016) 15.

Latoo J, Mistry M and Dunne F, 'Physical Morbidity and Mortality in People with Mental Illness' (2013) 6 *British Journal of Medical Practitioners* 3.

Lauterpacht H, *International Law and Human Rights* (Stevens & Sons, 1950).

Leijten I, *Core Socio-economic Rights and the European Court of Human Rights* (CUP 2018).

Lester E, *Making Migration Law: The Foreigner, Sovereignty and the Case of Australia* (CUP 2018).

Liebenberg S, 'The Value of Human Dignity in Interpreting Socio-economic Rights' (2005) 21(1) *South African Journal on Human Rights* 1.

'Between Sovereignty and Accountability: The Emerging Jurisprudence of the United Nations Committee on Economic, Social and Cultural Rights under the Optional Protocol' (2020) 42(1) *Human Rights Quarterly* 48.

Locke J, *Second Treatise of Government* (first published 1690, Hackett Publishing 1980).

Lougarre C, 'What Does the Right to Health Mean? An Interpretation of Article 11 of the European Social Charter by the European Committee of Social Rights' (2015) 33(3) *Netherlands Quarterly of Human Rights* 326.

'The Protection of Non-nationals' Economic, Social and Cultural Rights in UN Human Rights Treaties' (2020) 9 *International Human Rights Law Review* 252.

Lyon B, 'Inter-American Court of Human Rights Defines Unauthorized Migrant Workers' Rights for the Hemisphere: A Comment on Advisory Opinion 18' (2003) 28 *NYU Review of Law & Social Change* 547.

MacDonald E and Cholewinski R, *The Migrant Workers Convention in Europe: Obstacles to the Ratification of the International Convention on the Protection of the Rights of All Migrant Workers and Members of Their Families: EU/EEA Perspectives* (UNESCO Publishing 2007).

Mackenzie C, Rogers W and Dodds S (eds) *Vulnerability: New Essays in Ethics and Feminist Philosophy* (OUP 2014).

Macklem P, *The Sovereignty of Human Rights* (OUP 2015).

MacNaughton G, 'Beyond a Minimum Threshold: The Right to Social Equality' in Minkler L (ed) *The State of Economic and Social Human Rights* (CUP 2013) 282.

MacNaughton G and Frey D, 'ALMA-ATA at 40: From Siloes to Synergy – Linking Primary Health Care to Human Rights' (Health and Human Rights Journal Blog, 7 October 2018).

MacNaughton G, and McGill M, 'The Office of the UN High Commissioner for Human Rights: Mapping the Evolution of the Right to Health' in Mason Meier B and Gostin L (eds) *Human Rights in Global Health: Rights-Based Governance for a Globalizing World* (OUP 2018).

Mann J, et al., 'Health and Human Rights' (1994) 1 *Journal of Health and Human Rights* 6.

'Medicine and Public Health, Ethics and Human Rights' (1997) 27 *Hasting Centre Report* 6.

*Health and Human Rights: A Reader* (Routledge 1999).

Marmot M, *Status Syndrome: How Your Social Standing Directly Affects Your Health and Life Expectancy* (Bloomsbury 2004).

et al., 'WHO European Review of Social Determinants of Health and the Health Divide' (2012) 380 *Lancet* 1011.

Marmot M and Wilkinson R (eds) *Social Determinants of Health* (2nd edn, OUP 2006).

Marshall T H, *Citizenship and Social Class* (CUP 1950).

Mazzetti M, *Strappare le Radici. Psicologia e Psicopatologia di Donne e di Uomini che Migrano* (L'Harmattan Italia 1996).

*Il Dialogo Transculturale. Manuale per Operatori Sanitari e altre Professioni d'Aiuto* (Carocci 2003).

McAuley A, 'The Challenges to Realising the Right to Health in Ireland' in Toebes et al. (eds) *The Right to Health: A Multi-Country Study of Law, Policy and Practice* (Springer 2014) 375.

McCorquodale R, *International Law beyond the State: Essays on Sovereignty, Non-state Actors and Human Rights* (CMP 2011).

McCrudden C, 'Legal Research and Social Science' (2006) 122 *Law Quarterly Review* 632.

Meier B and Bras Gomez B, 'Human Rights Treaty Bodies: Monitoring, Interpreting and Adjudicating Health Related Human Rights' in Gostin L and Mason Meier B (eds) *Foundations of Global Health and Human Rights* (OUP 2020).

Meier B and Kastler F, 'Development of Human Rights through WHO' in Mason Meier B and Gostin L (eds) *Human Rights in Global Health: Rights-Based Governance for a Globalizing World* (OUP 2018) 111.

Meier B et al., 'ALMA-ATA at 40: A Milestone in the Evolution of the Right to Health and an Enduring Legacy for Human Rights in Global Health' (Health and Human Rights Journal Blog, 5 September 2018).

Meier B and Gostin L (eds) *Human Rights in Global Health: Rights-Based Governance for a Globalizing World* (OUP 2018).

Miller D, 'Grounding Human Rights' (2012) 15(4) *Critical Review of International Social and Political Philosophy* 407.

Moeckli D, Shah S and Sivakumaran S (eds) *International Human Rights Law* (3rd edn, OUP 2018).

Morsink J, *The Universal Declaration of Human Rights: Origins, Drafting, and Intent* (University of Pennsylvania Press 1999).

Mullally S, 'Gender Equality, Citizenship Status and the Politics of Belonging' in Fineman MA (ed) *Transcending Boundaries of Law: Generations of Feminism and Legal Theory* (Routledge 2011) 192.

Murphy T and Müller A, 'The United Nations Special Procedures: Peopling Human Rights, Peopling Global Health' in Mason Meier B and Gostin L (eds) *Human Rights in Global Health: Rights-Based Governance for a Globalizing World* (OUP 2018) 487.

Myrdal G, *Beyond the Welfare State: Economic Planning in the Welfare States and Its Economic Implications* (Duckworth 1960).

Nafziger J, 'The General Admission of Aliens under International Law' (1983) 77(4) *American Journal of International Law* 804.

Neuman G, 'Subsidiarity' in Shelton D (ed) *The Oxford Handbook of International Human Rights Law* (OUP 2013) 360.

Nifosi-Sutton I, *The Protection of Vulnerable Groups under International Human Rights Law* (Routledge 2017).

Nivard C, *La Justiciabilité des Droits Sociaux: Etude de Droit Conventionnel Européen* (Bruylant 2012).

'Précisions sur les droits de la Charte sociale Européenne bénéficiant aux étrangers en situation irrégulière' (2014) *La Revue des Droits de L'Homme – Actualité Droits-Libertés* 1.

Noja G et al., 'Migrants' Role in Enhancing the Economic Development of Host Countries: Empirical Evidence from Europe' (2018) 10(3) *Sustainability* 1.

Nolan A, Freedman R and Murphy T, *The United Nations Special Procedures System* (Brill 2017).

Noll G, 'Why Human Rights Fail to Protect Undocumented Migrants' (2010) 12 *European Journal of Migration and Law* 241.

Nussbaum M, *Women and Human Development: The Capabilities Approach* (CUP 2000).

*Frontiers of Justice* (Harvard University Press 2006).

'Human Rights and Human Capabilities' (2007) 20 *Harvard Human Rights Journal* 20.

*Creating Capabilities: The Human Development Approach* (Belknap Press 2011).

O'Cinneide C, 'Austerity and the Faded Dream of "Social Europe"' in Nolan A (ed) *Economic and Social Rights after the Global Financial Crisis* (CUP 2014) 169.

O'Connell P, *Vindicating Socio-economic Rights* (Routledge 2012).

O'Flaherty M, 'Towards Integration of United Nations Human Rights Treaty Body Recommendations: The Rights-Based Approach Model' in Baderin M and McCorquodale R (eds) *Economic, Social, and Cultural Rights in Action* (OUP 2007) 27.

O'Neill O, 'The Dark Side of Human Rights' (2005) 81 *International Affairs* 427.

Oberleitner G, *Global Human Rights Institutions: Between Remedy and Ritual* (Polity Press 2007).

Odello M and Seatzu F, *The UN Committee on Economic, Social and Cultural Rights: The Law, Process and Practice* (Routledge 2013).

Oliver M, *Understanding Disability: From Theory to Practice* (St. Martin's Press 1996).
 'Defining Impairment and Disability: Issues at Stake' in Emens E (ed) *Disability and Equality Law* (Routledge 2013) 39.

Oppenheimer G, Bayer R and Colgrove J, 'Health and Human Rights: Old Wine in New Bottles?' (2002) 30(4) *Journal of Law, Medicine & Ethics* 522.

Örücü E, 'The Core of Rights and Freedoms: The Limits of Limits' in Campbell T et al. (eds) *Human Rights from Rhetoric to Reality* (Blackwell 1986) 47.

Parran T, 'Charter for World Health' (1946) 61 *Public Health Reports* 1265.

Pascale AD, 'Italy and Unauthorized Migration: Between State Sovereignty and Human Rights Obligations' in Rubio-Marín R (ed) *Human Rights and Immigration* (OUP 2014) 278.

Perkowska M, 'Illegal, Legal, Irregular or Regular: Who Is the Incoming Foreigner?' (2016) 45(58) *Studies in Logic, Grammar and Rhetoric* 187.

Perlin M, *International Human Rights and Mental Disability Law: When the Silenced Are Heard* (OUP 2012).

Peroni L and Timmer A, 'Vulnerable Groups: The Promise of an Emerging Concept in European Human Rights Convention Law' (2013) 11(4) *International Journal of Constitutional Law* 1056.

Peters C, 'Equality Revisited' (1997) 110 *Harvard Law Review* 1211.

Pickett K, James O and Wilkinson R, 'Income Inequality and the Prevalence of Mental Illness: A Preliminary International Analysis' (2006) 60 *Journal of Epidemiology and Community Health* 646.

Pinzón-Espinosa J, 'The COVID-19 Pandemic and Mental Health of Refugees, Asylum Seekers, and Migrants' (2021) 280 *Journal of Affective Disorders* 407.

Posner R, 'Legal Scholarship Today' (2002) 115 *Harvard Law Review* 1314.

Potts H, 'Public Health, Primary Health Care, and the Right to Health' in Backman G (ed) *The Right to Health: Theory and Practice* (Studentlitteratur 2012) 93.

Preuss U, 'The Concept of Rights and the Welfare State' in Teubner G (ed) *Dilemmas of Law in the Welfare State* (Walter de Gruyter 1986) 151.

Rachovitsa A, 'Treaty Clauses and Fragmentation of International Law: Applying the More Favourable Protection Clause in Human Rights Treaties' (2016) 16 *Human Rights Law Review* 77.

Ramji-Nogales J, 'Undocumented Migrants and the Failures of Universal Individualism' (2014) 47 *Vanderbilt Journal of Transnational Law* 740.
 '"The Right to Have Rights": Undocumented Migrants and State Protection' (2015) 63 *Kansas Law Review* 1045.

Rawls J, 'The Law of People' in Shute S and Hurley S (eds) *On Human Rights: The Oxford Amnesty Lectures* 1993 (Basic Books 1983) 41.

Raz J, *The Morality of Freedom* (Clarendon Press 1986).

Riedel E, 'The Human Right to Health: Conceptual Foundations' in Clapham A et al. (eds) *Realizing the Right to Health* (Rüffer und Rub 2009).

Rinaldi A et al., 'Salute, Lavoro e Immigrazione: Il Ruolo degli Operatori della Salute in una Prospettiva di Sanità Pubblica' in Calafà L, Iavicoli S and Persechino B (eds) *Lavoro insicuro: salute, sicurezza e tutele sociali dei lavoratori immigrati in agricoltura* (Il Mulino 2020) 279.

Robeyns I and Byscov M, 'The Capability Approach' in Zalta E et al. (eds) *The Stanford Encyclopedia of Philosophy* (first published Thu 14 April, 2011; substantive revision Thu 10 December, 2020).

Rosen G, A *History of Public Health* (first published 1958, Johns Hopkins University Press 1993).

Ross D, *The Nicomachean Ethics/Aristotle*, Ackrill JL and Urmson JO (eds) (OUP 1980).

Ruger J, 'Towards a Theory of a Right to Health: Capability and Incompletely Theorised Agreements' (2006) 18 *Yale Journal of Law & the Humanities* 273.

Ryan B and Mantouvalou V, 'The Labour and Social Rights of Migrants in International Law' in Rubio-Marín R (ed) *Human Rights and Immigration* (OUP 2014) 177.

Sainsbury D, *Welfare States and Immigrant Rights: The Politics of Inclusion and Exclusion* (OUP 2012).

Salvatore M et al., 'Work Related Injuries among Immigrant Workers in Italy' (2013) 15 *Journal of Immigrant Minority Health* 182.

San Giorgi M, *The Human Right to Equal Access to Health Care* (Intersentia 2012).

Scheinin M, 'Core Rights and Obligations' in Shelton D (ed) *The Oxford Handbook of International Human Rights Law* (OUP 2013) 527.

Sekalala et al., 'An Intersectional Human Rights Approach to Prioritising Access to COVID-19 Vaccines' (2021) 6 *BMJ Global Health* 1.

Sen A, *Inequality Re-examined* (Clarendon Press 1992).

  *Development as Freedom* (OUP 1999).

  'Elements of a Theory of Human Rights' (2004) 32(4) *Philosophy and Public Affairs* 315.

Sepúlveda Carmona M, 'Alternatives to Austerity: A Human Rights Framework for Economic Recovery' in Nolan A (ed) *Economic and Social Rights after the Global Financial Crisis* (CUP 2014) 23.

Shaw, M, *International Law* (7th edn, OUP 2014).

Shue H, *Basic Rights: Subsistence, Affluence, and U.S. Foreign Policy* (first published 1980, Princeton University Press 1996).

Slinckx I, 'Migrants' Rights in UN Human Rights Conventions' in De Guchteneire P, Pécoud A and Cholewinski R (eds) *Migration and Human Rights: The United Nations Convention on Migrant Workers' Rights* (CUP 2009) 122.

Smits J, 'Redefining Normative Legal Science: Towards an Argumentative Discipline' in Coomans F, Grünfeld F and Kamminga M (eds) *Methods of Human Rights Research* (Intersentia 2009) 45.

Smyth C, 'Why Is It so Difficult to Promote Human Rights-Based Approach to Immigration?' in O'Connell D (ed) *The Irish Human Rights Law Review 2010* (Clarus Press 2010) 83.
— 'Towards a Complete Prohibition on the Immigration Detention of Children' (2019) 19(1) *Human Rights Law Review* 1.

Spencer S and Hughes V, '*Outside and in: Legal Entitlements to Health Care and Education for Migrants with Irregular Status in Europe*' (Oxford, COMPAS Report 2015).

Spencer S and Triandafyllidou A (eds) *Migrants with Irregular Status in Europe: Evolving Conceptual and Policy Challenges* (Springer 2020).

Spronk-van der Meer S, *The Right to Health of the Child* (Intersentia 2014).

Ssenyonjo M, *Economic, Social and Cultural Rights in International Law* (Hart Publishing 2016).

Straßmayr C et al., 'Mental Health Care for Irregular Migrants in Europe: Barriers and How they are Overcome' (2012) 12 *BMC Public Health* 367.

Stronks K et al., *Social Justice and Human Rights as a Framework for Addressing Social Determinants of Health: Final Report of the Task Group on Equity, Equality and Human Rights* (WHO Publishing 2016).

Tamanaha B, *Law as a Means to an End* (CUP 2006).

Thakur R, 'The Use of International Force to Prevent or Halt Atrocities: From Humanitarian Intervention to the Responsibility to Protect' in Shelton D (ed) *The Oxford Handbook of International Human Rights Law* (OUP 2013) 815.

Tjernberg M, 'The Economy of Undocumented Migration: Taxation and Access to Welfare' (2010) 12 *European Journal of Migration and Law* 149.

Tobin J, *The Right to Health in International Law* (OUP 2012).

Toebes B, *The Right to Health as a Human Right in International Law* (Hart Publishing 1999).
— et al., *Health and Human Rights in Europe* (Intersentia 2012).

Toebes B, and Stronks K, 'Closing the Gap: A Human Rights Approach towards Social Determinants of Health' (2016) 23 *European Journal of Health Law* 510.

Turner B, *Vulnerability and Human Rights* (The Pennsylvania State University Press 2006).

Uprimny R, Chaparro S and Castro A, 'Bridging the Gap: The Evolving Doctrine on ESCR and Maximum Available Resources' in Young K (ed) *The Future of Economic and Social Rights* (CUP 2019) 624.

Üstün T B et al., 'The International Classification of Functioning, Disability and Health: A New Tool for Understanding Disability and Health' (2003) 25(11–12) *Disability and Rehabilitation* 565.

Van Duffel S, 'Moral Philosophy' in Shelton D (ed) *The Oxford Handbook of International Human Rights Law* (OUP 2013) 32.

Venkatapuram S, *Health Justice: An Argument from the Capabilities Approach* (Polity Press 2011).

Vermeer-Kunzli A, 'Diplomatic Protection as a Source of Human Rights' in Shelton D (ed) *The Oxford Handbook of International Human Rights Law* (OUP 2013) 250.

Villareal P, 'The (Not So) Hard Side of the IHR: Breaches of Legal Obligations' (Global Health Law Groningen Blog, 26 February 2020).

Von Werthern M et al., 'The Impact of Immigration Detention on Mental Health: A Systematic Review (2018) 18 *BMC Psychiatry* 382.

Wadsworth M and Butterworth S, 'Early Life' in Marmot M and Wilkinson R (eds) *Social Determinants of Health* (2nd edn, OUP 2006) 31.

Warwick BTC, 'Socio-economic Rights during Economic Crises: A Changed Approach to Non-retrogression' (2016) 65(1) *International and Comparative Law Quarterly* 249.

Way S, Lusiani N and Saiz I, 'Economic and Social Rights in the "Great Recession": Towards a Human Rights–Centred Economic Policy in Times of Crisis' in Riedel E, Giacca G and Golay C (eds) *Economic, Social, and Cultural Rights in International Law: Contemporary Issues and Challenges* (OUP 2014) 86.

Weber M, *Economy and Society: An Outline of Interpretive Sociology* (University of California Press 1978).

Wentholt K, 'Formal and Substantive Equal Treatment: The Limitations and Potential of the Legal Concept of Equality' in Rodrigues P and Loenen T (eds) *Non-discrimination Law: Comparative Perspectives* (Kluwer/Brill 1999) 54.

Westen P, 'The Empty Idea of Equality' (1980) 95(3) *Harvard Law Review* 537.

Whelan D and Donnelly J, 'The West, Economic and Social Rights, and the Global Human Rights Regime: Setting the Record Straight' (2007) 29(4) *Human Rights Quarterly* 908.

Whelan DJ, *Indivisible Human Rights* (University of Pennsylvania Press 2011).

WHO Commission on Social Determinants of Health, 'Closing the Gap in a Generation: Health Equity through Action on the Social Determinants of Health – Final Report of the Commission on Social Determinants of Health' (2008).

'Mental Health Atlas 2017' (2018).

'Mental Health: Strengthening Our Response' (Factsheet, 30 March 2018).

'Technical Series on Primary Health Care – Building the Economic Case for Primary Health Care: A Scoping Review' (2018) WHO/HIS/SDS/2018.48.

WHO and Calouste Gulbenkian Foundation, 'Social Determinants of Mental Health' (2014).

WHO and United Nations Children's Fund (UNICEF), 'A Vision for Primary Health Care in the 21st Century: Towards Universal Health Coverage and the Sustainable Development Goals' (2018).

WHO and WONCA, 'Integrating Mental Health into Primary Care: A Global Perspective' (2008).

WHO European Region, 'Mental Health Promotion and Mental Health Care in Refugees and Migrants (Technical Guidance on Refugee and Migrant Health)' (2018).

WHO European Region/Italian National Institute for Health, Migration and Poverty (INMP), 'Report on the Health of Refugees and Migrants in the WHO European Region' (2018).

Wickramage K et al., 'Migration and Health: A Global Public Health Research Priority' (2018) 18 *BMC Public Health* 987.

Wilkinson R, *The Impact of Inequality: How to Make Sick Societies Healthier* (New Press 2005).

'Ourselves and Others – For Better or Worse: Social Vulnerability and Inequality' in Marmot M and Wilkinson R (eds) *Social Determinants of Health* (2nd edn, OUP 2006) 341.

Winslow C, *The Evolution and Significance of the Modern Public Health Campaign* (Yale University Press 1923).

Woods J, 'Justiciable Social Rights as a Critique of the Liberal Paradigm' (2003) 38 *Texas International Law Journal* 763.

Yamin A, *Power, Suffering and the Struggle for Dignity: Human Rights Frameworks for Health and Why They Matter* (Penn Press 2016).

Yamin A, and Cantor R, *Litigating Health Rights: Can Courts Bring More Justice to Health?* (Harvard University Press 2011).

Yamin A and Lander F, 'Implementing a Circle of Accountability: A Proposed Framework for Judiciaries and Other Actors in Enforcing Health-Related Rights' (2015) 14(3) *Journal of Human Rights* 312.

Yamin A and Norheim O, 'Taking Equality Seriously: Applying Human Rights Framework to Priority-Setting in Health' (2014) 36(2) *Human Rights Quarterly* 296.

Young K, 'The Minimum Core of Economic and Social Rights: A Concept in Search of Content' (2008) 33 *The Yale Journal of International Law* 113.

   (ed) *The Future of Economic and Social Rights* (CUP 2019).

# Index

Ingram Content Group UK Ltd.
Milton Keynes UK
UKHW020719120723
424982UK00029B/505